Microservices with Spring Boot and Spring Cloud

Develop modern, resilient, scalable and highly available apps using microservices with Java, Spring Boot 3.0 and Spring Cloud

Tejaswini Jog

Mandar Jog

Orangeava.com

First published: September 2023

Published by: Orange Education Pvt Ltd, AVA™

Address: 9, Daryaganj, Delhi, 110002

ISBN: 978-93-88590-91-4

www.orangeava.com

Dedicated to

Ojas *and* **Neko**

About the Authors

Tejaswini Jog is a professional educator with over a decade of experience. She has helped hundreds of thousands of students all over the world find their way into Java, and that number continues to grow day by day. She has also authored some of the best books in the industry, which work as a reference point for amateurs and professionals alike.

When she's not teaching or editing her books, she loves following along with the likes of Bob Ross and Picasso to create her own tour de force masterpiece. Not only is she an excellent acrylic artist, but her cooking skills also corroborate her being a culinary maven, and the plants in her home garden definitely flaunt her horticultural adroitness.

Mandar Jog Equipped with more than two decades of experience, over the last few years, Mandar Jog, a professional educator and consultant, has been helping students everywhere enter the ravishing, captivating, and fascinating world of Java.

He is the author of three books that help amateurs and professionals, alike, to get a different outlook on Java while simultaneously piquing their interest and making them fall in love with Java over and over again.

When he's not on his computer, writing or editing a new book, or even teaching, he loves to play chess. Also, being very fond of singing, he always finds time to hone his skills and better himself. He is a hardworking software enthusiast who strives to become the best version of himself.

About the Reviewers

Gil Zilberfeld has been in software since childhood, writing BASIC programs on his trusty Sinclair ZX81.With more than 25 years of developing commercial software, he has vast experience in software methodology and practices.

Gil has been applying agile principles for software development for more than a decade. From automated testing to exploratory testing, design practices to team collaboration, scrum to kanban, traditional product management to lean startup – he's done it all.

He is still learning from his successes and failures.

Gil speaks frequently at international conferences about unit testing, TDD, agile practices, and product management. He is the author of "Everyday Unit Testing" and "Everyday Spring Testing", blogs and posts videos, co-organizer of the Agile Practitioners conference, and in his spare time he shoots zombies, for fun.

Ankit Kumar is currently working as a lead software engineer for a backup and recovery company based out in Minnesota. He is passionate about designing scalable microservices applications using Spring Boot. He is based in Toronto, Canada. He graduated with a bachelor's in computer science from North Dakota State University (USA) and did a master's in Software Engineering from the University of Minnesota (USA). He has worked for about 10 years in various industries retail, backup and recovery, and healthcare to name a few as a backend software engineer. When he is not learning or doing coding for fun and work; he loves to cook, try new restaurants, go for hikes with his wife (Shaurya Chawla), and travel the world. He believes that programming is a true art that requires nurturing by constant learning, but once you start enjoying this art you realize that sky is the limit.

Acknowledgement

Without any doubt, writing a book is a formidable undertaking, demanding extensive teamwork and coordination. Right from the first task of choosing the book title to take it to publication, we were fortunate to receive continuous support from the exceptional team at Orange Education, AVA. Their dedication made this endeavor possible, and we are immensely grateful to the entire team for their invaluable contributions.

Moreover, we extend our heartfelt appreciation to our parents and friends, whose constant encouragement motivated us to share our knowledge with others through the pages of this book. Their belief in our vision was an inspiration that spurred us forward.

We sincerely thank each and every individual who contributed to making this book a reality.

Preface

This book is a complete guide for building and designing microservices. The book not only focuses on the theoretical concepts of microservices but also shows how to use different tools in order to make sure that the microservices are scalable, maintainable and highly available.

The book starts by explaining the basic skills required for microservices. In this book, the microservices are developed using Spring Boot. So, one must be aware of Spring Boot and how to create REST endpoints using Spring Boot. Both these concepts are explained thoroughly in this book.

The second part of the book is mainly aimed towards different concerns that one should take care of while designing the software using microservice architecture. This section talks about inter-service communication, service discovery, API Gateway Service, etc.

The last part of the book typically talks about advanced concepts like handling service failures, securing services and deploying the same. The section covers different tools like Resilience4J and Oauth2 and also container-based deployment of the services.

Chapter 1 will explore the fundamentals of Spring Boot. It covers how to develop, configure and deploy simple Spring Boot applications.

Chapter 2 will cover the basics of REST. This chapter talks about what the endpoint or service is. Along with this, it also covers how to handle different types of data and database communication in the REST. There is also a section about handling exceptions and writing self-descriptive messages.

Chapter 3 will introduce the reader to the concept of microservices. The chapter deals with in detailed discussion about why we need microservices, their advantages and limitations, etc.

Chapter 4 will cover the approach of centralized management configuration in microservices. The chapter emphasizes on using GIT as a centralized repository for Spring Cloud configuration.

Chapter 5 will deep dive into inter-service communication. This will cover different ways to establish inter-service communication using RestTemplate and Feign Client, etc.

Chapter 6 will cover the concept of service discovery. The chapter will discuss in detail about how to register your service and locate it using the Eureka Discovery Server.

Chapter 7 will talk about the need for Gateway API Service and the usage of the same. The chapter will also cover different GatewayFilter Factories used while we implement the routing.

Chapter 8 is all about monitoring. The chapter will discuss what is distributed tracing and how to use the Zipkin server to monitor the behavior of the service.

Chapter 9 will cover the concept of dealing with service failure. The chapter will discuss the reasons for service failure and approaches to handle such failures. It will also cover the usage of Resilience4J.

Chapter 10 will discuss how to secure the services. It will explore how to implement OAuth2 Token for security.

Chapter 11 will cover deployment. The chapter will discuss the container-based deployment of microservices.

Downloading the code bundles and colored images

Please follow the link to download the
Code Bundles of the book:

https://github.com/OrangeAVA/Microservices-with-Spring-Boot-and-Spring-Cloud

The code bundles and images of the book are also hosted on
https://rebrand.ly/1b9169

In case there's an update to the code, it will be updated on the existing GitHub repository.

Errata

We take immense pride in our work at Orange Education Pvt Ltd and follow best practices to ensure the accuracy of our content to provide an indulging reading experience to our subscribers. Our readers are our mirrors, and we use their inputs to reflect and improve upon human errors, if any, that may have occurred during the publishing processes involved. To let us maintain the quality and help us reach out to any readers who might be having difficulties due to any unforeseen errors, please write to us at :

errata@orangeava.com

Your support, suggestions, and feedback are highly appreciated.

DID YOU KNOW

Did you know that Orange Education Pvt Ltd offers eBook versions of every book published, with PDF and ePub files available? You can upgrade to the eBook version at **www.orangeava.com** and as a print book customer, you are entitled to a discount on the eBook copy. Get in touch with us at: **info@orangeava.com** for more details.

At **www.orangeava.com**, you can also read a collection of free technical articles, sign up for a range of free newsletters, and receive exclusive discounts and offers on AVA™ Books and eBooks.

PIRACY

If you come across any illegal copies of our works in any form on the internet, we would be grateful if you would provide us with the location address or website name. Please contact us at **info@orangeava.com** with a link to the material.

ARE YOU INTERESTED IN AUTHORING WITH US?

If there is a topic that you have expertise in, and you are interested in either writing or contributing to a book, please write to us at **business@orangeava.com**. We are on a journey to help developers and tech professionals to gain insights on the present technological advancements and innovations happening across the globe and build a community that believes Knowledge is best acquired by sharing and learning with others. Please reach out to us to learn what our audience demands and how you can be part of this educational reform. We also welcome ideas from tech experts and help them build learning and development content for their domains.

REVIEWS

Please leave a review. Once you have read and used this book, why not leave a review on the site that you purchased it from? Potential readers can then see and use your unbiased opinion to make purchase decisions. We at Orange Education would love to know what you think about our products, and our authors can learn from your feedback. Thank you!

For more information about Orange Education, please visit **www.orangeava.com**.

Table of Contents

Chapter 1
The Foundation

It's around 2.00 midnight, somewhere in Silicon Valley. Rakesh, a Software Architect, was still working on his desk. He was stressed and frustrated with lots of questions in his mind. He and his team have been developing a large-scale business solution for the last few months. They have formulated many of the business needs into small programs which can be integrated into the software. Their Product Owner was equally happy with the overall performance of the team. But a few days back, the one of the developer came up with a recommendation of choosing the framework over traditional application development. The idea was right because the framework would have made the application development more efficient, maintainable, and standardized. But the idea was abstract. The team had to take a call on which framework to choose. From that day one, a lot of brainstorming was generated in the scrum meetings. A few of the team members were using the convergent thinking approach and others were not reluctant to use the divergent thinking approach to come up with some solution. But following all that research, it was difficult to choose the framework, which would fit a hundred percent of all the business needs.

Rakesh is not the only software professional, who is facing to choose the correct option question. He represents a group of all such software professionals who are in dire need of finding the answers to all the questions that she is facing. This chapter aims to help you understand which is the best framework you can use for most of your business needs.

Structure

In this chapter, we will discuss the following topics:

- Framework: The savior
- Introduction to Spring framework
- Spring Boot: The solution
- Quick start
- Introduction to Bootstrapping
- Exploring Runners
- Executing the application
- Working with properties
- Short visit to deploy to server

Framework: The savior

Writing code is not an uphill task nowadays. We all are so well versed in the technical skill sets required to accomplish the required solutions. But nowadays mere coding skills are not enough for successful enterprise application development. Apart from just coding, developers also need to take care of security aspects, scalability, *and so on*. To be very honest, life is too short to do everything. While you strive to accomplish everything, you might end up achieving nothing. Many great philosophers and businessmen also faced similar issues in their early life. One of the famous authors and entrepreneurs *Gary Keller* quotes, *What's the ONE Thing I can do such that by doing it everything else will be easier or unnecessary*?. Well, that's what the *f*ramework does for developers.

Framework provides you with different services like centralized configuration, code standardization, logging, data flows, *and so on*. All the services which developers used to write manually earlier are now configured or wired automatically by the framework. The life of a developer was not so easy before. Fantastic, *isn't it*? When we decide to develop an enterprise application, *what questions come to our mind*? Obviously, the very first thing is the technology, or frameworks from the technology to choose. Today, as a developer, we have a wide range of choices to choose from. And that is where things get a little tricky. The richest person on the earth sometimes seems confused, because he has multiple options to choose from. Choosing the best framework is solely dependent on what criteria you apply. Let us discuss one by one of different criteria that play a vital role in framework selection.

Type of application

The very first question we need to answer is, *what is the sole purpose for which we need a framework*? We need to check if the framework we are looking for is suitable for a web application, web services or standalone application. There are different frameworks available for the different types of applications, they are specialized for that type of application.

Licensing of framework

Are we looking for distributing the application commercially? If the answer is *yes*, we need to check if the framework which we are going to choose needs some licensing. Extra licensing costs may increase the cost of our application. Also, the license might need regular updates with some additional cost. So, one of the options is to choose an open-source framework like Spring framework.

Design pattern

When we are developing web services, it is important for us to keep the data separate from that logic. One of the design patterns which very well allows us to keep the data, that is, the **Model**, the logic that is, the **Controller**, and the user interface, that is, the **View** separate from each other is - *yes, you've guessed it correctly*! MVC design pattern. So as we are interested in MVC, we need to precisely look for the framework which can support MVC architecture design.

Persistency

Not every application needs a persistence layer, but many of them require it. Most of the time, we need to perform **CRUD operations** on the data. Writing the code for such CRUD operations is really painful. It involves the tedious use of APIs for database connectivity, transaction management, and so on. Using the DB layer involves forming SQL queries to perform CRUD operations on data stored in the database. Developers will be immensely pleased if someone else takes up the responsibility of writing this code. If any framework can provide this service, then the developer can focus more on business logic rather than investing more time in database-related APIs. Not only this, but sometimes we need also services using which we can migrate the database very easily. This means the framework should provide ease in DB integration as well as migration. ORM *frameworks* available in the market offer us automated SQL queries for DB operation which make DB communication simpler.

Deployment process

Once we are done with application development followed by testing in the development environment, it's time to deploy the application. **Deployment** is obviously a complicated process, as it involves the packaging of the application along with the dependencies, and so on. Once that is done, we need to deploy the application on the deployment server. Often it is observed that after the application goes live, based on the feedback we need to make modifications to the application. This modification will force the redeployment of the application which is a *tedious* process if done manually. We need a way by which we can achieve easy packaging and an easy deployment process. And if any framework makes it easy for us, why not to choose it?

Scalability

What pleasant days those were! We used to sit back and relax when the application was deployed successfully and business was flourishing. But, trust me, now things are not so easy when it comes to enterprise applications. You will need to monitor the application continuously. On one fine day, you will observe that your application is a big hit in the market. The number of visitors is increasing, which is a soothing feeling. But suddenly, you may observe that the application is not able to respond or not able to sustain when the load is increased. As we have deployed only one instance of the application, it is not able to provide the service to a greater number of users at the same time. In order to achieve this, we also need to make use of a **load balancer**. We need something by which our application will be scaled up automatically when the load increases. We need such a framework using which we can preconfigure the load balancer, which will be *fired* as and when the need arises.

Learning curve

Now that we know all the criteria for choosing a framework, we need to choose the best-suited framework out of say, *ten frameworks*. We may have the best framework to tackle all the criteria but the learning curve could be very steep. Often the framework has its own set of rules for naming convention, package structure, configuration, and so on. On the other hand, some frameworks provide flexibility in terms of naming conventions and package structures, and so on. These frameworks do provide some default strategies but support customization whenever you need them. One point we cannot overlook is the language that the framework uses. *What if we need to learn the language right from scratch? And how easy or difficult will it be?*

Documented

When the framework is well documented, it is easy to learn. If it has enough configuration and sample examples with explanations, along with tutorials it will be easy to follow. It will also become popular among developers and bring them in. The framework with confusing, distributed documentation will confuse the developers. It's always better to choose a framework which is *well-documented.*

Community

An easy-to-learn and well-documented framework will attract more developers. If we are beginners, or spend some time with the framework, *what if we stuck?* If you have an issue or need help to perform a certain thing in a proper way, *what should you do?* In such a scenario, the community behind the framework will help us, teach us to learn the framework and get the work done. A framework with strong community support will make the framework a success. Try to choose a framework with strong community support.

In this book, we will be discussing the highly available, loosely coupled microservices sometimes talking to DB and to be deployed to cloud taking advantage of load balancers, configuration management, any many more. Let's start with a quick introduction of Spring framework with an answer why we are choosing it over others.

Introducing Spring framework

The very first version of Spring was written and released by *Rod Johnson*, in *October* 2002. In *June* 2003, it was first released under the license of the *Apache Foundation*. It's flexible and provides a variety of modules to develop both standalone as well as *server-side enterprise* applications. The framework allows developers to leverage **Dependency Injection**, **Inversion of Control**, and templates for repetitive code. This provides developers ease to develop and test the application. However, developers using the Spring framework need to have a thorough knowledge of the framework. Developers should know how to do configuration, which annotations are available, server configuration for deploying applications on the server, and so on.

Let us assume that you want to develop a console-based application with minimum configuration which should be easy to launch or you want to develop web application/web services with minimum configuration. The question is *Shall I use Spring Framework?* Well, if I had not known of any other alternative, I would have chosen Spring as the best solution. But, as I know the alternative, I would suggest, *You can go with Spring if you want to develop applications where object management, templates for repetitive codes and cross-cutting concerns were managed by the framework*. But the point of concern is we need to configure the objects, templates, or aspects either in the XML file or the class definition using annotations which we need to learn.

It is a big relief that now we are not responsible for the object lifecycle as it is managed by the framework. In spite of that, we need to learn the configuration. We need to know it thoroughly to leverage the services of the framework. Often, you would get frustrated with the learning and tend to go back to the traditional approach of object creation. But trust me, this happens with every new concept you try to learn. Let it be from technology or daily routines. **Spring** is no exception.

In *April 2014*, **Spring Boot 1.0** was launched as an extension of Spring, so as to develop applications in a faster and easier way with minimum or no configuration. The latest version 3.*x* was released in *November 2022*. We can develop stand-alone as well as web applications using Spring Boot. Many times, we read or come across the Spring framework or Spring Boot framework. And then curiously we start thinking *are these two different frameworks? Is there something common in them? Which one shall I choose for my application development?* Let's get into a detailed comparison of Spring and Spring Boot before discussing it.

Spring 1.0 was released in 2003 to provide flexibility in managing the instances and allowing them to focus on business logic which is the main task of a developer. Spring uses **Inversion of Control** to manage the application instances which can then be used in another part of the application using **Dependency Injection**. *Does Spring Boot support IoC and DI?* Of course, it does. Spring Boot being an extension of Spring supports all the features provided by Spring with minimum fuss.

In Spring, when we develop a web application or web service, we need to configure the external web server. However, Spring Boot comes with an inbuilt server like **Tomcat** or **Jetty**.

When it comes to database communication in Spring, we need to configure the Driver class name, URL, Username and Password of the database either in the XML file or in the configuration class using annotation. Spring Boot makes it much easier for *two* reasons:

- Firstly, Spring Boot has zero XML configuration.
- Secondly, we can configure these properties in the properties file which is just a *key-value* pair combination.

Spring comes in modules and to use these modules in the application we need to add some **.jar** files to the application. Being developers we are all aware of how painful it is to select jars with specific versions and also their dependent jars. Spring applications need each and every module to be configured separately.

But Spring Boot comes with handy starters to configure in a file managed by tools such as **Maven** or **Gradle**. We will discuss many of these in detail in the upcoming discussions. So just *relax*.

> **"Life is really simple, but we insist on making it complicated."**
> – *Confucius*

Consider developing an application for the *Student Management System*. We need to create an application, choose the jars to include, choose the database to persist the student-related records, and choose the server on which applications need to be deployed. Once the difficult choices are made, it is now time to manage the application and the required instances. For example, the connection instance using which CRUD operation can be performed. *Oh, come on!* You might not have expected a simple Student Management System to be so complicated. *It's a lot to do! Do we have a better choice?*

Spring Boot: The solution

Spring Boot makes the development of the web as well as stand-alone applications easy and is ready for production. We need *Just to run* the application and it's done. It allows the developers to quickly bootstrap the application along with arrangements to maintain and monitor it in the production environment. The way by which Spring Boot manages the beans configured is much easier than Spring as it basically uses the properties for dependency injection rather than managing complicated XML files. This means one can configure database properties and Spring Boot will manage the beans. *Am I going to learn altogether a new thing just to get an instance? Do you think I am crazy? Wait*, have patience dear. As I just told you, there is still a lot to explore. It's not so straightforward to cover everything in a paragraph. You are a big fan of database CRUD operations so let me explain the power with its help.

When you want to add a new record for a student to a database, what do you do?, I was asking this question to one of the new software developers, *Joy*, who was part of my team in one of the projects. *Are you kidding?*, *Joy* was surprised by this question as everybody knows the answer. *Yes, everybody knows, but still just once let me know what will you do?*, I was still expecting an answer from *Joy*.

I will get the connection for the database with which I want to communicate and insert the record in its table. I will obtain an instance of PreparedStatement using that connection. Using the PreparedStatement instance, we will fire a query to insert a record of a new student in the table, Joy was bang on! Brilliant! Now, what will you do to insert a record for an employee or a company or product for that matter?. Joy was looking a bit frustrated now, I will repeat the same steps just by changing the name of the table and values of the columns along with the number of columns. But, why are you asking?

With a little smile, I asked further, Joy, have you ever thought of the code redundancy you are doing?, Redundancy? Where is that generating from? First, I worked with student records, then employee, then product, and so on. I don't see any redundancy. Joy wanted to prove himself in every possible way now. Let me give you another perception. I totally agree when you said I worked with different types of records. However, observe the steps that you followed effectively by establishing a connection, obtaining a PreparedStatement, creating a query, and firing it with different values. What did you change? Absolutely nothing. The steps mean the lengthy process, remains the same, only the parameters of the query and the column name changed. While I was explaining this to Joy, I observed his eyes lighting up, as if he had won some lottery. Many of the developers think in the same way as Joy used to. Such redundancy issues can be handled by Spring Boot effectively. In Spring Boot, we can configure the database connection properties in the configuration file and use templates to perform CRUD operations. Even at some point of time in future the team decides to change the database nothing will change in the code, only configuration changes and database migration will take place smoothly as compared to Java enterprise applications.

Now, think of the **.jars** you need to include to use JPA in the application. Yup, more than 15 *jars* are needed just to go with JPA, then *Spring -JPA integration* jars and *how can we forget* ***.jars*** *for supporting modules of Spring such as core, bean, context, or EL? Are we going to include each of these entries one by one in the project configuration file*? It will be too lengthy and complex to manage. *Dear friends*, Spring Boot comes with handy starters to add all the basic **.jars** required for the module we need.

From time to time, we need to customize the properties of the application. It may be properties to communicate with the database or properties of the server where the application is deployed such as the port number of the server. Spring boot supports externalizing the configuration either in the properties file or the YAML file. *Cool!* However, *does Spring boot support the type safety of these properties*? Yes, it provides a strong type safe configuration, so as to govern as well as validate the configuration written. In day-to-day development, we need to test the application in different environments, the Spring Boot allows the developers to configure these different environments under different configuration files.

Once you are ready with the application development, it's time to go to the production stage. *Do you need to follow the lengthier process of war creation followed by its deployment*? Frankly, it's the choice you have to make wisely. If you decide to use an internal server for the deployment, Spring Boot comes with **Tomcat** or **Jetty** server with minimum or no configuration. Once we start with the code and configuration, we will discuss this in detail, so for the time being just relax and remember it's possible. At the same time, if you decide to deploy the application on the external server, it's also possible.

Application deployment is not the end of the project lifecycle. In fact, sometimes the real problem starts after that. Suddenly the application starts behaving weirdly and throws some exceptions. Remember everything has a reason. You must act like a *metaphysician* and find the reasons causing such exceptions. You should also be able to get information about JVM memory, the application's health, its readiness probe, environmental properties, and so on. Under normal scenarios, finding this information is very *tedious*. However, Spring Boot provides the Actuator as the module which enables the developers to expose application-related information which can be used by the administrator to monitor the application.

The list continues.....

Quick start

Let's take a pause for a while before we go in-depth and create our Spring Boot application. Basically, it's a **Maven-based Java** project. We can start from scratch and create the structure. However, it's a bit lengthy and unnecessary. I am saying it is unnecessary because we have other easy ways to create the project.

Using CLI for creating Spring Boot project

Spring Boot CLI is a command line tool that we can use to bootstrap a new project developed from **start.spring.io**. It has a **Groovy** compiler and it uses **Grape** as a dependency manager. The Spring Boot CLI supports *Groovy Scripts* without external installation.

Installing CLI

As we are going to use *Spring Boot 3.x.x* version, it internally is based on JDK 17. This is the minimum Java version requirement for Spring Boot 3.x.x. So, the very first thing before you start is to check the Java version on your system, and if you don't have JDK 17 then continue with the installation. You can refer to the following link and set up your Java:

https://www.oracle.com/java/technologies/downloads/

Don't forget to check that you are pointing to the correct version of Java from the Command Prompt just by entering, **java --version**.

If you already have the required Java version, proceed further, and download Spring Boot CLI from the given link as follows:

https://repo.spring.io/ui/native/release/org/springframework/boot/spring-boot-cli/3.0.1/

It will download a **.zip** file. Please unzip it to some location. I am using the Windows platform, so I just created a folder **Spring Microservices Book** on **D** drive and unzipped the CLI at that location.

To use the Spring commands, you need to set up the path as shown:

```
set path=D:\Spring Microservices Book\spring-boot-cli-3.0.1-bin\spring-3.0.1\bin;%PATH%
```

We can cross-check if the path is correctly set by the command, **spring --version**. It should display, **Spring CLI v3.0.1** if the downloaded version is **3.0.1**.

Cool, the stage is all set. Now it is time to create our first project. I will not add anything custom right now. We will do that next time. Execute the following command on the Command Prompt from any directory where you want your project to be stored:

```
spring init Spring_CLI_Demo_Basic
```

It will create a Spring Boot project having *Java* 17 for the 3.0.1 *version*. You can confirm it from the build file from the project structure.

In the same way, we can develop a **Maven-based project** having web as the dependency by the following command:

```
spring init-d=web --build=maven Spring_CLI_Demo_Basic_Maven
```

The preceding command will create a Maven-based project with support for the Spring web module. If you are very much curious, refer to the **pom.xml** file and confirm the Java, Spring Boot version, and supported module under the **dependency** tag. We will be discussing the dependencies in depth shortly.

Let's now focus on how the basic structure of the project can be developed using **Spring Initializr** from the **start.spring.io** site.

Using Spring Initializr

The **Spring Initializr** provides an extensible API to the developers for generating JVM-based projects. It allows the developers to inspect the metadata used for generating the basic structure of the projects. It also enables choosing the Spring Boot version from the list as well as the available dependencies for the modules which the developers want to use in the application.

Let's visit the page **start.spring.io**:

- The *first* section allows developers to select the type of project as *Maven-based* or *Gradle based* along with the basic language as **Java**, **Kotlin**, or **Groovy**.
- In the *second* section, we can choose the *Spring Boot version.*
- In the third section, project metadata as name of the project, ArtifactId, Group name, Version of Java, and so on.
- In the *fourth* section, we can include modules to be included in the application such as *web*, JPA, LDAP, and so on, under the **Dependencies** tab.

You will observe the GUI as shown in *Figure 1.1*:

***Figure 1.1**: Using Spring Initializr*

Here, we have selected a *Maven-based Java* 17 project with *Spring* Boot 3.0.1 version to be packaged as JAR with web module support. Now, click on the **GENERATE** button which will download a **.zip** file having the name **demo** which is the field value of **Name** under the **Project Metadata** section. We can now unzip the file and import it into the IDE of our choice and start developing the application further.

Using IDE

Now the final way of using IDE to generate the Spring Boot project. IDEs such as **IntelliJ**, **Eclipse**, and **Visual Studio** support the development of Spring Boot-based applications. You can use any of them as per your choice. Here, we will be discussing where to download the specific IDE and use it.

Let's start with **Eclipse**. The Eclipse IDE comes with **Spring Tools Suites** plugin, which you can integrate into your Eclipse for Spring Boot development. Or you can download the Spring tools suite separately and that's it. Here we will discuss both ways.

Integrating the STS plugin in the Eclipse

If you have already eclipse IDE installed then it is great. Just before going ahead, find the Java version support as we need a minimum Java 17 to go further. If you don't have an IDE, you can download it from **https://www.eclipse.org/downloads/packages/site** as per your platform.

Once the download is complete, extract it, and launch a workspace using it. I have launched the workspace and will now start integrating the STS plugin from the marketplace by clicking the **Install** button shown in *Figure 1.2*:

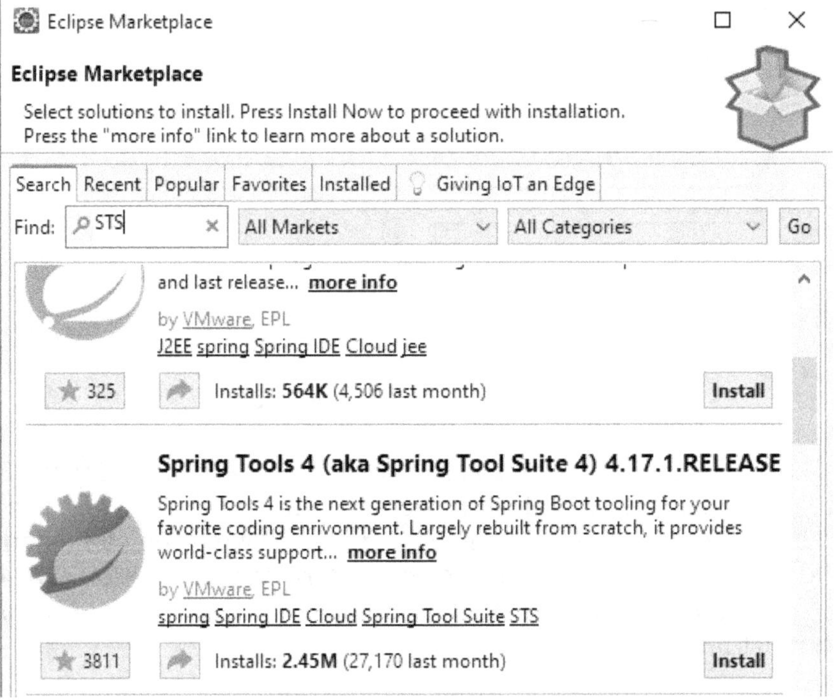

***Figure 1.2**: Installing Spring Tools in Eclipse*

Select the default choices and continue with the process. Once the process of downloading is complete, a dialog will appear to restart the workspace and the changes will be reflected. After the workspace is restarted, we can check the changes by clicking on **File** -> **New** -> **Spring Starter Project** option, we will get the following dialogue confirming our plugin is installed properly and we can use it as shown in *Figure 1.3*:

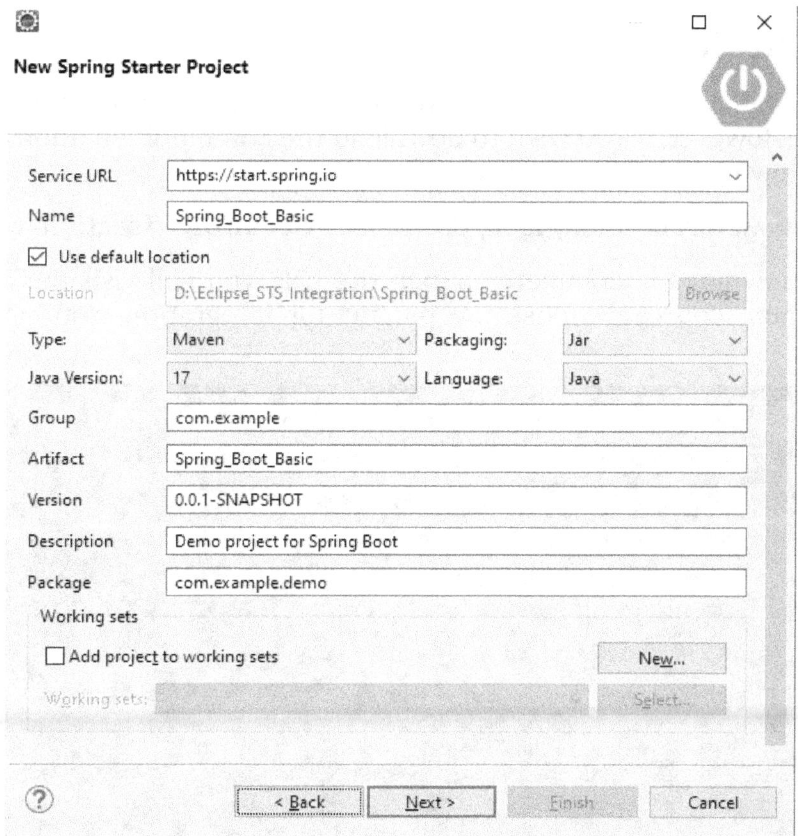

***Figure 1.3**: Spring boot project creation in Eclipse*

The **STS tool** communicates to the same site **http://start.spring.io/** and fetches the details. As we did in the earlier step, here too we will add the details and dependency by clicking on the **Next** button and adding web module dependency in the application.

Using STS

Spring Tools Suite (**STS**) is a specialized version of eclipse dedicatedly used for Spring Boot-based development. The latest version can be downloaded from **https://spring.io/tools** as per your preferred platform. I am downloading a

Windows-based version. Once the executable **.jar** is downloaded, double-click it. Once the extraction is done you will get the **sts-4.x.x.RELEASE** folder. Now, launch the workspace using an application file named, **SpringToolSuiteX**. Once the workspace is launched, follow the same steps to create an application as we did in the earlier step. We in the book will use STS extensively, but as I said you can choose any IDE as per your choice.

Using Intellij

If you already have the community edition, you can continue with integrating the plugin. However, if you wish to download the community edition of **Intellij**, use the following link for windows:

https://www.jetbrains.com/idea/download/?fromIDE=#section=windows

Once the download is complete, launch the IDE, you will visit the dialog box directly where you can choose the plugins for integration. You can refer to *Figure 1.4*:

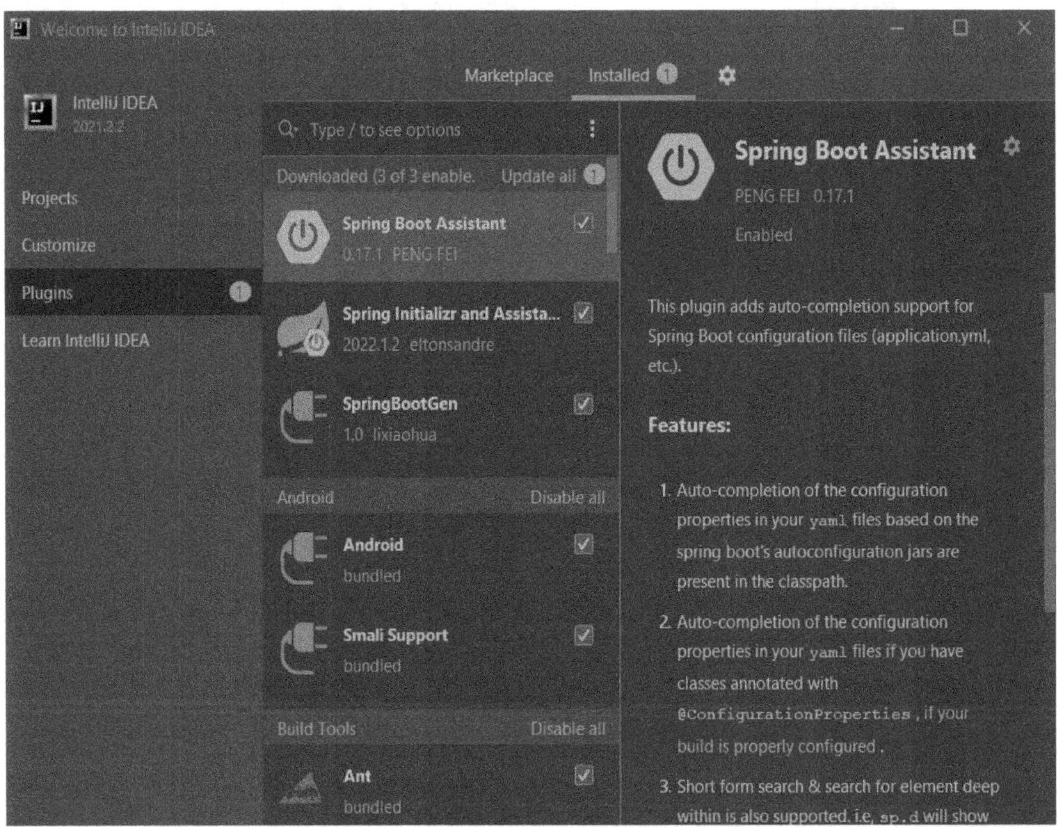

Figure 1.4: *Adding Spring plugins in Intellij*

We need to choose **Spring Boot Assistant** and **Spring Initializr and Assistant plugins** for integration. Follow the instructions and complete the STS plugin integration. After the integration is done, you can now choose the type of project as **Spring Initializr** as shown in *Figure 1.5*:

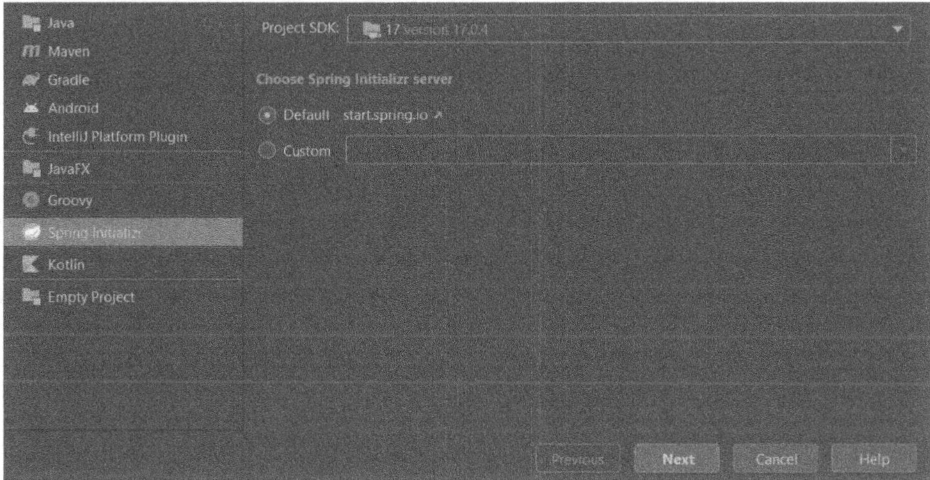

***Figure 1.5**: Creating spring boot project in Intellij*

Now continue to provide values such as the name of the project, type of project, language to use, and other metadata information along with the version of the Spring Boot application and its dependencies. The look and feel are different, but the process is very much the same, as we did in earlier steps for new application creation as shown in *Figure 1.6*:

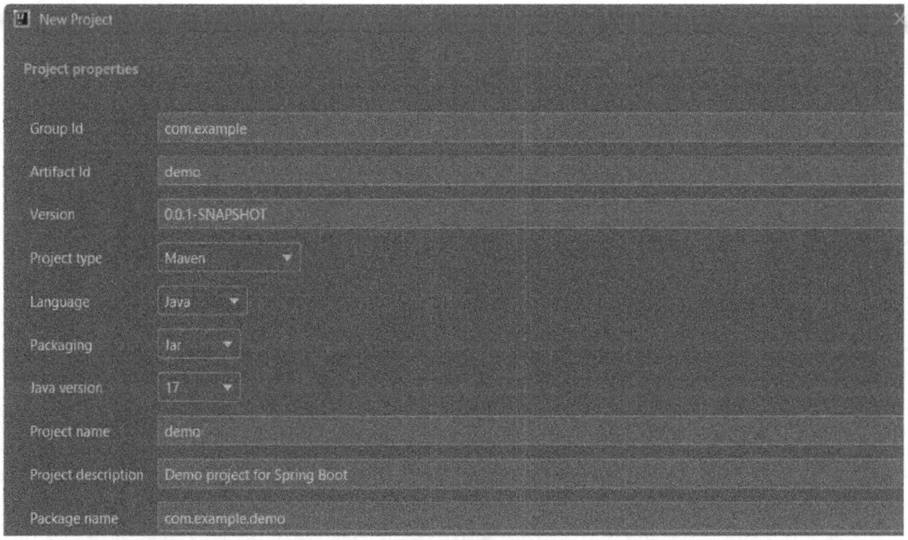

***Figure 1.6**: Configuring Spring boot project in Intellij*

Apart from this, you can also download the ultimate edition of Intellij from this link:

https://www.jetbrains.com/lp/intellij-frameworks/. The ultimate edition comes with inbuilt support for spring boot application development.

We can also use the VSCode Editor to create Spring boot application. Please refer to *Appendix*-1, to know how to configure VSCode to achieve the same.

Introducing Bootstrapping

Bootstrapping is to start with only essential minimalist resources needed to kickstart the application. The **bootstrap loader** is the first piece of the code, which executes to start the initial part of the application and then, the rest of the complicated part of the **application loads**. It not only enables the developers to choose what they need in the application, along with structure, and configuration but also provides ways of customization.

The easiest and widely accepted way of bootstrapping a Spring Boot application is by using **Spring Initializer**. We, in the earlier section, already have used the Spring Initializr in various ways to get the basic infrastructure of our application. It may be *Maven-based* or *Gradle based*, but it provides you with some basic structure. Before going further with development, let us first explore the basic structure, the files, their importance, and if we need customization then how to do it. Let's start with the file structure. The project structure for Gradle as well as Maven based project is as shown in *Figure 1.7*:

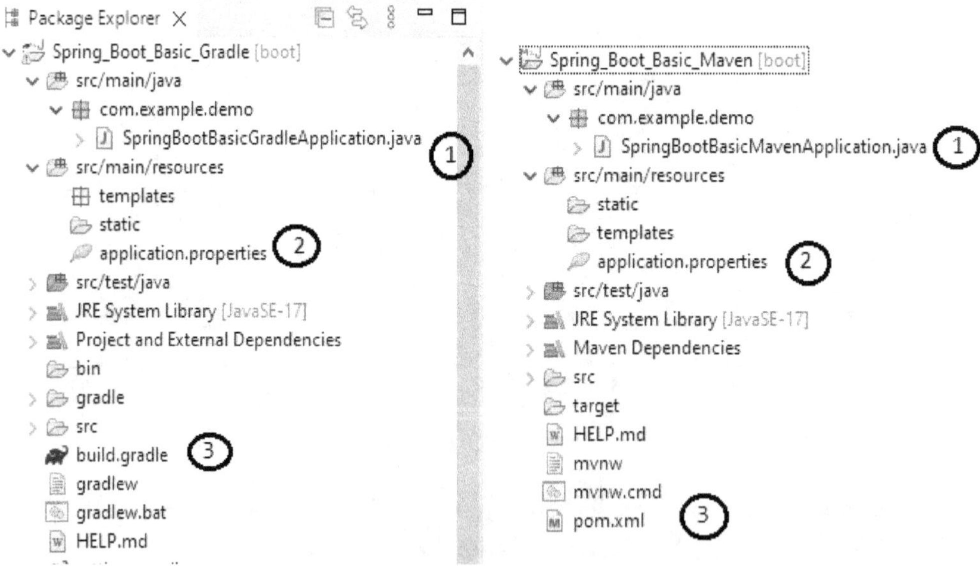

Figure 1.7: *Project structure of Spring Boot application in Grade and Maven*

The main components of the projects are:

- The main application file
- The application configuration file
- The metadata configuration file to set up Java, dependencies, packaging, and so on.

The Spring Boot application has the main class definition by default generated by Spring Initializr. The name of this class can be any *user-defined name*. However, the default naming convention for this class is the *name of the application* post fixed by **Application** word. In our case, you can observe the class name is the *Name of Application + Application* as, **`SpringBootBasicGradleApplication`** or **`SpringBootBasicMavenApplication`**.

This class is annotated by a class-level annotation **`@SpringBootApplication`**. This annotation is called **meta-annotation**. This is a combination of three different annotations:

The first is class-level annotation, **`@Configuration`** which indicates, the annotated class provides an application configuration that is located automatically.

The second is, **@ComponentScan** which enables scanning the packages for the **`@Component`** annotation.

The third annotation is **`@EnableAutoConfiguration`**, which enables the automatic configuration mechanism of the application. This auto-configuration takes place automatically depending upon the **.jars** added to the class path.

This class definition contains a standard **public static void main()** method. As in any Java application, it indicates the entry point within the application. In our case, it also acts as the entry point. The main method then delegates the application class by calling the **run** method as follows:

```
SpringApplication.run(SpringBootBasicMavenApplication.class, args);
```

The Spring application bootstraps our application by launching the Spring container and starts to auto-configure the web server depending upon the metadata configuration. Here, if needed, we can also send some command line arguments to add customization.

Now, the question is *what exactly happens when we say configuration is located and actions are taken?* Spring container locates the configuration and the beans are configured and stored for future use. In Spring, the XML *file* or *annotation-based configuration* is located and the action is taken. However, Spring boot has no XML configuration. So, all the action needs to be taken based upon the annotations applied to the classes or methods. The application also needs some application-level beans such as DataSource, **LDAP** or **RabbitMQ**. Our application is going to be either *Gradle* or *Maven based*. The Gradle has **build.gradle** and Maven has a **pom.xml** file containing the dependencies tag providing the information about which Spring modules are supported by the application as shown in *Figure 1.8*:

pom.xml

```
<dependencies>
  <dependency>
    <groupId>org.springframework.boot</groupId>
    <artifactId>spring-boot-starter-web</artifactId>
  </dependency>

  <dependency>
    <groupId>org.springframework.boot</groupId>
    <artifactId>spring-boot-starter-test</artifactId>
    <scope>test</scope>
  </dependency>
</dependencies>
```

build.gradle

```
dependencies {
      implementation 'org.springframework.boot:spring-boot-starter-web'
      testImplementation 'org.springframework.boot:spring-boot-starter-test'
}
```

Figure 1.8*: Setting dependencies in Maven and Gradle project*

As we only have added a web module at the time of application creation only one dependency has been added. The test module is by default for writing test cases. But, *have you observed that it is not only just a dependency; it's actually a starter for the dependency*? Yes, Spring Boot provides **starters** to include. Before Spring Boot was introduced, the developers needed to add each and every individual required dependency one by one. Though the tools like *Gradle* and *Maven* make this process easy, the developers still need to spend lots of time. The starters make this time-consuming and complex process *easy*. This enables the developers to easily add the modules we need to include in the application and all its dependent jars will be included in the classpath automatically. Spring boot has 50+ *such starters*. Here we have included web-starter, the basic Spring jars such as **`spring-beans`**, **`spring-context`**, and **`spring-core`** along with **`spring-boot`**, **`spring-autoconfigure`**, **`spring-boot-starter`**, and so on, are included in the classpath and which jars to include are completely dependent upon the dependencies added in **`pom.xml`** or **`build.gradle.build`** file as shown in *Figure 1.8*.

We just discussed the process of adding third-party **`.jars`**. But *what about bean management? How does Spring Boot manage the beans needed by the application?* As Spring Boot is *zero XML based*, the configuration is much simpler. At the time of application start-up, the container looks for class level and method level annotations to create the instances and manage their lifecycle. It also scans classpath to find the information about the modules included and accordingly which beans are needed. When we include **web-module** in the classpath, application needs at least a bean for the front controller. If the **spring-jdbc** module is included, then the bean for **DataSource** and **JdbcTemplate** will be managed by the container. But now the question is *how the container finds the values of the URL, username, and password for the database connectivity*. The container will use the values configured in the application's properties file and use them to generate a bean and further manage its life cycle. *Be careful!* When you add a dependency in the **pom.xml** file, the **.jars** are downloaded and added to the classpath. The classpath is scanned to manage the required beans. So, if you add some dependencies without providing values of its properties, for sure bean cannot be managed, and hence, the application will fail to start.

Exploring Runners

Now we are aware that, at the time of application start-up, bootstrapping will take place and the application will be launched. But still, one question is unanswered. *Will the application be started as a standalone application or will it be a web application?* To answer this question, we need to discuss the runners.

By default, whenever we create a Spring Boot application, it is a type of *web application*. One can have it as a full-fledged web application having its presentation layer, or it can be a web service-based application which exposes the endpoints. If you are considering using **CommandLineRunner** to develop standalone applications, you are guessing it wrong. The **ApplicationRunner**, as well as **CommandLineRunner**, are used to run some logical code just at the time of application startup, along with passing runtime arguments to it. Both **ApplicationRunner** and **CommandLineRunner** have **run()** methods which need to be overridden to execute the custom logic. The following code snippet will show how to access command line arguments in the **run()** method:

```
@SpringBootApplication
public class SpringBootBasicMavenApplication implements
                                                  CommandLineRunner {
 public static void main(String[] args) {
     SpringApplication.run(SpringBootBasicMavenApplication.class, args);
 }
 @Override
 public void run(String... args) throws Exception {
     System.out.println("Displaying the command line arguments");
     for (String arg : args) {
        System.out.println(arg);
     }
   }
 }
```

You can execute the application by command:

java -jar SpringBootBasicMavenApplication.jar argument1 argument2

This will show the output as:

```
Displaying the command line arguments
argument1
argument2
```

Unfortunately, **CommandLineRunner** only allows us to pass values to the application and then by remembering the order or by applying the String parsing methods we may need to parse or use the values as per the scenario. *Is there a better way to send the values for a particular property?*

The **ApplicationRunner** is a savior here. Using **ApplicationRunner**, one can pass the *key-value* pair from the command line argument and can be used in the application's run method as shown by the following code snippet:

```
@SpringBootApplication
public class SpringBootBasicMavenApplication implements
ApplicationRunner {
  public static void main(String[] args) {
    SpringApplication.run(SpringBootBasicMavenApplication.class, args);
  }
  @Override
  public void run(ApplicationArguments args) throws Exception {
    System.out.println("Displaying the command line arguments");
    for (String arg : args.getOptionNames()) {
           System.out.println(arg);
    }
    System.out.println(args.getOptionValues("application.name"));
    System.out.println(args.getOptionValues("server.port"));
    }
}
```

You can execute the application by command:

```
java -jar SpringBootBasicMavenApplication.jar application.name=sampleapp
   server.port=8081
```

This will show the output as:

```
Displaying the command line arguments
sampleapp
server.port
[sampleapp]
[8081]
```

Executing the application

The Spring Boot application is basically a Java application with the **main()** method. So, one can execute it as a Java application. However, we have STS plugin integrated. We can also execute this as a Spring Boot app. It will also be executed as a Java application with a few extra options as shown in *Figure 1.9*:

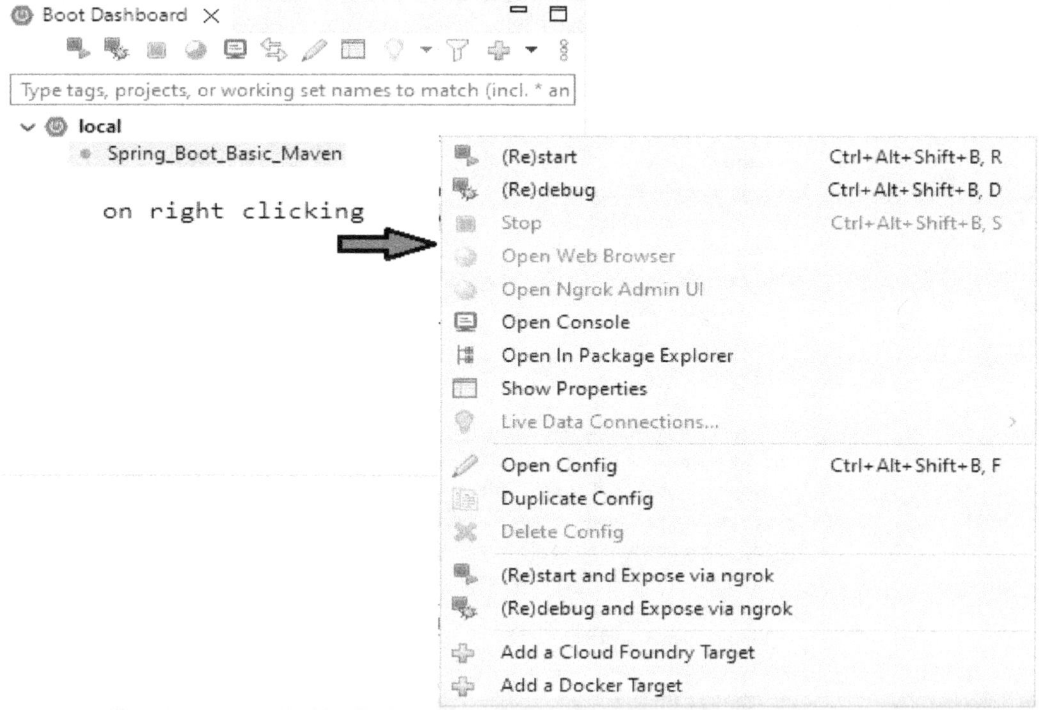

***Figure 1.9**: Executing Spring Boot application*

This is how we execute the application from IDE. But *what if I want to execute the application from the Command Prompt?* Good question. Well, you have various options to choose from. The easiest one is when you are the developer and want to execute it using the Maven tool. We created this as a Maven based application so we can use the **mvnspring-boot:run** from the Command Prompt.

Working with properties

Spring Boot is a highly customizable application, the easiest way. One can set up various application-related properties in the **application.properties** or **application.yml** file. Though the list of these properties is unceasing, it is not feasible to discuss all of them here. We can categorize these properties into 16+ *different categories* such as **Core**, **Cache**, **Mail**, **JSON**, **Database and**

Transaction,**Web**, **Templating**, **Server**, **Security**, **Actuator**, **Dev-tool**, and **Testing**. We are aiming to develop a service, so let's start by customizing some server-related properties. For the first time, we are adding some details to the application.properties file. The beginning might look a little difficult to digest, but that's what the learning process is all about. If the kid gives up, the moment he falls, then he will never be able to learn how to walk. Let's open the **application.properties** file from the **resources** folder and press *ctrl* + *space* to get the properties as shown in *Figure* 1.10:

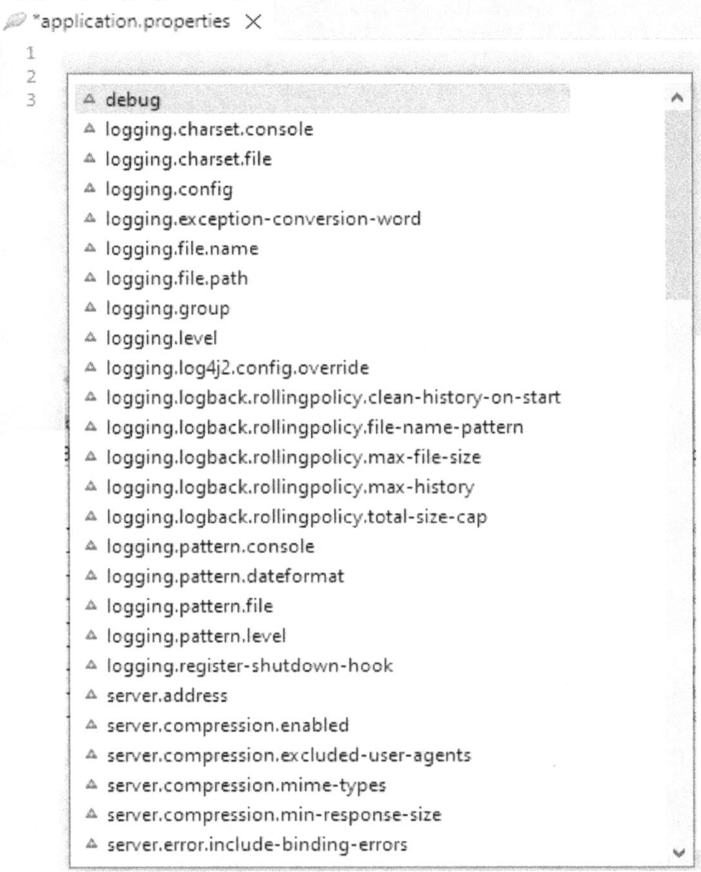

***Figure* 1.10**: *Setting server port*

If on your system some applications are already running on port **8080**, then launching a Spring Boot application on the same port number is not possible. *What shall we do in such a case*? Very easy, to change the port number for the Spring Boot server, in our case Tomcat, by setting **server.port=XXX**, where **XXX** can be any valid available port number on the system, where we want our server to launch. Once you set this property to **8081**, your application will be launched on **8081** as shown in *Figure* 1.11:

```
application.properties
1 server.port=8081
2
3

Problems  Javadoc  Declaration  Console  Progress
Spring_Boot_Basic_Maven - SpringBootBasicMavenApplication [Spring Boot App] C:\Users\LENOVO\Downloads\sts-4.17.1.RELEASE\plugins\org.eclipse.justj.openjdk.hotspot.jre.full.win32.x86_64_17.0.5.v2022

13012 --- [    main] o.apache.catalina.core.StandardEngine    : Starting Servlet engine: [Apache Tomcat/10.1.4]
13012 --- [    main] o.a.c.c.C.[Tomcat].[localhost].[/]       : Initializing Spring embedded WebApplicationContext
13012 --- [    main] w.s.c.ServletWebServerApplicationContext : Root WebApplicationContext: initialization completed in 1020 ms
13012 --- [    main] o.s.b.w.embedded.tomcat.TomcatWebServer  : Tomcat started on port(s): 8081 (http) with context path ''
13012 --- [    main] c.e.d.SpringBootBasicMavenApplication    : Started SpringBootBasicMavenApplication in 1.942 seconds (process running for 2.795)
```

Figure 1.11: *Spring Boot project launch with a modified port*

In the same way, we can change the other properties of the server. You can get all the properties on the fly by pressing the server, followed by, *ctrl* + *space* as shown in *Figure 1.12*:

Figure 1.12: *Loading the properties*

Let us do an *interesting* thing. When we start the application, a banner appears on the console. Let us play along and disable it or change it. To disable the banner from both consoles as well as log files, we can set the **banner-mode** to **off** as **spring.main.banner-mode=off**. Sometimes we want to print the banner on the console or in the log file only. In this case, we can set the **banner-mode** to **log** or **console**. Hey, *but what if we want the banner but not the boring Spring*

Boot one? *Is it possible to achieve that*? Obviously, we can change it anytime by adding a **banner.txt** file in the classpath. If you add a file with text with some *asterisk* as **This is a new banner** you will observe the change in the banner text as shown in *Figure 1.13*:

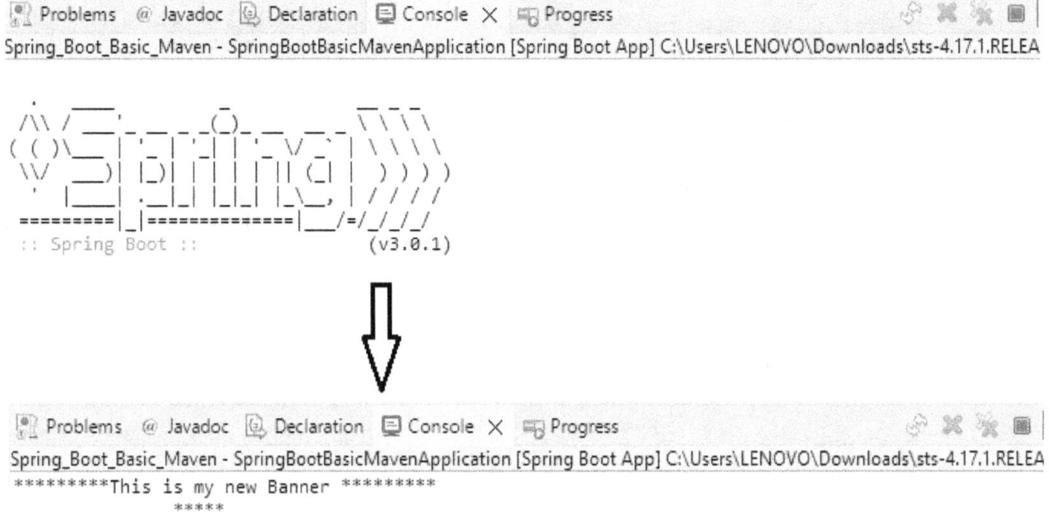

***Figure 1.13**: Setting up the banner text*

You can also use the **application.yml** instead of the **application.properties** file. The properties that you configure do not change. But the structure of the file changes. YAML file is structured as compared to the **application.properties** file.

For example, the server port configuration can be written as:

```
server:
  port: 8081
```

As you can observe, this is more structured. All the properties related to the server can be configured similar to the port.

Short visit to deploying to the server

Once you have tried and tested the application and you are satisfied with it, you want your teammates to use the application, or you want to distribute the application. *What should we do*? We have again various choices for how to distribute the application. But before going into details, I would like to discuss a bit about what happens when we run the application.

A Spring Boot application is ready to run a *production-grade application*. That means we literally do nothing or very little to get into production mode. When we create an application, we have selected the packaging mode as JAR. So, when we run the application, an executable **.jar** will be generated by the IDE and it will be executed. At the time of **.jar** execution, it will launch a Tomcat server in which our application is deployed. Once the Tomcat server is ready, one can start using the application either from the browser if it's a web application or the client consuming it if it is a web service. What I am trying to say is we don't need to rely on the external configuration of the server and then follow the application deployment process. It saves a lot of time. The executable **.jar** is dedicated to a server hosting an application. Here, we are following the application per server design pattern. Don't worry we will discuss the deployment design patterns in detail in the respective chapter. For the time being just remember, by default our application will be hosted on the Tomcat server when we run the application in IDE.

Once we know in detail about the process of what happens when we run the application. Now, let's focus on the distribution process.

This is very easy and many of you might have already guessed it as well. We can get the application packaged in the JAR and distribute the JAR. On the client system, run the executable **.jar** and that's it. May it be a normal system or a cloud we only need to fire the Java command to run the JAR. Now, you might be wondering how to get the JAR. I said it might be because many of you have packaged the application as an executable **.jar** a number of times, or are at least aware that the IDE has such a system. However, we have developed our application as a Maven application, it will be the best choice to use the tool for packaging. In the Command Prompt, you can use the **mvn install** command or in IDE right *click the application* → **Run As** →**Maven install** as shown in *Figure 1.14*:

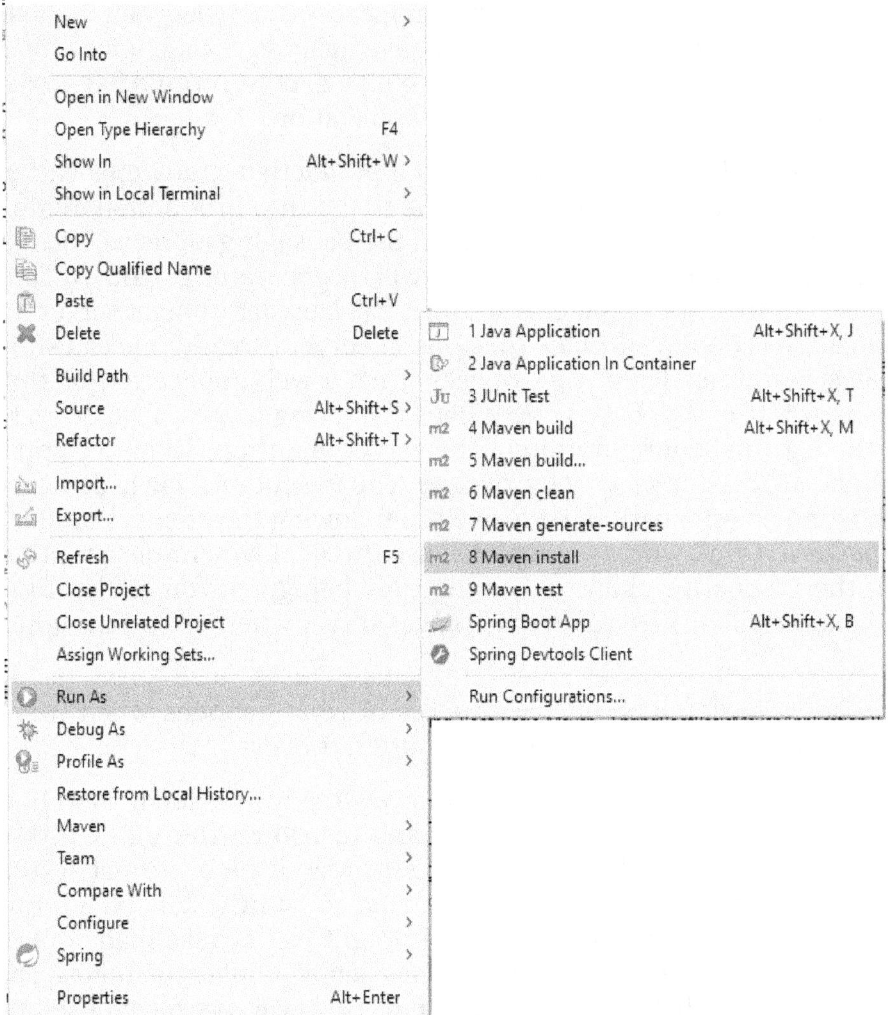

Figure 1.14: *Deploying the Spring Boot application*

It will generate a **`.jar`** in the target folder. Once you have the jar you can upload it to the cloud or execute it on the client system. The application will be ready to use. *Isn't it simple?*

Sometimes we want the application to be packaged as **`War`** to deploy it in the server of our choice. We can select the packaging as **`War`** at the time of creating an application as shown in *Figure 1.15*:

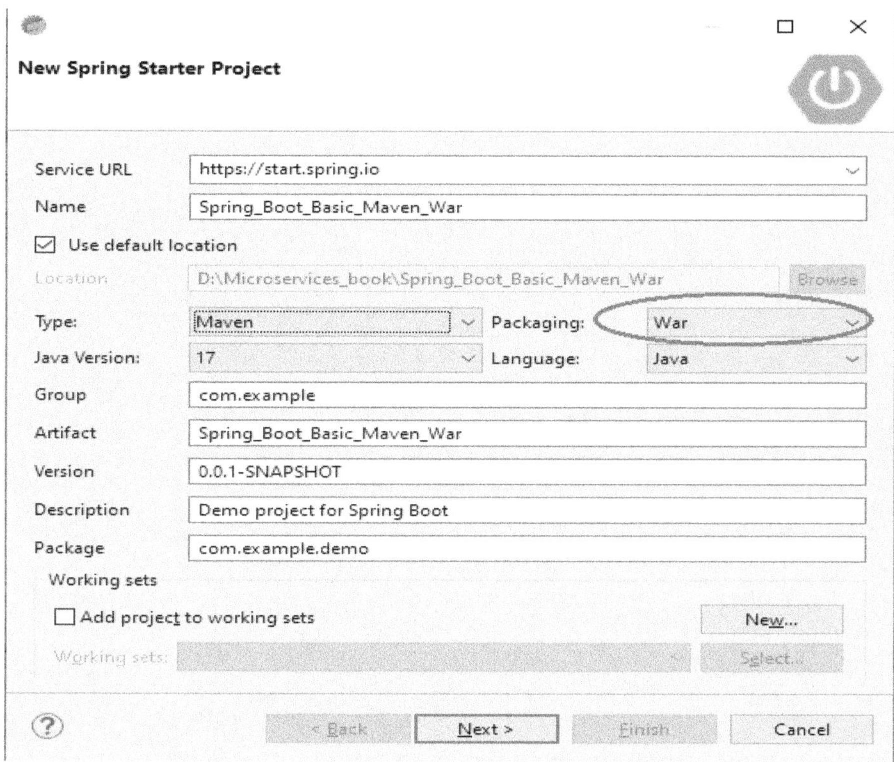

***Figure 1.15**: Generating the war or jar file*

Once the application is ready, we can get the **`war`** file by **`mvn install`** command to get the **war** file in the target folder. We can then deploy the application on the external server of your choice.

Conclusion

In this chapter, we discussed the basics of the Spring Boot framework. We talked about how to develop the simple Spring Boot application and execute it. We also discussed the different types of runner lines **`ApplicationRunner`**, and **`CommandLineRunner`**, and their usage. Also, we learned the basic structure of the application and how to customize different properties of the application using the properties file. Finally, we discussed how to deploy the application on the Tomcat server. In the next chapter, we will discuss the basics of REST application, and develop an *end-to-end service* talking to database, and then test it using **Postman**.

CHAPTER 2
Decipher The Unintelligible

In the previous chapter, we discussed the need for framework and *why to use the Spring Boot framework*. Obviously, it was an introductory chapter. So, we only dealt with very basic concepts. Once we decide to use Spring Boot, we can leverage the different modules provided by it. You all know that creating an application itself is a very tricky task. But gone are the days when you create a complete application using a single technology. Some technologies offer better UI development features, which can be used to create UI like **Angular** and **React**. While some technologies do offer better API for writing flexible business logic like Java or .NET. So, one may think to create UI in Angular and business logic in Java. In such a case, the UI layer created in Angular should be able to pass the data to the business layer created in Java and vice versa. Tough job, *isn't it*? We are expecting that one application should communicate with another application that is developed in a different programming language or framework. In such a scenario, we need services to establish communication and share the data independent of the technology used at the other end.

Most of the time, we might know about the consumer in detail. Sometimes, it is unrevealed. We might know what language it uses, or in which format the consumer is expecting the response from the service provider. Accordingly, we can create a service provider who understands the language used by the consumer. But *what if we do not know if the service and the consumers use the same language, versions, or even the framework they used*? Or they are using the same platform? The services for the consumer are always tricky. In such cases, we need to create the service which can generate a *language-independent response* to the consumer. This is achieved by the REST services. This chapter will introduce the basics of the Spring Boot REST. We will learn how to create REST-based services using Spring Boot to support different HTTP requests.

Structure

In this chapter, we will discuss the following topics:

- Basics of application development
- Need of a service
- Developing simple REST service
- Handling different media types
- Communication to database
- Exception handling in REST
- Writing self-descriptive messages

Basics of Application Development

Frequently, we come across terminology such as *software*, *software application*, *application*, or simply **app**. Whatever we call it, it is identical. In simple words, *an application is a program which is designed to perform some tasks and related operations as well*. In general, when we say it is an application, we are aiming to design a one-stop shop for all the client's needs. Let's take an example of *online shopping*. *What does a consumer need from an Online Shopping Application*? A *consumer* might want to find a list of all the products or a list of the products by category. Consumers also might want to buy some products, pay online if they wish to, and also want to track the *order*, and so on. In the same way, you can think of *School Management*, *Company Management*, *Banking Applications*, and *Share Market applications* which can be developed using *different languages*, *frameworks*, and *platforms*. Nowadays, console-based applications are rare due to their reach. They are more complicated to install. Also updating the console application on the client's system is a tedious job. Today is the world of web applications, with *client-server connectivity* which is achieved via the internet. The web application can be accessed easily from any browser remotely. The browser acts as the consumer of the application and sends the request to the server. We are not here to learn web architecture. So, let us skip all of that for now. In case you are new to web applications, please *Google* to find further details, and don't avoid the topic as it's very important to clear the basic concept. The best part of web applications is, they are hosted on the server and the version changes on the server. The client doesn't need to do any updates on their systems to use the newer version of the application. One can develop web applications using many languages such as .NET, Python, Java, PHP, and so on. Typically, if we think of Java, we can use **Servlets** and **JSPs** to develop enterprise applications. The **Spring MVC** and **Struts** frameworks also have strong APIs for developing web applications.

Along with web applications, nowadays mobile apps are also very much in use. Mobile applications are developed typically for mobile platforms and hence are *lightweight*. **Android**, **IOS**, **Flutter**, and so on can be used to develop mobile-based applications.

The Enterprise web applications are *complex*, *lengthy*, and *crucial* to developing from a security aspect as well. The market is demanding and the team cannot afford to spend months together to develop and then test the applications. A team needs to decide numerous things like the language for the application, the framework to use, the design patterns to use, and finally, after development the way by which the application will be tested. When an application development is done from scratch, it takes *time* and *effort*. Moreover, it requires highly experienced developers. The frameworks in this perspective, provide a basic infrastructure for faster development.

Can we imagine an application without data? Well, it's not improbable. But it is highly difficult to identify such applications. According to the scenario, one can go ahead and use SQL or NoSQL databases. Of course, there is no specific advice as to which is the best database and which one to use at this point of time. In this book, we will be using MySQL database. However, if one doesn't want to install any database, then we will also discuss the **in-memory H2 database**.

Apart from the scenario, we have discussed most of the things which are required to start the application development. But, *are we going to develop a Spring Boot web application or mobile application?* We are not going to develop either of them. You heard it right. *None of them! Why?* Before going into why, let me tell you that, we will be developing web services. Our service will handle the request and will generate the response after performing some business logic. It might even communicate to the database. Obviously, our service will not be all written in a single class. We will be developing a multilayer application to handle *request*, *logic*, and *database* communication in dedicated layers. Not to worry, we will discuss all this in detail in upcoming sections.

You must be having a whole bunch of questions. *The master key of knowledge is, indeed, a persistent and frequent questioning* - *Peter Abelard* once said. Don't worry, if you are a beginner and keen to know details about services, the next section is for you. I assume some of you might be already developing services and not so interested in all these details. If that is so, skip the section and start with the developing REST application section directly. Those who are interested to continue get relaxed in your chair and enjoy the next light discussion on service.

Need of a service

John, the PO of *Agile Team* was excited today. His team had already completed one of the sprints planned and he was about to present the same to the stakeholders. The development team completed the sprint using traditional UI components like **HTML**, **CSS**, and **Bootstrap** which were integrated with the business logic built in Java or Servlet/JSP. But when *John*, presented the current sprint to the stakeholders, they came up with a new requirement. They were expecting the UI to be converted to Angular rather than the traditional UI components. They wanted to leverage the advantage the application will get from Angular. Though the overall look and content were the same, this was a complete U-turn for the team. Also, when *John* communicated this to his team, the team was a bit reluctant to go for this change. Of course, *that was not an option!*

Being Agile, sounds really fascinating. But when after every sprint, the stakeholders propose new requirements, it is painful. The team needs to change the application code. Sometimes the task might be easy. But many times, the data to handle needs to change, lot of code needs to change which might generate a lot of conflicts in the team. We want our clients to always be happy, but *what about the team?* You know, this time the client is asking for the new functionality. It's new for them but my team has already developed a similar kind of solution in some other projects. The team now has to work again, this time obviously they will take less time as the solution is almost ready.

The solution code is so lengthy and *complex* in one technology, while other technology might achieve it easily. Now, *does the team need to migrate from one technology to another*? If there is no other choice, we need to do that. But it needs a lot of rework and frankly, the team might not want all the pain again. It would be great if we can develop a part of the solution in one technology and a part in another technology. Then these *two* applications will communicate with each other. Further to this, any of the solutions created in any technology can be independently used by anyone else as well.

Let us assume that we are designing a web application. The team had worked rigorously on the business logic and it is working fantastic. However, the team needs a better UI. The team can use some templates, CSS, and themes in the UI. But still, something is missing, and need to work for a better UI. This might be because of the technology we are using to develop web applications. The technology we are using might be providing us the best API for writing business logic but it is not giving the best results in terms of UI. In such conditions, we need to rework using new technology which will be able to provide us a way to design impressive UI. But this does not guarantee that the technology we are choosing will provide similar services for business logic development like the earlier technology. *Is there any technological solution where I can take leverage the best UI as well as enterprise solution?* All you need is a service. A way of communication between different parts of a software system to exchange data over the network is a service or precisely a web service. One part of the software system requests for the data and the other part or parts provide the details. The part of the system which requests the data is a **Service Consumer** and the one who provides the details is called a **Service Provider**.

The different parts of the software system may use different programming languages. The languages have their own *data types*, *ways of declaration*, and *its use*. When we want to communicate between heterogeneous languages, we need to take care of a couple of things. The very first, all such communication needs lots of work in terms of API for cross-language communication. Second, due to technical differences even if the communication happens, it will *futile*. That means we need a method for the data exchange that is not dependent upon a particular programming language. Instead of executing a logic of another application's module, we request the module to take the resource, execute the logic and return the modified or expected payload response.

The service-based applications exchange the data in between them over one or multiple calls. As we know, this communication is between heterogeneous applications the most important what they need is the data of some common format which all of them should understand with less or no work. Most of the languages can interpret, understand and have APIs for XML and JSON. So, it is obvious most of the services use XML and JSON to exchange the data.

Developing a simple REST service

Lots of discussion and theory, we can write a separate book on this concept. Lots of materials are available on this in tangible and intangible formats. So, let us not get into much detail. It is time for action now. Let's start then.

Here, we will be developing a service for *hospital management* that will communicate with the database for performing CRUD operations._Our application is a *multi-layered service* deployed on the server along with a few other applications as shown in *Figure 2.1:*

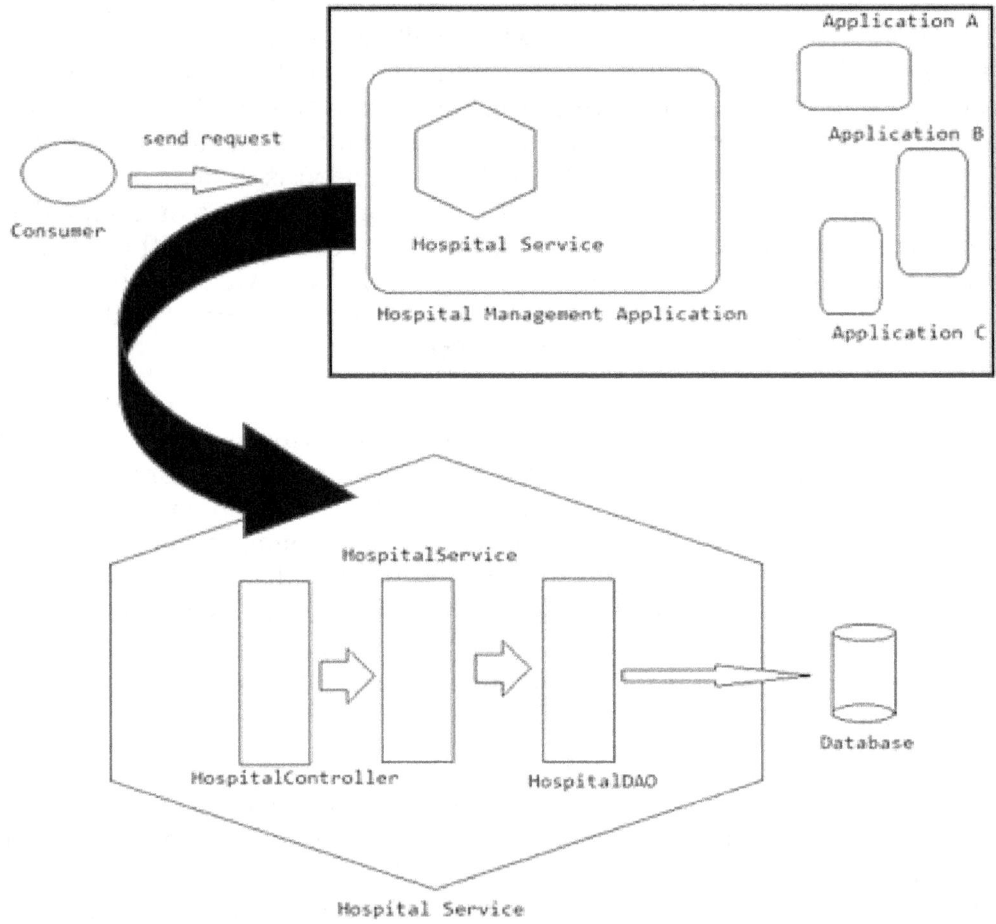

Figure 2.1: *Hospital Service Management*

Let's get started. We will develop a Spring Boot application in **Eclipse STS** having **Spring web**, **JDBC**, and **MySQL** as dependencies. Those who want to use **H2** or any other database such as **Oracle**, **PostgreSQL**. Please select the respective dependencies from the SQL section_as shown in *Figure* 2.2:

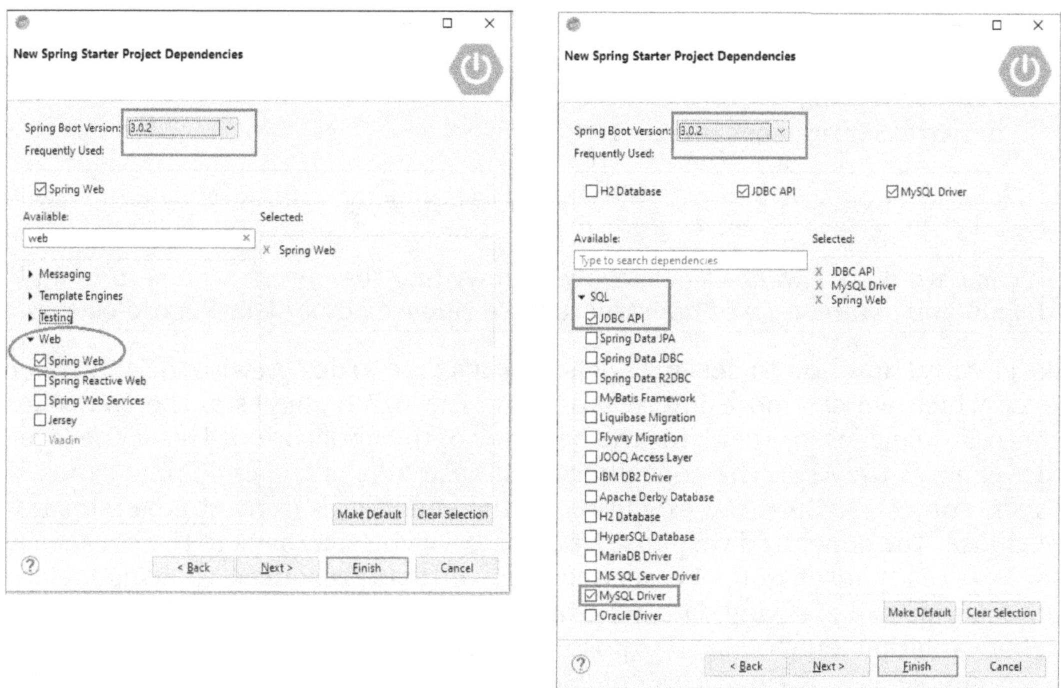

***Figure 2.2**: Creating spring boot app with dependencies*

Once the application is generated, observe the starters added in the **pom.xml** file. Just a quick reminder - in *Chapter 1: The Foundation*, we already have discussed the starters. In case you want to revise, please visit the *Quick start* section in *Chapter 1, The Foundation*. Our application is a multi-layered application as shown in *Figure 2.1*. Now in general, when we are aware of what concept we are going to implement to complete the application, the choice is ours; either to start with the *code* or with *configuration*. It is usually preferred to start with code, but that is just an individual's preference. So, here we are going to follow the pattern of *code first*. Our application needs a service for the *doctors*. It means along with other layers to take the data from one layer to another, we also need some domain objects. In our application, we need a *Hospital*, *Doctor*, *Patients*, and so on as domain objects. To start with, here we are going to define a POJO for *Doctor*, having some *data members*, *constructors*, and *accessor* and *mutator* methods. The need of **`toString()`** and **`hashCode()`** is scenario based. We don't need them here. The following code shows the actual content of the POJO:

```
public class Doctor {
 private int doctorId;
 private String doctorName;
 private String specialization;
}
```

Note

In case, we do not want to get involved in writing the getters and setters and default and parameterized constructors we can use Lombok or Record classes.

We already know how to design POJOs; now it's time to design with the controller layer which we are more interested in. As the name suggests, the *controller* controls, manages, or regulates the behavior of the application. This is the layer that exposes the APIs. The consumer uses these APIs or the endpoints exposed by the controller. Once the execution on the endpoint is done, it generates the response. The generated **response/ payload*** will be sent back to the *consumer*. As we already discussed, the service deals in **data/resource** exchange. Here onwards instead of saying data, we will use the term **resource**. So, the *controller* defines multiple endpoints to expose the resources. In general, a resource can be as simple as, a **String** or as complex as a video file. Anything which can be shared to and from the *consumer* such as *object*, *file*, *image*, and more, can be considered as a resource. Here, we will be dealing with an object as a resource.

Note

* A payload in web services is the data that is sent in HTTP request or response. The payload is this information which is exchanged between the consumer and the provider. The payload can be of various formats such as text, XML, and JSON, and so on.

REST controller layer

Let's declare the **DoctorController** with end-points to perform CRUD operations on the **Doctor** resource. The very first end-point we will be declaring is the endpoint that accepts the instance of the **Doctor**. We are not going to add this resource to the database as of now. But we will surely do that in our next sections. In this section, we will focus on how to declare, implement, and use the end-points:

```
package com.example.demo.controllers;
@RestController
public class DoctorController {
   @PostMapping("/doctors")
   public Doctor createNewDoctorRecord(@RequestBody Doctor doctor) {
     // Logic to add record in table will go here
   return doctor;}
}
```

The controller class is annotated by a stereotype annotation **`@RestController`** which is a specialized version of **`@Component`** annotation and this is auto-detected through the **classpath** scanning. The **`@PostMapping`** annotation applied to the handler method **`createNewDoctorRecord()`** is expected to read the incoming HTTP request containing details of a *doctor*. The annotation **@PostMapping** annotation, is a shortcut for **`@RequestMapping(method=RequestMethod.POST)`** which is available since *Spring* 4.3, along with a few other annotations. We will discuss the other annotations later in this section. The **`@PostMapping`** annotation is used when we want to create a new resource at the provider end. Observe the way the endpoint is declared:

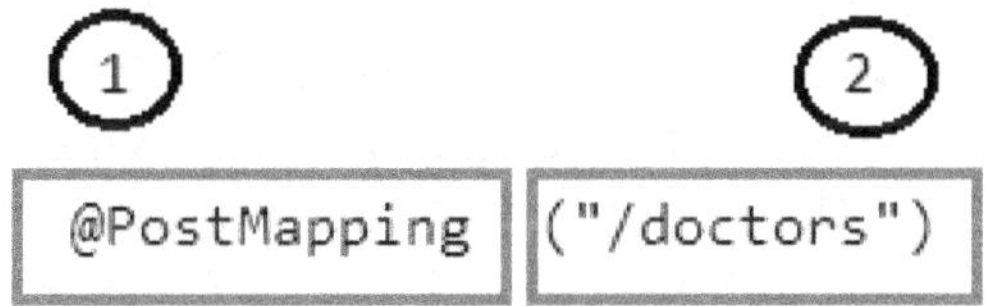

***Figure 2.3**: End point for resource creation*

The *first* part defines a *uniform interface*. A **uniform interface** declares the **HTTP method**, for which the incoming request is mapped. The *second* part defines the path for which the *endpoint* is defined. This second part is usually a plural form of a noun, instead of a verb as usually we declare in Java. Also, this path value should always start with a slash **/**. A pair of HTTP methods and the path is always unique for an application, so be careful while re-using it.

Now, take into consideration the *handler* method and observe its argument:

```
public Doctor createNewDoctorRecord( @RequestBody Doctor doctor )
```

***Figure 2.4**: Accepting RequestBody in method argument*

The method accepts an argument of type **Doctor**, which is annotated by the **`@RequestBody`** annotation shown in the preceding figure. The **`@RequestBody`** annotation maps the incoming **`HttpRequest`** having the body to a domain object. In our case, it is *doctor*. It enables the automatic deserialization of the inbound **`HttpRequest`** body to an instance. Here, as we are using the default deserialization mechanism, the JSON data sent by the consumer will be de-serialized to our *doctor* instance using the deserialization APIs by Spring Boot framework. For the time being, we are keeping the return type as **Doctor**. Of course, we are free to decide, what to return from the handler method. One thing we always need to remember is, services are meant for communication between *two* applications or services. When the response is received at the consumer end, the *consumer* needs to take the decision, on what action to perform depending upon what happened at the provider end or the endpoint. It can be void, if we don't want to send any information to the consumer. It can be also the number of records affected in the table, or an instance as we have returned in our snippet. Though here we have returned an instance, we will revisit the method to change it. *But not now!*

Let's test the endpoint now using Postman as a client. The **Postman** is a tool that enables the developers to explore, test, and debug the controller APIs easily. Using **Postman**, we can use all HTTP methods such as **GET**, **POST**, **PUT**, **PATCH** as well as **DELETE**. Along with HTTP requests, we can also define the complex API requests for **REST**, **SOAP**, **WebSockets** as well as **GraphQL**. It also has *built-in support* of authentication for a wide range of protocols including **AWS Signature**, **OAuth 1.0**, **OAuth 2.0**, and so on. Postman is one of the testing tools, we will also provide information and relative download links in *Appendix-2* instead of including all of them here. The Postman can be downloaded from **https://www.postman.com/downloads/**. Please go ahead and download it for your respective platforms. After the download, when you launch it for the very first time, it may ask you to sign in. Not to worry, you can skip the sign-in process just by clicking the **skip** link which is placed below the *username* and *password* text fields. In case you are struggling, please refer to *Appendix-2*.

Time to use Postman after launching! You will get the UI as shown in *Figure 2.5*:

***Figure* 2.5**: POSTMAN *dashboard*

Let's now start the application and hit our endpoint to create a new resource. Please follow *eight* steps one by one, to send the request as shown in *Figure* 2.6:

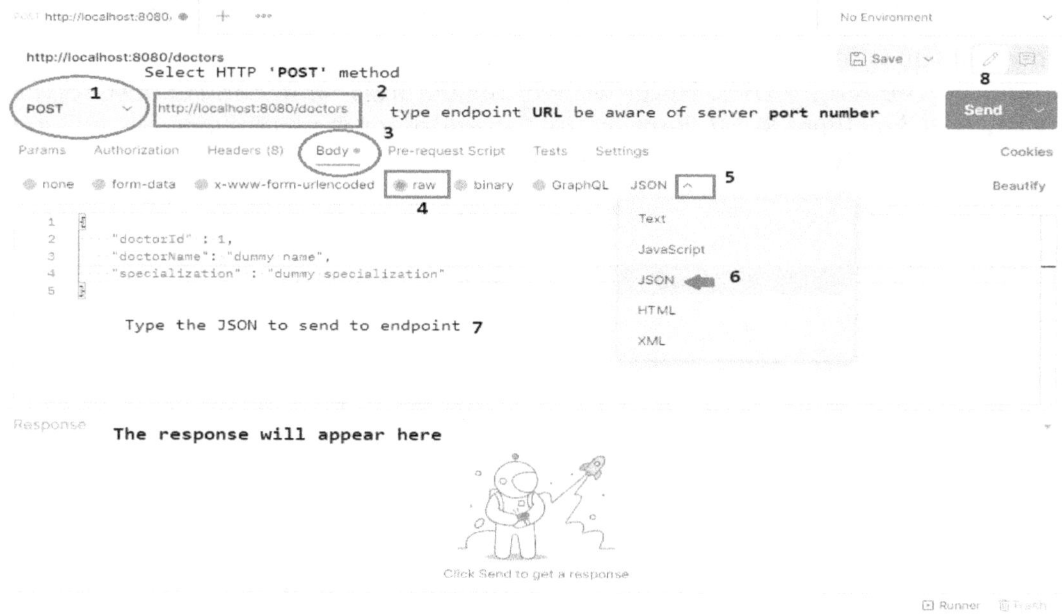

Figure 2.6: *Using* POSTMAN

Once you click on send button, a **HTTP POST** request will be sent to **http://localhost:8080/doctors** endpoint. If the matching URI **/doctors** is available, the *handler* method will be invoked and the logic will be executed. Finally, a *response* is generated and sent to the *consumer*. In our case, it is a dummy object of type *Doctor* is received at the *consumer* end as shown in *Figure* 2.7:

Figure 2.7: *Observing HTTP status 200 in* POSTMAN

In the response, the most important thing is **the status code**. The status code enables the *consumer* to understand what happened to the request sent to the provider. It normally denotes if the action is executed without issues, or if any exception is raised, and so on. Here, we are fortunate to get the status code **200** which means everything is fine on the server. The request endpoint is available, it is executed without any exception and the response is also generated.

Now, the question is, *what if the endpoint doesn't exist?* Let's edit the URL and enter the wrong URL. Here, we will deliberately send the request to the URL **http://localhost:8080/doctor1**. As the endpoint is *unavailable*, we will get the status code **404** as shown in *Figure* 2.8:

***Figure* 2.8:** Observing HTTP status 404 in POSTMAN

Sometimes the URI is *correct*, but our server is *stopped* or not available on the specified *port* number or at the specified *IP address*. In such case, we will get the connection error as shown in *Figure* 2.9:

***Figure* 2.9:** *Connection error in POSTMAN*

For the *developer*, it is important to test the endpoints in all the possible scenarios. Depending on the test result the *developer* will be able to know which *status code* the consumer will receive at their end in the given situation. The testing will allow *developers* to write code with better quality and also to write documentation for reference in a proper way. This will also help the *consumer* in understanding the reason for the response received and to take appropriate action. Here, we have sent a request body of type JSON and we have received status code **200**. You might want to send **XML** or **Text** in the request body or you may want to respond to the consumer with **201** as status code instead of **200**. We will discuss this all in detail very soon.

In the earlier case, the provider reads a resource of type object, now the question is, *is it possible to read primitives as well?* Obviously, you can. The Spring Boot has made the process very easy to accept primitives. Let's declare the endpoint which will be requested by the consumer to fetch the records depending upon the **doctorId**. The following code snippet shows how to write the handler method for the same:

```
@GetMapping("/doctors/{id}")
public Doctor findDoctorById(@PathVariable int id) {
  // logic to find doctor by id will go here
  return new Doctor(id, "dummy name", "dummy specialization" );
}
```

The **@GetMapping** handles the HTTP GET method. The endpoint to find a resource depending on some criteria is declared using **@GetMapping** annotation. The *consumer* needs to send the criteria to search for the matching record or records. If the information to exchange is sensitive or lengthy, it's always preferred to use **@RequestBody** annotation and send the resource via body, so that it will not be visible publicly. However, most of the time it is not *sensitive* and one can send it in the **URI** itself. Observe the endpoint declaration as shown in *Figure 2.10*:

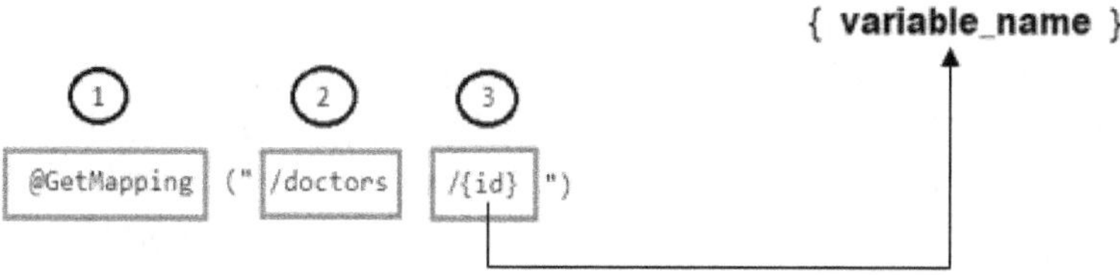

Figure 2.10: *GetMapping with data appended in URI*

The *first* part defines the mapping for incoming HTTP requests to the *controller* method. The *second* part is the base URI path. For us, the *third* part which is also part of the path is most important, as it is the first time when we are sending some values to the provider. It is typically called a **URI path variable.** It is always declared in the pair of curly brackets **{ }** holding the valid *variable name.* The *curly* brackets act as a placeholder, where the *consumer* is going to send the actual information.

Now, the values sent by the *consumer* must be available to the provider for use. The **@PathVariable** annotation enables the provider to access the value from the path. When the consumer adds the value in the URI, technically it is of **String** type, but we are accessing it directly as an **integer**. We are able to do so, as Spring Boot reads the values from the **URI** path when it reads the **@PathVariable** annotation. Then depending on the data type we declared for the *argument* type, the framework parses the **String** value to that respective data type. We as a *developer* just have to use it. Let's test the **GET** endpoint in Postman as shown in *Figure 2.11*:

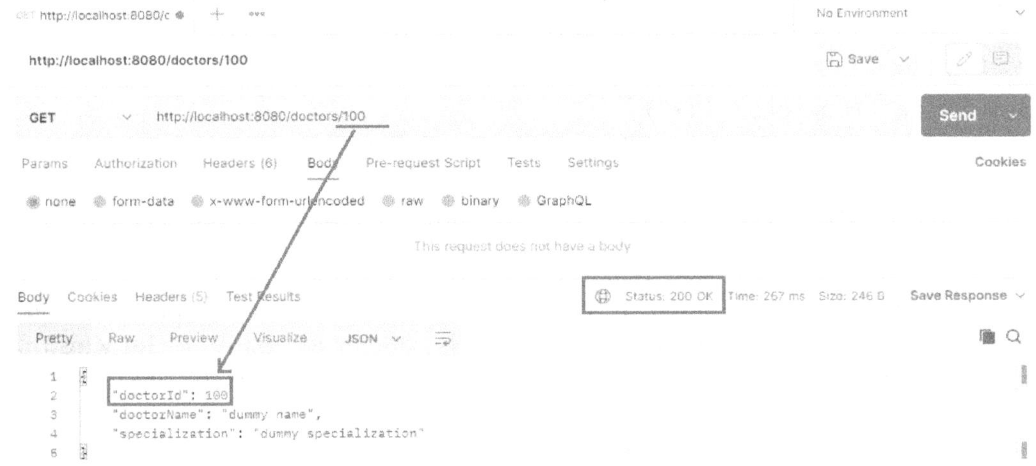

Figure 2.11: *Passing path variable in* POSTMAN

As the figure clearly shows, we requested for the **GET** endpoint having a path variable value for **doctorId** as **100**. As the endpoint is available, we got the response status code as **200**. The JSON response also shows a value for **doctorId** attribute, equals to **100** proving the proper binding of **path** variable value to the function argument as discussed earlier. We need to remember one thing, by default the *name of the argument* should match with the **path** variable name. This is just a default strategy, and one can follow their own conventions as well. To achieve this some extra work is required at the developer end. *Chill!* It is easy and we will discuss in the next handler method.

So, without wasting time, let's start declaring the *handler* method to search the *doctors* by their specialization as shown here:

```
@GetMapping("/doctors/{specialization}")
public List<Doctor> findDoctorBySpecialization(@PathVariable
String doctor_specialization) {
    // Logic to find all doctors by specialization will go here
    return Arrays.asList(new Doctor(1, "dummy name",
                              doctor_specialization ));

}
```

We already have discussed the **@GetMapping**, **@PathVariable** annotations. *Do you remember, the pair of HTTP method and URI is unique? Aren't we redeclaring the same pair here?* No! In the first **GetMapping** we had **/doctors/{id}** and here it is **/doctors/{specialization}**. *Where is the similarity? Very true.* It is the same for normal human being or non-technical persons, but it is not the same technically:

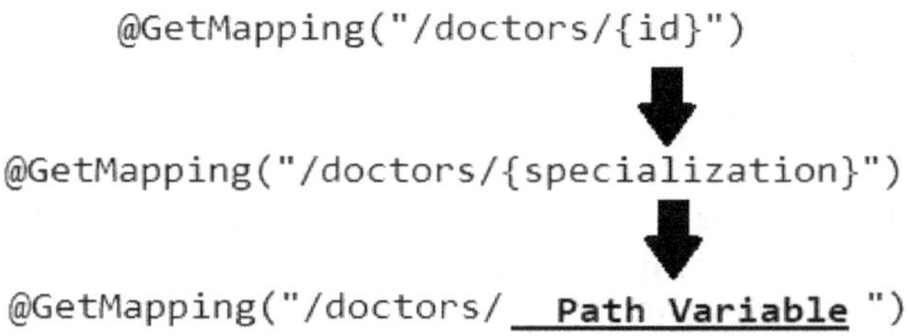

***Figure 2.12**: Ambiguous end points*

Both the URIs are having the same format. So, when the *consumer* tries to send a request like **http://doctors/10 or http:8080/doctors/heart** from the Postman will raise the **IllegalStateException** due to ambiguous handler mappings. You can cross-check the occurrence of the exception. Please run the application and try to hit one of the preceding URI from the Postman. You will get the *internal server error* with a *white label*. Please visit the application console where we will get the stack trace as shown in the *Figure* 2.13:

```
java.lang.IllegalStateException: Ambiguous handler methods mapped for '/doctors/12': {
                                  public com.example.demo.pojo.Doctor  com.example.demo.controllers.DoctorController.findDoctorById(int)
                                 ,public java.util.List com.example.demo.controllers.DoctorController.findDoctorBySpecialization(java.lang.String)
                                 }
```

***Figure 2.13**: IllegalStateException for ambiguous end points*

We instead of responding to the consumer with *white label error* can respond with custom response. We will discuss the exception handling in detail under *Exception Handling* section.

For time being, let's update the mapping to overcome the exception as:

```
@GetMapping("/doctors/specialization/{specialization}")
public List<Doctor> findDoctorBySpecialization(@PathVariable String doctor_specialization)
```

Figure 2.14: *Handling IllegalStateException*

Now, keenly observe the **path** variable name and the name of the method argument in shown in preceding *Figure* 2.14. Unfortunately, they don't match and we will not be able to use it. If a *consumer* sends the request for this endpoint, he will get the **500 Internal Server Error** and if we observe the application console, we will get the message about the absence of URI path variable as shown in the *Figure* 2.15:

```
Resolved [org.springframework.web.bind.MissingPathVariableException: Required URI template variable
'doctor_specialization' for method parameter type String is not present]
```

Figure 2.15: *MissingPathVariableException for end points*

The exception message straight forward suggests the **path** variable is not bounded. Here we have *two* choices. One is to change the *method argument declaration*, to match with the path variable name. However, if for some reason that's not possible then we can use the second choice of using *attribute of path variable* which enables the binding of variable in the path to the argument of the method. Let's update the **@PathVariable** annotation as follows:

```
@GetMapping("/doctors/specialization/{specialization}")
public List<Doctor> findDoctorBySpecialization(@PathVariable("specialization") String doctor_specialization)
```

Figure 2.16: *Handling MissingPathVariableException*

Great! Now, we are flexible enough to declare a different name of the function argument from that of the path variable name. We can test the endpoint using Postman for the URL **http://localhost:8080/specialization/heart**. Don't forget to launch the application before you test. Observe that, you are getting the correct response.

Now, our endpoint is working fine. We are the *developers* and want to handle some permutation combinations of the URIs. We can send the information via the **path** variable. But *do we have the flexibility to choose whether to provide the path variable or not?* In short, *can the **path** variables be optional? Or can the **path** variables have default value? Lucky you are!* We have the flexibility to do so just by adding the attributes. Let us do a quick check on ***@PathVariable*** annotation to have more insight of *what we can do?*

The annotation has *three* attributes: **name**, **required**, and **value** to modify its default behavior. The default value of the **name** attribute is the same as that of the **path** variable. But we can change it, as we did in **findDoctorBySpecialization()** method. Also, we can use the **value** attribute to add aliases for the **path** variable. One can either use the **name**, or the **value** attribute to specify the binding of the **path** variable to the argument. As we were having a single attribute, we don't need to specify the **name** attribute. The second attribute **required** takes a value of type **boolean**. By default, **required** has value **true**, which means the consumer needs to specify it, and if is not specified an error occurs. One can use it to make the path variable *optional*. As we are now going to specify more than one attributes, we have to specify the name of each attribute. So, the possible modifications available to use are as follows:

Case 1: Using the required attribute specifying the *path* variable is optional

```
@GetMapping(value={"/doctors/specialization","/doctors/specialization
                                              /{specialization}"})
public List<Doctor> findDoctorBySpecialization(@PathVariable(
 name="specialization",required = false) String doctor_
                                      specialization)
```

Case 2: Using *value* attribute

```
@GetMapping(value={"/doctors/specialization","/doctors/specialization
                                               /{specialization}"})
public List<Doctor> findDoctorBySpecialization(@PathVariable(
 value="specialization",required = false)
                        String doctor_specialization)
```

Case 3: Using both value as well as *name* attribute

```
@GetMapping(value={"/doctors/specialization","/doctors/specialization
                                              /{specialization}"})
public List<Doctor> findDoctorBySpecialization(@PathVariable
 (name="specialization",required = false,value="specialization")
                                      String doctor_specialization)
```

Case 4: Using *java.util.Optional* for path variable

After JDK 1.8, instead of using **required** as an attribute, one can also use the type **java.util.Optional** for the argument, whenever we want the **path** variable to be optional. We need to make certain changes in the code to declare the type of argument as **<Optional> String** instead of **String**, and in the code, we now have to check the presence of the **path** variable logically. The following sample code does the same:

```
@GetMapping(value = { "/doctors/specialization", "
                    /doctors/specialization/{specialization}" })
public List<Doctor> findDoctorBySpecialization(
                    @PathVariable(name = "specialization")
                    Optional<String> doctor_specialization) {
 // logic to find all doctors by specialization will go here
 String specialization = "all";
 List<Doctor> doctors=new ArrayList<>();
 if (doctor_specialization.isPresent()) {
  doctors= Arrays.asList(new Doctor(1, "dummy name",
                     doctor_specialization.get()));
 }
 return Arrays.
         asList(new Doctor(1,"dummy name", "any specialization"));
}
```

We can execute the application and test each one of them by sending a GET request from Postman using the URLs as, **http://localhost:8080/doctors/specialization/child** or **http://localhost:8080/doctors/specialization**.

We have here more than one case for the same URL mapping. So, please add one case at a time otherwise you will get an *ambiguous* mapping exception.

In all the examples for the HTTP GET method that we just discussed; we were expecting the **path** variable. One may also with to get the list of all the doctors. In that case, we simply have to give up the **path** variable as shown in the following code to find all *doctors*:

```
@GetMapping(value="/doctors")
public List<Doctor> findAllDoctors() {
   // logic to find all doctors will go here
   return Arrays.asList(new Doctor(1,"dummy name", "all" ));
}
```

Now the question is *do we really need this* URL? Frankly, not required. We already have the URL with the *optional* path variable we can reuse it anytime. One thing to note is **/doctors/specialization/{specialization}** when starts handling request for searching the resource for a specific specialization or all the *doctors* then load on it will increase and the performance may get hampered. Think *twice* before you write an endpoint to handle multiple conditions and *then make your choice!*

We now have the information about how to create a new resource, and find the existing resource. Now, let's modify the resource. The **@PutMapping** annotation enables the mapping of HTTP PUT requests to a specific *handler* method. It is the shortcut for the **@RequestMapping(method = RequestMethod.Put)** annotation. The HTTP PUT method is used to update or *modify* the available entire resource. Let's add a *handler* method to update the resource as shown in the code:

```
@PutMapping("/doctors")
public Doctor modifyDoctorInfo(@RequestBody Doctor doctor) {
   // logic to update the doctor's information if the id exists will go
   // here otherwise we will create a new record in DB
   return doctor;
}
```

The way we requested GET or POST, in the same way, we can test this endpoint as well. Just make sure to select the PUT method from the drop down and don't forget to send the JSON request body as well. We will test this after the database connectivity, as here we are dealing with dummy values. *Hope that's fine!* Let's move on to the next HTTP method PATCH. Here, we used the **@PutMapping** to update the entire resource. However, now we want to partially update the resource. *Can we use the same? Can we do it in the following way?*

```
@PutMapping("/doctors/{id}/{specialization}")
public Doctor modifyDoctorInfo(@PathVariable int id,
@PathVariable String specialization) {
   // logic to update the doctor's information will go here
   return new Doctor(id, "abc", specialization);
}
```

It's a *legal* declaration. This endpoint will search the *doctor* with the given *id*, and update its specialization. Then the question might be, *why we are not using the earlier endpoint and creating a new one to update some fields? Good point! Shall we try to do so first before going ahead with the discussion?* Let's test the endpoint just by sending the specialization.

If we send partial values, the rest of the unset fields will be set to their respective default values. It means we want to update the *doctor*'s specialization and we are sending only a value for that particular field. In this case, the value of the name of *doctor* will be null and the *doctorID* being an integer will be *zero*. And we don't want this to happen. Let's give it another try to get a better idea. This time we are providing the values assuming the *id* and *name* is already present and only the specialization field value is *new*.

Under such a scenario **@PatchMapping** comes to rescue us. Let's try another better approach to use when we want to partially update the resource. We can use HTTP PATCH method instead of the PUT. Let's modify the endpoint mapping of the code for **Patch** method as:

```
@PatchMapping("/doctors/{id}/{specialization}")
public Doctor modifyDoctorInfo(@PathVariable int id,
@PathVariable String specialization) {
   // logic to update the doctor's information if the id exists will go here
      return new Doctor(id, "abc", specialization);
}
```

Go ahead and test it in Postman, as we did for all other endpoints.

Congratulations! You can now create new resources, update them, and search them as well. The resource we created with so much interest I don't want to delete it. However, that is our final mapping in discussion, *how to delete an existing resource?* We now will be mapping the HTTP DELETE request to a handler method using **@DeleteMapping** which is a shortcut for the **`@RequestMapping(method = RequestMethod.Delete)`** annotation.

The following *handler* method will delete the existing resource:

```
@DeleteMapping("/doctors/{id}")
public Doctor deleteDoctorById(@PathVariable int id) {
   // logic to delete the doctor's information if the id
exists will go here
   return new Doctor(id, "abc", "dummy specialization");
}
```

And with this, we covered the frequently used HTTP methods with dummy data to clear the concept of how to declare the *handler* methods for a specific type of HTTP request for a JSON type of data to declare an endpoint. Now, in the next section, we will focus on handling data of type XML or HTML or from form submission, and so on.

> **Note**
>
> When we use, PUT, POST, or PATCH method to modify or create a new resource the client hitting the API, should be informed of the activity that happened at the endpoint. And because of this, every time we have returned the resource, for example, Doctor. The same thing we adapted even for HTTP DELETE. But we also can declare the return type as void or HTTP status code.

Updates for handling URL formats in Spring Boot 3.0

In the earlier versions of Spring Boot, if we use **/xxx** or **/xxx/** URLs, the *trailing slash*, that is **/** is not considered significant. However, with the updated version

Spring 6.0, the trailing slash matching configuration option has been deprecated. This means that **/xxx** and **/xxx/** are not identical. If you do not follow the exact configuration of URL then you will end up with HTTP **404** error. So, we need to be careful while adding the trailing slash to the URL.

Handling different media types

As discussed earlier, by default the endpoints in Spring Boot web services consume as well as produce JSON. However, some *consumers* may want to send or receive XML representation. Spring Boot uses **Jackson Data Binder** library to handle the *serialization* and *deserialization* of incoming requests and outgoing responses to and from the XML. As we know we need to use APIs to perform the conversion. Just by placing the library on the *classpath*, the container will not be able to choose the conversion or the converters automatically as we know the JSON is the default conversion type. We also need to specify on the *handler* method to consume the request body having XML or producing the response having XML presentation. The **consumes** and **produces** are the attributes of the **@XXXMapping** annotations that enable the handling of different media types instead of using JSON as a default media type.

The most interesting part is one *handler* method can handle more than one media type. Hence, let's update our defined handler method **createNewDoctorRecord()** to handle XML media type along with JSON using **consumes** attribute each separated by a comma as follows:

```
@PostMapping(path = "/doctors", consumes = {
    MediaType.APPLICATION_JSON_VALUE, MediaType.APPLICATION_XML_VALUE})
```

Don't forget to add **Jackson** library in the class path so as provider message converter to and from the XML in **pom.xml** by the tag shown as follows:

```
<dependency>
     <groupId>com.fasterxml.jackson.dataformat</groupId>
     <artifactId>jackson-dataformat-xml</artifactId>
</dependency>
```

We have services exposing endpoints. Many times, our services will be used by the front ends such as **Angular** or **React-based applications**. Now consider we have a front-end application that we are accessing from the browser. The *client* now will fill up the form to send a *doctor's* information to create a new record of the *doctor*. When the form is submitted, a HTTP request will be sent from the *front-end* to the *back-end* service hitting the respective endpoint. Now, in our case, as we want to create a new resource it should hit the POST endpoint to accept the values from the submitted form. Let's add an endpoint to handle the form submission as shown in *Figure 2.17*:

Figure 2.17: *Working with Form data*

The figure clearly shows the response of type JSON as it is a default presentation by Spring Boot. However, sometimes the scenario demands XML, HTML, or text-based presentation. The attribute **produces** enables us to specify the expected response type. Let's update the endpoint to generate the response of type XML consuming data from the form submission as:

```
@PostMapping(path = "/doctors/form",
  consumes = MediaType.APPLICATION_FORM_URLENCODED_VALUE,
  produces = MediaType.APPLICATION_XML_VALUE)
```

Now, let us execute the application and send the request from Postman. *Luckily*, we have the earlier request sent from Postman. We need to click on the **Send** button. Once we do this, we will receive the response having the same value as that of earlier but now we will get the response which will not be of type JSON but of XML presentation as shown in *Figure 2.18*:

Body Cookies Headers (5) Test Results Status: 200 OK

Pretty Raw Preview Visualize XML

```
<Doctor>
    <doctorId>1</doctorId>
    <doctorName>ABC</doctorName>
    <specialization>Medicine</specialization>
</Doctor>
```

Figure 2.18: XML *response*

A *question*! We can consume multiple media types. In the same way, *can we produce a response having multiple media types*? *Yes, we can*. Depending on the client's requirement the *producer* can generate the response of type JSON by default or the specified one. To do so let's update the produces attribute as:

```
@PostMapping(path = "/doctors/form",
            consumes = MediaType.APPLICATION_FORM_URLENCODED_VALUE,
            produces = {MediaType.APPLICATION_JSON_VALUE,
                        MediaType.APPLICATION_XML_VALUE})
```

Let's re-execute the application and submit a request to a specific endpoint from Postman. *Are you getting the response of type* XML? You can observe that, it is not of type of XML. You are getting the response having a JSON presentation because it is default. *Does it mean we can't get* XML *response*? We will get the XML response if we ask for it and to specify *what kind of response presentation the consumer expects*, the consumer has to add a header **Accept** in the request. Let's add the header in the request to ask for the XML presentation as shown in *Figure* 2.19:

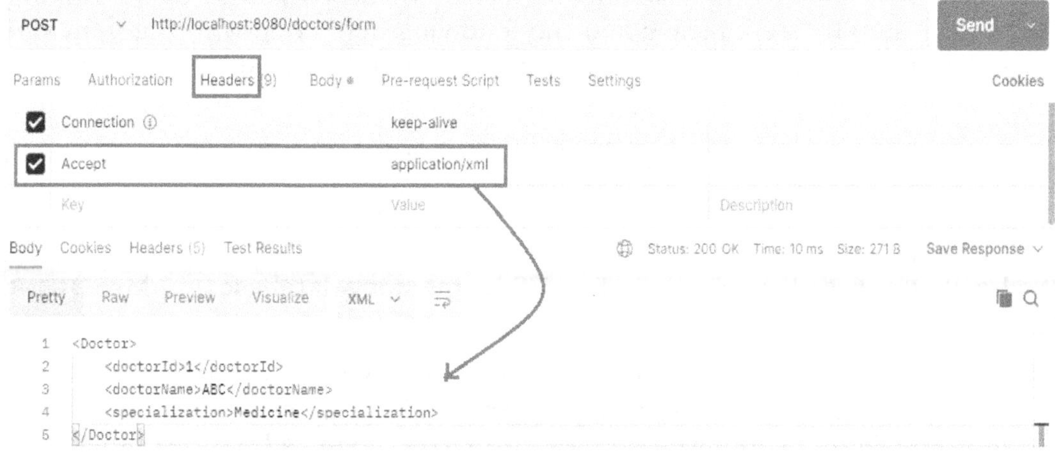

Figure 2.19: *Working with XML data*

Communicating with database

Well Done!!! We very well understood the handling of request and response by the *handler* method of the *controller* in the service. However, to focus on one factor at a time we did not pay attention to the persistency layer. Also, being all of us from JAVA background we are pretty confident and aware of the concepts involved in JDBC. The thing we might need to discuss is a couple of queries such as how Spring Boot handles JDBC *integration*, *classes*, and *interfaces* involved in this process, and how the connection is obtained.

The **spring-jdbc** starter provides all the relevant definitions of classes and interfaces involved to use JDBC API in our code. As we are developing a multi-layered application we are having a dedicated DAO layer to communicate with the database and to handle CRUD operations. Spring is flexible enough to support JDBC API use in our code in Java style. It means we can obtain the connection, get the relevant type of statement, fire the query, and finally process the result. So, let's start by adding the starter in the application if you don't have it already. We have created the application including the **spring-jdbc** starter, so we do not have to add it explicitly. In case anyone missed the dependency or developing the project step by step, please add the following dependency in the **pom.xml** file and don't forget to add relevant driver for the databases dependency as well:

```
<dependency>
  <groupId>org.springframework.boot</groupId>
  <artifactId>spring-boot-starter-jdbc</artifactId>
</dependency>
```

As already discussed, we will be using **H2 in-memory database** and **MySQL** for the demonstration.

Now, we want to create a flexible application that is easy to migrate from one database to another, without changing the code. The *major reason* for not achieving flexibility is to have database properties such as URL, *username*, and *password* in the class definition. Spring Boot enables easy configuration of these and similar other properties by externalizing them in **application.properties** or **application.yml** file. In this way, we can achieve flexibility in the database connectivity as it is not configured as static values in any class definition. In the next section, we will discuss the connectivity using in **memory H2 database**. In case, you don't want to use it and want to continue with MySQL please skip the next section.

The **H2 in-memory database** gives us the advantage of using it with no or minimum properties in the configuration file. So, let us go ahead and execute the code and observe the console log for H2 database connectivity. *Are you getting H2 related any logs on the console*? Unfortunately, *not*! It is because by default the H2 console is *disabled*, let us add the property to *enable* the H2 console, observe the highlighted part of your console in the *Figure* 2.20:

```
main] com.zaxxer.hikari.HikariDataSource          : HikariPool-1 - Starting...
main] com.zaxxer.hikari.pool.HikariPool           : HikariPool-1 - Added connection conn0: url=jdbc:h2:mem:9045507e-5d32-40cf-815a-b38bbf8f46c5 user=SA
main] com.zaxxer.hikari.HikariDataSource          : HikariPool-1 - Start completed.
main] o.s.b.a.h2.H2ConsoleAutoConfiguration       : H2 console available at '/h2-console'. Database available at 'jdbc:h2:mem:9045507e-5d32-40cf-815a-b38bbf8f46c5'
```

***Figure* 2.20**: *Enabling H2 console*

This is providing us the database URL to connect.

You got a default URL to connect with **H2 database**. *Isn't it cool? Yes, it is*. But we can't forget one thing, this is an *in-memory database* and hence we are at risk of losing all the persisted data once the application is restarted and the URL will change each time. Let's try to open H2 console using the default URL **http://localhost:8080/h2-console** as shown in *Figure* 2.21:

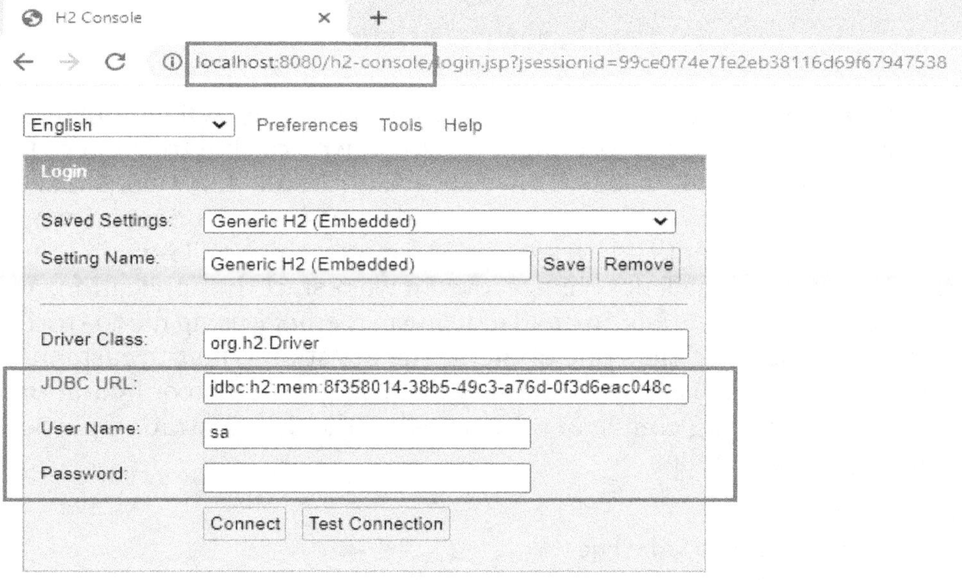

***Figure* 2.21**: *Launching H2 console*

Enter the URL which you obtained from the console. We can use the default username as, **sa** with *no* or *blank* password. Try to first test the connectivity by clicking the **Test Connection** button. If it works and displays message as **Connection successful**, please *go ahead*, and connect to the database. We will land on a page where we get the *editor* to type the queries and multiple options to execute them. Also, on the left-hand side, we will get the H2 database structure as shown in *Figure 2.22*:

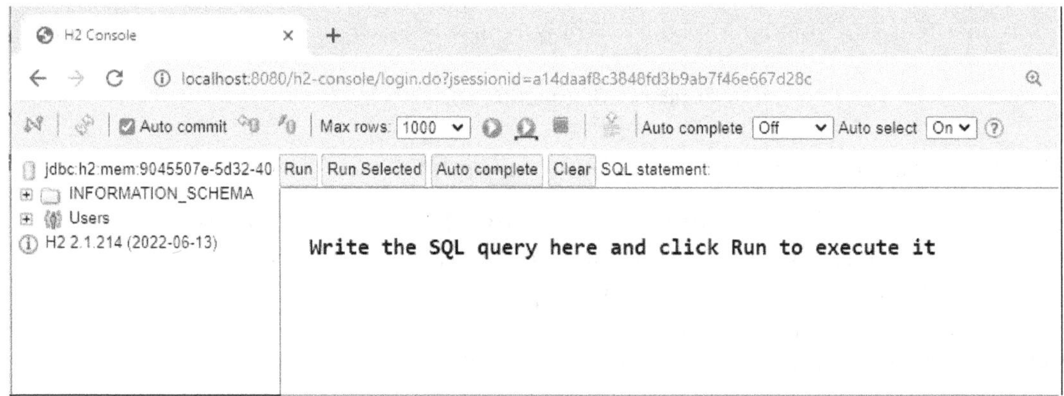

Figure 2.22: *Exploring H2*

The playground is all yours, go ahead and try some of the SQL commands just to make sure the database is working fine. *Great*, we are able to connect to the database with the default values. However, using the default values make our application vulnerable. We may want to provide a password for security or may want to provide a different URL to access H2 *console* which will remain the same on every execution and will not change, even if we restart the application. A URL, *password*, or other *credentials*, instead of using in memory using file to store data we are able to customize each one of them. The question is *how to customize the H2database properties*? The answer is very *simple*, update the configuration file. Here, we are configuring couple of properties for the demonstration purpose in **application.properties** file:

```
#default is false
spring.h2.console.enabled=true
# default is /h2-console
spring.h2.console.path= /h2
spring.datasource.url=jdbc:h2:mem:sample_db
# default is sa
spring.datasource.username= service
# default is blank
spring.datasource.password= service
```

Just restart the application and check the logs for H2 URL. The console logs will display **/h2** which we have configured in the properties file just now. Let's use **http://locahost:8080/h2** to access the database console along with values of URL, *username*, and *password* same as that of **application.properties** file. *Great!* Now you have successfully connected to the H2 database.

It's time to use the MySQL database for persistency and` to do so we need to change the dependency for driver from H2 to MySQL connector in the **pom.xml** and then configure MySQL connectivity properties as specified in *Figure 2.23*:

```
spring.datasource.url=jdbc:mysql://localhost:3306/doctors
spring.datasource.username=root
spring.datasource.password=mysql
```

database schema to connect

***Figure 2.23**: Configuring MySQL*

The schema specified must exist before you start using it, in case it is not existing you have to create one in the MySQL. Once our database is *ready* to connect now let's focus on the code.

We want to perform CRUD operations for the data received from the *consumer*. We are developing a *multi-layered application*, so let's add a layer for database operation. The DAO *layer* consists of a contract having functions for performing CRUD operations as:

```
public interface DoctorDAO {
   int addDoctor(Doctor doctor);
   boolean updateDoctor(Doctor doctor);
   boolean updateSpecialization(int doctorId,String specialization);
   int deleteDoctorById(int doctorId);
   Doctor findDoctorById(int doctorId);
   List<Doctor>findAllDoctors();
   List<Doctor>findAllDoctorsBySpecialization();
}
```

You can add more functionalities depending upon the scenarios you have.

The **classpath** contains the starter for JDBC which enables the container to create a bean of **DataSource** using the properties configured in the **application.properties** file. We can use this bean to communicate with the underlying database to perform CRUD operations in plain JDBC style using SQL APIs. However, the Spring provides **JdbcTemplate** to perform similar operations without using SQL APIs. So, let's autowire it in the implementation class and perform CRUD operations using it, as shown by the methods in the following code:

```
public int addDoctor(Doctor doctor) {
   int added = 0;
   String INSERT_DOCTOR = "insert into doctor values(?,?,?)";
   added = jdbcTemplate.update(INSERT_DOCTOR, doctor.getDoctorId(),
         doctor.getDoctorName(),
   doctor.getSpecialization());
   return added;
}
public boolean updateDoctor(Doctor doctor) {
  boolean isUpdated = false;
  String UPDATE_DOCTOR = "update doctor set doctorName=?,
     specialization=? where doctorId=?";
  int updated = jdbcTemplate.update(UPDATE_DOCTOR,
          doctor.getDoctorName(), doctor.getSpecialization(),
          doctor.getDoctorId());
  if (updated > 0) {
    isUpdated = true;
  }
 return isUpdated;
}
public int deleteDoctorById(int doctorId) {
  int deleted = 0;
  String DELETE_DOCTOR = "delete from doctor where doctorId=?";
  deleted = jdbcTemplate.update(DELETE_DOCTOR, doctorId);
  return deleted;
}
public Doctor findDoctorById(int doctorId) {
  Doctor doctor = null;
  String FINDDOCTORBYID = "select * from doctor where doctorId=?";
  doctor = jdbcTemplate.queryForObject(FINDDOCTORBYID,
        (rs, rowNum) -> {
             Doctor d = new Doctor();
             d.setDoctorId(rs.getInt(1));
             d.setDoctorName(rs.getString(2));
             d.setSpecialization(rs.getString(3));
             return d;
        }, doctorId);
  return doctor;
}
public List<Doctor> findAllDoctors() {
  List<Doctor> doctors = new ArrayList<>();
  String FINDDOCTORBYID = "select * from doctor";
```

```
  doctors = jdbcTemplate.query(FINDDOCTORBYID, (rs, rowNum) -> {
      Doctor d = new Doctor();
      d.setDoctorId(rs.getInt(1));
      d.setDoctorName(rs.getString(2));
      d.setSpecialization(rs.getString(3));
      return d;
    });
 return doctors;
}
```

We now have the DAO layer and controller layer *ready*. I thought it would be very monotonous to have all the code here and being fine developers we all can write the rest of the code. The GIT repository has all the code as a ready reference. Here, we are using JDBC which means we need to create a **doctor** table in the database which we are going to use. Here, as I am working with MySQL, I am adding a new table in MySQL under *doctor*'s schema using the following DDL statement having **doctorId** as Primary Key:

```
create table doctor(doctorId integer PRIMARY KEY,
     doctorNamevarchar(20),specialization varchar(20));
```

Once the database is set *up*, now it's time to set up the communication between them in order to perform CRUD operations on the data received from the *consumer*. The way we did autowiring of the **`JdbcTemplate`**, we now will set up the autowiring of the **`DoctorDAO`** in the **`DoctorController`** by adding the following piece of statement:

```
@Autowired
DoctorDAO doctorDAO;
```

As the instance of DAO is available in the controller, *what are we waiting for*? Let's invoke the DAO method and complete the logic of inserting a new row in the table in the *controller* handler method:

```
Doctor d = null;
int added = doctorDAO.addDoctor(doctor);
if (added == 1)
  return doctor;
return d;
```

Code is *ready*, we can now run the application and test the POST request to add a new record using Postman.

We already have discussed the way Postman can raise the POST request using JSON as media type such as:

```
{
    "doctorId" : 1,
    "doctorName": "Dr. Mandar",
    "specialization" : "Orthopedic"
}
```

Please refer to the section where we have written **DoctorController** in case you need reference. We will get the status code as **200** and even the **Doctor** table in MySQL will now have a new row having the column values as specified in the JSON.

Try sending the same request without changing the request body. *Oops!* We got an *Internal Server Error* 500 and from the application console it's clear that we got the exception for the duplicate entry for the Primary Key. We can handle the exception in the DAO layer but not now. We in the controller have **createNewDoctorRecord_Form()** method to deal with form submission. The logic of the earlier code and this code is the same. You can refer to the code from the repository and test endpoint using Postman. Now, we are having *two* records in the table. Let's now update controller **findDoctorById()** method to fetch the record from table using the DAO layer as:

```
Doctor doctor = doctorDAO.findDoctorById(id);
return doctor;
```

Now it's time to test the endpoint **http://locahost:8080/doctors/{id}** using Postman, make sure you are requesting for the record with the **doctorId** which is existing in the table. Try the endpoint, but this time request for record with id which is not in the table. *Exactly!* We will get **EmptyResultDataAccessException** on the console and the Postman will receive the response as, **500** *Internal Server error*. Don't worry, we have a dedicated section to deal with exception handling in detail.

Once we successfully tested the **/doctors/{id}** endpoint, we now can start with finding *doctors* by *specialization* by using the following code block for the first *three* case scenarios discussed in the *controller* section:

```
List<Doctor> doctors= doctorDAO.findAllDoctorsBySpecialization
                        (doctor_specialization);
return doctors;
```

For the fourth scenario, when we are using **java.util.Optional** to handle *optional* **path** variable, we first have to find out whether the specialization is obtained from the *consumer* request or not and then accordingly take the decision which DAO method to invoke as:

```
List<Doctor> doctors = new ArrayList<>();
if (doctor_specialization.isPresent()) {
   //Logic to find all doctors by specialization will go here
   doctors= doctorDAO.findAllDoctorsBySpecialization(
   doctor_specialization.get());
   return doctors;
}
   //Logic to find all doctors as specialization is not
   //present will go here
doctors= doctorDAO.findAllDoctors();
return doctors;
```

Try to test code using URL,

http://localhost:8080/doctors/specialization/{specialization}

or

http://localhost:8080/doctors/specialization

When we specify the specialization in the request URL, we will receive the response with an array of JSON objects matching the specified value. Otherwise, we will get JSON array of all the doctors from the table. Similarly, other *controller* methods can be updated to communicate to the DAO layer. You can refer the code from the repository.

Exception handling in the REST

We are now getting the payload response of type JSON, or XML depending on the mapping specified for the positive scenario, such as *sending new resources*, *requesting for the resources* with matching **doctorId**, *deleting the resource which exists*, and so on. Cool! This is done and dusted. In practice, a *consumer* can also provide the resource which is already in the database, or request to search for doctored which doesn't exist. Whenever the consumer requests to fetch or *update* or *delete* the resource which does not exist, *what response does the consumer receive?* Yes, 500 *Internal Server Error. Is anything wrong with the response?* No, nothing is wrong in this. That's what is going on at the server side and it is just informing the consumer about it. *Wait, wait, what are you doing? Aren't you exposing the weaknesses of your application to the consumer? Is the Internal Server Error explaining the cause of the error to the consumer? Is the consumer able to take an appropriate action based on status code* 500? Well, a very simple answer to all the questions is; No, *not every time!* The *consumer* understands that something went wrong. But he is unaware of the reasons. He is *clueless. Are there any issues with the request he sent or is it because the application code raised some exceptions?* We are repeatedly mentioning about *consumer*, don't forget we are expecting the *consumer* to be an application who is requesting to *service-endpoints*. And to make the decision about what to do further, the service has to give a response clearly. *Don't keep the consumer clueless!* It's the responsibility of the service. Think about the scenarios which raise the *exception*, *process them*, and *respond appropriately* to the consumer. It's a *two-step process*. *Firstly*, we need to handle the exception and then we need to generate the customized response. In the next section, we will focus on learning how to handle the exception in different ways.

Using try-catch

As we all are Java developers, we know the traditional way of handling exceptions with **try-catch**. Let's consider the **addDoctor()** method. Here, the exception will be raised in the DAO layer at *update* method invocation of **update()** method of **JdbcTemplate**. It's obvious to handle it here using **try catch** and we have various ways to do it. Following is one of the ways:

```
try {
     added = jdbcTemplate.update(INSERT_DOCTOR, doctor.getDoctorId(),
         doctor.getDoctorName(), doctor.getSpecialization());
} catch (Exception e) {
    System.out.println(e.getMessage());
    //Log the message or Log the stack trace
}
```

This is a better approach to log the cause of exception for the *developers* at the application level and not to expose it to the *consumer*. Here, even we can define the custom exception class such as **DoctorAlreadyExistsException** and handle it in the controller and then expose it to the consumer. For the time being, let's define the *custom* class for the scenario when *doctor* already exists as:

```
public class DoctorAlreadyExistsException extends RuntimeException
{
   private String message;
   public DoctorAlreadyExistsException()
   {
      // TODO Auto-generated constructor stub
      this("We have similar record");
   }
   public DoctorAlreadyExistsException(String message)
   {
      super(message);
      this.message = message;
```

```
    }
}
```

Now, let's use it by updating in the DAO method to expose specialized message to the *controller* such as **RECORD EXISTS**:

```
public int addDoctor(Doctor doctor) {
    int added = 0;
    String INSERT_DOCTOR = "insert into doctor values(?,?,?)";
    try {
        added = jdbcTemplate.update(INSERT_DOCTOR, doctor.getDoctorId(),
            doctor.getDoctorName(), doctor.getSpecialization());
    } catch (Exception e) {
    System.out.println(e.getMessage());
    throw new DoctorAlreadyExistsException("RECORD EXISTS");
    }
     return added;
}
```

Now, the raised exception by the DAO will get propagated to the *controller* and we can handle it as:

```
public Doctor createNewDoctorRecord(@RequestBody Doctor doctor) {
  Doctor d = null;
  int added = 0;
  try {
    added = doctorDAO.addDoctor(doctor);
  } catch (DoctorAlreadyExistsException e) {
    System.out.println(e.getMessage());
  }
  if (added == 1)
    return doctor;
  return d;
}
```

We later will expose it to the *consumer*. Now, we will execute the code and send the JSON based response for the record which already exists in the table. Obviously, it will be raising an exception and we can observe how this mechanism of *try-catch* works by the Postman as well as on the console. *Figure 2.24 shows* the part of the *stack trace* that displays our message set for the custom exception on the console:

```
com.example.demo.DoctorAlreadyExistsException: RECORD EXISTS
at com.example.demo.dao.DoctorDAOImpl.addDoctor(DoctorDAOImpl.java:34) ~[classes/:na]
```

Figure 2.24: *Custom Exception in application*

However, the Postman shows the output as shown in *Figure* 2.25:

```
{
    "timestamp": "2023-02-01T17:19:09.386+00:00"
    "status": 500,
    "error": "Internal Server Error",
    "path": "/doctors"
}
```

Figure 2.25: *Custom exception in* POSTMAN

It means out exception handling worked at the DAO as well as the layer. Unfortunately, we still are exposing the details to the consumer. Let us work on it.

Using @ExceptionHandler

The **@ExceptionHandlerannotation** provides flexibility for handling exceptions by applying to the method which handles exceptions. Such a *handler* method accepts an exception or a list of exceptions as an argument, which we want to handle in the defined method. The *container* will detect this annotation and then will register this method as an exception handler. This method is responsible for handling the specified exception as well as its subclasses passed to the annotation. Let's define a handler method in the controller as:

```
@ExceptionHandler(value = DoctorAlreadyExistsException.class)
public String handleDoctorAlreadyExistsException(
   DoctorAlreadyExistsException blogAlreadyExistsException) {
       return "Doctor already exists";
}
```

Whenever the **`DoctorAlreadyExistsExceptionis`** is raised the **`handleDoctorAlreadyExistsException()`** method will be invoked and generate the response. The *controller* method needs to be updated to raise the exception instead of handling **with try-catch** as we did in the earlier code. The updated code of the controller is as follows:

```
@PostMapping(path = "/doctors", consumes = {
MediaType.APPLICATION_JSON_VALUE, MediaType.APPLICATION_XML_VALUE })
public Doctor createNewDoctorRecord(@RequestBody Doctor doctor)
                    throws DoctorAlreadyExistsException{
   Doctor d = null;
   int added = 0;
   added = doctorDAO.addDoctor(doctor);
   if (added == 1)
      return doctor;
   return d;
}
```

Now execute the code and send the request for the endpoint **/doctors** having the same JSON object in the request body. This will raise the exception and we will get the **Doctor already exists** as a message on the Postman response. *Pretty Cool!* Now we are communicating the message to the *consumer* without exposing the error message or its cause. But the *handler* method which we just wrote is for a dedicated *controller* class, *what if we need to deal with a bit broader way.*

Using @ControllerAdvice

We have just used **@ExceptionalHandler** to handle the exception for a specified *controller*. It means it is active for a specific controller where we declared it. *Sounds good.* But let us assume that we want to handle the same exception in the different controllers. *Are we going to declare another method in those different controllers and that too for the same exception?* Unfortunately, YES! *Weird, isn't it?* Developers have invested the whole of their life in learning the concepts like code reusability. But now the approach that we are recommending promotes the redundant code. Maybe we would have chosen the approach because we are dealing with a pretty simple application. For complex multi-controller enterprise applications, defining a specific *handler* method for the same exception in different *multiple-controller classes* will not be a good idea. *Can we define exception handler methods that will be used anywhere in the application? Yes, we can.* Trust me, you need to *philomath* while you deal with new technology.

Aspect Oriented Programming (**AOP**) is one of the fantastic modules provided by Spring to handle cross-cutting concerns such as *logging*, *transaction*, and *exception handling*. The AOP provides support to write the code once which can be applied wherever applicable. AOP takes out repetitive code for *logging*, *exception*, *security*, or *transaction* out of the business logic methods, which is spanned across the layers at one single place which is termed as **Advice**. This advice then is plugged in at various *join-points* in the application such as *before the method*, *after the method*, *around the method*, or when an exception is raised by the code. The **Pointcut** helps in defining the expressions so that for which *class*, *method*, *argument*, or their *combination* the join point will be plugged can be defined. We will not go in all of these details. It's just a process that takes place behind the scene when we use global exception handlers.

The **@ControllerAdvice** is used to define the global exception handler along with **@ExceptionHandler** annotation. We will not define a global exception handler class defining various handler methods for a specific or general exceptions as:

```
@ControllerAdvice
@RestController
public class GlobalDoctorExceptionhandler {
  @ExceptionHandler(DoctorAlreadyExistsException.class)
  protected Object handleMyException(Exception ex, WebRequest rq) {
     return "Doctor already Exists";
  }
  @ExceptionHandler(Exception.class)
  protected Object handleAllException(Exception ex, WebRequest rq) {
     return ex.getMessage();
  }
}
```

As we have a global exception handler defining how to handle exceptions, let's comment out the **handleDoctorAlreadyExistsException()** method from the **DoctorController** class.

Now execute the code and send the request for the endpoint **/doctors**, having the same JSON object in the request body. This will raise the exception and a message will appear on the console and will get the **Doctor already exists** as a response in the Postman. It's very similar to the earlier *handler* method but we don't need to repeat the code. Please just *go ahead* and define the various exception handler methods which you want to try.

Writing self-descriptive messages

A *consumer* is sending a request to the service provider. He is willing to have some resources of his preferred choice. The *endpoint* may or may not be having the resource. These to-and-fro travel of the *request* and *response* usually happens between a *consumer* and *provider* application. When a client sends the correct request, it can be processed well and the response is sent. However, nothing is perfect. The *consumer* may send *in-sufficient information* in the request, or he may send the information in the wrong form which is unexpected by the provider makes the provider unable to process it.

Also, the response has to be in a format, which is expected by the *client*. Otherwise, even upon receiving the response client may not be able to process it. Both the *consumer* and *provider* didn't follow the basic rules of communication which leads to a chaotic situation. Always remember to send self-descriptive messages between the consumer and provider. When a client sends a request, he should pass the information about, *what is the expected response type along with the correct form of the path variables, path parameters, or request body*. Similarly, the *response payload* should also contain information about the *status code, type of payload sent*, and the *actual value of the expected resource*. When the client receives such a descriptive message, he can wisely take the decision on what should be the next processing step for the response. The controller layer which we discussed earlier was providing the resource, but *was it self-descriptive*? While sending the POST request, we already faced this scenario. Let me discuss this in more detail. Consider, we are sending a request to add a new resource using POST mapping. We will send the request body having a **doctorId** which we don't have in the table. *What status code do we receive*? Let's find this out together by executing the actual request for **/doctors** endpoint by Postman as shown in *Figure* 2.26:

Figure 2.26: HTTP Status code 200

What the status code is suggesting? It suggests everything is fine on the server. *Does it mean the resource creation successfully took place*? In our case, exception occurred as the request body has resource with existing doctorId. But it didn't get propagated to the consumer. *Does it mean the exception is properly handled and the consumer doesn't have to worry about it? What conclusion the consumer will draw*? To be very honest, *no idea!* It's obscure. *How to handle this situation? What all things need to be changed?* Don't worry, it's not that difficult. All this confusion at the *consumer* end can simply be avoided by sending a well-defined status code. For example, when a successful resource creation took place, the provider will send **201**. When the *consumer* asks for a resource and it doesn't exist, then send the **204** as a status code to the *consumer*. Now the question is, we have a resource of type **Doctor** and it doesn't contain the status code field, then *how to do this? Are we going to change our* POJO? No! We have a class which takes care of this and many other related things. The **HttpEntity** class represents the HTTP request entity or response entity which consists of a body, which contains the expected resource value and some headers. The **HttpEntity** class is extended by the **ResponseEntity** which adds an **HttpStatusCode** presenting the result as HTTP response status code. It's time to have a reality check. Let's update the controller code for POST mapping as to return **ResponseEntity** instead of **Doctor** POJO as:

```
@PostMapping(path = "/doctors", consumes = { MediaType.APPLICATION_JSON_
VALUE, MediaType.APPLICATION_XML_VALUE })
public ResponseEntity<Doctor> createNewDoctorRecord(@RequestBody Doctor
doctor)  throws DoctorAlreadyExistsException{
   // Logic to add record in table will go here
   Doctor d = null;
   int added = 0;
   added = doctorDAO.addDoctor(doctor);
   if (added == 1)
      return new ResponseEntity<Doctor>(doctor,HttpStatusCode.valueOf(201));
   return new ResponseEntity<Doctor>(HttpStatusCode.valueOf(204));
}
```

Let's try with the Postman sending a POST request for a resource with a different **doctorId** and with an existing **doctorId**. For a new resource, we will get the following output. Observe the status code in *Figure 2.27*:

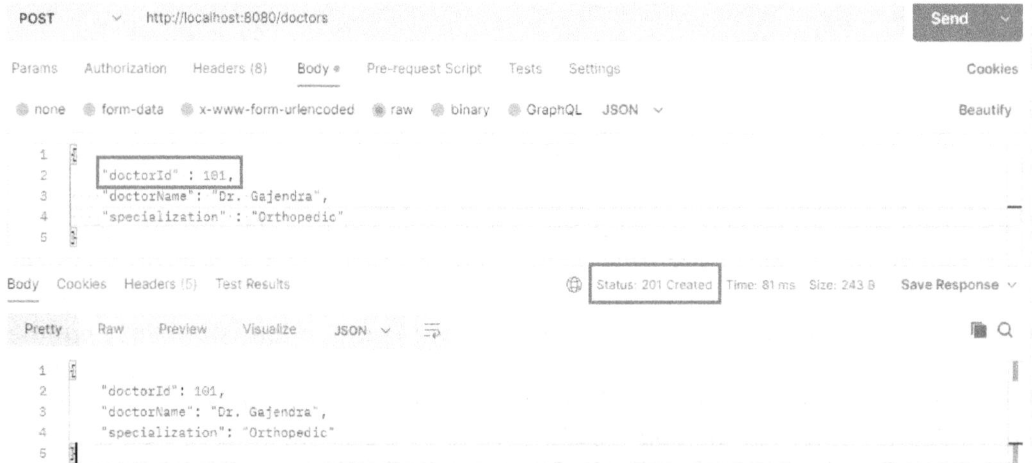

***Figure 2.27**: HTTP Status code 201*

Let's retry sending the same request, *don't change the request body*! We will get **Doctor already Exists**, but *what about the status code? It's still the same old* 200 OK! Oh! come on. If **Doctor** already exists and no new record has been added, *how could it be* OK? *Agreed*! We got the output message from the **GlobalExceptionHandler** class as **DoctorAlreadyExistsExceptiongot** raised. So, let's update the *handler* method to return the correct status code and not the boring **200 OK** message by annotation it with **@ResponseStatus** as:

```
@ExceptionHandler(DoctorAlreadyExistsException.class)
@ResponseStatus(code = HttpStatus.NOT_MODIFIED)
protected Object handleMyException(Exception ex, WebRequest rq) {
 return "Doctor already Exists";
}
```

This code change will lead to the output which states the status code as **304** shown in *Figure* 2.28:

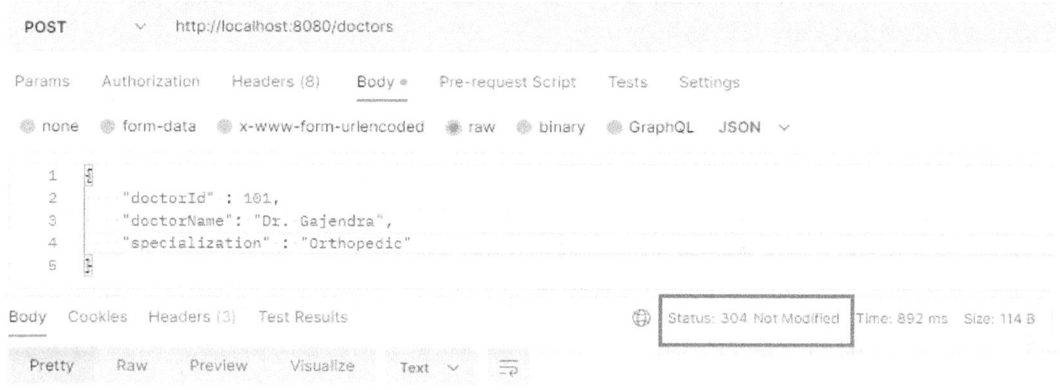

Figure 2.28: *Status code 304*

But *where is the message*? Before answering this question, I have a more important question to answer. If the status code is going to provide information about what happened at the *provider* and accordingly the *consumer* will be able to take the decision then *why do we need a message*? We don't need the message every time. The status codes such as **204**, **304** which are raised by the **PUT**, **POST**, and **DELETE** methods decline to send the message or presentation of the response in the payload. One needs to wisely take the decision, whether they need a custom response message or not. In case some consumers want, they can process the *error message* and then will load their page or take the further decision. We can create a custom response and send it to the *client* which will give him a clear idea about what exactly went wrong at the server. Here, we are creating the POJO for **ExceptionResponse** class, which is responsible for the custom response message as:

```
public class ExceptionResponse {
  Date timeInfo;
  String message;
  String details;
  //default parameterized constructor
  //getters and setters
}
```

As per the scenario, we can add a few more fields to expose in detail information. Now, it's time to use the response in the *exception handler* method as:

```
@ExceptionHandler(DoctorAlreadyExistsException.class)
//@ResponseStatus(code = HttpStatus.NOT_MODIFIED)
protected ResponseEntity<Object> handleMyException(Exception ex,
                                                    WebRequest rq) {
  ExceptionResponse exceptionResponse =
              new ExceptionResponse(new Date(),ex.getMessage(),
  rq.getDescription(false));
  return new ResponseEntity<Object>(exceptionResponse,
                                    HttpStatusCode.valueOf(400));
}
```

We commented the **@ResponseStatus(code = HttpStatus.NOT_MODIFIED)**, as we are setting it in the **ResponseEntity** instance.

Time for action, let's execute the POST request in Postman as shown in *Figure 2.29*:

Figure 2.29: *Handling exception with self-descriptive message*

The POST request body contains the resource with the **doctorId** which is already existing in the table. This will lead to duplicate key exception and be handled in the **try-catch** block of **addDoctor()** method. Then the **DoctorAlreadyExistsException** with **RECORD EXISTS** message will be thrown. A *callback exception handler method* will be called and the custom response will be generated as shown by the preceding output response.

Updates in logging

We are not intended to talk much about logging at this point of time. But we need to know the updates provided by current version of Spring Boot. Till *Spring Boot 2.x.x*, the *date* and *time* components were aligned with ISO-8601, which can be utilized by both the **Logback** and the **Log4j2**. But from *Spring Boot 3.x*, the format is modified to **yyyy-MM-dd'T'HH:mm:ss.SSSXXX**. For more clarity, please observe *Figure 2.30*:

```
2023-05-14T21:08:23.323+05:30  INFO 31160 --- [           main] c.e.d.SpringBootRestBasicsApplication

2023-05-14T21:08:23.328+05:30  INFO 31160 --- [           main] c.e.d.SpringBootRestBasicsApplication
2023-05-14T21:08:26.687+05:30  INFO 31160 --- [           main] o.s.b.w.embedded.tomcat.TomcatWebServer
2023-05-14T21:08:26.702+05:30  INFO 31160 --- [           main] o.apache.catalina.core.StandardService
2023-05-14T21:08:26.703+05:30  INFO 31160 --- [           main] o.apache.catalina.core.StandardEngine
2023-05-14T21:08:26.882+05:30  INFO 31160 --- [           main] o.a.c.c.C.[Tomcat].[localhost].[/]
2023-05-14T21:08:26.886+05:30  INFO 31160 --- [           main] w.s.c.ServletWebServerApplicationContext
2023-05-14T21:08:27.893+05:30  INFO 31160 --- [           main] o.s.b.w.embedded.tomcat.TomcatWebServer
2023-05-14T21:08:27.907+05:30  INFO 31160 --- [           main] c.e.d.SpringBootRestBasicsApplication
```

***Figure 2.30**: Modified log message format*

Also, notice that the new format now uses a character **T**, as a separator between the *date* and the *time* instead of white space. Additionally, it also appends the time zone offset towards the end.

Conclusion

In this chapter, we fast-forwarded about how to create REST-based application using Spring boot framework. Spring Boot is a huge concept to discuss. But to go further with microservices, we should have at least the basic idea about different concepts of REST-based services that support the HTTP requests and responses for the endpoints. This chapter was about what a service is and how to design it to expose endpoints with annotations to handle the HTTP request for GET, POST, PUT, DELETE, and so on methods. We also talked about how to handle the different media types which can be consumed by the service and response can be generated. Exception handling is dealt in a different way in the REST application, as the exception rose in the service need to communicate with the consumer concisely. Here, we discussed what are the different ways to handle the exceptions raised in the service. Lastly, we talked about how to send a self-descriptive message to the consumer from the service.

We are now well equipped with the basics of REST-based applications using Spring Boot. However, we started this journey to understand microservice-based architecture. That is the aim of our next chapter. In the next chapter, we will have in depth discussion about microservice-based architecture, how is it different from *traditional monolithic architecture*, the features of microservices and many more. A lot to come, *pull of your socks and get ready for the journey!*

CHAPTER 3
Scale it Down

The previous chapter opened the doors of a whole *new*, *interesting*, and *growing* world of services. We developed REST services using Spring Boot. It's just one of the frameworks, we used for developing services. However, there are many ways to develop them. And you may experience them in the near future. Once we are aware of REST concepts, the implementation we are using is just syntactically different. The chapter laid the pretty concrete foundation of Spring Boot REST. We now are well equipped to start the first stage of our battle.

Once we are done with services, *what else is remaining? Nothing and everything! Confused?* Don't be. We develop a service to have one-stop shop for all the needs of the consumer who wants to consume the *doctor's* service. *Do we need all these functionalities together up and running at the same time?* It was easy and less complex so we wrote it easily. However, in reality, all services might not be so straight-forward and may need complex algorithms. It's obviously time consuming and we may not be able to write all the functions together and make them available for the *consumers*.

In enterprise applications considering the complexities, the time taken for the *designing*, the *amount of code involved*, the *time to test each one*, and then *releasing them takes time*. By the time we come up with a solution, the consumer's needs might change, or the consumer already has started using some other service. Then *what about our services? Did we do something wrong? Frankly no!* We just took a *well-defined*, *tried*, and *tested traditional* approach. The only thing we overlooked is the time factor. Imagine you are at a *bookstore* to purchase one of the best seller, *The Da Vinci Code*. Unfortunately, the book is out of stock and the storekeeper even told you that he has already ordered the copies and the parcel will be arriving in a couple of days. Great, *isn't it*? Now some of you might wait also, but the impatient buyer like me will go to another shop or sometimes hunt for the shop having that book. I will go and get it. Now, *what's the fault of the storekeeper here*? Not at all, he already placed the order but the parcel was not delivered. It is all about the availability of the book when it was required by the buyer. The *customers* from the world of software are no different than this. If they do not get the services that they expect, they will simply switch to another browser or tab to fulfill their requirements.

In this chapter, let's start understanding what was there in traditional application designing like *monolithic architecture* and now what *microservices architecture* is offering. We will also design microservices and start the migration from monolith to microservices.

So, *shall we start*? Let's go on a tour of microservices.

Structure

In this chapter, we will discuss the following topics:

- Getting acquainted to microservices
- Motivation to choose microservices
- Features of microservices
- Migrating from monolithic to microservices
- Limitations of microservices

Getting acquainted with microservices

Mandar's team is building a project for transport service providers to offer facilities for applying for *booking a cab*, *registration*, *recharging wallets*, *billings*, *travel history*, *changing passwords*, and so on. This application was developed for browsers and mobile clients, both. The *team* spends hours developing the Spring Boot REST application and also deployed well in time. *Mandar* and the team are happy and ready for the *Friday* night celebration. The *drink* and *food* were ordered and all were set for a happy weekend. While everyone was about to raise glasses, a request for an upgrade arrived. The application is working well, however, it also needs additional functionality to *book a cab* not for the *customer* but for some other person as well. It was not the initial functional requirements provided by the client. But the team needs to upgrade the application. After all, we need to satisfy the customer. The *developer* team needs to work on this new feature now. *What do they require*? May be a new POJO for an unregistered *customer*, or the earlier POJO needs an extra field to get the information so that booking can be mapped. It also requires new functionality to accept requests for booking from unregistered customers, DAO layer to support the mapping of data related to this new type of booking request. It means the team has to do lots of re-work from the controller layer to the database design. This will take more time to release the updates in the application. For sure that was not so pleasant *Friday* for the entire team.

Let us take another scenario. My team will be starting to work on a new project. When the initial communication happened, the team got an overall idea about what the project is all about and the basic modules to implement. When we were discussing the technologies, a framework to choose for implementation, we got various suggestions. And we also know one *framework*, *language*, and *technology* are not full-fledged in providing solutions to all the modules which we want to develop. Some technologies are good at one, while others are at something else. And that applies to us as well. We may be good or expert in one technology, aware of another but not having hands on it. We may not come up with one unique technology to choose. But *are we going to use all of them*? Yes, we need to use all of them, and we already discussed the same in our earlier chapter when we decided to start with service-based development. So *now what's different? Have patience dear friends! Patience* is a universal key to success.

The technology to choose is a point of discussion amongst developers and they might come up with some agreement for the same. However, *time availability* is another important factor and it's impossible to finish everything in a limited period. We do not want to lose the project, but *how we are going to tackle the hours needed to complete the work*? We must have to have a bigger team size. This was the only solution. And that may not be possible right now. *How are we going to plan, so that the application will be released in time? Don't you think a large code base adds extra complexity in development Can we reduce the code size*? Well, we are developing enterprise applications not demo applications for some internal presentation. It involves a high level of algorithm, a tremendous amount of flow management, and various business logics. It's next to impossible to reduce the code size as it might not be possible considering the business values your software should build. *We are in a panic situation for sure!*

In this situation, instead of reducing the code base, we can develop the code base in parts. We can bifurcate the code. What I mean to say is, instead of developing the entire application together, let's develop them in small chunks. Once the chunk is ready, release it. This approach of continuous delivery plays a very important role, as the customer will able to test it or use it, by the time your team is working on some other code. As we will be building the project in small chunks, we will develop it efficiently and in less time as the complexity is also built chunk by chunk. Now, *instead of saying chunk may we call that a module?* So now, we will not be focusing on the entire application. We will be investing our time and efforts in the smaller tasks or modules. One by one all such small parts that are modules will be developed and then will be integrated, and communicated with each other to provide a full-fledged solution. We now are free to use it as one complete solution, or if we want to use some part of it somewhere else is totally up to us to promote reusability.

We now will focus on one module at a time. It's like mini meals. Instead of having large portions of food at a time, we will take smaller portions and will enjoy them. This way, we can try more flavors of meals and we will not feel *stomach heaviness*. Software services are like a complete meal with starters, a main course, and *how can I forget the deserts*? The smaller services are like mini meals; one at a time. *You got me!* Mini meals, precisely mini services are smaller pieces of our actual application. Though we say that we are working with mini services, it is still a responsibility. I would still want to step down and cut it down into smaller pieces or miniature. You guessed it right, we are talking about **micros**, smaller than *minis*, which is microservice when we talk about software designing.

Microservices are a tiny part of our application, which then can be integrated or utilized by the consumer. The microservice enables the developers to achieve rapid and reliable delivery frequently to develop complex enterprise applications in parts. The motivation behind the microservice is to develop the solution in parts that are *self-sufficient*, *reusable*, *replaceable*, *testable*, *easy to deploy*, *quick at startup*, and last but the most important, *highly available*. Let's take an example of a custom cloth stitching unit. We visit to the store, a store representative will take us to first select the clothing for stitching, then he will take measurements, and provide us the catalogue to select the style of stitching. He will then generate a receipt and finally, we will need to pay and exit the store. You all will agree this is a time consuming and very lengthy process, wait, this is again customer specific. When we have *ten representatives* to attend to the *customers* and when they alone perform everything from start to end, they are dedicated to a single client. Now, let's divide the store into *departments*. We have the *clothing unit*, *style unit*, *measurements unit*, and then the *billing unit*. We will move from one to another department and get the services. *What did we do differently*? We took an entire solution, cut it down into *smaller self-manageable parts*, and now they are on their own to serve. In case we know which style to choose, we simply move from the clothing department to measurements. Nothing strict, everything is flexible. So, are our microservices.

Motivation to choose microservices

Hey, we are using monolithic applications for such a long time and we still want to continue with that. If it is not serving the purpose, we would have already given it up. But that's not the reality, still in the industry we use the word monolith with much respect. Then *what is this new microservice architecture, going to make a difference in our life*? *Why am I beating the bushes around*? Let's dive deep and find out the reasons to choose microservices architecture.

Reduced code base complexity

We are discussing the development of enterprise applications. As we all are aware, the moment we say enterprise, the *first* thing that strikes our minds is now we will be developing many components which obviously tend to increase in the application code: *different modules*, *their structure*, *definitions*, and then *testing*. With a larger code base comes complexity. We are the experts so code base size doesn't matter to us. *Cool! What if we need to modify it to accommodate the proposed changes or new requirements*? Now, we certainly need to look into the code thoroughly and that will not be an easy task at all. We now need to understand all the modules associated with our changes at least. Then we design what needs to change. Many times, one module is dependent on another. So, when we change certain declarations, and definitions in one place, that might impact other modules or components, and even that module starts showing up errors. Though we very often say *our application is loosely coupled*, when it comes to modification and incorporating the changes, we start feeling *uncomfortable*, *hesitant*, and *reluctant*.

In microservice, we cut down the application or application modules into *smaller independent pieces* which are often reusable and have some business meaning as discussed earlier. Now we are not looking at a bigger picture but a piece of it. We will focus on this independent part, as it's small when the changes are expected we just need to change our service. As the services we will be developing are loosely coupled they have fewer dependencies and it becomes much easier to roll back the changes. When the code is less to *modify*, *understand* or *develop*, the developers get more flexibility.

Development time

In *monolithic applications*, as just discussed, the code size is *enormous*, and the complexity is more. So, it's very common that such application development is a bit of a lengthy task. The development is one of the phases, which is followed by the most important step testing. With more code to develop, even the time taken for testing is more which leads the team to take more time in development.

Now, this is when we develop a code, *what if we want to update something*? The application might have higher interdependency on each other; any change in one module may cause problems in some other modules. Sometimes, the *development team* may also need to incorporate all together a new module. Once this new module is developed then it needs to be incorporated with all other older modules. So, incorporating a new module is always a time-consuming task. Now, let's take into consideration the time taken in development when we adopt microservices. Microservices are a bunch of *independent* intercommunicating tiny services performing single responsibility. As we are focused, we will deliver services with the best quality in minimum time. We will be developing these services in smaller teams so a team will *develop*, *test*, and then *release* them quickly to be used and reused by other teams or services.

Ease in deployment

In *monolithic applications*, we need to deploy a single file. Deploying a single file is always going to be easy. *Agreed? Yes*, that's true, we have consensus here. However, even a very minor change to a monolithic application needs the redeployment of the entire application. When we target the deployment of an entire application in a single go all the modules are going to be deployed together as a single module. It means we are at a very high risk even for a single change. Now assume we are done with deploying monolithic applications now we have to test each of its individual functionality. It means the application can't go live without rigorous testing. This is really going to be time consuming.

The deployment takes time so the complete production deployment needs need to be scheduled. As more time is taken in the deployment task, it results in *high downtime*. Now, we had planned for the deployment which means we may have to inform our users about the downtime, still, the downtime affects both the business as well as the customers due to the unavailability of the system. This may cause loss of revenue to the business.

As compared to monolithic, in microservice we develop multiple smaller applications which leads to frequent and faster release of individual applications with ease in independent deployment. Earlier in monolithic we might push updates once per week. However, now as we are developing smaller applications, we may release it *two to three times* a day. The smaller applications are easy to test. In case of any changes taking place in any of the service, only that service needs to be updated and then redeployed. Now, the service which is under deployment, the clients who consumes that service will face issues if proper contract testing is neglected. The *consumers* of other services still continue using their services smoothly.

Availability

What is meant by availability? The application availability is a measure which is used to estimate whether an application is performing well for its functionalities and also whether it fulfils the requirements. Anytime, when for a reason application instance is going down, it hampers the customer experience and for that time the application is said to be down. We can take measures to restart the instance or to start all together a new instance, but again that will not change the user experience. For them the application is still unavailable due the size and the amount of resource allocation.

Now, when we deal with microservices, we are having services with single responsibility and limited resources to allocate. So, as compared to monolithic, the microservices will take less time to start. *Why*? This is pretty simpler to guess; the service has a single responsibility. It means limited resource allocation; *which obviously requires minimum startup time*. Let's now think about *what if requests are overloaded*? The chances of overloading the service with requests is less as we already limited the service for what task it is going to perform. For multiple instances and all we will discuss in the next point.

Scaling

We just discussed the availability of the application and how it impacts the client experience. We are talking about real-world applications and not just conceptual applications. So, whatever care we take there always are chances of application failure, it's inevitable. One of the very important reasons for the failure is a sudden increase in the request load. Managing the increasing load is always difficult. But we can take some early measurements as well. The easiest thing will be finding the maximum and minimum load which the application needs to handle, then according to that find the resource allocation to find the memory requirements. Once we know this, we can go ahead and take a call about what memory configuration to use when we deploy the application. This applies to all kinds of applications. Now, let's discuss this in teams of monolithic and microservices in detail.

The monolithic application needs more resource allocations and all kinds of requests will always hit the same application. We need to allocate more memory to launch the application as compared to microservices. At any moment when we understand the earlier memory is insufficient, we need more memory, and we need to scale our application. As we are talking about upgrading the hardware, it's a vertical scaling. We use the term vertical scaling usually in terms of upgrading the server hardware in terms of increasing *Input and Output Operations*, *amplifying* CPU *or* RAM *capacity*, or sometimes even increasing the disk capacity. Now, in terms of monolithic application, this will always be costly and I don't have to mention why, we very well know the reason. When it comes to microservices, the application and resources required are very less as compared to monolithic applications and that means even if the application has to scale vertically it will be less costly.

Now, we have instance with sufficient memory. But this requirement can change at any moment. *Are we again going to change our instance configuration? Sometimes yes, but should we do that always?* We should not. For *two* reasons:

- *First*, frequent changes in memory means *un-deploying* and *re-deploying* the application. This will lead to unnecessary downtimes and we don't want that.
- *Second, how many times we will change our server or its configuration?* On top of that, we don't know whether in the future this server configuration is sufficient, we need *more* or *less*.

In case, we have more which is not required, then it's just a waste of resources and money as well. In such a situation when we are not sure, how much more load my instance needs to handle instead of just dumping the memory we need to allocate the instances dynamically. *You guessed it right again*; I am talking about horizontal scaling.

The monolithic application when deployed as a single instance keeps it busy serving requests and many times the requests are queued, basically hampering the performance. Let's take an example. We are having an *online shopping application*. The festive season is coming up. This obviously will increase the number of requests hitting the application. And that's what we want. However, we have an issue to tackle. We get so many requests that the instance is unable to handle them and becomes unhealthy. *Why*? There are *many* reasons, let's not jump into the details. Right now, what is most important for us is that the application should be available maximum time. This will make customers happy. But that's not happening. If the instance is *unhealthy*, the application will be unavailable. We are talking about the *real-time world* where we are expecting the application to be up and running all the time, technically we called this as highly available application. So, it's the question of being available. The instance can become unhealthy due to many reasons and it's really impossible to predict each and every reason. *Does it mean it's fine to have an unavailable application?* No! We need highly available applications. The very easy way to handle this situation is instead of having one instance we will have more than one instance deployed on different regions and then routing will be done by the router. *Great!* Now, this is better, at least we have a substitute instance to replace unhealthy. *Did we get the highly available monolithic applications? Frankly, no.* Still, there is a chance of having applications down and then hampering the customers. Also, when any instance is down that instance will try to restart again. The application is bulky with lots of resources to allocate and is going to take time at startup. More time in restarting the application instance makes the application less available. In microservices, *we are saying our instance will never be unhealthy*? No! In real time it can be *unhealthy*. However, similar to monolithic we will make sure a minimum of *two* instances will be made available all the time so that at least one instance is available all the time. *What if both are getting restarted*? Ok, it's quite possible. Here we need to remember we are developing microservices so we are having service with a single responsibility. It means *less code size*, *lesser resource allocation*, and *less startup time*. So, even application goes down another instance can be spun up and will be ready to serve in minimum time. In the worst scenario, even if the instance can't be turned up, only the consumers who are going to request that instance endpoint will face discomfort while all other microservices will be happily servicing their consumers.

Reusability

We now are developing small well-defined services which have their single responsibility. As the services are following basic REST principles more inter service communication can be made to reuse the solution.

In monolithic applications, we will be able to share the APIs. In one application we have APIs we can add them to JARs and use the JARs in another application. In such a way we reuse the code. The microservices reuse the solution but in a bit different way. In microservices, when a solution is required and another service has it, we will use interservice communication. So instead of using the code, we will ask the service to execute the code and provide the result as a response. Additionally, one can also go with common library or source duplication where we have a scope of diverging versions.

Flexibility to use the right tool

In the *monolithic architecture*, the application is one bulky code using various third-party APIs, and tools. However, we use those tools because they were the best in the market when the application was under development. Software development is *not* an overnight task. Sometimes, it may take few years. It might happen that, by the time we are in middle of the development some new frameworks or tools are introduced in the market. The services provided by such new frameworks or technology could be better than the frameworks that we are using currently. But unfortunately, we may not able to replace our existing APIs or the frameworks by the new one. *Why framework*? Even if we think to change the version of any API or simply Java we need to think thoroughly, as it might affect our code at multiple places. And we would never prefer that.

Our microservices are simple and decoupled from other services. It means if there is a version change or we want to adopt a new technology we can take that leverage without affecting other services very easily. The only thing we need to worry about is not to change the contract between the provider and the consumer.

Quick development

Oh, that's a tricky one. How can we achieve the quick development? Frankly, development is never easy and it has to pass various parameters of testing before we start using it. One thing you all will be agree that enterprise application development is always time consuming and when the entire application has to develop in one go it will be more complicated. The adoption of change is also time demanding. Though to develop enterprise applications multiple teams work together, each team will be taking their own time for development and some teams keep waiting for others to finish their work. Coordination between teams is also important to keep track of progress. Any miscommunication may increase the cost of development in a large amount.

When it comes to microservices, we have each service loosely coupled and can be integrated into other applications with ease. The moment a change is required, instead of changing the service implementation, one can develop all together a new service and replace a new one. Smaller size teams with expertise, work in microservice development and as each team is developing its *independent* services overall application development will be much faster.

Let us take an example of a *Food Delivery Application*. Instead of designing the application as a monolith application, we can think of converting it to microservice-based application. We can divide our application in different services like searching the menu, selecting the menu to create a cart for delivery, a payment process, and followed by the delivery services. In this way, different teams will work in different services simultaneously and each of these services can be launched independently.

Infrastructural cost

The monolithic applications are not only complicated to develop, but at the same time they are *resource-demanding* when it comes to deployment. To achieve high availability, one can deploy the application at multiple instances and then can use the external load balancer to route the request to one of the instances. This *external load balancer* will increase the cost of the application. The microservices allow us to optimize resources due to the size and its responsibility. The microservices have internal load balancers and depending on situation we may take the decision to use external load balancer.

Continuous delivery

The monolithic applications are developed by multiple teams who are experts in their areas of handling UI, *database*, or *backend*. Even though the one team is done with their work, along with its testing they need to wait for others to finish. This becomes critical when we are expecting continuous delivery. Though continuous delivery is achievable in the monolith, it is difficult as the teams need to wait for other modules to get completed so as to release working software.

Unlike the monolithic applications, for microservices we use *cross-functional teams* to handle the application development and then it is followed by a continuous delivery model. In microservice development, the code is continuously *developed*, then *tested*, and finally *deployed* easily and instantly. The continuous delivery may be impacted if our services are dependent on other services as it needs integration testing.

Features of microservices

Once we know the reasons for which we should build microservice-based applications, let us now understand the different features of microservices.

Decoupling/flexibility

Each microservice performs its unique responsibility independently. The services can be used by other services and each service is open for inter-service communication. However, these services when *changed* or replaced, impact very little on other services as they follow basic principles of service development as well as contract between *consumer* and *providers*. So, when it comes to change the *developers* can make changes without worrying about other services. Each service can be *developed*, *built*, *deployed*, *replaced* and *monitored* independently.

Responsibility

Microservices follow a **single responsibility principle**. Each microservice has its unique responsibility which makes it more *focused*, *easy to develop*, and *maintain* as well. Even if the service for some reason is *down*, it will impact the consumers who are using the service and the rest all can enjoy the other functionalities easily.

Independently deployable components

The micro components are developed in smaller easily *manageable* pieces that allow faster deployment without impacting other parts of the application. This makes the new features to deploy in smaller and manageable parts.

Decentralized

The microservice directly or indirectly leads to the distributed systems having decentralized data management as well. Irrespective of the traditional monolithic applications, the microservices have a distributed database. It means each of the services will have ownership of the data needed for the particular functionality. You might be having a question, *why*? *Why can't we have all the data in one place which we were having traditionally*? The answer is very *simple*, the decentralization helps in isolating the impact of schema changes. In case the database is impacted again, it's not for the entire functionalities, it will be limited to only the impacted data.

Resilient

Every service is independently *developed*, *tested*, and *deployed* as well. In case the service is unavailable, the failures are localized only to those functionalities performed by the service without impacting the entire application. The *microservices-based application* is resilient as it continues to function in despite of the failures of some services in the system.

Migrating from monolithic to microservices

Now, we are well aware of microservice architecture and how it's different from monolithic architecture. So, let's start our exciting journey with microservices. *Hold your brakes!* We just discussed microservices and now we are planning to migrate from monolithic. The very important question is *how do you achieve that? How are we planning to cut down our application into smaller discrete, manageable parts?*

Decomposing application

We need a stable architecture having focused, strongly related testable functionalities which can be easily *developed* by a team and *deployed* independently without worrying about others.

Decompose based on business capabilities per team

Let's take an example of an *online food delivery application*. The application includes capabilities such as *order management*, *food catalogue management*, and *delivery management*. It means we can have a team dedicated to *developing*, *testing*, and *deploying* a module independently. As each specialized team is taking care of their own business capabilities, the developed service will be focused on the business values rather than concentrating on technical functionalities and features:

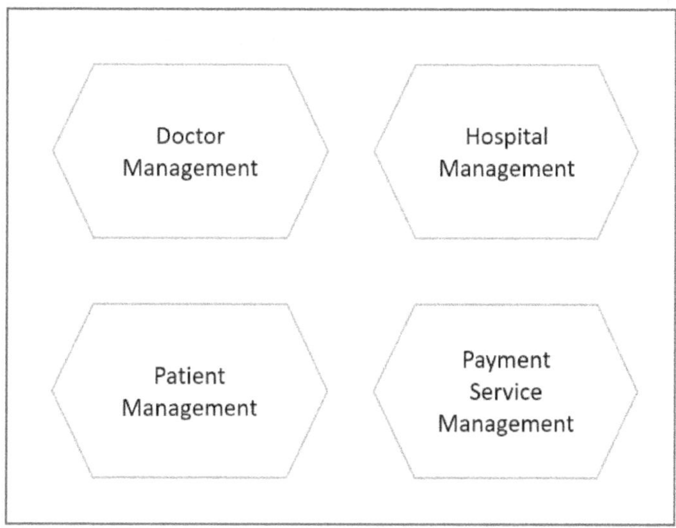

***Figure 3.1**: Decomposition based on business capability*

Strong domain knowledge plays a vital role to identify the correct business capabilities. The high-level domain model knowledge with understanding of different groups involved in organization structure helps to design microservices using business capabilities.

Decompose based on subdomain

We also can define the microservices according to domain and its corresponding subdomains with **Domain Driven Design**. Now the question is, *how to identify the subdomain as we already know for which domain we are designing the services.* One can consider subdomains which are the core part of the applications which consist of the main functionalities, then services providing the supportive functionalities followed by the subdomain having services with generic functionalities.

Let's take the same example of a Hospital Management Application. The subdomains of this domain can be Doctor Management, Hospital Management, Patient Management, and Payment Service Management:

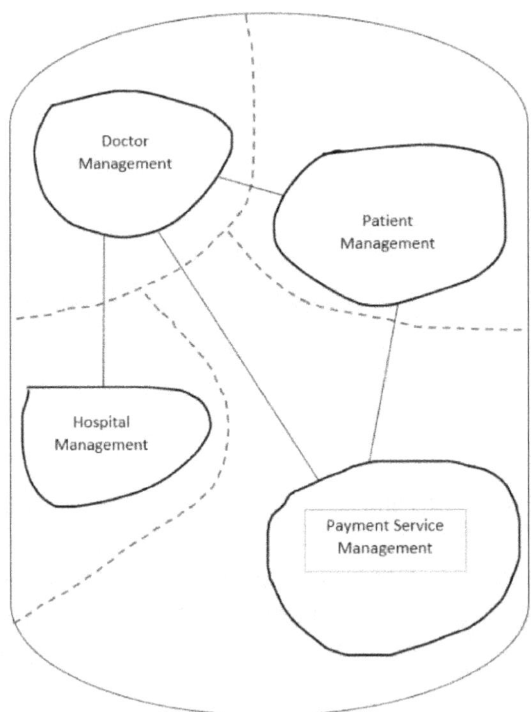

***Figure 3.2**: Decomposition based on sub-domains*

A strong business understanding helps in identifying the subdomains, which is very similar to the earlier business capabilities. One can decompose the application using subdomains efficiently by understanding overall organizational structure with high-level domain model understanding. A subdomain may have one or many subdomains to further divide the functionalities to have a subdomain for a subdomain.

Using the **Domain Driven Design** (**DDD**), the developers along with the domain experts use a *Unified Language* for sharing the knowledge, documents, and code. In DDD, a **bounded context** (**BC**) is the circumstance under which a particular term has a definite. These bounded contexts of various subdomains have some setup relationships. Let's take the same example of *online delivery*. Once a *customer* checks the *menus* and pace the *order payment* needs to be done and finally, once the order is *ready*, we need to check with the delivery department for the dispatch. Here *catalogue*, *order*, *payment*, and *delivery* share some relationship which is known as **context map**. Similar to *multi-layer enterprise applications*, the DDD also facilitates us with *domain model layer*, *application layer*, and *infrastructure layers*, and so on.

Decomposing the services by Single Responsibility Principle

As discussed, and emphasized a number of times, it's all about having small independent services, following *single responsibility* and *high availability*. Now the question is, *what to consider as a single responsibility*? Let's revisit the doctor management service, which we have developed in the earlier chapter. We were having a *Doctor* service to perform CRUD operations. Here, the *Doctor* service performs operations on only the *Doctor* subdomain; it can be considered as a *single-responsibility service*. It's a service; but, *is it a microservice*? If you ask me, I will strongly say *no*! The *first* reason is, it's *not micro*. *Second*, its SRP service is only from the surface but internally it's taking various responsibilities of performing various DB operations. *Thirdly*, from the high availability perspective, if one endpoint has issues it will be penetrated to others and all *consumers* will face the impact.

In *Chapter 2, Decipher the Unintelligible*, we already have the doctor service performing CRUD operations as shown in the *Figure* 3.3:

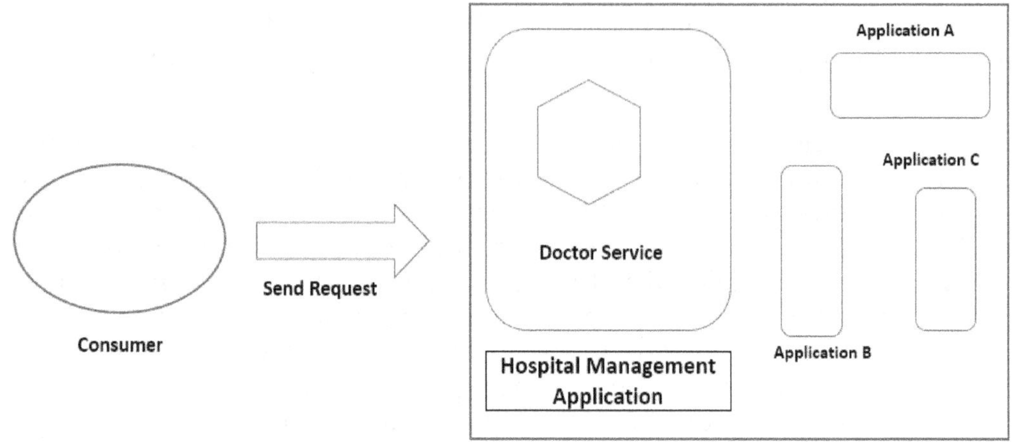

***Figure* 3.3**: *CRUD operations by Doctor service*

It means now we are going to cut down our earlier version of *doctor* service into multiple services based on SRP. Here, **Doctor** is our subdomain having **AddDoctorService**, **UpdateDoctorService**, and so on as shown in *Figure* 3.4:

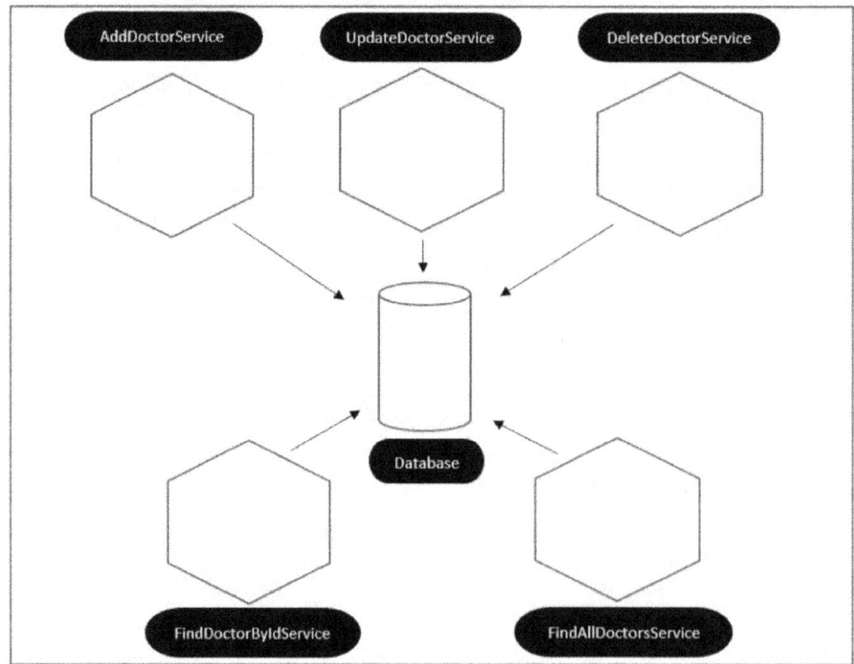

***Figure* 3.4**: *Services and subdomains*

In the same way, we will further consider subdomains for *Patients*, *Hospitals Payment*, and so on. Each subdomain may contain one to many services as per their responsibilities. So, *shall we start breaking down doctor service?*

Here, we are creating a Spring Boot microservice application for adding a *Doctor* to the table. As we already created a similar application, we can *skip* the stepwise application creation process. Just to be on the same page, we need to add starters for **web**, **jdbc**, and don't forget to add the **database driver**. We will be using the same *doctor* domain class and DAO *implementation* from our earlier application as per the project outline shown in *Figure* 3.5:

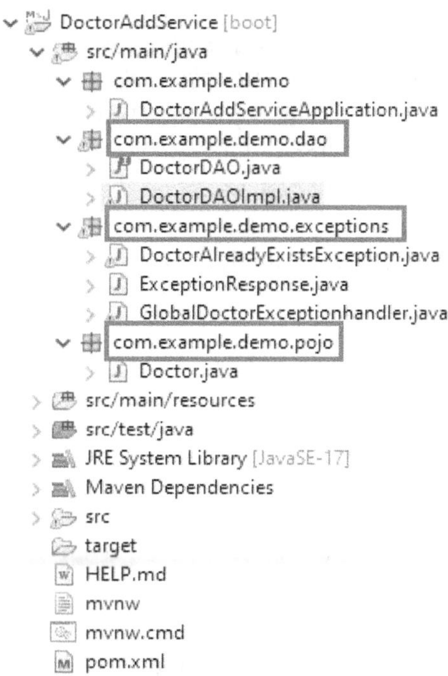

Figure 3.5: *Project Structure for DoctorAddService*

Let's add the **DoctorAddController** having single endpoint for adding a new **doctor** resource as shown in the following code:

```
@RestController
public class DoctorAddController {
 @Autowired
 DoctorDAO doctorDAO;
 @PostMapping(path = "/doctors",
              consumes = { MediaType.APPLICATION_JSON_VALUE,
                           MediaType.APPLICATION_XML_VALUE })
```

```
public ResponseEntity<Doctor> createNewDoctorRecord(@RequestBody
            Doctor doctor) throws DoctorAlreadyExistsException{
   // logic to add record in table will go here
   Doctor d = null;
   int added = 0;
   added = doctorDAO.addDoctor(doctor);
   if (added == 1)
   return new ResponseEntity<Doctor>(doctor,
                       HttpStatusCode.valueOf(201));
  return new ResponseEntity<Doctor>(HttpStatusCode.valueOf(204));
}
@PostMapping(path = "/doctors/form", consumes =
   MediaType.APPLICATION_FORM_URLENCODED_VALUE, produces = {
   MediaType.APPLICATION_JSON_VALUE, MediaType.APPLICATION_XML_VALUE })
public Doctor createNewDoctorRecord_Form(Doctor doctor) {
   // logic to add record in table will go here
   Doctor d = null;
   int added = doctorDAO.addDoctor(doctor);
   if (added == 1)
      return doctor;
   return d;
}
}
```

Now it's time to add *database*, *application*, and *server* properties in the **application. properties file** as shown:

```
spring.application.name=doctor-add-service
server.port= 8081
spring.datasource.url=jdbc:mysql://localhost:3306/doctors
spring.datasource.username=root
spring.datasource.password=mysql
```

For the very first time we have configured the name of the application. It's one of the very important properties in microservices architecture. We will not be discussing it in detail here, let us wait for a few more chapters but for every application we will configure this without fail.

Let's *run* and *test* the application for the **/doctors/form** endpoint as shown in *Figure 3.6*:

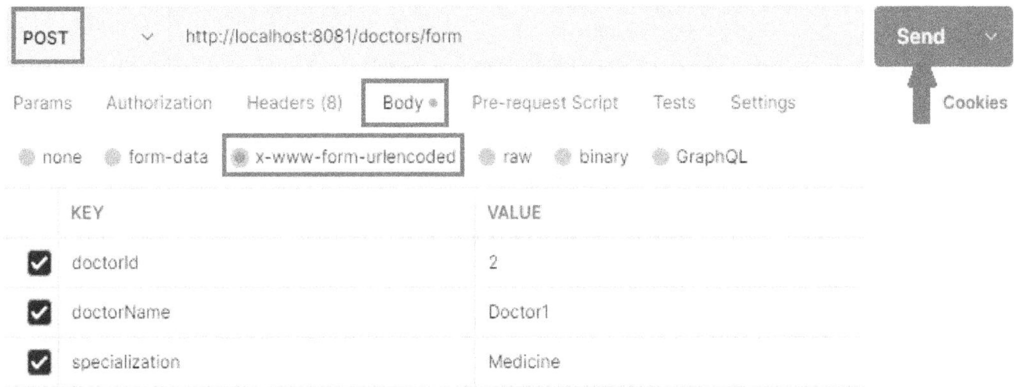

***Figure 3.6**: Creating new Doctor resource*

The request will be processed by the controller adding a new record to the **doctor** table and get the following response:

```
{
    "doctorId": 2,
    "doctorName": "Doctor1",
    "specialization": "Medicine"
}
```

***Figure 3.7**: JSON response for /doctors/form* API

In the **DoctorAddService**, we are exposing more than one endpoint. One may consider this as an application with multiple responsibilities. However, we are only creating a new resource which is a single responsibility.

Now, let's create a new Spring Boot microservice application to find all *doctors*. Each of the microservice is independent of the other and can all together be a different stack of technology. Here, we will use JPA repositories instead of JDBC

API to communicate with tables in MySQL. The project will have the following outline:

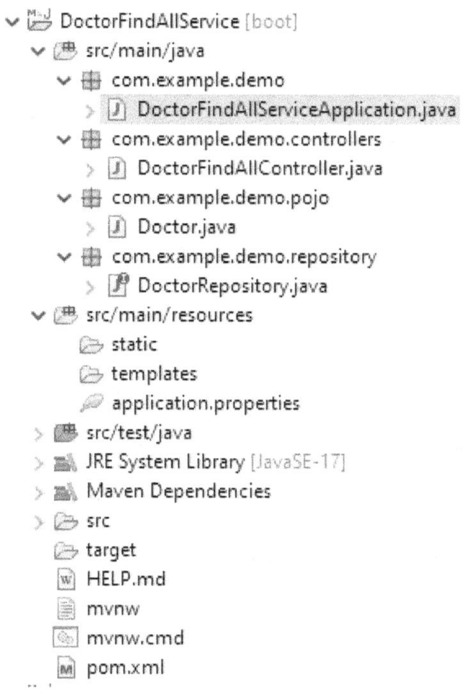

Figure 3.8: *Project structure for DoctorFindAllService*

As we are going to use JPA, let's update **Doctor** to map as *entity*. The code snippet shown in *Figure* 3.9 elaborates, how to connect JPA API to map the **Doctor** as entity to the table:

```
import jakarta.persistence.Column;
import jakarta.persistence.Entity;
import jakarta.persistence.Id;

@Entity <------------------  maps the class to the table
public class Doctor {
      @Id <---------------  maps a data member to the Pirmary Key
      @Column(name="doctorid") <-- maps the column name to data member
      private int doctorId;
      @Column(name="doctorname")
      private String doctorName;
      private String specialization;

}
```

Figure 3.9: *Mapping JPA with Doctor*

Note

The Java EE has been changed to Jakarta EE and Spring Boot 3.0 has also upgraded from Java EE to Jakarta EE APIs. The Spring Boot possible, have opted Jakarta EE 10 compatible dependencies. Observe that the import statements for the package names which were earlier starting with javax has now been changed to jakarta.

We are using a JPA repository to communicate with the database. You need an interface in order to declare the contract between JPA and *Doctor*. *Figure 3.10* shows how to declare such interface:

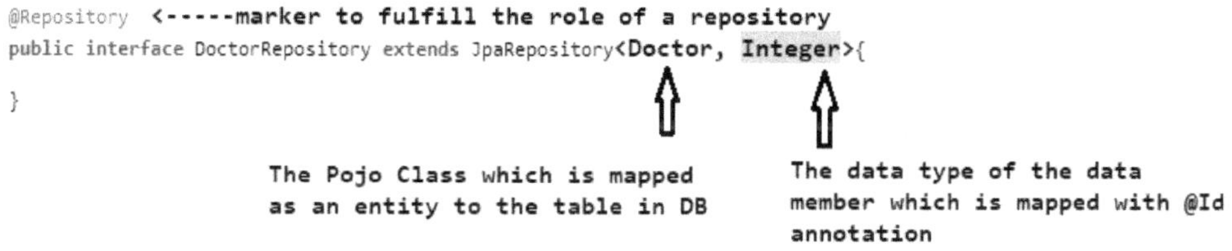

```
@Repository  <-----marker to fulfill the role of a repository
public interface DoctorRepository extends JpaRepository<Doctor, Integer>{

}
```

The Pojo Class which is mapped as an entity to the table in DB

The data type of the data member which is mapped with @Id annotation

***Figure 3.10**: JPARepository interface for Doctor*

Spring Data JPA is a library which adds an extra layer of abstraction on the top of the JPA provider such as Hibernate or eclipseLink. Let us now update the configuration for JPA configurations along with the DB properties as follows:

```
spring.jpa.properties.hibernate.dialect = org.hibernate.dialect.
                                          MySQL8Dialect
spring.jpa.show-sql= true
```

The final step is to add the *controller* having an endpoint exposing the *doctor* resource as shown in the following code:

```
@RestController
public class DoctorFindAllController {
 @Autowired
 DoctorRepository repo;
 @GetMapping(value = "/doctors")
 public ResponseEntity<List<Doctor>> findAllDoctors() {
    // logic to find all doctors will go here
    List<Doctor> doctors = new ArrayList<>();
    doctors = repo.findAll();
    if(doctors.size()>0) {
       return new ResponseEntity<List<Doctor>>(doctors,
                                  HttpStatusCode.valueOf(200));
    }
    return new ResponseEntity<List<Doctor>>(HttpStatus.NO_CONTENT);
  }
}
```

Here, instead of using DoctorDAO, we have autowired and used functionalities of the **DoctorRepository** to find all *doctors* and then expose them as a *resource*.

In the same, we may create microservices for *updating*, *deleting*, and *finding* the resources by doctorId. Each of these microservices has been *developed* and *deployed* separately.

Let's test the **/doctors** endpoint as shown in *Figure* 3.11:

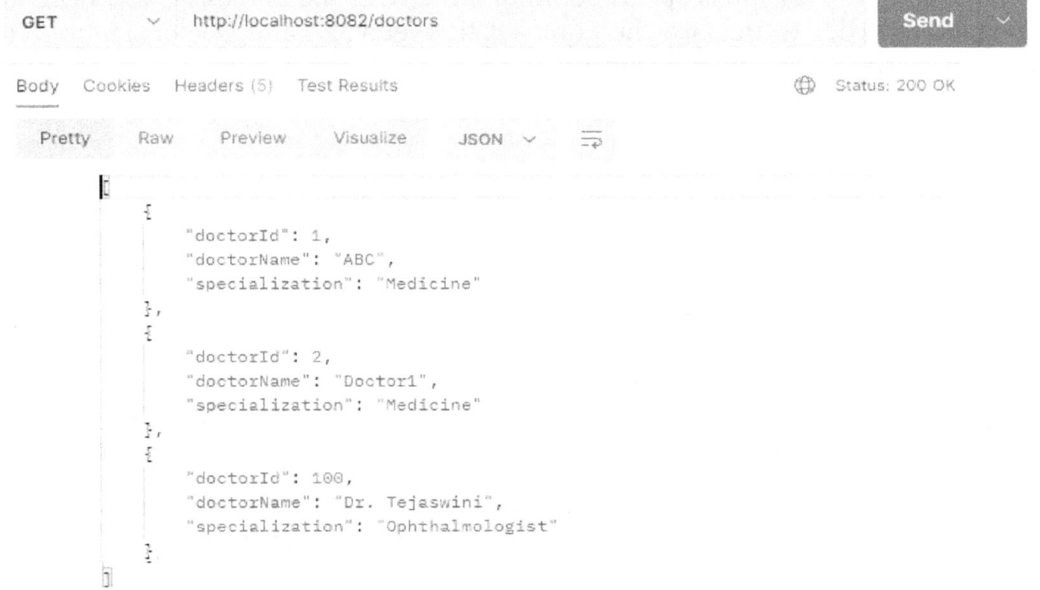

***Figure* 3.11**: *Response for /doctors API*

Observe the response which is in the form of JSON array. It may contain more or less records depending upon the records available in the database. *Are we using JDBC to communicate to the doctor's table?* No, we are not. In the **AddDoctorService**, we have used JDBC integration. But here we have used JPA integration. *Isn't it cool?* We are using a different technology stack without changing the other service.

In this way, we can create our other services as well. So, in all, we will have a group of a minimum of *five* to *six* services developed and deployed separately. Some of you might be thinking *why do we all have headache; can't we just use the earlier service as it is?* Yes, we can. But *what if the service is loaded with requests? Will it be able to handle the increasing workload? When we deploy the application will be with the same ease as that of microservices deployment?* If more instances are required at runtime to launch, *will they be launched as quickly as that of microservice instances? Is it possible to use JDBC API and JPA's at the same time? Will the application development time be less or more as compared to microservice-based development?*

Hope we now know very well why we are choosing microservices. But we need to closely discuss the need of creating these many services. *Do we need all of them?* At one point to follow SRP we need them. However, one can apply the thumb rules before designing the microservice. The workload plays a very important role when it comes to SRP. The **AddDoctorService**, **UpdateDoctorService**, or **DeleteDoctorService** obviously will have less request load as compared to the services to find all *doctors* or find doctors by *specialization* service. Even if we combine the endpoints of these services it will be able to tackle the requests without any workload issue. Again, even if this service with many endpoints *fails* it will not impact the end users, *max to max* the administrative functionalities may be impacted. And it will not be a major issue. Now, for development and deployment also, it's not a very complex code. It means it's possible to take advantage of microservices even when we are not following SRP.

Figure 3.12 shows our first subdomain with microservices:

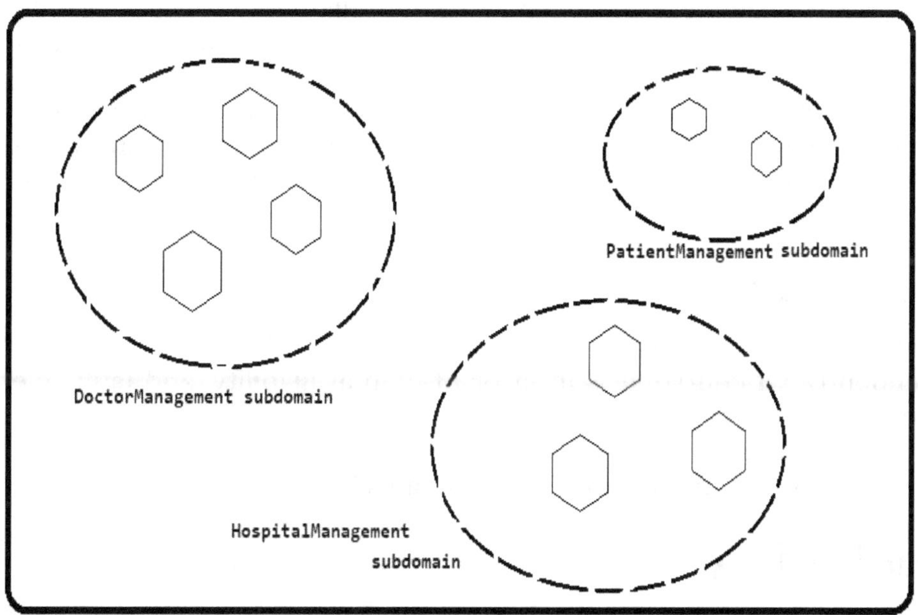

Figure 3.12: *Complete subdomains with microservices*

We have designed our service to handle the increasing load, which will be highly available and developed as well as deployed separately. *Excellent!!!* But I have a question. We developed more than 3-4 *services* and *what we did to connect to the database*? Exactly, we configured database properties in **application.properties** file individually. *Isn't it the repetition of configuration*? And *will it not be an issue in maintenance*? Let's park it for the time being. We will take this into discussion in the next chapter.

Limitations of microservices

Till now we discussed many advantages of the microservices. But every coin has *two* sides. Let's now find out what is on the *other side of the coin.*

Complexity

We are now migrating from monolithic to microservices. However, it comes with a higher degree of complexity. The complexity of designing, mapping the services having single responsibility, managing what goes where, testing them, and debugging is more as compared to monolith.

Network traffic

As already discussed, the microservices will be following single responsibility and they are designed in such a way that they will highly support reusability. It means one microservice will talk to multiple services to complete the task. This interservice communication is heavily rely on the network. More interservice communication results in network latency. One microservice may communicate with one or many services as each one follows **Single Responsibility Principle** (**SRP**), when one of the services fails due to any error it becomes very difficult to track it down.

Monitoring

Our microservices are not only developed independently but also deployed independently. Of course, it is in favor of high availability, and fault tolerance but *what about maintenance*? Now, we need to manage various servers which might be separated region wise. When the number of services increases their maintenance as well monitoring is just a headache.

Conclusion

In this chapter, we covered the basics of microservices. We discussed *why should we go for microservices instead of the monolith.* We discussed different features provided by microservices architecture, which makes it one of the best choices for developers. Along with this we also talked about the limitations of microservices which we need to know before choosing microservice as a part of your software design. At the end of the chapter, we learned how we can decompose the software in different parts or modules as to migrate the monolith approach to microservices.

In the next chapter, we will discuss how to work with the centralized configuration by using the Config server.

Chapter 4
Reflective Composition

In most of the applications, we use various properties. Most of the time the application-related properties such as the *name of the application*, *database configurations*, *port* on which the application is running, and so on., remains constant. However, it does not mean we do not wish to change them at runtime. When the values are part of the code, they are *static* and then any changes we wish to make ultimately requires *re-compilation* and *re-packaging* followed by *re-deployment*. To avoid this, we can externalize the configuration using environmental variables, command line arguments, and with the help of configuration files. One of the thumb rules we as developers should follow is, not to include the frequently changing values in the code. The properties and **YAML** files are very common ways to externalize configuration. Then we can load the configuration files as and when required. We may choose to keep such properties in the external location so that it will be easy to make changes to the configuration as and when needed. As configuration properties are available at the external location; one does not necessarily have to visit the application to make any changes. Also, all the properties are at one centralized location, so the updates become easier.

We can use it for configuring application properties, properties related to the database such as Oracle, MySQL, and so on. Additionally, we can also configure the communication channels like **Kafka** and **RabbitMQ**, and so on, and sometimes the URLs which will be frequently used for the communication between client and server application.

Structure

In this chapter, we will discuss the following topics:

- Approaching centralized configuration management
- Performing centralized configuration
- Exploring Cloud Config server
- Locating the properties in GIT
- Using Profiles
- Limitations in using centralized configuration system

As already discussed many times, the *traditional monolithic architecture* has all functionalities running in the same instance. The application requires various configurations. However, the best part was all of them found at the same location irrespective of whether we configured them in one file or separated them across multiples. Now, we are dealing with microservices architecture which mostly runs in a cloud environment. Our microservices will be spanned across multiple containers separated by geographical regions. Each one of them will have their own configurations. However, many of them will have similar configurations with the same values. Indeed, we are duplicating configurations from one service to another. But then managing so many services and their configuration is a very complex job. When it comes to managing configuration settings with dozens of services, it will be much more difficult. All these duplicate copies of the configurations when spanned across different locations, can become error-prone. We might change the configuration at one place while some other service for the same task may be using the older configurations. This makes it difficult to maintain consistent configuration. As services are referring to two different sets of configurations, it straightforwardly leads to the data inconsistency. That means managing and maintaining consistent configuration plays a very critical role in microservice's architecture.

Approaching centralized configuration management

Now, our approach is to separate the configuration from the code and store it separately at a location where the application will read it as needed. The configuration is separated, one can now update it separately as and when required without connecting to the application. The services do not have to store the configuration locally, it means even multiple services are using the same configuration. We can change the configuration at one place and without knowing who all are using it, the changes will be reflected across all the locations.

Let us observe *Figure 4.1*, where we have the duplication of the configuration for the DB communication across various services:

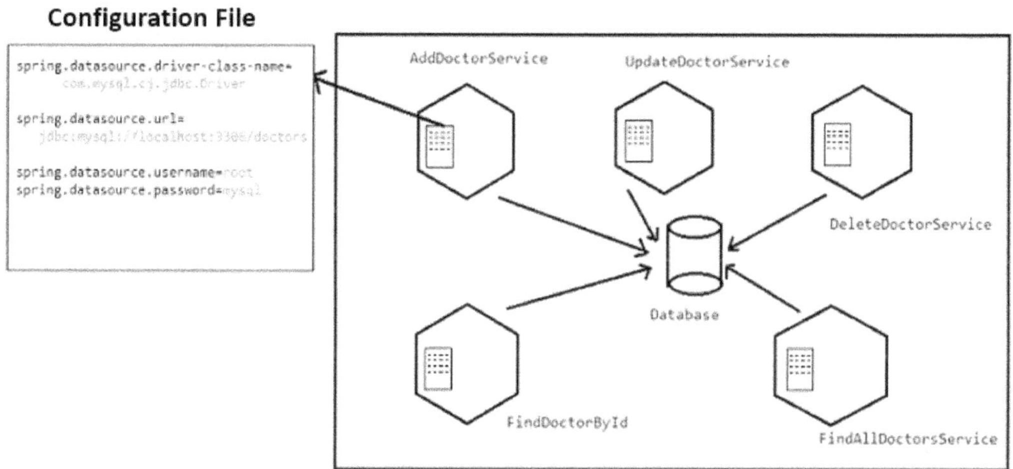

Figure 4.1: *Redundant configuration settings*

In application development, once a scenario is DONE, we always wish to test the application for certain environmental parameters such as the *platform*, *different databases*, *messaging tools*, *logging configurations*, and so on. We are now referring to the same configuration as these are very common and all the services will need them. *Does that mean we will keep on changing the configurations in each file for testing environments?* We know very well the way the Spring profiles support segregating the parts of our application configuration and making them available under certain environments. In the same way, we now can store multiple configurations for various environments such as *dev*, *test*, or *production*.

Earlier we used to configure our most secure information of *usernames* and *passwords* for various services. Maintaining them was one headache; however, securing them is bigger and of at most importance. Now, the configuration is centrally placed in a secure environment; it's now the most reliable. And that is what we want to achieve. *Figure* 4.2 shows the approach to implementing centralized configuration:

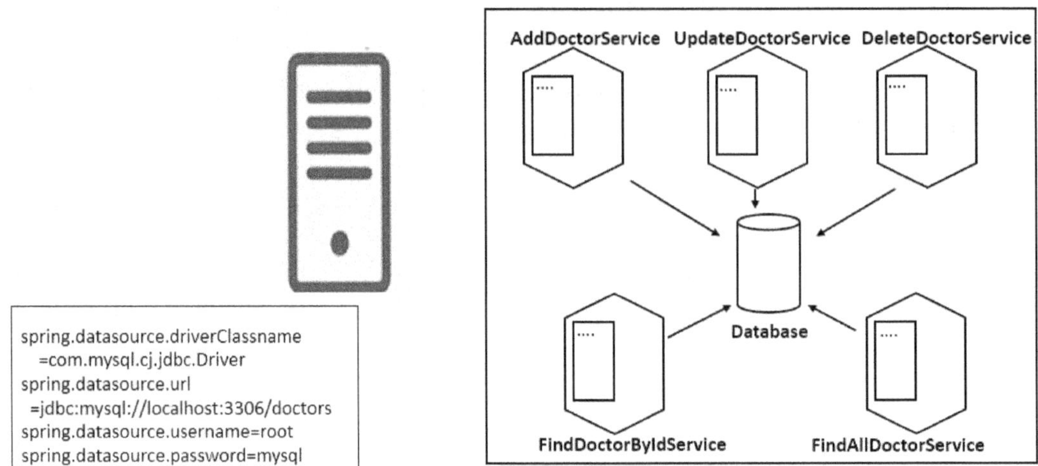

Figure 4.2: *Centralized configuration*

Performing centralized configuration

The **Centralized Configuration System** enables us to conquer the complexity of configuration management by separating the reusable configuration from the application code at one centralized location which can be accessed by the applications to read the configured properties. We can update the configuration without accessing the applications and any updates at the configuration will be reflected at the application level automatically. **Spring Cloud Config** module supports both *server-side* as well as *client-side* approaches for externalizing the configuration in the distributed system.

The system consists of the **Config Server** (1), **backend stores** (2), and the **services**(3) which want to read the properties as shown in *Figure* 4.3:

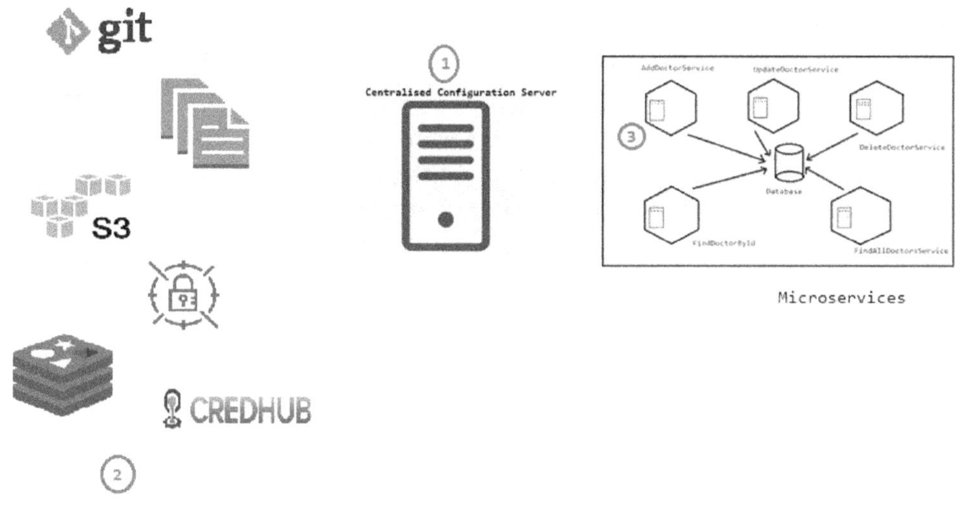

Figure 4.3: *Externalized configuration system*

The figure is certainly not a straight highway. We need to explore different components of it.

For simplicity when we decide to opt for the centralized configuration, we can consider the following steps to follow:

1. Decide the properties to externalize and keep them at the centralize location to access.
2. Decide from available backends which one to use such as **JDBC**, **Vault**, **CredHub**, or **Redis** and so on.
3. Add the properties to externalize to the backend.
4. Take the decision how to locate the properties such as application name and profile, configuration file name, using the label and the configuration file name, application name, profile, and the label.
5. Decide how many profiles to maintain such as *test*, *dev* or *prod*, and so on.
6. Set up the Config Server and add the connectivity to the backend by setting property **spring.cloud.config.server.XXX** where **XXX** will be replaced by the name of the backend and followed by its connecting properties.

Exploring Cloud Config Server

Now that we know the steps, let us set up and keep our *Cloud Config Server* ready to communicate with the backend once it is set. The **Config Server** is a central place that manages our externalized properties for the applications. The properties are externalized but the question is *where are we going to store these configurations*? Depending on the backend store the configuration of the Cloud Config Server changes. Let us start by creating our Config Server.

Let us create a Spring Boot application **Cloud_Config_Server** having **spring-cloud-config-server** as the dependency. As the service needs the ability to be a server, we will add **@EnableConfigServer** annotation as shown in the *figure* 4.4, as follows:

```
@SpringBootApplication
@EnableConfigServer
public class CloudConfigServerApplication {

	public static void main(String[] args) {
		SpringApplication.run(CloudConfigServerApplication.class, args);
	}

}
```

Figure 4.4: *Using @EnableConfigServer*

Great! We know how to create a Config Server. By default, it will try to communicate to GIT. However, we do have various other backend stores to locate the configuration. Let us discuss the other ways one by one.

Selection of backends

There are different backend stores options available. Let us discuss those in detail:

Vault Backend

Most of the application has various *passwords*, API *keys*, *certificates*, or some *very sensitive information* that needs to be kept secure to access various resources securely. This secret can be stored in Vault. The **Vault** is a tool that allows accessing secrets securely. The Vault provides a unified interface with tight access control and records a detailed audit log.

When we decide to use Vault as the backend, we need to add the **spring-cloud-starter-vault-config** in the dependencies and then configure **spring.profiles.active=vault** in the **application.properties** of the Config Server. We need to set the following configuration to communicate to the Vault as backend as shown in *figure* 4.5:

```
# This configures the Vault endpoint with an URI in case we have host, portnumber or scheme
configured URI always takes precedence
spring.cloud.vault.uri=
# The hostname of the Vault host which uses SSL certificate validation
spring.cloud.vault.host=
# the Vault port number. The default is 8200
spring.cloud.vault.port=
# the read timeout expressed in milliseconds
spring.cloud.vault.connection-timeout=
#the order for the property source
spring.cloud.vault.config.order=
```

***Figure 4.5**: Setting Vault backend*

JDBC backend

We can use JDBC as a backend for the configuration of the properties. Once we decide to use JDBC for storing the configuration, the very first thing needed is to include a **jdbc-starter** and database driver as the dependencies. We can use **PostgreSQL**, **MySQL**, and other RDBMS and NoSQL to store the configurations. Now, it is time to configure the properties to communicate to the database as:

```
spring.application.name=cloud-config-server
server.port= 8888

spring.datasource.driver-class-name=com.mysql.cj.jdbc.Driver
spring.datasource.url=jdbc:mysql://localhost:3306/configuration
spring.datasource.username=root
spring.datasource.password=mysql
```

***Figure 4.6**: Setting JDBC backend*

Now, we need to add the **Properties** table under the schema **configuration** as shown in *figure* 4.7:

```
mysql> desc Properties;
+-------------+--------------+------+-----+---------+----------------+
| Field       | Type         | Null | Key | Default | Extra          |
+-------------+--------------+------+-----+---------+----------------+
| id          | int          | NO   | PRI | NULL    | auto_increment |
| APPLICATION | varchar(255) | YES  |     | NULL    |                |
| PROFILE     | varchar(255) | YES  |     | NULL    |                |
| LABEL       | varchar(255) | YES  |     | NULL    |                |
| PROP_KEY    | varchar(255) | YES  |     | NULL    |                |
| VALUE       | varchar(255) | YES  |     | NULL    |                |
+-------------+--------------+------+-----+---------+----------------+
6 rows in set (0.00 sec)
```

***Figure 4.7**: Structure of Properties table*

Let's add a few rows. The following figure shows all the entries in the table:

```
mysql> select * from Properties;
+----+---------------------------+---------+--------+------------------------------+------------------------------------------+
| id | APPLICATION               | PROFILE | LABEL  | PROP_KEY                     | VALUE                                    |
+----+---------------------------+---------+--------+------------------------------+------------------------------------------+
|  1 | doctor-find-all-service   | default | latest | spring.datasource.url        | jdbc:mysql://localhost:3306/doctors      |
|  2 | doctor-find-all-service   | default | latest | spring.datasource.username   | root                                     |
|  3 | doctor-find-all-service   | default | latest | spring.datasource.password   | mysql                                    |
+----+---------------------------+---------+--------+------------------------------+------------------------------------------+
3 rows in set (0.00 sec)
```

***Figure 4.8**: Records of the Properties table*

The **Prop_key** is the name of the property, expected by the client application. Here, we have inserted the value for the application as **doctor-find-all-service**, which is the name of our client application.

The default configuration of the Cloud Config Server will try to connect to GIT. However, now we want it to communicate to JDBC. The following configuration enables the communication to the backend database as:

```
spring.profiles.active=jdbc
spring.cloud.config.server.jdbc.order=2
spring.cloud.config.server.jdbc.sql= SELECT PROP_KEY,VALUE from PROPERTIES where APPLICATION=? and PROFILE=? and LABEL=?
```

How to select the configuration associated with a client application

***Figure 4.9**: Communicating to database*

Let us start and test how the application configuration is loaded in Postman. Once you hit the **doctor-find-all-service/default/latest** to fetch its configuration, you will get the output as shown in *Figure 4.10*:

***Figure 4.10**: JDBC-based configuration*

CredHub backend

CredHub is a component used for managing the credentials centrally in the *Cloud Foundry*. It also allows generation of secure credentials, their storage, and management along with mechanisms to access them. It also supports encryption management.

We need to include the **spring-credhub-starter** dependency to enable integration of CredHub to use it as a backend store. Along with it, we also need to include the following properties in the Cloud Config Server:

```
spring.profiles.active= credhub
spring.cloud.config.server.credhub.url= <CredHub URL>
```

Figure 4.11: *Setting CredHub backend*

Redis Backend

The Spring Cloud Config Server supports the use of **Redis** as a backend for storing the configurations. One can use it by adding a dependency Spring Data Redis in the application. Now the configuration must include the URL for Redis server along with active profile as **redis** as shown in the *Figure* 4.12:

```
spring.application.name= cloud-config-server
spring.profiles.active= redis
spring.redis.host= < REDIS URL >
```

Figure 4.12: *Setting Redis Backend*

AWS Secrets Manager Backend

AWS Secrets Manager is an AWS service which makes it easier to manage secrets such as *database credentials*, *passwords*, *third-party* API *keys*, and so on. The Secrets Manager console enables managing, storing and controlling access to these secrets centrally via **command-line interface (CLI)**, the Secrets Manager API as well as SDKs. Along with adding the dependency **software.amazon.awssdk**, we also need to configure other properties as shown in *Figure* 4.13:

```
spring.profiles.active= awssecretsmanager
spring.cloud.config.server.aws-secretsmanager.region= < name of region >
spring.cloud.config.server.aws-secretsmanager.endpoint = <URL endpoint >
spring.cloud.config.server.aws-secretsmanager.origin= < value of origin >
spring.cloud.config.server.aws-secretsmanager.prefix= <value of prefix>
spring.cloud.config.server.aws-secretsmanager.profileSeparator= <value of seperator>
```

Figure 4.13: *Setting AWS Secrets Manager Backend*

AWS S3 Backend

AWS S3 can also be used as a store for the configuration. For this, we need to include the **software.amazon.awssdk** dependency and configure the properties as:

```
spring.profiles.active=awss3
spring.cloud.config.server.awss3.region= < name of region >
spring.cloud.config.server.awss3.bucket= < name of bucket >
```

***Figure 4.14**: Setting AWS S3 Backend*

AWS Parameter Store Backend

The **AWS Parameter Store** can be used as the Spring Cloud Config Server backend store. The **software.amazon.awssdk** dependency needs to be included to add support for AWS Parameter Store backend. Along with dependency, we also need to configure the following properties:

```
spring.profiles.active= awsparamstore
spring.cloud.config.server.awsparamstore.region= < name of region >
spring.cloud.config.server.awsparamstore.endpoint = < endpoint URL >
# The default value is aws:ssm:parameter:
spring.cloud.config.server.awsparamstore.origin= < name of origion >
# The default is /config
spring.cloud.config.server.awsparamstore.prefix = <value of prefix>
spring.cloud.config.server.awsparamstore.profile-separator = < value of seperator >
# The default value is true
spring.cloud.config.server.awsparamstore.recursive = <true / false>
# The default value is true
spring.cloud.config.server.awsparamstore.decrypt-values= <true / false>
```

***Figure 4.15**: Setting AWS Parameter Store Backend*

Composite environment repositories

Till now, we discussed how to configure the backend where the configuration can be stored. Can there be a condition where one needs to use more than one backend store to store the configuration and then to pull configured data from multiple environment repositories? Yes, this is possible. It can be enabled by using the composite profile in our configuration of the config server application. We can have various options to pull the data. Let us discuss a couple of them.

Case 1: Using the subversion repository as well as Git repositories to store the configuration

The following configuration shows, how to configure Git repository along with the subversion repository:

```
spring.profiles.active= composite
spring.cloud.config.server.composite[0].type=svn
spring.cloud.config.server.composite[0].uri= file://path to svn
spring.cloud.config.server.composite[1].type=git
spring.cloud.config.server.composite[1].uri= file://path to git
```

Figure 4.16: *Using subversion repo with Git repo*

Case 2: Using the Git repository and a Vault server to store the configuration

Following configuration shows, how to configure Git repository and Vault server:

```
spring.profiles.active=git, vault
spring.cloud.config.server.git.uri= file://path to file
spring.cloud.config.server.git.order= 2
spring.cloud.config.server.vault.host= <host name>
spring.cloud.config.server.vault.port= <port number >
```

Figure 4.17: *Using Git and Vault*

File System Backend

Tortoise SVN, **GIT**, **Apache SVN**, and **CMS** are some of the version control tools. The **GIT**, **SVN** are the tools that support cloning the local file systems. The properties **spring.cloud.config.server.git.basedir or spring.cloud.config.server.svn.basedir** enables the backend location support. The **spring.profiles.active=native** enables setting the profile to **native** so that the configuration files can be loaded from the local classpath or from the file system. We will discuss this in detail very soon.

Git Backend

The default implementation of the server to store the backend uses git. It makes it easy to support the labeled versions of the configuration environment and them accessible to a wide range of tools. However, *Spring Cloud Config Server* supports various ways to connect to the backend where the configuration properties are stored. It's now time for a long-awaited store, the GIT. Let us get started then.

Let us take into consideration our **FindAllDoctorService** which earlier was having the properties for database connectivity configured in **application.**

properties file. Now, we are going to take those properties out of the service and place them in the git repository as described in *Figure 4.18*:

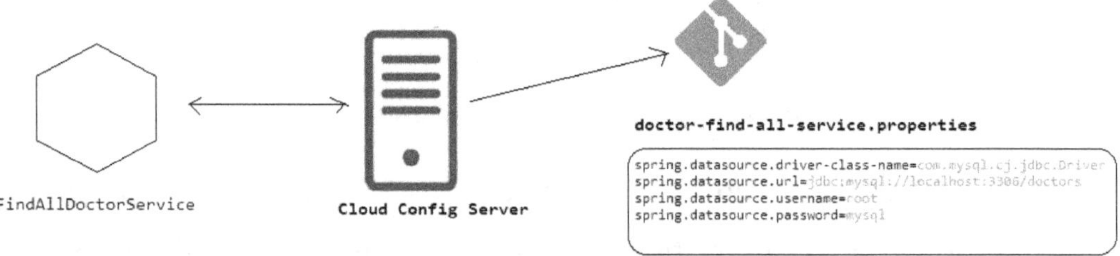

***Figure 4.18**: Working with properties from Git*

Our system consists of *three* parts; the Git repository has the property files, the Cloud Config Server, which communicates to the backend store Git, and then the **FindAllDOctorService** which wants to import the configured properties. First, we now need to build a Git repo having properties file. In practice, we will create the repository at Git located remotely. However, for testing, we may choose to use the local Git repository. Here, we will cover both these scenarios to create and configure the repos:

Scenario 1: Remote repository

At **http://Github.com**, we will be creating a repository. We can use any name of your choice. Don't forget to copy the URL to use it in the configuration. Now, create or upload a file **doctor-find-all-service.properties** having the following content:

```
spring.datasource.driver-class-name=com.mysql.cj.jdbc.Driver
spring.datasource.url=jdbc:mysql://localhost:3306/doctors
spring.datasource.username=root
spring.datasource.password=mysql
spring.jpa.properties.hibernate.dialect = org.hibernate.dialect.MySQL8Dialect
spring.jpa.show-sql= true
```

***Figure 4.19**: Working with remote repository*

And *commit* the file to your repo.

Why the name of the properties file is ***doctor-find-all-service****? Can we change this?* Well, there is a reason, we are going to discuss that when we will talk about config clients. For the time being, just remember the file name must be equal to the name of the client config microservice whose properties we are willing to externalize.

Scenario 2: Local repository

For testing purposes instead of using the Git account, one may choose to use a local repository. We need to create an empty folder to initialize the repository and then add the **doctor-find-all-service.propetries** file to it and commit it locally rather than pushing it to remote. The following figure describes *step-by-step* process of creating repository:

```
MINGW64 /d
$ mkdir config-repo      <--- creating repository folder

MINGW64 /d
$ cd config-repo        <--- changing to working directory

MINGW64 /d/config-repo
$ git init              <--- initializing repository
Initialized empty Git repository in D:/config-repo/.git/
```

Figure 4.20: *Creating local Git repository*

Once we have a repository, let's add a file **doctor-find-all-service.propetries** to the **config-repo** folder. Follow the following sequence of commands to commit the file to **config-repo** repository:

```
MINGW64 /d/config-repo (master) <-- label for repo
$ git add doctor-find-all-service.properties   <--- adding the file for indexing
warning: in the working copy of 'doctor-find-all-service.properties'

MINGW64 /d/config-repo (master)
$ git commit -m "DB properties"    <--- commiting the file to repo
[master (root-commit) 6c57ee1] DB properties
 1 file changed, 8 insertions(+)
 create mode 100644 doctor-find-all-service.properties
```

Figure 4.21: *Committing the file to repository*

Once the backend store is ready, let's now create a new Spring Boot application named **Cloud-Config-Server** service to communicate to the Git having **spring-cloud-config-server** dependency. You can refer to, *Setting up Cloud Config Server* section in case you don't have an application already created. We will be reusing the same project.

We need to add the configuration in **Cloud-Config-Server** to locate the backend and the port on which it should launch as:

```
spring.application.name=cloud-config-server
server.port= 8888
#Using Git as backend store where repository is located remotely
spring.cloud.config.server.git.uri=< the repo URI having the configuration>
spring.cloud.config.server.git.password= < The Access Token >
```

Figure 4.22: *Configuring Cloud Config Server*

In case we are using a local repository there is no need to add the *password* and the URI will be prefixed by **file://** for Windows-based systems and **file:///** for others. It is then followed by the repository path. To facilitate the selection of our local repository, **myrepo** on Windows-based systems, we can configure it as follows:

```
spring.cloud.server.git.uri= file://E:/dir1/dir2/myrepo
```

And for non-Windows we can use the following command:

```
spring.cloud.config.server.git.uri: file:///dir1/dir2/myrepo
```

Once you complete this task, the Config Server is set. Now, let us test the loading of the configurations using **Postman** as a client:

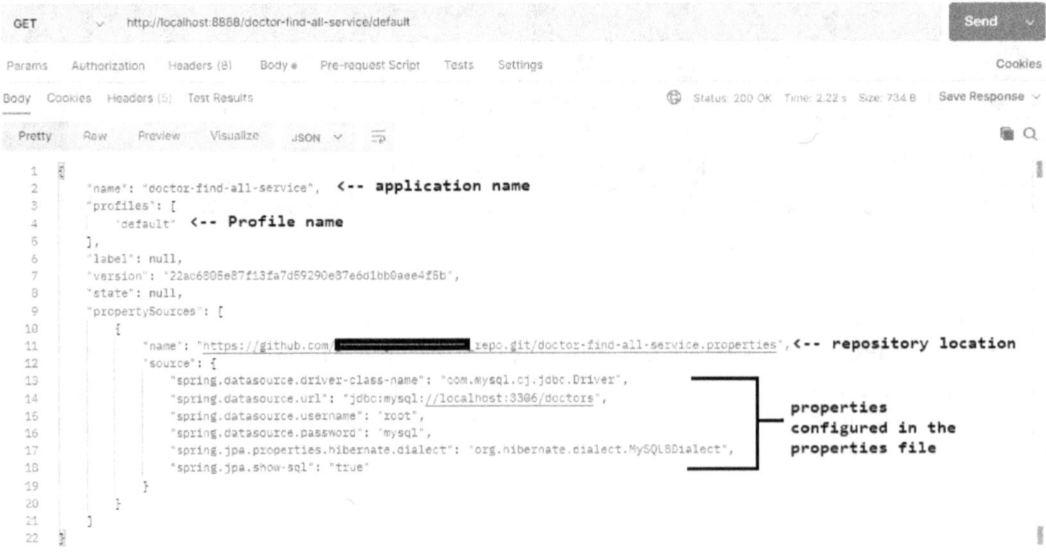

Figure 4.23: *Testing the configuration*

Congratulations!!! Our configurations are getting located. Happy?

Hey Tejaswini, but why are we using ***/doctors-find-all-service/default*** as request? Can we use something else? Or are there some predefined URIs? Before discussing new concepts, first, let us address these questions.

Locating the properties in GIT

The Spring Boot application's environment is used to enumerate the property sources and then publish them at a JSON endpoint scenario-wise. Here, are some of the scenarios to locate the configuration:

Scenario 1: Requesting the resource using the application name and profile

We request the resource using the *application name* and the *profile* associated with it. *Figure* 4.24 shows how a client can give the request in a similar way:

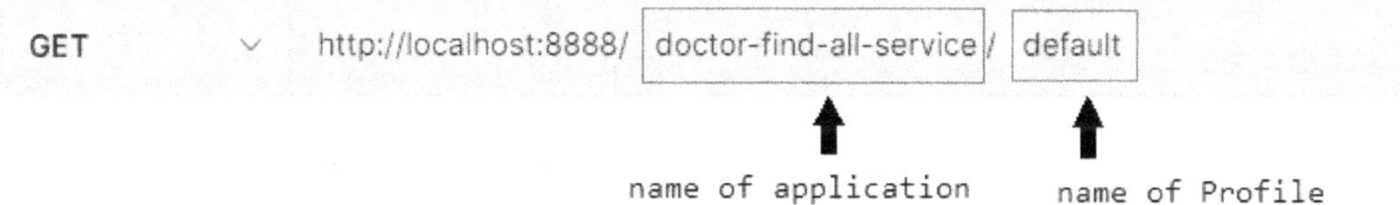

Figure 4.24: *Resource request using application name and profile*

The name of the application is the value set in application.properties file for the property **`spring.application.name.`** This is the same request we made for the discussion we just had.

Scenario 2: Requesting the resource using the configuration file name

You can also request the resource using the configuration file name. *Figure* 4.25, shows how to request the resource based on the configuration file name:

Figure 4.25: *Resource request using file name*

Scenario 3: Requesting the resource using the label and the configuration file nameing the label along with the configuration file name. *Figure* 4.26 shows you how you provide such type of request:

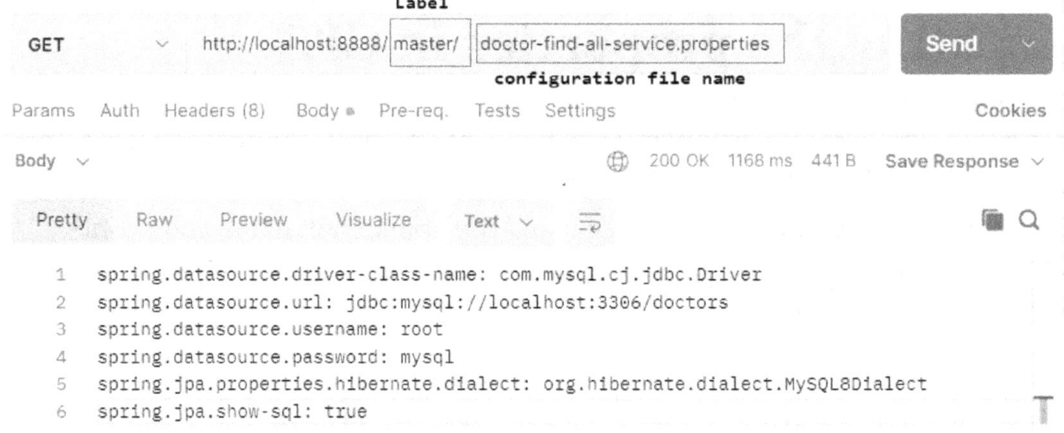

***Figure 4.26**: Resource request using label and configuration file name*

Scenario 4: Requesting the resource using the application name, profile and the label

You can also provide the combination of the *application name*, *profile*, and *label* to generate the resource as shown in *Figure* 4.27:

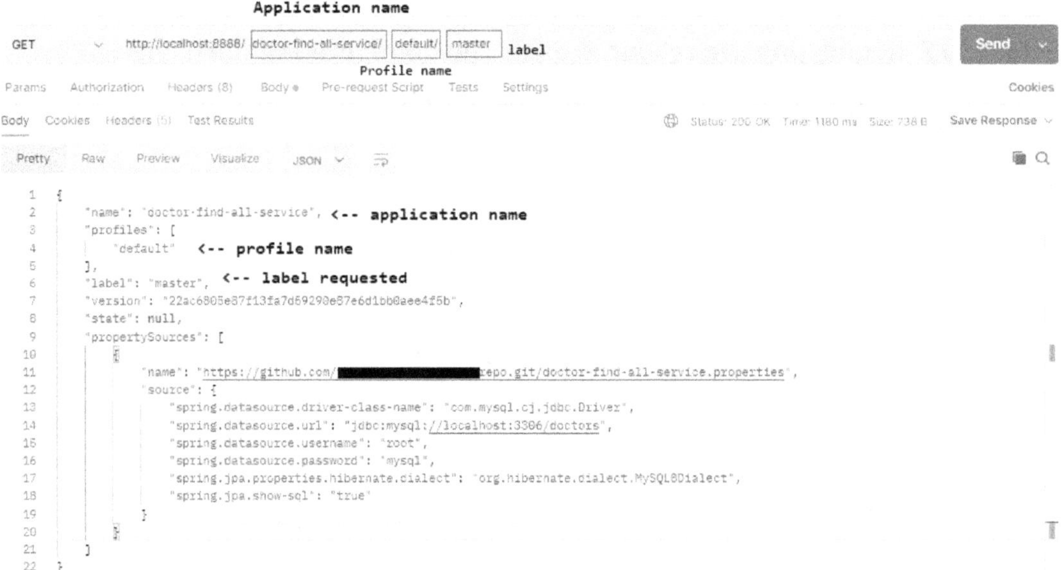

***Figure 4.27**: Resource request using application name, profile and the label*

The request can also be made for the resource for a specific profile for an application. However, for the time being, let's keep it on the board as we have an entire section dedicated for the profiles.

Once everything is set at the Config Server with a backend store, now let's focus on the Config Client. Let's continue ahead with our most awaited component in the cloud config ecosystem, the service which will act as config client.

Configuring the client service to communicate with Config Server

Let us create **DoctorFindAll_ConfigService** as a Spring Boot application which is our client to the Config Server. This microservice will have **spring-boot-starter-data-jpa**, **spring-boot-starter-web**, **mysql-connector-j**, and **spring-cloud-starter-config** as dependencies. The **spring-cloud-starter-config** is very special as it enables the features of being the client of the Cloud Config Server asking for some configuration that is missing at its end.

Now, let us add the **RestController**, **Repository**, and **Pojo**. For simplicity here, we will be reusing the **Doctor.java**, **DoctorFindAllController**, and **DoctorRepository** which we already had written in *Chapter 3, Scale it Down*, for **DoctorFindAllService** which will have project structure as shown in *Figure 4.28*:

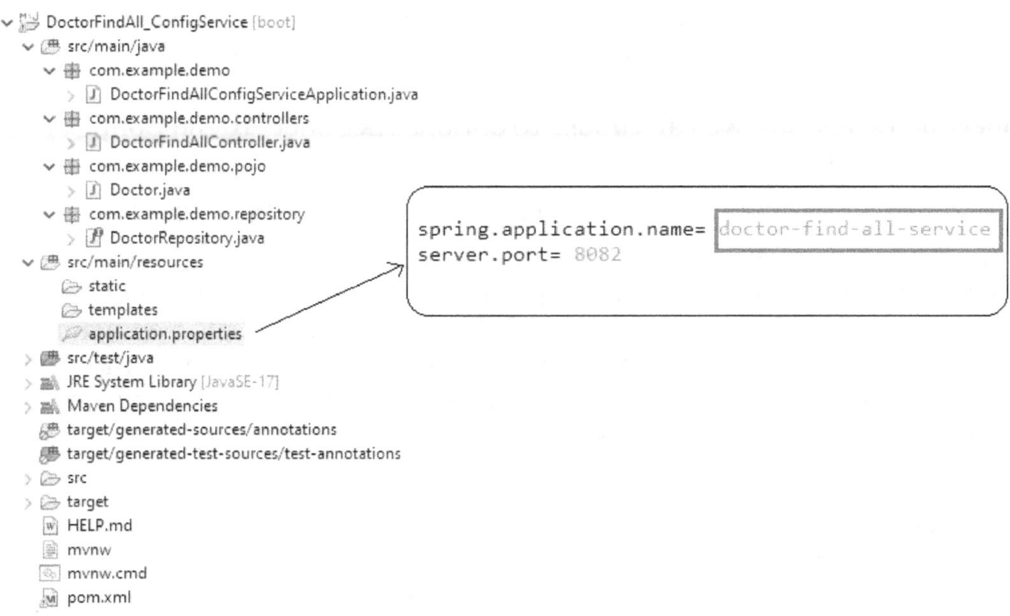

Figure 4.28: *Project structure for DoctorFindAll_ConfigService*

You can choose to use the earlier microservice, do not forget to add the new dependencies to enable the config client module. We are having the **spring.application.name** as **doctor-find-all-service** which exactly matches the property file which we are having on Git. One more thing to observe is, we are not adding any DB as well as JPA-related properties in the **application.properties** file. *Why?* Well, we want to load them from the remote repository. Obviously, as we want to load them from the remote repository. The service has the **spring-cloud-starter-config** dependency which at the startup will force the service to locate the Cloud Config Server and request it for importing the configurations. Here, in our case DB and JPA properties will be imported. The **spring.config.import**, property enables the client to bind to the Config Server. Prior to *Spring Boot 2.4*, we were setting the **spring.cloud.config.uri** property in client service to communicate with Cloud Config Server where the value will be the location where the Config Server is running. However, *Spring Boot 2.4* introduced a new way to import configuration data. Now, we use the property **spring.config.import** to bind to Config Server as:

```
spring.config.import=configserver:http://Location_of_the_config_server
```

We have configured it as:

```
spring.config.import=configserver:http://localhost:8888
```

Once we configure the property, it becomes mandatory to bind to the Config Server and the config client. The config client will fail if it is unable to connect to the Config Server. Sometimes, the Cloud Config server may be unavailable or in some cases, the configuration is not available on the server then we may expect to overlook the configuration and may choose to start the service normally. Under such scenarios, we can choose to optionally connect to the Config Server by setting the property as:

```
spring.config.import=optional:configserver:http://localhost:8888
```

Let us start our config client service, the **DoctorFindAll_ConfigService**. Make sure the Cloud Config Server is up and running. *Hope your service has started smoothly? Congratulations!* You successfully have externalized the configuration by using Git as a backend store. Now observe the console log of the service which proves at startup the configuration data is getting imported from the config server. For ease, I am sharing the console snapshot with you as shown by *Figure 4.29*:

```
Starting DoctorFindAllConfigServiceApplication using Java 17.0.5 with PID 10372
No active profile set, falling back to 1 default profile: "default"
Fetching config from server at : http://localhost:8888
Located environment: name=doctor-find-all-service, profiles=[default], label=null,
```

Figure 4.29: *Fetching configuration from server*

Sometimes when we use a Git repository, we may get the exception as **NoSuchLabelException** and your Config Server console log matches with *Figure* 4.30:

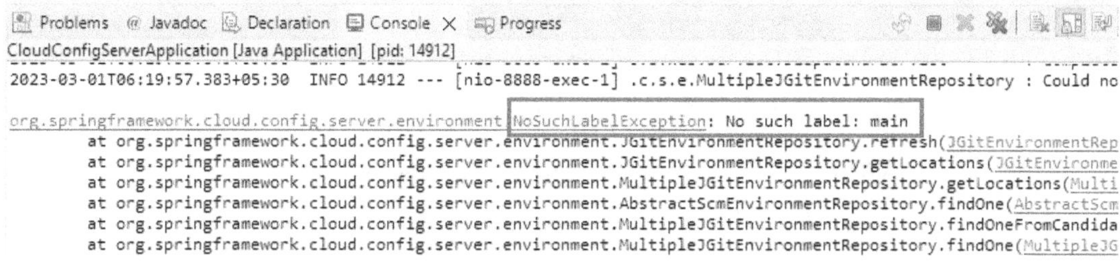

***Figure 4.30**: ConfigServer log for NoSuchLabelException*

We just need to configure **spring.cloud.config.server.git.defaultLabel=master** in the

Cloud Config Server configuration where master is the **repo** label. You can easily find it from the console as well as from Git. *Figure* 4.31 will help you to find more details about it:

***Figure 4.31**: ConfigServer configuration in Git*

The console also displays the log messages of detecting the dialect and initialization of the JPA **EntityManagerFactory**. It means, now we can obtain the information about all doctors by hitting the **/doctors** endpoint in Postman. We will receive the information as shown in *Figure* 4.32:

GET http://localhost:8082/doctors

Params Authorization Headers (8) Body Pre-request Script

Body Cookies Headers (5) Test Results

Pretty Raw Preview Visualize JSON

```
[
    {
        "doctorId": 1,
        "doctorName": "ABC",
        "specialization": "Medicine"
    },
    {
        "doctorId": 2,
        "doctorName": "Doctor1",
        "specialization": "Medicine"
    },
    {
        "doctorId": 100,
        "doctorName": "Dr. Tejaswini",
        "specialization": "Ophthalmologist"
    },
    {
        "doctorId": 101,
        "doctorName": "Dr. Gajendra",
        "specialization": "Orthopedic"
    }
]
```

Figure 4.32: *Getting all the doctor's informatiov n using ' /doctors' endpoint*

And with this, we have an ecosystem set where the Cloud Config Client (MicroService), the Cloud Config Server and the backend store (Git) work together to separate the code from the configuration. Once we have a working demo now the question is, *how is it working*?

How does the microservice make the request and the cloud config server locates the configuration?

Internal process of locating the properties

The **EnviornmentRepository** governs the strategy of storing the details and then serves the environment as an object. The repository implementation behaves as good as a Spring Boot application which loads the configuration files from the backend (where we stored the configuration). We are going to have multiple services which may need the properties to load. It means our backend repository may contain various configuration files. Now, the question is how the configuration is located.

The configuration is located by following *three* strategies:

- Our service is going to have a name which is configured using the **spring.config.name** which provides the value for the **{application}** parameter.
- Our service may also configure an active profile using the configuration **spring.profiles.active** equal which provides the value for the **{profiles}** parameter. If no profile is configured **{profiles}** will take value as **default**. When it is configured, the specified profile will take precedence. We can also configure the multiple profiles then the last configured profile will take precedence.
- Service may have the label property configured this will provide the value for **{label}** which is the server-side feature for labeling a set of files under versioning.

At the microservice start up, when the service finds the **spring-cloud-starter-config** dependency in the classpath, it tries to locate the Cloud Config Server by the property mentioned by **spring.config.import** property. Now, the request is made to the config server as, **http://localhost:{cloud-config-server-location}/{application-name}/{profile}**. There are few more scenarios to locate the configuration and all those scenarios we have already discussed. In our case it is, **http://localhost:8888/doctor-find-all-service/default**. The Cloud Config Server knows the backend store Git to search for the configuration **doctor-find-all-service.properties** for the **default** profile. And, that is the reason we have named the configuration file as, **name-of-service** which is the config client.

Using profiles

The Spring Boot profiles provide a way to separate the parts of our application's configuration under different available environments. In the *development* stage, one may need a certain set of properties. In the *testing* stage, we may want to test how the application works against some different set of properties; so that in *production*, the application will run smoothly. Instead of changing the same configuration file again and again just to find the working of the application, Spring Boot profile allows us to create sets of configurations and then choose one of them which will be utilized by the application. We just imported the data set of default configuration properties for

`DoctorFindAll_ConfigService.`

Let us now add a **test** and **dev** profile in the repo as shown here.

The following configuration is used for configuring dev profile in the file **doctor_find_all_service-dev.properties**:

```
spring.datasource.driver-class-name=com.mysql.cj.jdbc.Driver
spring.datasource.url=jdbc:mysql://localhost:3306/doctors_dev
spring.datasource.username=root
spring.datasource.password=mysql
spring.jpa.properties.hibernate.dialect=org.hibernate.dialect.MySQL8Dialect
spring.jpa.show-sql= true
```

The following configuration is used for configuring **dev** profile in the file **doctor_find_all_service-test.properties**:

```
spring.datasource.driver-class-name=com.mysql.cj.jdbc.Driver
spring.datasource.url=jdbc:mysql://localhost:3306/doctors_test
spring.datasource.username=root
spring.datasource.password=mysql
spring.jpa.properties.hibernate.dialect=org.hibernate.dialect.MySQL8Dialect
spring.jpa.show-sql=true
```

For the sampling purpose, I have created **doctors_test** and **doctors_dev** schemas and have added some test data as shown in *Figure* 4.33:

```
mysql> use doctors_test;
Database changed
mysql> select * from doctor;
+----------+------------+---------------------+
| doctorId | doctorName | specialization      |
+----------+------------+---------------------+
|       20 | test name  | test specialization |
+----------+------------+---------------------+
1 row in set (0.00 sec)

mysql> use doctors_dev;
Database changed
mysql> select * from doctor;
+----------+------------+---------------------+
| doctorId | doctorName | specialization      |
+----------+------------+---------------------+
|       50 | dev name   | dev specialization  |
|       51 | dev name1  | dev specialization1 |
+----------+------------+---------------------+
2 rows in set (0.00 sec)
```

***Figure* 4.33**: *Data under doctor_test and doctor_dev schemas*

We have *three* profiles **default**, **test**, and **dev**. Now, all we need is to set the profile in the **DoctorFindAll_ConfigService** by setting the active profile as:

```
spring.profiles.active=dev
```

After running the application, the console log will display the active profile as **dev** and importing relevant data as shown in *Figure 4.34*:

```
Starting DoctorFindAllConfigServiceApplication using Java 17.0.5 with PID 14004
The following 1 profile is active: "dev"
Fetching config from server at : http://localhost:8888
Located environment: name=doctor-find-all-service, profiles=[dev], label=null,
```

***Figure 4.34**: Console output for DoctorFindAllConfigService Application*

The Postman will also prove that the data associated with the **dev** profile is getting loaded as shown in *Figure 4.35*:

```
GET  http://localhost:8082/doctors
[
    {
        "doctorId": 50,
        "doctorName": "dev name",
        "specialization": "dev specialization"
    },
    {
        "doctorId": 51,
        "doctorName": "dev name1",
        "specialization": "dev specialization1"
    }
]
```

***Figure 4.35**: Loading the data and configuration for dev profile*

In this way, we can get the response for the test profile after setting **spring.profiles.active** to test. I guess this is the right time to reinitiate the scenarios for which the data is imported.

We already have discussed four scenarios. Now let's continue further in terms of profile-based imports.

Scenario 5: Requesting the resource using the profile and the name of application

You can also request the resource using the *profile* and the *name* of the application as shown in *Figure 4.36*:

***Figure 4.36**: Requesting the resources using the name of the application and profile name*

You can observe we have requested for the dev profile. However, in the property resources shows the files related to default as well as dev profile will be provided. The question is *why the default profile file is associated*? This is a strategy to ensure high availability. Sometimes the config client may request to import the data associated with a profile, but there is no configuration associated with that profile. In such a case, the config client will fail. However, due to this strategy when the specified profile is unavailable, the default profile will be imported. *Isn't it cool!*

Scenario 6: Requesting the file using the name of the file

You can request for the file content using the name of the file directly as shown in *Figure 4.37*:

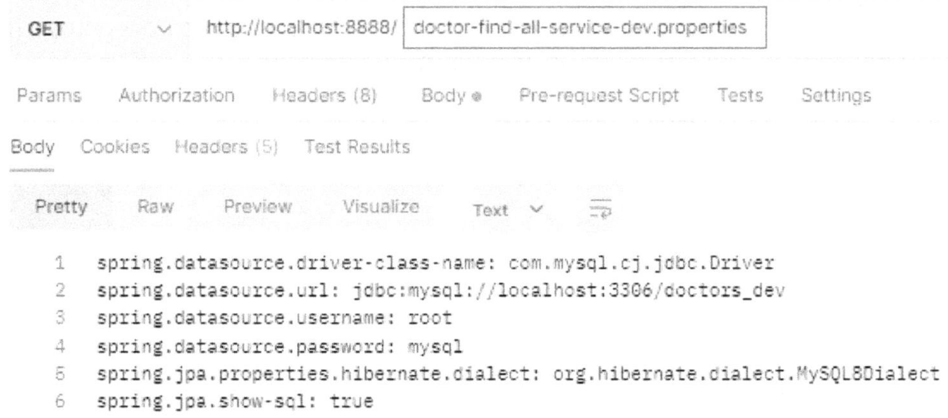

***Figure 4.37**: Requesting for the file using the file name*

Note

The HTTP service have the following forms to fetch resources:

```
/{application}/{profile}[/{label}]
/{application}-{profile}.yml
/{label}/{application}-{profile}.yml
/{application}-{profile].properties
/{label}/{application}-{profile}.properties
```

We now are very well aware of how the configuration resource is requested. Before starting the discussion we said, this ecosystem separates the configuration from the code and makes it flexible to update the configuration independently. *Shall we try updating the configuration?* Here, to update the configuration we will be updating the schema of the database to **doctors_dev_new** for the **dev** profile and then commit changes.

To test the committed changes, we have created a new schema, and then created the **doctor** table without any data as shown in *Figure* 4.38:

```
mysql> use doctors_dev_new;
Database changed
mysql> select * from doctor;
Empty set (0.00 sec)
```

***Figure* 4.38**: *Status of the doctor_dev_new schema*

Let us find how the changes are reflected at the config client's end using the **/doctors** endpoint in the Postman as shown in *Figure* 4.39:

```
GET    http://localhost:8082/doctors

Params  Authorization  Headers (8)  Body  Pre-request Script  Tests  Settings

Body  Cookies  Headers (5)  Test Results

Pretty  Raw  Preview  Visualize  JSON
```


```
[
    {
        "doctorId": 50,
        "doctorName": "dev name",
        "specialization": "dev specialization"
    },
    {
        "doctorId": 51,
        "doctorName": "dev name1",
        "specialization": "dev specialization1"
    }
]
```


***Figure* 4.39**: *Updated list of doctors*

The response clearly shows the changes are not reflected at the config client's end and the client is still using the older schema. *Why*? The reason is very straightforward, the application imports the configuration at startup, any updates taking place after the application startup will not be notified, and the application continues to use the same properties. This is *not good*. The updated changes must be reflected otherwise the application will face issues such data inconsistency. The simplest solution is to restart the application, after which it will pick up the changes. However, this is practically difficult to achieve. We may not know when to restart the application, as we do not know when the update will take place.

Highly available Config Server

The Cloud Config Server can fail to start for some reason, in turn the client service fails to start as it cannot connect to the Config Server. We can set **spring.config.import** to **configserver:http://location_of_server** instead. When we use **spring.config.import** to set **optional:configserver:http://location_of_server**, the client service tries to connect to the config server, but it will still start as the connection is *optional*.

We cannot stop the Config Server from failing. It's a service and due to a number of reasons it may fail. When we know there is a possibility of occasional failing of the Config Server and we are not even in favor of setting the connection to the server as *optional*, then the only possibility is the client will also *fail*. We choose microservices for being highly available, but this seems to go in other direction. *What is the choice we have here?* Our service is failing because of the unavailability of the Config Server. If the Config Server is unavailable when our application starts, it will keep on trying to reconnect to Config Server. Our microservice will retry six times with an initial backoff interval of **1000ms**, which is its default behavior. However, if we can override it by setting the **spring.cloud.config.retry.*** in the configuration. The **spring-retry** and **spring-boot-starter-aop** dependencies need to be added to the classpath to take advantage of the **retry** feature. Alternatively, we can set the **import** property as:

```
spring.config.import=configserver:http://location_of_server?fail-
   fast=true&max-attempts=Number_of_attempts&max-interval=timeinterval&
   multiplier=multiplier value&initial-interval=initial_interval_time
```

One strategy is to retry and get connected with the Config Server. It works very well when there are occasional failures. In the same way, the Config Server might be busy in handling the request and the service waiting in the queue for a long time may face failures. The service fails due to the default timeout. We also can set the timeout thresholds. The property **spring.cloud.config.request-read-timeout** enables us to set the read timeouts and **spring.cloud.config.request-connect-timeout** allows us to set the connection timeouts.

Limitations in using a centralized configuration system

When it comes to *scaling*, the Cloud Config Server has limitations. The Cloud Config Server can be scaled up vertically. However, vertical scaling also has a limit. After a limit, even if we increase the hardware or software capabilities of the server, its performance cannot be increased after a certain point.

To make the Cloud Config Server highly available, it needs to be up and running all the time. Config Server can be horizontally scaled up, all instances of the server must point to the same repository, and it is possible only under the shared file system.

Conclusion

In this chapter, we discussed what is the importance of a centralized configuration management system and the different ways to achieve it. We talked about how to work with Git backend in detail to store the configuration in a centralized way. We also discussed different scenarios to load the resources based on the application name, profile, and file name which can be pulled from the centralized configuration system. We discussed how to locate the properties and how to use the concept of profiles to pull those properties. We can even change the configuration based on our requirements and we observed how to reload the modified configurations from the centralized configuration management system. At the end of the chapter, we discussed what are the limitations of using a centralized configuration system.

In the next chapter, we will discuss how we facilitate communication between the services and the different ways to implement it.

Chapter 5
Liaison Among Services

Aniket was *Production Manager* for one of the top garment factories in *San Francisco*. His company was serving many well-known brands for their clothing products. Considering the workload, the factory was divided into *multiple units*. One unit was just producing the fiber required for the specific companies, whereas the other unit was using the *fiber* produced by that *department*.

Aniket's company was working with a traditional approach to production. Whenever the factory bags any order, the production manager is supposed to inform each of the units separately. That means the first order was placed with the fiber manufacturing department. Once the fiber was manufactured, a further order was placed with the fabric manufacturing unit. The system was working pretty fine over the years. The number of clients was increasing and the production going well matching the orders they receive. But suddenly on one fine day, *Aniket* was shocked to observe that the cycle time for the production was increasing. This was not expected at all, as this was impacting the lead time as well. This was impacting the manpower utilization as well, as few of the resources were observed to be in an idle state. *Aniket* was in panic till he found where the actual problem was, which he found after relentless efforts and analysis. He observed that the fiber manufacturing and the fabric manufacturing team were working independently. The *fiber manufacturing team* was not having much idea about how much fiber was required on priority for how much fabric order. On the other hand, the *fabric manufacturing department* was kept in waiting mode until they get the stock of fibers, without any clue as they do not know what production is being done in the *fiber manufacturing department*. There was no communication at all. *How to resolve this?*

The solution was pretty *simple*, instead of giving separate manufacturing orders to separate departments, the order should have followed the sequence. That is, the order should be placed in the fabric manufacturing department, which internally should communicate with the fiber manufacturing unit. This will make sure that the fiber production unit knows exactly how much the requirement is from the fabric manufacturing unit. When this approach of intercommunication among different units was implemented in *Aniket*'s factory, it turned out to be miraculous results in terms of the cycle time of the product. The units were inter-connected which generated more business values for the organization.

By this time, you all know how to design **microservice**. You all know that every microservice has the responsibility for which it is designed. But many times, we might need to communicate between different microservices. In such cases, the microservices should able to exchange data with each other. This is typically the *Producer-Consumer architecture* that all of you know. The microservice that produces or has the data is our producer or provider. And the microservice, which consumes the data, is a *consumer* or *subscriber*. In our *microservice-based application*, we will be having many services which will communicate with each other and follow the *Producer-Consumer model*. It's high time to discuss the ways to organize the data and then how to exchange the data among microservices. We have various approaches to deal with.

Structure

In this chapter, we will discuss the following topics:

- Revisiting microservice decomposition
- Strategizing inter-service communication
- Using RestTemplate for interservice communication
- Shifting from RestTemplate to feign client
- Using a message broker to exchange messages
- Matching the demands

Revisiting microservice decomposition

We now are designing microservices that are loosely coupled. They are *developed*, *deployed*, and *scaled* independently. When we deal with data, the transaction is closely associated with it. But as opposed to monolithic applications, now transactions will be spanned across multiple services. For example, when we want the *doctor* to be associated with the *hospital*, first we need to check the details of the *doctor* and then add it to the mapping table. In the same way, when someone wants to find the list of doctors in the *hospital*, a list of doctors having some specialization in the *hospital*, we need to query data owned by multiple services, in our case from the *doctor* and *hospital* tables. We are not only going to query the data from different tables, but once the data is obtained, we also need to join the data that is owned by multiple services. We also have to be sure of keeping our data safe and secure. We can't overlook the fact that the data is persisted on a physical server and there is always a possibility that the server may fail. *Do I sound pessimistic by nature*? Surely, *not*. Famous author *Stephan King* once said, *there's no harm in hoping for the best as long as you're prepared for the worst*. For us, the data is an embryo of our microservice ecosystem. We cannot afford to lose it. On a serious note, if we need to tackle this situation, we need to have a strategy for database scaling as well as replication. At the same time, we cannot overlook the fact of different requirements of data storage. We may have multiple services with their requirements. Some of them may need relational databases and some may need NoSQL databases such as MongoDB. We need our microservices to persist the data which is private to that individual microservice. Matter of fact is, *we need to share such data*. To share the data, we have various design patterns. Let us discuss them before we start sharing the data among microservices.

Shared database

Under a *shared database approach*, we use a single database that is shared among multiple services. Every service is free to access the data owned by the other services, using local transactions.

Benefits:

- Being with *monolithic architecture* for years together, the developers are very much familiar with the ACID transactions for data consistency.
- It's always very easy and simple to work with a single database.

Drawbacks:

- The *development time* is slow as the developers need to coordinate all the changes so that other services can access the same tables.
- As the database is shared among various services, the operations performed by one microservice can interfere with one another.
- Various services may have their requirements for storing data, but when we use a single database, it might not satisfy the data storage requirements of some of the services.

Database per service

The microservice may have APIs to expose this data. And most importantly the service's transactions only revolve around its database. *Figure* 5.1 shows a typical structure of such an approach:

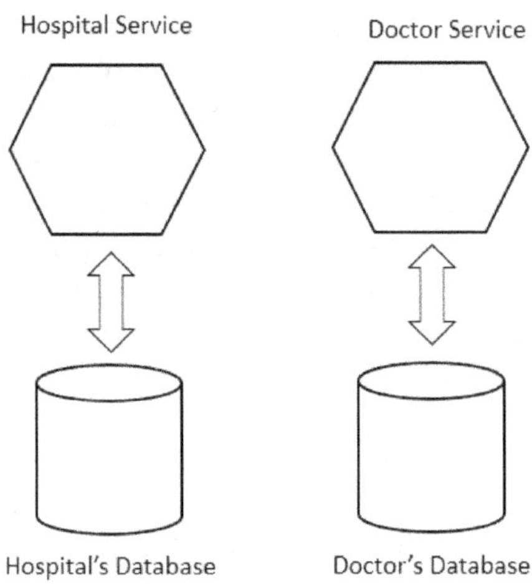

***Figure* 5.1**: *Database per service*

The *microservice* will own the data, specific to it, and cannot be accessed by any other services directly. As the data is private, the question is *what are different ways to keep persistent data private to the service*? We don't need a separate database server for each microservice. Here are some strategies to keep the data private to the service:

- **Table per service**: Each service will owe a set of tables, which will be accessed by that service.
- **Schema per service**: Each service will have a database schema, which is private to that service.
- **Database server per service**: Each service will owe its database server.

Benefits:

- *Database per service* helps to ensure the services are loosely coupled and a change made in one service's database will not affect any other services.
- Depending upon the need for a microservice, it can use the database which is best suited to its needs.

Drawbacks:

- The most complex thing is handling *transaction management* which spans multiple services. Many of the databases don't support them.
- When the environment deals with multiple databases, the implementation of the queries which join data becomes challenging.
- In the environment according to the need of the service, it may handle SQL or NoSQL databases, managing these SQL and NoSQL databases is complex.

Saga

We just discussed *database per service*, where each service has its database. However, in *day-to-day life*, some business transactions may span across various microservices. When the tables are in different databases or different types of databases that are owned by different services, we cannot use a local ACID transaction in our applications.

You may have heard or read about the **Two-Phase Commit** (**2PC**). The 2PC is *a standardized atomic commitment protocol* that ensures the ACID properties of the transaction. The 2PC uses a transaction manager for the data integrity of the database by participating in the transaction as well as monitoring the commits and rollbacks of the distributed transactions. The 2PC acts like a single request. However, we just discussed *database per service*, which means each service will have its transaction manager and one request may be completed in multiple steps and not in a single step. This is where *Saga* plays an important role.

A **Saga** is a sequence of local transactions where each local transaction that updates the database publishes a message or it may trigger an event for the next local transaction. Because of some reason, if the local transaction fails the Saga executes a series of compensating transactions which will undo the changes made up till now in the database.

Benefits:

- The **Saga** design pattern enables to maintain data consistency across multiple services without using distributed transactions in the application.

Drawbacks:

- Saga programming is complex programming.

API composition

We just discussed the services owing their private data and how to manage the transactions span across services. It means, whenever we decide to use a database per service our required data may come from various services. Combining such data is a complex process. We need an easy way to fetch the data from multiple services and then combine it whenever needed. This is where API composition comes into the picture which enables implementing queries that join data from multiple services.

In API composition, we have **API Composer** which invokes the services from whom we need to fetch the data and then perform an *in-memory join* to produce the results.

Benefits:

- It provides an easy way to query data in a complex microservice architecture.

Drawbacks:

- Queries may result in an efficient dataset when we try to join large datasets.

Command Query Responsibility Segregation (CQRS)

As we know the data is segregated among multiple services which own their private data. This generates a need for the implementation of multiple queries to join data from multiple services. We can have a service command that typically needs to update the database. Once updated, it will send messages. However, even if we apply the *Event-Sourcing pattern* then the data can't be easily queried.

In CQRS, we define a view database, which is *a read-only replica* designed to support the query. The application then keeps the replica up to date with data by subscribing to the domain event which is published by the service which owns the data.

Benefits:

- The pattern supports various de-normalized views which are scalable.
- It supports the separation of concerns, where we will have a simpler command separated from the query models.

Drawbacks:

- Pattern implementation increases the complexity of code duplication.
- After discussing different ways of data management, let us move on to data sharing between the services.

Strategizing inter-service communication

We now have microservices with SRP. As discussed already, we design the microservices for reusability. It means one of the microservice now will be the consumer of other microservices. When it comes to interservice communication, we can have *two* distinct ways to deal with it - **synchronous communication** and **asynchronous communication**.

Synchronous communication

In this approach, the *consumer service* as a client sends a request to the provider service and then waits for the response. The client will not be able to proceed further as the response is important for the next stage and it keeps on waiting. Let's take a classic example of currency conversions as shown in *Figure* 5.2:

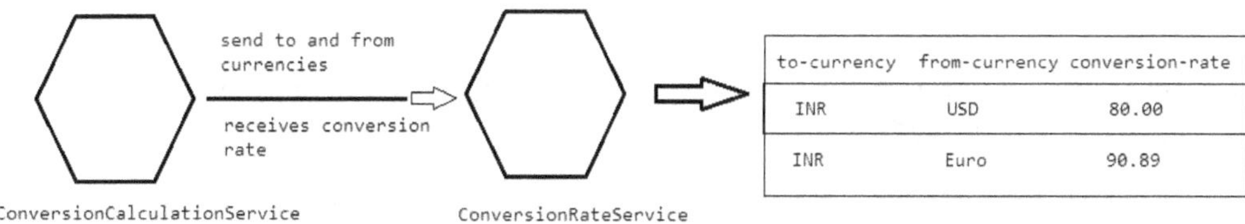

***Figure* 5.2**: *Synchronous inter-service communication*

We have a **ConversionRate** microservice communicating to the database where the currency conversion rate is stored. Now, when we want to calculate the currency conversion for a certain amount, we need the rate of conversion. The **ConversionCalculationService** needs to communicate to the **ConversionRateService** to fetch the data of conversion rate and then using the rate of conversion further calculation can be done. Now, here for calculating the conversion amount it is necessary to have the conversion rate and without which the calculation can't be performed. Here, the **ConversionCalculationService** has to choose the *synchronous communication* between the microservices and it waits for the response.

Asynchronous communication

Instead of waiting for the response, the service may choose to move on which makes the application more *responsive*. Now, the *client service* can choose not to wait for a response if the underlying service is taking more time.

The asynchronous communication uses the *publisher-subscriber pattern*. The *provider* service publishes the data and the *consumer* service subscribes to published data. Under this scenario, even if the publisher service fails to respond, due to *asynchronous communication* it will not affect the overall flow.

So, without wasting time, let us continue our discussion with synchronous communication. We will be discussing in detail how to use **RestTemplate** to achieve synchronous inter-service communication.

Using RestTemplate for inter-service communication

The *easiest*, *simple*, *most popular*, and most *straightforward* option available to use is **RestTemplate**. The **RestTemplate** is based on template design patterns offering various HTTP methods for common scenarios. Along with these methods, **RestTemplate** also provides the generalized **exchange()** and **execute()** methods. The RestTemplate is the best choice for requesting services for synchronous clients.

Before starting the demo first, let's have a look at the frequently used methods available from the **RestTemplate** class:

- **getForObject():** The method retrieves a representation by requesting the resource exposed at the specified URL on HTTP GET method. If required, the method can send expected URI *Template* variables to the provider.
- **getForEntity():** The method retrieves an entity by requesting the resource exposed at the specified URL on the HTTP GET method. The received response is then converted and stored in the **ResponseEntity** instance. If required, the method can send expected URI template variables to the provider.
- **headForHeaders():** The method retrieves all the headers of the resource specified by the URI template in the argument. If required, the method can send expected URI *Template* variables to the provider.
- **postForLocation():** The method enables the creation of a new resource by POSTing the instance to a specified URI. It then returns the value of the *Location header* which indicates the location where the new resource is stored. If required, the method can send expected URI *Template* variables to the provider. It also can contain the argument of type request which can be of the type **HttpEntity** to add any additional HTTP headers in the request. The request contains the body for the POSTing object which can be a **MultiValueMap** to create a request having multipart having values of

any *Object* representing the body of the part, or an instance of HttpEntity representing a part having the *body* and *headers*.

- **postForEntity():** The method enables the creation of a new resource by POSTing the instance to specified URI and returns the response of type ResponseEntity. If required, the method can send expected URI Template variables to the provider. It also can contain the argument of type request which can be of type HttpEntity to add any additional HTTP headers in the request. The request contains the body for posting object which can be a MultiValueMap to create a request having multipart having values of any *Object* representing the body of the part, or an instance of HttpEntity representing a part having the *body* and *headers*.
- **put():** The method enables the creation or modification of a resource by PUTing the supplied object to the specific URI. The URI allows us to supply the *URI variables* in the URI. The request parameter can be of type HttpEntity to provide additional HTTP headers to the request.
- **patchForObject():** The method enables the modification of the resource using the **PATCH** method for the given object to the URI template and then returns the representation in the response. If required, the method can send expected URI Template variables to the provider. The request parameter can be of type HttpEntity to send some additional HTTP headers in the request to the provider.
- **delete():** The method enables the deletion of the resources at the URI specified in the argument.
- **optionsForAllow():** The method returns the value of the header **Allow**, for the specified URI. If required, the method can send expected URI *Template* variables to the provider.
- **exchange():** The method enables execution of the specified HTTP method on the given URI using the entity in the request and then returns the response of type ResponseEntity. If required, the method can send expected URI *Template* variables to the provider.
- **execute():** The method enables executing the HTTP method to the given URI along with preparing the request with the RequestCallback and then reading the response using the ResponseExtractor.
- **doExecute():** The method provides the ability to execute the specified HTTP method on the given URI. The ClientHttpRequest is then processed with the help of RequestCallback and the response obtained from the ResponseExtractor.

Updates in Spring 6.0

```
@Nullable
protected <T> T doExecute(URI url,
   @Nullable String uriTemplate, @Nullable HttpMethod method,
                              @Nullable RequestCallback requestCallback,
   @Nullable ResponseExtractor<T> responseExtractor) throws
                              RestClientException
```

Let us start implementing the inter-service communication using RestTemplate. As shown in *Figure* 5.3, we will be developing *two* services: **DoctorFind_By_DoctorId**, which provides the doctor data, and **Hospital_FindDoctors**, which consumes the data. Both these services have stored the data in their schema. We can also have *two* different types of databases.

Now, one can debate how the design of the database can be better or what alternatives can be chosen. However, here our point is not to discuss how to design a database but we want to understand inter-service communication to share the data between the services using **RestTemplate**:

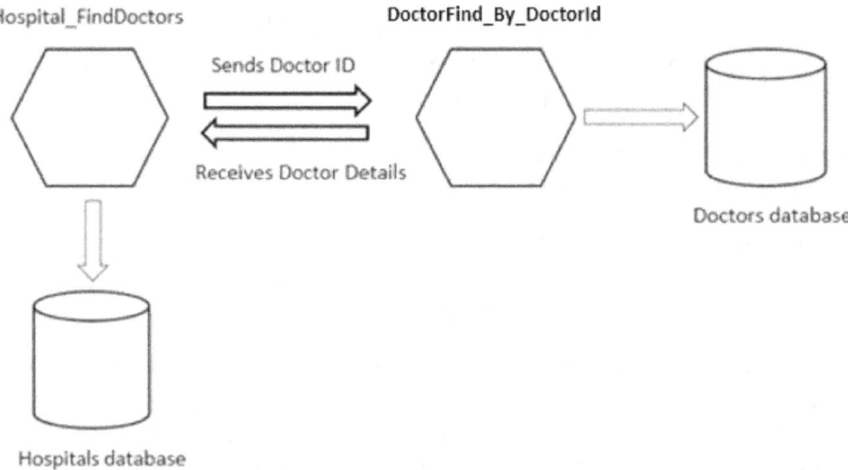

***Figure* 5.3**: *Synchronous inter-service communication using RestTemplate*

Let us start with the **DoctorFind_By_DoctorId** microservice having **starter-web**, **starter-data-jpa**, and the database driver dependencies added. This service will talk to the **doctors** database to fetch the data from the **doctor** table. This is the same table that we used in our earlier chapter. It also has the same **DoctorRepository** interface which gets extended from **JpaRepository** as shown in *Figure* 5.4:

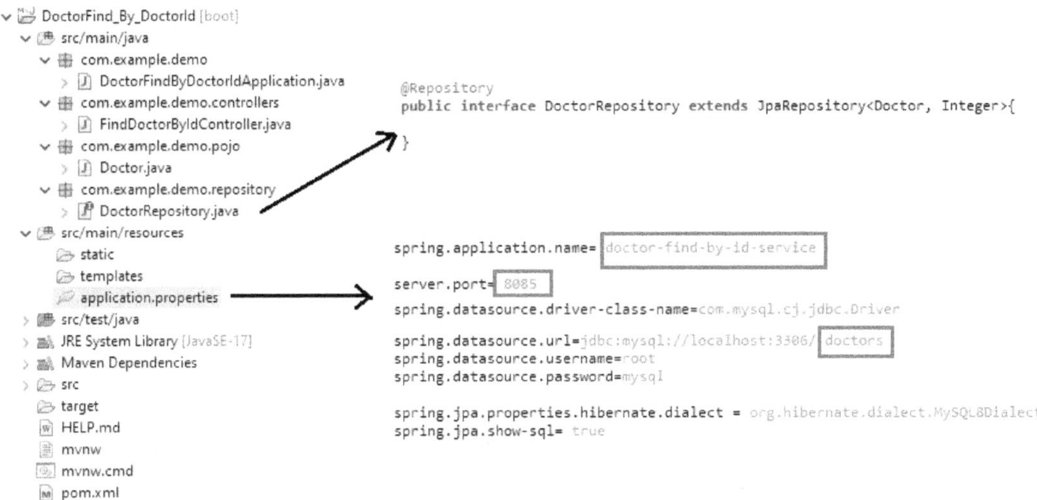

***Figure 5.4**: Project structure DoctorFind_By_DoctorId*

Let us add the endpoints to the **`FindDoctorByIdController`** to fetch the data from the database based on the **`doctorId`** as using **`DoctorRepository`**:

```
@RestController
public class FindDoctorByIdController {
       @Autowired
       DoctorRepository repo;
       @GetMapping("/doctors/{doctorId}")
       ResponseEntity<Doctor> findDoctorById(@PathVariable int doctorId){
        Optional<Doctor> optional=repo.findById(doctorId);
        if(optional.isPresent()) {
              Doctor doctor=optional.get();
                     return new ResponseEntity<Doctor>(doctor,HttpStatus.OK);
        }
              return new ResponseEntity<Doctor>(HttpStatus.NO_CONTENT);
       }
}
```

Once everything is set, start the application and test the **`/doctors/{doctorId}`** endpoint on Postman with available **`doctorId`** as follows:

***Figure* 5.5**: *Response from FindDoctorByIdController for available doctorId*

Next, test it again with non-available **`doctorId`** from the **`doctor`** table, as shown in *Figure* 5.6:

***Figure* 5.6**: *Response from FindDoctorByIdController for non-available doctorId*

We have to make sure that the provider must be *up* and *running* at all time to attend the incoming requests from the consumer. Let us keep it running and we will focus on the **Hospital_FindDoctors** service.

The service has its data under the hospital's schema. The *service* will fetch the data from the **`hospital`** table to find the details associated with the *hospital* along with the details of the doctors. As already discussed, for case study purposes, here we are creating *two* tables. The **`hospital`** table stores *hospital-related information* and **`doctor_hospital_mapping`** table to map a hospital with *doctors*. Finding the doctors who are associated with a hospital may be challenging since there is no relationship between the hospital and doctor tables, and they are not part of the same schema. Furthermore, it is possible that they belong to separate databases.

I remember one situation when I was working as a *Software Architect* in one of the top MNCs. The developers were all experts in designing the database, normalizing it and so on. One of the smart engineers reached out to me. *Hey Mandar! Can't we apply normalization here? Why can't we go for joins? Our life will be easier*. I stared at him for a moment and before I could explain him, he cheered up, Oh! *I am so sorry that I raised this question. These tables are from different schemas, we cannot consider those for normalization. But then how can we handle this situation?* It was a really sigh of relief for me; at least I didn't need to explain to him the basic database concepts. Of course, the team was then new to microservice architecture. Expecting the team knows the concept *shared-database* or *database-per-service* was *unrealistic*.

Currently, we are facing the same situation in our demonstration. We can't use normalization to write queries for generating *joins*. So, we need to take an alternative approach. Here we need to set communication between the *hospital* service and *doctor* service to find the details of the *doctor* and then we will set the fetched data to the hospital instance. Here to set up the communication, we will be using **`RestTemplate`** for synchronous communication.

The **`Hospital_FindDoctors`** microservice will have **`starter-web`**, **`starter-jdbc`**, and database driver dependencies as shown in *Figure* 5.7:

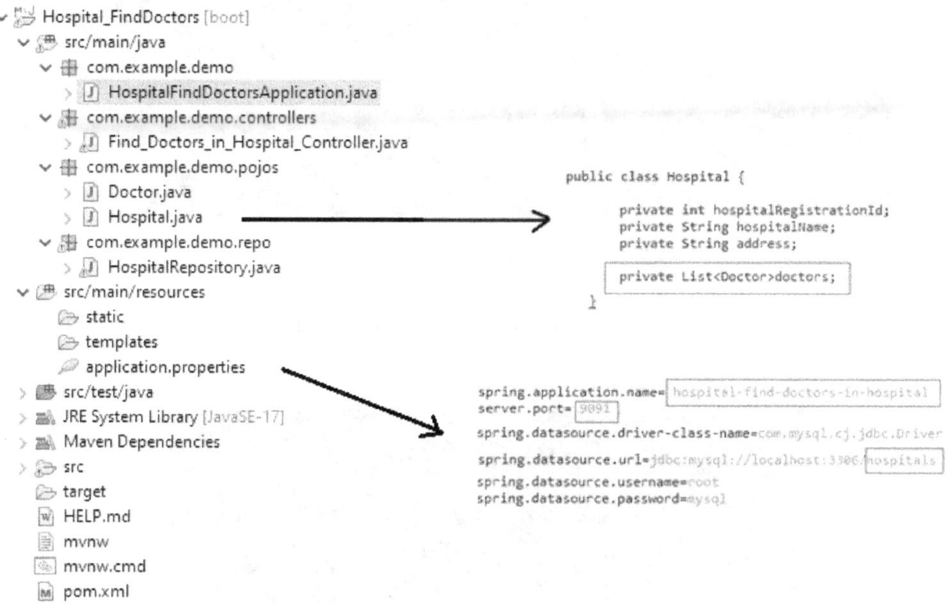

Figure 5.7: *Project Structure for Hospital_FindDoctors*

Once the application is *ready*, let us add the configuration in **application.properties** file. The project also contains the *hospital* and *doctor* POJO. We have shown the hospital POJO and the contents of the configuration file in *Figure* 5.7. We are using the same **Doctor.java** class which we have defined in *Chapter* 2, *Decipher the Unintelligible.*

Here, we are using the JDBC to communicate with the database. So, we also need to create a hospital and **`doctor_hospital_mapping`** table under the **`hospitals`** schema.

Following is the table structure and the sample data for your reference:

```
create hospitals schema

mysql> create database hospitals  ;
Query OK, 1 row affected (0.30 sec)

select the schema

mysql> use hospitals
Database changed
```

***Figure* 5.8**: *Setting hospital database*

Figure 5.9 shows the **`hospital`** table:

```
hospital table

mysql> desc hospital;
+--------------------------+--------------+------+-----+---------+-------+
| Field                    | Type         | Null | Key | Default | Extra |
+--------------------------+--------------+------+-----+---------+-------+
| hospital_registration_id | int          | NO   | PRI | NULL    |       |
| address                  | varchar(255) | YES  |     | NULL    |       |
| hospital_name            | varchar(255) | YES  |     | NULL    |       |
+--------------------------+--------------+------+-----+---------+-------+
3 rows in set (0.00 sec)
```

***Figure* 5.9**: *Describing hospital table*

Figure 5.10 displays the **`doctor_hospital_mapping`** table:

```
doctor_hopital_mapping table

mysql> desc doctor_hospital_mapping;
+------------+------+------+-----+---------+-------+
| Field      | Type | Null | Key | Default | Extra |
+------------+------+------+-----+---------+-------+
| doctorId   | int  | YES  |     | NULL    |       |
| hospitalId | int  | YES  |     | NULL    |       |
+------------+------+------+-----+---------+-------+
2 rows in set (0.06 sec)
```

***Figure* 5.10**: *Describing doctor_hospital_mapping table*

Following is the sample data for demonstration:

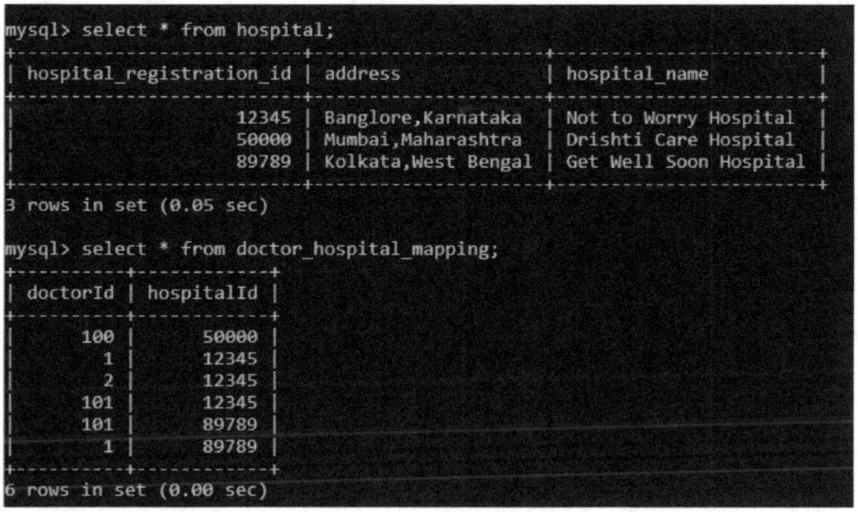

```
mysql> select * from hospital;
+--------------------------+--------------------+-----------------------+
| hospital_registration_id | address            | hospital_name         |
+--------------------------+--------------------+-----------------------+
|                    12345 | Banglore,Karnataka | Not to Worry Hospital |
|                    50000 | Mumbai,Maharashtra | Drishti Care Hospital |
|                    89789 | Kolkata,West Bengal | Get Well Soon Hospital |
+--------------------------+--------------------+-----------------------+
3 rows in set (0.05 sec)

mysql> select * from doctor_hospital_mapping;
+----------+------------+
| doctorId | hospitalId |
+----------+------------+
|      100 |      50000 |
|        1 |      12345 |
|        2 |      12345 |
|      101 |      12345 |
|      101 |      89789 |
|        1 |      89789 |
+----------+------------+
6 rows in set (0.00 sec)
```

***Figure 5.11**: Data in hospital and doctor_hospital_mapping table*

That's it! Our database is set. Let us now use **`JdbcTemplate`**, to find *hospitals* by **`hospitalId`** and records from the mapping table with matching **`hospitalId`**:

```
public List<Integer> findDoctorIds(int hospitalId) {
  String query = "select doctorId from hospital h inner join "
    + "doctor_hospital_mapping ON h.hospital_registration_id=
      doctor_hospital_mapping.hospitalId where h.hospital_registration_id=?";
  return jdbcTemplate.queryForList(query, Integer.class, hospitalId);
}
public Hospital findHospitalById(int hospitalId){
  Hospital hospital=null;
  String Find_HospitalBy_Id="select * from hospital where
                              hospital_registration_id=?";
  try {
   hospital = jdbcTemplate.queryForObject(Find_HospitalBy_Id,
                                         new RowMapper<Hospital>() {
   @Override
   public Hospital mapRow(ResultSet rs, int rowNum) throws SQLException {
    Hospital hospital=new Hospital();
    hospital.setHospitalRegistrationId(rs.getInt(1));
    hospital.setAddress(rs.getString(2));
```

```
    hospital.setHospitalName(rs.getString(3));
    return hospital;
    }
   },hospitalId);
  }
  catch(Exception e) {
                System.out.println(e.getMessage());
  }
  return hospital;
 }
```

The final step is to add the endpoint in the controller to fetch the record using **HospitalRepository** and expose it to the client:

```
@GetMapping("/hospitals/{hospitalId}")
ResponseEntity<Hospital> findAllDoctorsInHospitals(@PathVariable int
                                                   hospitalId) {
List<Doctor> doctors = new ArrayList<>();
Hospital hospital = repo.findHospitalById(hospitalId);
if (hospital!=null) {
  return new ResponseEntity<Hospital>(hospital, HttpStatus.OK);
}
  return new ResponseEntity<Hospital>(HttpStatus.NO_CONTENT);
}
```

Great everything is *done*, time to test the endpoint as shown in *Figure* 5.12 for **HospitalRegistrationId=12345:**

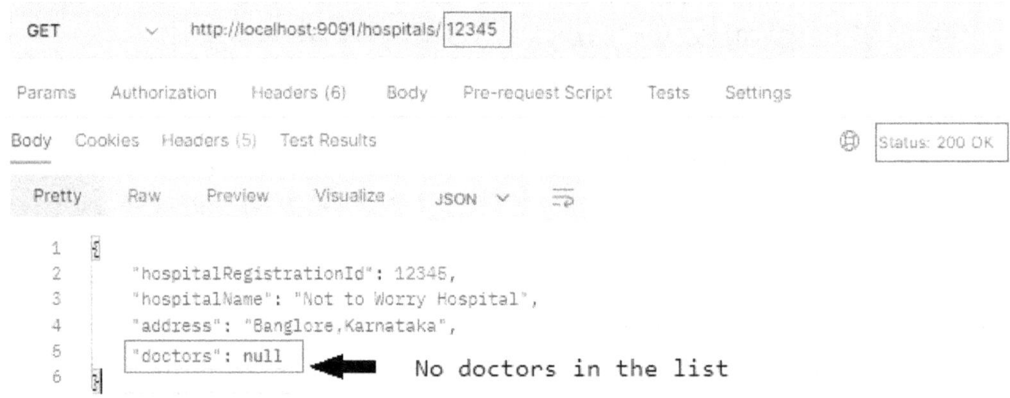

***Figure* 5.12**: *Response from findAllDoctorsInHospitals for matching hospitalRegistrationId*

We at the time of setting sample data have inserted record for hospitalId=12345, feel free to use hospitalId which you have inserted in DB

We received the response from the endpoint; however, there are no *doctors* in the list. But actually, we have *doctors* associated with the *hospital*. The *doctors* are present under the **doctor** table which is associated with the **DoctorFind_By_DoctorId** microservice.

Now, our **Hospital_FindDoctors** will request to the **DoctorFind_By_DoctorId** service to fetch the *doctor's* details and then will set it as:

```
@GetMapping("/hospitals/{hospitalId}")
ResponseEntity<Hospital> findAllDoctorsInHospitals(@PathVariable int
hospitalId) {
  List<Doctor> doctors = new ArrayList<>();
  Hospital hospital = repo.findHospitalById(hospitalId);
  if (hospital!=null) {
       List<Integer> doctor_ids = repo.findDoctorIds(hospitalId);
       RestTemplate restTemplate = new RestTemplate();
       for (int i = 0; i < doctor_ids.size(); i++) {
              ResponseEntity<Doctor>entity= restTemplate.
                     getForEntity("http://localhost:8085/doctors/
                     {doctorId}", Doctor.class, doctor_ids.get(i));
              if (entity.getStatusCode().equals(HttpStatus.OK)) {
                     doctors.add(entity.getBody());
              }
       }
       hospital.setDoctors(doctors);
       return new ResponseEntity<Hospital>(hospital, HttpStatus.OK);
  }
  return new ResponseEntity<Hospital>(HttpStatus.NO_CONTENT);
}
```

I know you are now keen to observe the output. You are more *inquisitive* than earlier. But *hold on!* Let us discuss the interservice communication in detail before moving ahead:

The **DoctorFind_By_DoctorId** is exposing the resource on the HTTP GET method at **/doctors/{doctorId}** endpoint. The **Hospital_FindDoctors** being the consumer will make the HTTP GET *request* (1) on the *endpoint* URI (2) and expect the response of type *Doctor* (3). Also the endpoint is expecting **`doctorId`** as a path *variable* (4) which will be sent by the argument in the method call as shown in *Figure* 5.13:

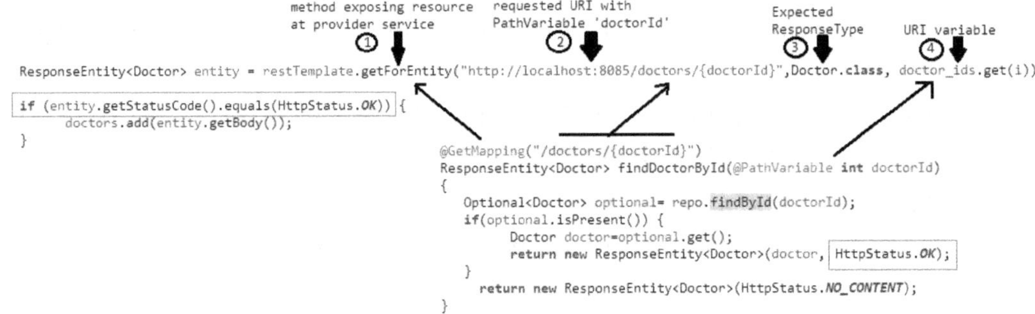

Figure 5.13: *Working of getForEntity() of RestTemplate*

Let us do a final check by requesting the same resource once again this time as we are intercommunicating with the service. We are expecting the list of doctors associated with the *hospital*. Observe *Figure* 5.14, where we are using the endpoint/hospitals, which internally requests the **`/doctors`** endpoint to generate the list of *doctors* associated with the corresponding *hospital*:

Figure 5.14: *Response from updated find All Doctors In Hospitals for matching hospital Registration Id*

Bingo!! We are now getting responses as predicted. We here have hit the provider service number of times, instead the better approach will be to add a service which will take hospitalregistrationId and return the list of doctors associated with it.

But here is a glitch about **`RestTemplate`**. It is not foolproof in all situations. There are some drawbacks of **`RestTemplate`**. Let us list out them.

Drawbacks of RestTemplate

He enlisted the following drawbacks of **`RestTemplate`**:

- The **`RestTemplate`** configuration does not support concurrent modification and all the configuration must be done at the startup.
- The code needs to be duplicated for different HTTP methods.
- The developers need to write each and everything which gives fine-grained control over inter-service communication which is a lengthier process.
- The *longer* the path variables, the *lengthier* the list to pass them to the provider.

Considering these drawbacks of **`RestTemplate,`** we can also opt for an alternative to **`RestTemplate`**, that is, **Fein client**.

Shifting from RestTemplate to Feign Client

The **Feign** is a declarative approach for being a REST client to the REST service. Using **`RestTemplate`**, we developers micromanage the request to another service. As discussed in the earlier demo, the process of using **`RestTemplate`** is lengthier and the developer needs to perform each activity which makes it unwieldy. Whenever the list of URI variables increases, the passing of values to the provider becomes tougher. The **Feign** module makes this process easy. It provides the declarative approach for being the REST client to the service just by annotating an interface.

Spring Cloud OpenFeign (4.0.1) enables the integration of **OpenFeign** in the Spring Boot application with easy auto-configuration along with binding to the Spring Environment. Using **Feign** is a declarative approach of being a client to communicate web service in the easiest way. **OpenFeign** provides support for using Feign through different annotations along with other annotations provided by **JAX-RS**. It also supports plugging of *encoders* and *decoders*.

What are we waiting for? Let us get into action.

This demo is an extension of our earlier demo where we used **RestTemplate**, for inter-service communication. To enable the support of **OpenFeign** module, we need to first add the **spring-cloud-starter-openfeign** dependency in **pom.xml** file as:

```
<dependency>
        <groupId>org.springframework.cloud</groupId>
        <artifactId>spring-cloud-starter-openfeign</artifactId>
</dependency>
```

Let us now add the interface to take advantage of the declarative approach for inter-service communication. Before we start the declaration, let us revisit a couple of things. Our microservice **Hospital_FindDcotors** is a client to the **DoctorFind_By_DoctorId** microservice, to consume the **endpoint /doctors/{doctorId}** exposed on the HTTP GET method at **http://localhost:8085**.

We will consider this information to declare the interface as:

```
@FeignClient(value="doctor-find-by-id-service",url ="http://localhost:8085" )
public interface Hospital_Doctor_Feign {
        @GetMapping("/doctors/{doctorId}")
        ResponseEntity<Doctor> searchDoctorById(@PathVariable("doctorId")
                    int doctorId);
}
```

When we start using this approach, a few questions will always pop up in your mind, such as:

- Are there any rules to declare the methods in the interface?
- Can we define more than one method?
- Can the methods be annotated by @PostMapping or any other Http mapping method annotation?
- How to decide the signature of the method?

Undoubtedly, this is a bunch of very important questions and to be confident in writing the interface, we need to know everything in detail.

Let us tackle them one by one.

The interface which we will be declaring can have any name. It is recommended that you be choosy to declare it in a self-descriptive manner. This interface is annotated by **@FeignClient** which accepts a minimum of *two* attributes:

- First is the value which holds the name of the provider service and
- Second is the URL, which holds the value of the location where the provider is running.

In this interface, one can declare more than one method which is annotated by the HTTP method. In our case, we are annotating it by **@GetMapping**. One is free to choose a self-descriptive method name. Now the most important part, the *return type* of method should be the expected response from the provider and we will need to specify the arguments of the same type expected by the **path** variable or request body at the provider. *Figure* 5.15 is the facsimile of all these recommendations same:

Figure 5.15: *Working of FeignClient*

Similarly, we can declare more methods. But it is advised not get carried away. We should keep in mind that we are working with microservices.

We had a long discussion about how to declare an interface. Now, let us use it for inter-service communication by auto-wiring it in our **Find_Doctors_in_Hospital_Controller** controller:

```
@Autowired
Hospital_Doctor_Feign feign_client;
@GetMapping("/hospitals-feign/{hospitalId}")
ResponseEntity<Hospital> findAllDoctorsInHospitals_feign(@PathVariable
                                                        int hospitalId) {
 List<Doctor> doctors = new ArrayList<>();
 Hospital hospital = repo.findHospitalById(hospitalId);
 if (hospital!=null) {
```

```
        List<Integer> doctor_ids = repo.findDoctorIds(hospitalId);
        for (int i = 0; i < doctor_ids.size(); i++) {
          ResponseEntity<Doctor> entity =
               feign_client.searchDoctorById(doctor_ids.get(i));
               if (entity.getStatusCode().equals(HttpStatus.OK)) {
                    doctors.add(entity.getBody());
        }
    }
    hospital.setDoctors(doctors);
    return new ResponseEntity<Hospital>(hospital, HttpStatus.OK);
    }
    return new ResponseEntity<Hospital>(HttpStatus.NO_CONTENT);
}
```

Isn't it so simple? We are not writing any code for creating an instance of **RestTemplate**, setting path variables, and all other lengthy processes that we did earlier. Now we have clean code without any boilerplate code.

Are we DONE? Shall we test the code? Hold it there for a minute! There is one last thing we have to do. You have to enable the feign client by adding **@ EnableFeignClients** annotations on our **main** class. This annotation enables the scanning of the components for the interfaces which are declared as Feign clients using **@FeignClient** annotation.

Now, we are all ready to test the microservice inter-communication. First of all, let us start provider **DoctorFind_By_DoctorId** and the consumer **Hospital_ FindDoctors** microservices. Once both services are *up* and *running*, test the endpoint **/hospitals/{hospitalId}** as shown in *Figure* 5.16:

***Figure 5.16**: Response from updated findAllDoctorsInHospitals_feign for matching hospitalRegistrationId*

The working of Feign client

The interfaces which are annotated with **`@FeignClient`** generate a synchronous implementation, where one thread is assigned per request. It means when the request is made a thread is assigned to it. This assigned thread is *blocked* until it receives a response from the provider service.

It should be noted that the request made by the Feign client keeps multiple threads *alive* and these open threads occupy the memory and the CPU cycles. When the traffic on the service increases, the threads will start piling up and keep on allocating the required resources. This subsequently degrades the performance of the service.

Now if you are asked to choose between the **`RestTemplate`** and Feign client, many of you will prefer Feign client for sure. It provides flexibility and enables us to take the advantage of the declarative approach. Now, we can relax in our chairs and enjoy a cup of coffee by just declaring with which service to communicate, what values to provide and what is the expected type of response. But that's not all. Along with the declarative approach, Feign Client can be integrated with **`Eureka,`** **`CircuitBreaker`**, and **`LoadBalancer`** to take advantage of location transparency and performance enhancement. We will discuss these concepts in the next chapter, in this chapter we will only focus on inter-service communication.

We just discussed synchronous ways of communication. Now let us focus on a couple of points.

Synchronous communication is a kind of face-to-face conversation in the real world, where both parties communicating with each other must be present. Unless and until the response is not received, further processing of the response or further communication will not be continued. Sometimes responder may take more time, which leads to a blocking system. This hampers the application's performance which is not something that we wish for.

In synchronous communication, one service may communicate with more than one underlying provider services. There are multiple scenarios we need to consider:

- In the *first* scenario, communication will be sequentially or interdependent. This means the response from one service can be utilized as input for consuming the other service. As more to and fro takes place, the final response will take more time and may lead to timeouts.
- In the *second* scenario, there is no dependency on the services, we are just going to collect some response from the underlying systems and combine it. The response received in the *second* scenario will be faster than in the first scenario. But *what if one of the services is taking more time to return the response*? When the underlying service or one of the underlying services takes more time, it ultimately leads to more waiting time and has an impact on application performance.

Our communication is among the services. But *what is the guarantee that all the services will be up and running all the time*? We didn't take into consideration the worst condition. Yes, the provider service can be unhealthy and not up for communication. Since it is unavailable, no communication will happen. Ultimately, this will lead to no predicted response or will generate a timeout exception.

In the real world, we found alternatives to face-to-face communication by using letters, phone calls, messages, video chats, emails, and many more. These alternatives are not synchronous and can be considered asynchronous communication. Over time we understood every time the other party to whom communication is to be made is not present and not necessarily to be present. We can start the communication from one end and whenever the other party is available, it will respond and further communication will continue. In the same way for our microservice communications, we now can use either *synchronous* or *asynchronous* communication appropriately based on the scenario. For asynchronous communication, we have a couple of models.

Let's first discuss the models before using one of them.

Asynchronous call-back

The functions are passed to another function that starts executing code in the background in asynchronous call-backs. Once the code running in the background finishes, then the **async call-back** function is called for notifying along with passing on the data to the call-back function which just finished the task in the background.

Publishing and subscribing based on the broker

The *Publisher-Subscription* is a form of asynchronous communication between the services. Here we have the *publisher* and the *subscriber* which rely on the most important unit, a message broker. The *publisher* publishes the message to the message broker. The *message broker* relays the messages from the publisher to the subscribers. The *subscriber* is the consumer of the message from the broker.

Polling-based communication

In the *polling-based asynchronous communication*, the client sends the HTTP requests to the application server after some equal intervals. Then, the server returns updates to the browser. In this way, the application keeps updating frequently.

Using a message broker to exchange message

Now, we will be discussing the publishing and subscribing based on the broker in detail.

In the *message-driven system*, the reactive system emphasizes the **async**, non-blocking messages. The messages are sent without waiting for a response in turn. The interested sender receives the response asynchronously. In *synchronous communication*, relying on the provider was the major challenge. In this model, the allocated resources can be released immediately without waiting for the response to release them. Even though the publisher is unhealthy, it has already published the message which means the subscriber already has the data. *What if the receiver is down?* In that case, we can set the broker in such a way as to queue up the messages and deliver them to the receiver when it is available. Both the *publisher* and the *subscriber* are decoupled from each other; the implementation changes in them will not have an impact on the other. In this case, as developers, we will have the flexibility to choose the implementation.

As decided to use the *publisher-subscriber model*, let us go ahead and discuss the support from Spring Cloud module in detail.

The **Spring Cloud Stream** is the extension product of the Spring Integration and Spring Boot together for data integration workloads. The Spring Cloud Stream is a framework for building message-driven microservice applications. The Cloud Stream enables us to build, test, and deploy the data-centric applications in isolation. It allows us to use messaging in microservices architecture patterns including composition. It enables us to develop de-coupled applications using event-driven architecture. Both consumer and provider are unaware of each other. It provides opinionated support for the integration of various message brokers starting from **RabbitMQ**, **Apache Kafka** to **Amazon Kinesis**. The framework supports a range of automatic *content-type* for common use-cases and allows the conversions of different data types along with publish-subscribe semantics, consumer groups, and partitions.

Now the question is how to include the module in the application. The answer is pretty simple, by adding a dependency **`spring-cloud-stream`** in the **`classpath`**. This enables the application to connect to the message broker which is exposed by the provided **`spring-cloud-stream`** binder. The latest version now supports a functional programming approach to implement the functional requirement.

Many of us might be already working with message brokers to send and receive the message in the applications. However, to be on the same page, let us quickly get acquainted with some of the concepts in the message-driven programming model. If you are pretty comfortable you can skip this section.

Let us refer to *Figure* 5.17 and understand how message brokers are useful in *real-time scenarios*:

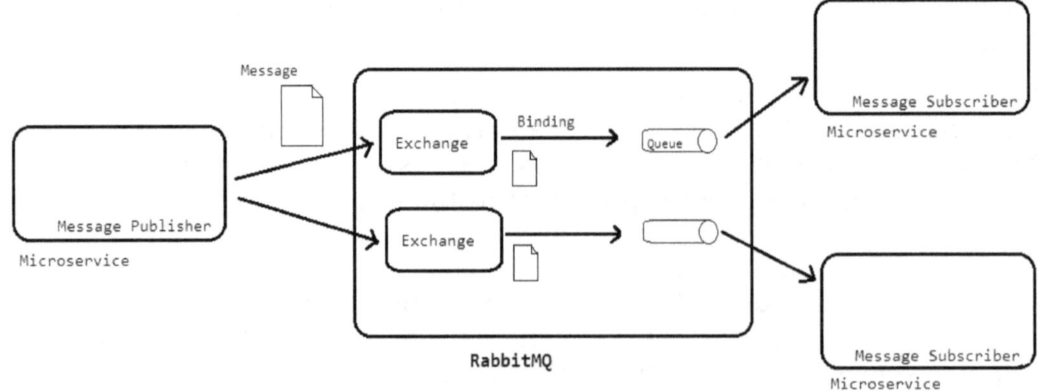

***Figure* 5.17**: *Message-driven communication*

The figure is self-explanatory. It depicts that the publisher publishes the message to the exchange in the binder which further uses the routing algorithms to bind it to the queue which further is subscribed by the subscriber. This might not have been perceived properly, as most of the terminologies are yet to be explained.

Let us first discuss the terminologies.

Destination binders

Destination binders is responsible for providing the integration with the external messaging systems. The destination binders are extension components of Spring Cloud Stream which is responsible for providing all configuration and implementation responsible for connectivity, delegation along with the routing of messages between the producers and consumers. It is also responsible for the data type conversion. When we provide the binding configuration, the binders handle a lot of the boilerplate code which otherwise has to be done by us.

Message

The **Message** is the canonical data structure that is used by both publisher and subscriber to communicate with the destination binders or to the other applications via the external messaging systems.

Bindings

The **destination binder** creates the **bindings** which act as the bridge between the external messaging systems queues, topic, and application provided publisher and subscriber of messages.

Exchange

The **exchange** is used as a routing mediator. It receives the messages from the publisher and pushes them to message queues using the rules provided by the RabbitMQ exchange type. Remember each exchange routes the message by using a separate set of parameters and bindings.

Queue

The **queue** is the container that holds all our messages which are processed in a **first in first out (FIFO)** manner. In FIFO, the processing as well as the delivery happens in the order it is received. The first message that is received by the queue is processed first and sent first, that is, processing, and delivery happens in the order it is received.

Publisher

The **publisher** is the application that creates the message and publishes it to the message broker.

Subscriber

The **subscriber** is the application that reads the message from the message broker.

Once we are aware of the technologies, it's the best time to discuss approaches to producing and consuming messages.

Prior to *Spring Cloud Version* 2.1, we were using the `@EnableBinding` for triggering binding, **@Output** and **@Input** to specify a customized channel name for the reading and writing channels subsequently allowing us to create **Source**, **Sink**, and **Processor**. As we are dealing with *Spring Cloud Version* 4.x.x, we will not go in detail with that model. For more understanding, we will be putting together the deprecated **annotations**, **classes**, and **interfaces** for this model.

This model supports us by providing a choice between implicit and explicit publishing or consumption of the messages. The first is a functional approach where the data is published or consumed implicitly and the second is to use StreamBridge for explicitly publishing the messages.

Sending/consuming messages using functional programming

In this version, our first approach is to choose build-in support for Spring Cloud Function. In this approach, we can express the beans of **`type java.util.function.Supplier, java.util.function.Function,`** and **`java.util.function.Consumer`** based on the requirement. One also needs to specify which functional bean is to bind to which external destination using the **spring.cloud.function.definition** property. The configuration of the **spring.cloud.function.definition** property is *optional*. Whenever we have a single bean of type *Supplier*, *Function*, or *Consumer*, such functional beans will be auto-discovered.

By configuring the **`spring.cloud.stream.function.autodetect`** property value to set *false* , we can disable this auto-discovery.

Let us observe the following code snippet:

```
@Bean
public Function<String, String> createGreetingMessage() {
  return s -> s. concate(" welcome to publishing and consuming messages");
}
```

In the preceding example, we have defined a bean of type **java.util.function.Function** called **createGreetingMessage().** This function acts as a message handler whose input and output must be bound to the external destinations exposed by the provided destination binder. By default, the input binding will have the name **createGreetingMessage-in-0**, and **createGreetingMessage-out-0** acts as the name for output binding. *How are these names defined?*

In the preceding example, we have an application with a single function that acts as a *message handler*. As we are having a function, it has an input as well as an output.

The naming convention used to name the input bindings is as follows:

```
input - <name_of_function> + -in- + <index_number>
```

The naming convention used to name the input and output bindings is as follows:

```
output - <name_of_function> + -out- + <index_number>
```

where:

- **in** and **out** corresponds to the type of input binding or output binding.
- The **index** is the index number of the input or output binding.

It is relevant for functions with multiple input and output arguments as its value is always **0** for single input or output function.

If we want to map the input of this function to a remote destination of type topic and queue named **my-queue**, you would do so with the following property:

```
--spring.cloud.stream.bindings.createGreetingMessage-in-0.destination=my-queue
```

Observe the way we have used **createGreetingMessage-in-0** as a segment in property name and the same goes for the output as **createGreetingMessage-out-0.**

Similarly, we can define **Consumer** and **Supplier** functions as shown in the following snippet:

```
@Bean
public Supplier<Double> generateNumber() {
 return () ->  Math.random();
}
@Bean
public Consumer<Double> readNumber() {
 return System.out::println;
}
```

Sending the message outside of Spring Cloud Stream context

Sometimes, we may need to create explicit bindings where bindings are not tied to any function and we need to explicitly publish the data. In such scenarios, we need to choose the second approach. **`Spring Cloud Stream`** allows us to define the input and output bindings explicitly by configuring the **`spring.cloud.stream.input-bindings`** and **`spring.cloud.stream.output-bindings`** properties. Note that, here we have used the plural in the property names. This allows us to define the multiple bindings by simply using ; (semicolon) as a delimiter. We can also define the custom bindings. If we are not going to use functions to publish or consume the data then *how we will be doing that*?

The **`StreamBridge`** enables us to support integrations with other frameworks to send the data to an output binding. In common scenarios, when we worked with the spring-cloud-stream application we rarely had to send data explicitly. However, when the sources of data are outside of spring-cloud-stream context, then we need to bridge the outside sources with spring-cloud-stream. We can have a source of the data that may be a REST endpoint. This class allows us to send data to an output binding by bridging a **`non-spring-cloud-stream`** application with Spring Cloud Stream while maintaining the type conversion and partitioning.

We now have a microservice with an endpoint, *shall we try it with a demo*?

Whenever a doctor is created, the **`DoctorAddService_Producer`** will publish the doctor data once it is added to the database. And then the **`Hospital_FindDoctor_Consumer`** service will consume the data for further processing.

Let us start with a producer **`DoctorAddService_Producer`**, `having the dependencies` **`spring-boot-starter-data-jdbc`**, **`spring-boot-starter-web`**, **`spring-cloud-stream`**, `and` **`spring-cloud-stream-binder-rabbit`** as shown in *Figure* 5.18:

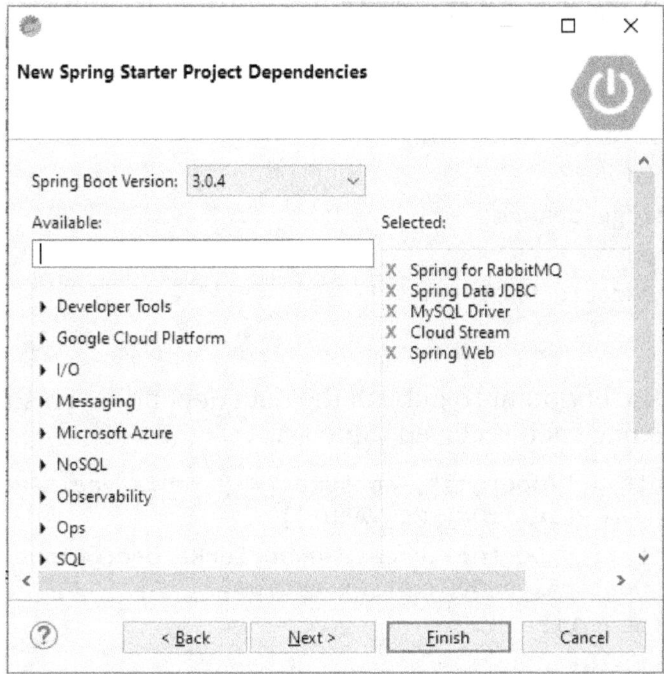

Figure 5.18: *Dependencies for DoctorAddService_Producer*

To simplify the coding, we will be reusing the code from **`DoctorAddService`** and focus on message publishing as shown in *Figure* 5.19:

Figure 5.19: *Project structure for DoctorAddService_Producer*

Let us create **DoctorAddController** and autowire the **DoctorDAO** and **StreamBridge** as follows:

```
@RestController
public class DoctorAddController {
	@Autowired
	StreamBridge bridge;
	@Autowired
	DoctorDAO doctorDAO;
}
```

Now, let us add the endpoint to publish the data depending on some logic. Here, we will be publishing each received value as:

```
@PostMapping(path = "/doctors", consumes = { MediaType.APPLICATION_JSON_
VALUE, MediaType.APPLICATION_XML_VALUE })
public ResponseEntity<Doctor> createNewDoctorRecord(@RequestBody Doctor
doctor) throws DoctorAlreadyExistsException{
	Doctor d = null;
	int added = 0;
	added = doctorDAO.addDoctor(doctor);
	if (added == 1)
	{
		boolean isPublished = bridge.send("doctorSupplier-out-0",
			MessageBuilder.withPayload(doctor).build());
		System.out.println("data published :"+ isPublished);
		return new  ResponseEntity<Doctor>
			(doctor,HttpStatusCode.valueOf(201));
	}
	return new ResponseEntity<Doctor>(HttpStatusCode.valueOf(204));
}
```

As already discussed, the **StreamBridge** is used to publish the data. It has the **send** method which publishes the payload to the output binding. Following is the syntax of **send()** method:

```
boolean send(String bindingName, Object data)
```

The method **send()** sends the *data* to an output binding specified by **bindingName.**

In the **send** method, we specify the binding name. However, to which exchange the data will be published to and where the broker is running is still unknown. This information now will be configured in the **application.properties** file as shown in the following code:

```
spring.rabbitmq.host=localhost
spring.rabbitmq.port=5672
spring.rabbitmq.username=guest
spring.rabbitmq.password=guest
spring.cloud.stream.bindings.doctorSupplier-out-0.destination=doctors-list
spring.cloud.stream.function.bindings.doctorSupplier-out-0.destination
                                                    =doctors-list
```

In the case of **kafka,** we need to add the following properties:

```
spring.cloud.stream.kafka.binder.brokers=localhost:9092
```

Figure 5.20 shows the working of **send()** method which communicates with the binder:

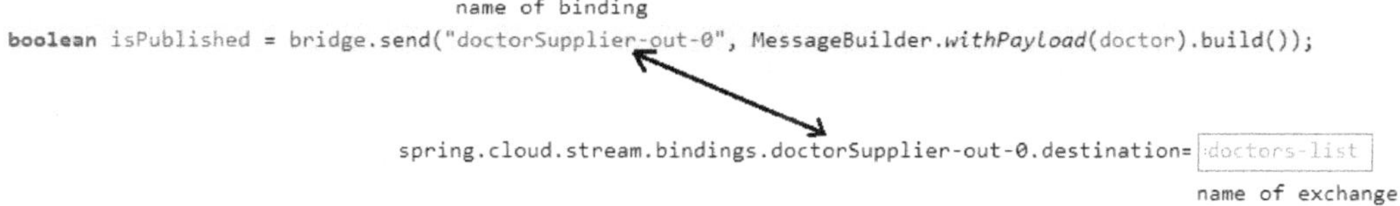

Figure 5.20: *Configuring and using bindings in producer*

Here for understanding purposes we will be using the **doctor_producer** table to insert the record for a doctor instead of the **doctor** table. If you want, you can update the same microservice with the same table. In case, if you wish to use the **doctor_producer** table you can use the following DDL to create the table:

```
create table doctor_producer(doctorId integer,doctorName
varchar(30),specialization varchar(20), PRIMARY KEY(doctorId));
```

And make sure you will change the name of the table to **doctor_producer** instead of **doctor** table in the **DoctorDAOImpl** implementation.

Let us continue ahead with creating the consumer **Hospital_FindDoctor_Consumer** microservice by adding the dependencies shown in *Figure* 5.21. Here, we have used the dependency for **spring-cloud-stream-binder-rabbit:**

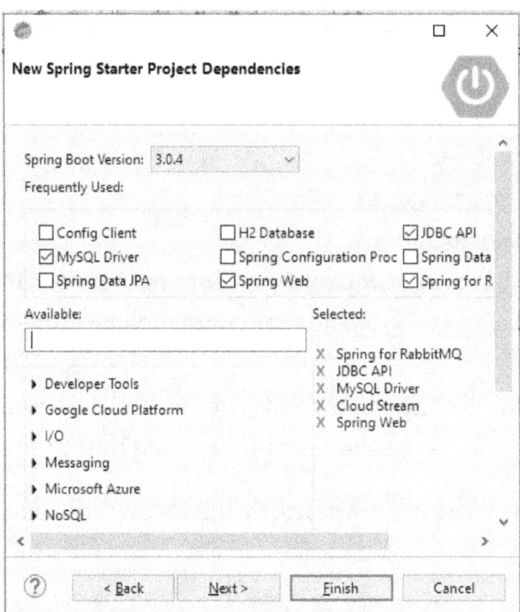

***Figure* 5.21**: *Dependencies for Hospital_FindDoctor_Consumer*

(In case you are interested to use **Kafka**, as a message broker you can include **spring-cloud-starter-stream-kafka** dependency instead of RabbitMQ).

This service acts as the consumer of the published data and then processes it as per the scenario. Here, we are reading the published *doctor* and adding it to the *doctor's* list. Further to relate, we will use this list to find the *doctor* associated with the *hospital*. Again to keep things simple, we will be reusing the **Hospital_FindDoctors** microservice. If you wish, you can reuse the same service instead of creating a new one.

Let us now add a handler **java.util.function.Function** as shown by the following code:

```
@Bean
public Consumer<Doctor> readDoctors() {
      System.out.println("***********received doctor details**********");
      return (doctor) -> {
            doctors_received.add(doctor);
            System.out.println("Consumer Received : " + doctor);
      };
}
```

The **`input`** and **`output`** of this handler must be bounded to the external destinations exposed by the provided destination binder as shown by the following configuration:

```
spring.cloud.function.definition=readDoctors
spring.cloud.stream.bindings.readDoctors-in-0.destination= doctors-list
```

The **`spring.cloud.function.definition`** property in the configuration specifies which functional bean is to bind to the external destination which is exposed by the bindings. And then the **`spring.cloud.stream.bindings.readDoctors-in-0.destination`** property specifies the consumer will consume the messages from the *doctor-list exchange*:

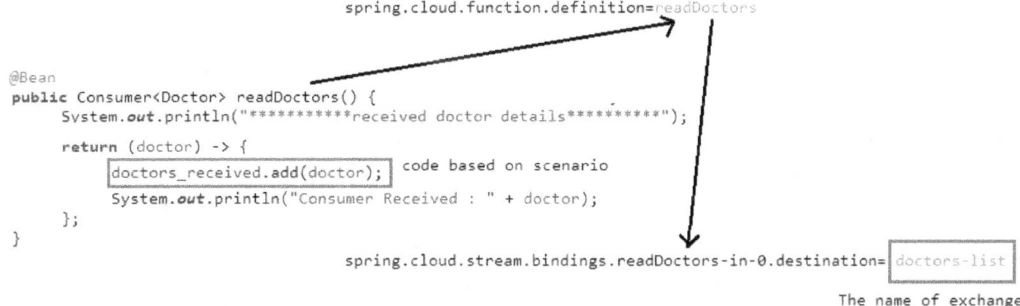

Figure 5.22: *Configuring and using bindings in consumer*

Observe the name of the method we have used to specify the destination bindings. The name of the *exchange* is the same as that of the *producer*. Also, we will add the RabbitMQ connection properties in the **`application.properties`** file same as that of the producer.

The scenario will decide how we will use the data received. Here, we will use the list to find the *doctors* associated with the *hospital*:

```
//list of the doctors which will update with every new entry to the
//doctor table
List<Doctor> doctors_received = new ArrayList<>();
@GetMapping("/hospitals/{hospitalId}")
ResponseEntity<Hospital> findAllDoctorsInHospitals(@PathVariable int
hospitalId) {
      List<Doctor> doctors = new ArrayList<>();
      Hospital hospital = repo.findHospitalById(hospitalId);
      if (hospital != null) {
            List<Integer> doctor_ids = repo.findDoctorIds(hospitalId);
            for (int i = 0; i < doctor_ids.size(); i++) {
```

```
                    for (Doctor d : doctors_received) {
                          if (d.getDoctorId() == doctor_ids.get(i)) {
                                      doctors.add(d);
                          }
                    }
              }
              hospital.setDoctors(doctors);
              return new ResponseEntity<Hospital>(hospital, HttpStatus.OK);
        }
        return new ResponseEntity<Hospital>(HttpStatus.NO_CONTENT);
}
```

Now, what we expect or predict is to find the *doctors* associated with the *hospital*. In reality, we will have a *doctor* registering with the system. Then that *doctor* will get associated with a *hospital*. It means the *doctor* and *hospital* ID will be mapped in the **doctor_hospital_mapping** table by the **Doctor_registration_service**. That sounds *cool*. But, we haven't written such a service till now and we will not write it now as well. We want to understand how the consumer reads and uses the data. So here, when we post a *doctor* to the producer service, we will manually map that *doctor* with one of the *hospitals*. In the future, we can cover the registration process. This should not be a problem. Now we are ready with the services. However, we need to have a message broker. We can install RabbitMQ or use Docker image. The following command shows how to use the Docker image for RabbitMQ:

```
docker run -it --rm --name rabbitmq -p 5672:5672 -p 15672:15672
rabbitmq:3-management
```

In case you choose to use a full-fledged installation, you can find the same at **https://www.rabbitmq.com/download.html**.

Once we have the broker installed, let us start both services. By now, you all might be excited to proceed and post the data. But before that, take a moment and visit RabbitMQ at **http://localhost:15672**. We will be prompted to enter the credentials, please enter **guest** as *username* and **guest** as *password*. All these values are default values, in case you wish to configure, please go ahead and use it. After entering the correct credentials, we will get RabbitMQ, listing our *doctors-list* under **Exchanges** section as shown in *Figure* 5.23:

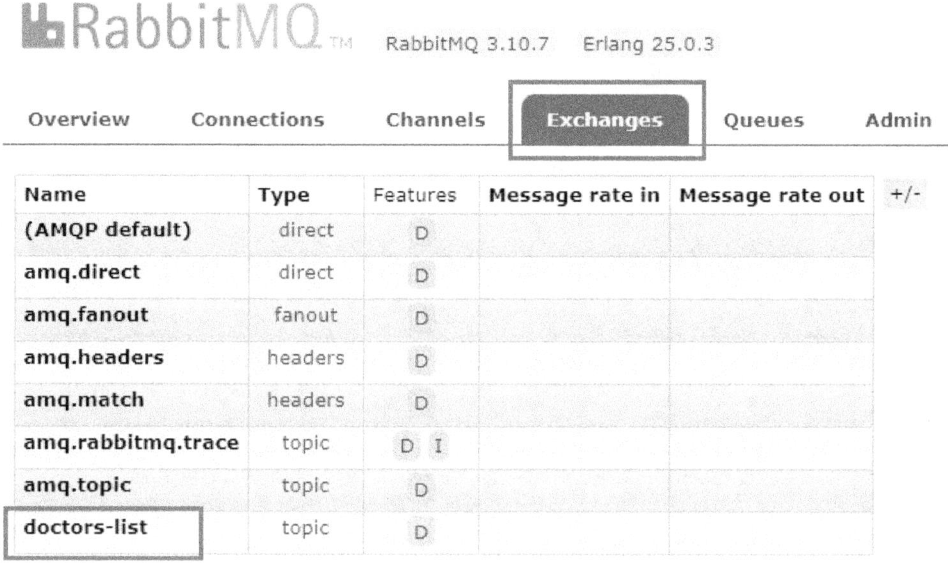

Figure 5.23: *RabbitMQ Exchanges dashboard*

You can also observe the RabbitMQ channel dashboard as shown in *Figure 5.24*:

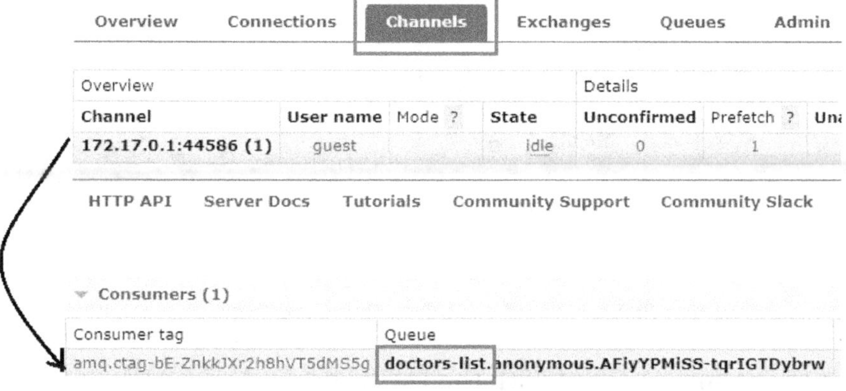

Figure 5.24: *RabbitMQ Channels dashboard*

Now for the final step, as discussed, we need to add some entries in the **`doctor-hospital-mapping`** table. Here are the records to enter. You can choose any records; just make sure the **`doctorId`** is the one which we will be using for our producer to publish. Also, it must match to the mapping table otherwise our logic will not work:

```
insert into doctor_hospital_mapping values(201,89789);
insert into doctor_hospital_mapping values(444,50000);
```

All set! Time to hit the **`endpoint /doctors`** as shown in *Figure 5.25*:

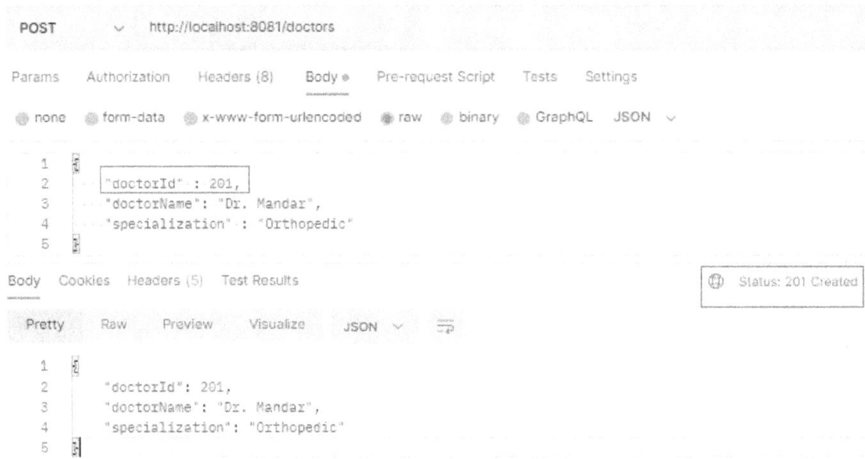

***Figure 5.25**: Response from createNewDoctorRecord*

Now visit the **`Hospital_FindDoctor_Consumer`** microservice console, you will observe the *doctor* details which we posted to the **`DoctorAddService_Producer`** has been consumed. You will find the similar statement on your console as highlighted by *Figure 5.26*:

```
Problems  @ Javadoc  Declaration  Console X  Progress
HospitalFindDoctorConsumerApplication [Java Application] C:\Users\LENOVO\Downloads\sts-4.17.1.RELEASE\plugins\org.eclipse.justj.
2023-03-19T13:38:51.735+05:30  INFO 8640 --- [           main] o.s.c.stream.binder.BinderErrorChannel
2023-03-19T13:38:51.789+05:30  INFO 8640 --- [           main] o.s.i.a.i.AmqpInboundChannelAdapter
2023-03-19T13:38:51.818+05:30  INFO 8640 --- [           main] .d.HospitalFindDoctorConsumerApplicatio
Consumer Received : Doctor [doctorId=201, doctorName=Dr. Mandar, specialization=Orthopedic]
2023-03-19T17:20:16.641+05:30  INFO 8640 --- [nio-9091-exec-3] o.a.c.c.C.[Tomcat].[localhost].[/]
2023-03-19T17:20:16.730+05:30  INFO 8640 --- [nio-9091-exec-3] o.s.web.servlet.DispatcherServlet
2023-03-19T17:20:17.269+05:30  INFO 8640 --- [nio-9091-exec-3] o.s.web.servlet.DispatcherServlet
```

***Figure 5.26**: Console output for Hospital_FindDoctor_Consumer*

Let us post one more record with the following values:

```
{
    "doctorId" : 444,
    "doctorName": "Dr. Tejaswini",
    "specialization" : "Opthalmologist"
}
```

Now, let us find the *doctors* associated with *hospital* using **`/hospitals/{hospitalId}`** endpoint as shown in *Figure 5.27*:

Figure 5.27: *Response from Hospital_FindDoctor_Consumer*

Here, we have used message broker to publish the data from the publisher to the consumer and the magic is both of the services are loosely coupled with each other. This is different from using **`RestTemplate`** or **`FeignClient`** for communication where both parties are tightly coupled with each other.

The deprecations

Following are the deprecated annotations for sending and receiving messages:

- Now it's more about functional programming. The annotation-based programming model uses annotations. The usage of **`@EnableBinding,`** **`@StreamListener`** and all related annotations are now deprecated.
- The **reactive** module provided by the **`spring-cloud-stream-reactive`** dependency is no longer supported in favor of native support via **`spring-cloud-function`**. However, for backward compatibility, we can still use it for the previous versions.
- The annotation **`@StreamMessageConverter`** is deprecated, as it is no longer required by the functional programming approach.

Matching the demands

We have microservices dedicated to their focused concern. The **`RestTemplate`** and Feign clients help a microservice to synchronously communicate with other *one-to-many microservices* to obtain the response and enable reusability. Similarly, message drive communication enables reusability without being tightly coupled with the microservices. And it worked very well for us. Here we have services that are consumers and providers. Let's focus on providers.

Do we have any idea how many requests will hit the microservices? The provider is now able to handle the load of requests. If the load increases in the future, will it be able to handle that? What if the provider not able to handle the load? Can we predict the increasing load and take some action? Hey, let's not play rapid-fire. All these are very important questions. Though they are related to inter-service communication, we also need some concepts such as **load-balancing**, **service-discovery** to **discover services**. We will be discussing many of these in the next chapter. So, see you in the next chapter.

Conclusion

In this chapter, we discussed in detail synchronous communication between the microservices using `RestTemplate` and Feign client. The `RestTemplate` enables micromanaging the inter-service communication while the Feign client is the declarative approach. Along with synchronous communication, we also discussed how to achieve asynchronous communication using RabbitMQ as the message broker. We discussed the functional approach provided by Spring Cloud Stream. This chapter is focused on communicating between the services. However, there are some real-time challenges which we might need to handle. In the next chapter, we will discuss such challenges, how to overcome those challenges, and most importantly how to maintain the location transparency for the microservices.

CHAPTER 6
Location Transparency

It was 9th *February*; the clock was ticking around 11.00 *am*. *Ryan* was busy with his daily routine work at his office. He was working as a website administrator for a trending *online gift portal*. His job was to maintain the record of the overall working of the portal. His key responsible area of work was to check if all the customers were getting efficient responses from all the services of the website. The website was internally communicating with *three* different services: one of the services was **Find Gifts**, which returns a list of available gift items to the end user from which the user can pick the gift item that he or she wants to purchase. This service was an embryo of the system which was utilized by other services on the website like **Update Gifts** and **Order Gift**. These services were used to update the status of gift items and serve the gift orders respectively. The portal was pretty hit in recent years and the business managers were excited to expand their business to some more gift categories. It was all well, until *Ryan* received the mail from one of their customer care representatives, stating that many customers are facing the issue of performance from the portal. When they tried ordering some gift items or updating the gift items, the portal became *non-responsive*. There were no responses generated from the portal. *Ryan* was surprised and thought that there might be some minor issue from the server and it will get resolved soon. But then, he observed that there are numerous emails similar to this and customer care representatives were perturbed as they needed to give justification to their customers. It is high time to take some action and find out the reasons behind this bug.

When *Ryan* tried to rectify this, he found that the application is generating a timeout exception. Clueless, *Ryan* reported this issue to the software maintenance team for further investigation. When the team started testing the API, services, and so on, they found the culprit. They observed that the core service which was responsible for the entire ecosystem of the application, that is, **Find Gifts** service was not functioning properly. It was *unhealthy*. It was not responding to the requests. The reason was a bit obvious. On the occasion of *Valentine*'s *Day*, the portal announced some lucrative offers for customers. Because of this suddenly the customers' requests increased. This created a drastic change in the load on the service and the service simply declined to accept such load. This was a worrisome situation for sure. Our service should be such scalable that it should be able to handle the extra requests dynamically. *How to achieve this*? *Ryan's team* worked with the concept of high availability of microservices and resolved this. The *portal* generated fantastic business on the occasion of *Valentine's Day*, irrespective of increased visitors to the portal. It was a win-win situation for business owners as well as the end customers. *Isn't it*?

Let us learn a few concepts in this chapter, which were implemented by *Ryan's team* as well.

Structure

In this chapter, we will cover the following:

- Revisiting matching demand
- A quick trip to deployment
- Locating services
- Understanding ways of service discovery
- Exploring service discovery
- Ways of providing service registry
- Approaching location transparency using the Eureka discovery server
- Developing highly available Eureka server
- Health check-ups
- Altering the load balancer algorithm

As we have already seen, the services which get more requests are always at high risk. The *resources* allocated for the services can handle a certain load and when the load increases the requests will be queued. The *services* still try to handle the increasing demand, but at one threshold point, the service becomes detrimental. The main observed reason is the *unpredicted load*. That's not the only reason, and frankly, it is not the reason. It is the impact. Various causes are there, which lead to the unavailability. It is a chain reaction due to a series of events occurring one after another. Let us start from the same point where we paused our discussion in the earlier chapter.

Revisiting matching demand

The very first thing which will impact the response is the number of requests hitting the microservices. Every microservice is capable of handling a certain number of requests and when the number of requests increases the story changes. Sometimes, it is not about the load at all. It is a laborious process. The task performed by the microservices is taking more time which impacts the response time and then ultimately performance. Yes, we know this and we are discussing this for a long time. But *what's the solution*?

There are multiple things that we can perform here. However, we will be discussing the most commonly used. No one can *predict the load* and it can increase exponentially at any time, the reasons for the increase are not the point of discussion. The responsibility of the services has to be performed but well on time. The point here is how to handle these.

Scalability

What is scalability? When you try to Google this, the straightforward definition we explore is, the capacity to change in size or scale, or the ability of a computing process to be used or produced in a range of capabilities.

Scalability is the ability of an application to continue to function well when we rescale its capacity to match the increasing demand of the load. Increasing the RAM and expanding the storage of different systems are some of the ways to achieve rescaling. Functioning well is one part, sometimes the microservice takes more time to respond. By using a larger operating system, it automatically enhances performance and can handle more loads. We here have *two* ways to deal with the situation. One is *horizontal scaling* and *vertical scaling* (*Figure* 6.1):

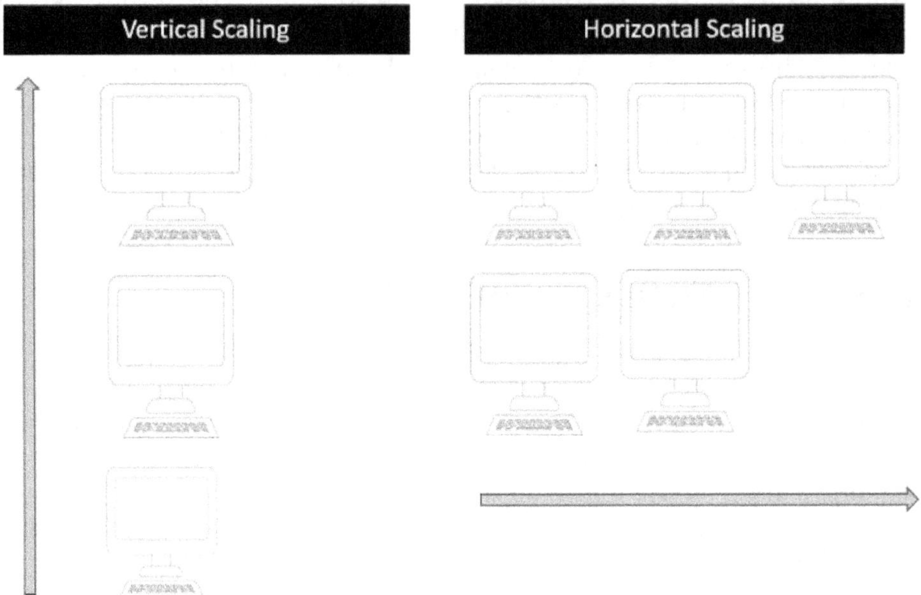

***Figure* 6.1**: *Vertical versus horizontal scaling*

Vertical scaling

It is also known as **scaling up**. In *vertical scaling*, the enhancement of the existing infrastructure is done. Sometimes by adding or replacing components such as CPU, HDD, and so on. As *vertical scaling* needs commissioning of the existing infra and then decommissioning, it has higher capability infrastructure.

Horizontal scaling

Horizontal scaling is also often called **scaling out**. The name says so, as it means adding new computing systems to enhance the processing and storage capabilities as well. *Horizontal scaling* is useful for applications that need *high availability*, *zero downtime*, *enhancement in performance*, and so on.

As compared to *vertical scaling*, the *horizontal scaling* is quicker, it is easier to achieve and cost effective. As compared to *horizontal scaling*, the *vertical scaling* may take longer as it needs major infrastructural changes. The *downtime* also be more as the entire system will be replaced. While choosing the scaling up option one needs to think about the load requirement and correctly calculate the resources otherwise the infrastructure will be just allocated without its proper use. In *vertical scaling*, a system is *upgraded* and when it goes down the application will face down time. In terms of *horizontal scaling*, we are free to allocate resources which are geologically separated and the downtime is almost *nil*. In terms of *flexibility*, the *horizontal scaling* is extremely *flexible*. It has no upper limit for how many instances to launch and enables to choose optimal configuration in terms of cost and performance. The *vertical scaling* is not as flexible as the system has restrictions on the upper capacity. The *horizontal scaling* has built in redundancy as compared to vertical scaling which has a single system and when it fails everything fails.

A quick trip to deployment

Before discussing how to design horizontal scaling for our microservices, we first need to know the basics of deployment. Of course, we will go for a detailed discussion about the deployment in the later chapter. That's a commitment I am giving you right away.

Now you might be wondering why we are discussing deployment, rather than discussing horizontal scaling. The *horizontal scaling* is launching the application multiple times. I can do this on the same system or multiple physically separated systems. And, this is the reason why we need to take into consideration deployment first.

Following are the major design patterns one can choose, to decide how the deployment will take place:

- Multiple service instances per host
- Service instance per host
- Service instance per VM
- Service instance per container

As the name suggests, we can have one or multiple services *per host system*. That plays a crucial role to decide where to launch the *second*, *third*, or n^{th} instance of our application. There are a lot of questions like, *what is the difference between these patterns*, *which is well suited for us*, and *how to use them?* We are going to address all these questions along with some other concepts in our final *Chapter 11, "Deployment"*. So, now let us focus back on *horizontal scaling*.

Let us reconsider the interservice communication between **DoctorFind_By_DoctorId** and **Hospital_FindDoctor** using **RestTemplate**. We did this demo in

Chapter 5, "*Liaison Among Services*", the summary of communication is as shown in *Figure* 6.2:

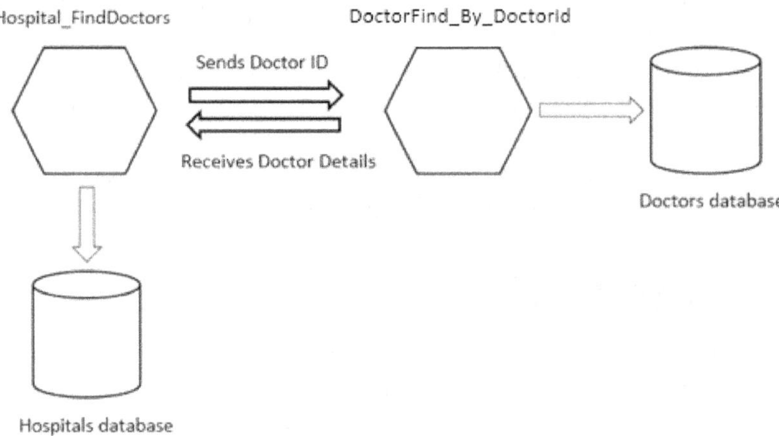

***Figure* 6.2**: *Inter-service communication*

Now, here the **DoctorFind_By_DoctorId** being the provider needs to be up and running always. It may also have some other consumers along with **Hospital_FindDoctors** service. We can have multiple instances of both of these services. However, here we are only launching multiple instances of **DoctorFind_By_DoctorId** which is the provider in our system. In real time, you may choose to launch the instance on a different system as per the deployment approach.

Let us launch the first instance of the **DoctorFind_By_DoctorId** server. We will be using an IDE to launch the second instance, as we are in the development stage by launching the configuration as shown in *Figure* 6.3:

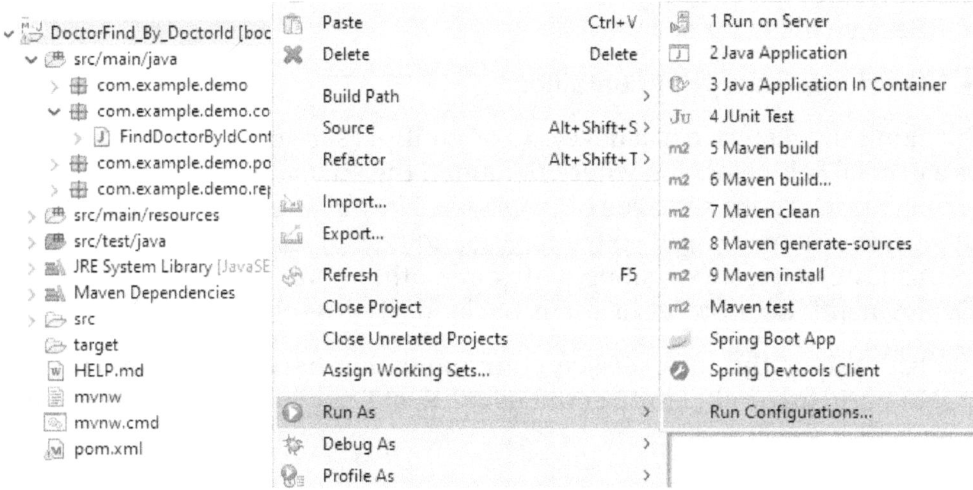

***Figure* 6.3**: *Selecting configuration option*

As shown in *Figure* 6.4, let us rename the configuration to **DoctorFindByDoctorIdApplication_8086**, it's just for our convenience. You can use any name of your choice. Now add the VM argument **-Dserver.port=8086**. Here **8086** is the port number, which we are choosing to launch our second instance. Again, you are free to choose any valid free port number. Click on **Apply** and then **Run** which will launch a second instance and we will get the confirmation from the *two* different consoles with *two* different port numbers.

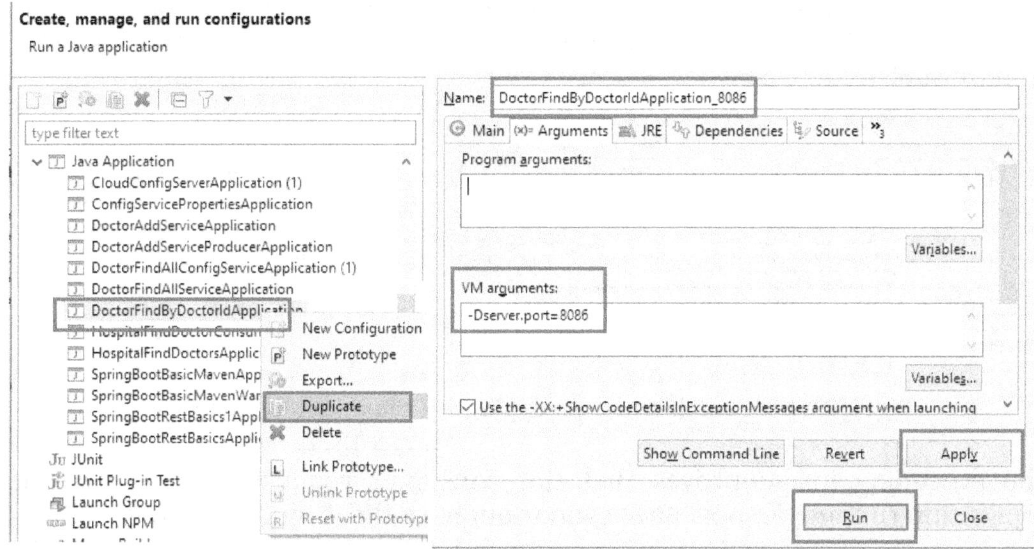

Figure 6.4: *Launching the second instance of DoctorFindByDoctorIDApplication*

Instead of assuming *why don't we test both of them by hitting the endpoint? Figure* 6.5 is the proof of having two instances that we just discussed:

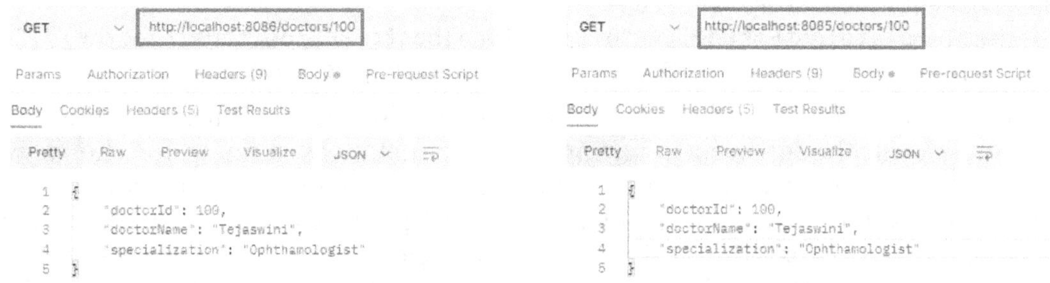

Figure 6.5: *Testing execution of two instances of service*

We can just follow the same process to launch any number of instances manually. Always remember in the production environment, we will be using different approaches to launch the instance. Many of you might be wondering, *Is this the horizontal scaling? Yes, it is. Isn't it easy?*

Let us launch the consumer as well and use Postman to test **/hospitals/{hospitalId}** endpoint. As we know very well, we will get the *hospital* details along with a list of *doctors*. Observe the provider consoles. One of the consoles will display the **Hibernate** query in the log. Try hitting the same endpoint a few more times. *Are we getting the query displayed on the same console or now it is displaying on another console as well?* Albeit, we have more than one instance, the message will be displayed only on the same console for the instance running on port **8085** (*Figure* 6.6):

```
Problems  Javadoc  Declaration  Console X  Progress
DoctorFindByDoctorIdApplication Java Application]
2023-03-23T20:56:15.249+05:30  INFO 48904 --- [           main] SQL dialect                              : HHH000400: Using dialect: org.hibernate.diale
2023-03-23T20:56:15.249+05:30  WARN 48904 --- [           main] org.hibernate.orm.deprecation            : HHH90000026: MySQL8Dialect has been deprecate
2023-03-23T20:56:16.170+05:30  INFO 48904 --- [           main] o.h.e.t.j.p.i.JtaPlatformInitiator       : HHH000490: Using JtaPlatform implementation:
2023-03-23T20:56:16.184+05:30  INFO 48904 --- [           main] j.LocalContainerEntityManagerFactoryBean : Initialized JPA EntityManagerFactory for pers
2023-03-23T20:56:16.903+05:30  WARN 48904 --- [           main] JpaBaseConfiguration$JpaWebConfiguration : spring.jpa.open-in-view is enabled by default
2023-03-23T20:56:17.790+05:30  INFO 48904 --- [           main] o.s.b.w.embedded.tomcat.TomcatWebServer  : Tomcat started on port(s): 8085 (http) with c
2023-03-23T20:56:17.803+05:30  INFO 48904 --- [           main] c.e.d.DoctorFindByDoctorIdApplication    : Started DoctorFindByDoctorIdApplication in 7.
2023-03-23T20:56:21.720+05:30  INFO 48904 --- [nio-8085-exec-1] o.a.c.c.C.[Tomcat].[localhost].[/]       : Initializing Spring DispatcherServlet 'dispat
2023-03-23T20:56:21.720+05:30  INFO 48904 --- [nio-8085-exec-1] o.s.web.servlet.DispatcherServlet        : Initializing Servlet 'dispatcherServlet'
2023-03-23T20:56:21.722+05:30  INFO 48904 --- [nio-8085-exec-1] o.s.web.servlet.DispatcherServlet        : Completed initialization in 2 ms
Hibernate: select d1_0.doctorid,d1_0.doctorname,d1_0.specialization from doctor d1_0 where d1_0.doctorid=?
Hibernate: select d1_0.doctorid,d1_0.doctorname,d1_0.specialization from doctor d1_0 where d1_0.doctorid=?
Hibernate: select d1_0.doctorid,d1_0.doctorname,d1_0.specialization from doctor d1_0 where d1_0.doctorid=?
```

***Figure 6.6**: Console output for application running on port* 8085

The preceding image proves that the consumer request is for a provider application running on port **8085** even though we did it multiple times. *Why?*

Now consider the **findAllDoctorsInHospitals()** method from the consumer service written under **Find_Doctors_in_Hospital_Controller** class. We will not discuss it again as we already discussed that in our earlier chapter. Here, our only focus is on the code for inter-service communication which is achieved by the code snippet shown as follows:

```
ResponseEntity<Doctor> entity =
   restTemplate.getForEntity("http://localhost:8085/doctors/{doctorId}",
                             Doctor.class, doctor_ids.get(i));
```

Observe this carefully. We are mentioning which instance to hit for getting the response even though we are having multiple instances running for the same server they never will be requested. Then, *what is the point of instantiating more than one instance?* Instead of putting the burden on the currently executing service, we wish that the available instance should be chosen for servicing. *Obviously*, the current code does not have that feature; we need to update the code.

Using RestTemplate as a load-balanced Client

Now, we need a **RestTemplate** which will pick up one of the available instances. But unfortunately, **RestTemplate** can't do it alone, it needs a helping hand. The **@LoadBalanced** annotation will perform balancing of the load between the available instances. So, now we need to register a bean for **RestTemplate** which is load balanced as:

```
@Configuration
public class MyConfiguration {
	@LoadBalanced
	@Bean
	RestTemplate restTemplate() {
		return new RestTemplate();
	}
}
```

Note that, the **@LoadBalanced** annotation enables the load-balancing feature.

This **RestTemplate** will be autowired in the **Find_Doctors_in_Hospital_Controller** and used for requesting as shown in the code snippet as shown:

```
@Autowired
RestTemplate restTemplate;
@GetMapping("/hospitals-balanced/{hospitalId}")
ResponseEntity<Hospital>
findAllDoctorsInHospitals_loadBalanced(@PathVariable int hospitalId) {
	List<Doctor> doctors = new ArrayList<>();
	Hospital hospital = repo.findHospitalById(hospitalId);
	if (hospital!=null) {
		List<Integer> doctor_ids = repo.findDoctorIds(hospitalId);
		for (int i = 0; i < doctor_ids.size(); i++) {
			ResponseEntity<Doctor> entity =
			    restTemplate.getForEntity("http://?/{doctorId}",
			            Doctor.class, doctor_ids.get(i));
			if (entity.getStatusCode().equals(HttpStatus.OK)) {
				doctors.add(entity.getBody());
			}
		}
	hospital.setDoctors(doctors);
```

```
        return new ResponseEntity<Hospital>(hospital, HttpStatus.OK);
        }
        return new ResponseEntity<Hospital>(HttpStatus.NO_CONTENT);
}
```

For simplicity, we have added here a new endpoint **`/hospitals-balanced/{hospitalId}`**. If you wish you can update the earlier code as well. Earlier we used the location of the instance, for example, **`localhost:8085`** or **`localhost:8086`**. But now, we don't know in real time *how many instances of the service are available, what is the location, where are the instances running*? It means now we cannot and we should not use static values. The available instance has to be chosen at runtime by the load balancer. But, *how the load balancer will locate the service instances*? Every service we have written up till now has a name, and load balancer will use it to choose the instances associated with that service.

The final code by replacing the *question mark* (?) which we will be using is:

```
restTemplate.getForEntity("http://doctor-find-by-id-service/doctors/
                            {doctorId}", Doctor.class, doctor_ids.get(i));
```

In the preceding code, we have used **doctor-find-by-id-service** which is the name of the service. *Where is it coming from? Have we declared it somewhere?* Yes, we already have registered this name in the properties file as:

```
spring.application.name=doctor-find-by-id-service
```

Observe the **`spring.application.name`** property, configured in the **`application.properties of DoctorFind_By_DoctorId`** as shown previously. And if you recall, we have configured this for every microservice.

We know we used the name of the service in the URL. But now we need to answer a more important question, how does the **`RestTemplate`** know **`doctor-find-by-id-service`** is associated with some service which is running at **`8085`** or **`8086`** or *both of them*? **`RestTemplate`** can't find it. It is not the job of **`RestTemplate`** to find where the service is running. Its job is to talk to the service with the specified URL. The load balancer will choose the instance for **`RestTemplate`** and we need a component that provides these instances. *We need a service locator!*

Locating the service

For high availability, we now are opting to launch multiple instances of service over a single instance. When **RestTemplate** requests a load balancer for instance the load balancer tries to locate the physical address from the entry in a routing table. This search is based on the path the consumer is trying to access. The *routing table* contains the entries of the services and its associated list of physical locations which are actually other servers. The *load balancer* then finds the entry and then picks one of the locations or servers which further be used by the `RestTemplate`. Now the load balancer is interested in finding the location for the service name, it needs a *service discovery mechanism.*

Understanding ways of service discovery

The **service discovery mechanism** uses a centralized server named **service registry**, which maintains microservices' network locations. This information is updated at fixed intervals when microservices update their locations. The interested clients connect to the service registry to fetch information related to the locations of other microservices.

This involves *two* service discovery patterns:

- Client-side service discovery
- Server-side service discovery

Let us discuss them one by one:

The client-side discovery

The **client** is responsible for discovering the locations of microservices and then *loading-balancing* requests between them. The client connects to the *service registry* and retrieves the locations. Then, this client uses its dedicated load balancer to select a microservice instance from the list obtained and then the request is sent to it.

The server-side discovery pattern

In *client-side discovery*, the client is tightly coupled to the service registry. The *server-side discovery* pattern solves this by decoupling the client and the service registry. Here, the load balancer is responsible for communicating with the service registry unlike the *client-side discovery*, it has a dedicated load balancer. Here, the client requests a microservice via the load balancer. Now, the load balancer sends the query to the service registry and then obtains location of the microservice. Using this information, the load balancer routes the request to the relevant microservice instance.

Note

Implement row-level security that restricts the Salespersons to view the data only for their assigned regions.

Exploring service discovery

The *service discovery mechanism* enables the services to discover the services and their locations. This further allows them to communicate with each other without hard coding the hostname along with a port number. *Have you ever used a telephone directory to look up numbers for a person or institution?* We search alphabetically for the name of a person or an institution and once we have it, we will get the associated phone number. The same pattern we use in our mobile phones as well. We search for a person by *name* and get his *phone number*. In offices, when we want to send an email to someone, we type the name in the *recipient text field*. That generates his registered email in our records. To make sure that the entries of phone numbers or email addresses are available in the phone directory, contact list, or email, someone has to follow the registration process. Without *registration*, such discovery will be *forlorn*. This rule is applied to a service discovery as well.

The *service discovery server* stores the information about the service. A service that is under the discovery process and a service that is interested in discovering other services are part of the ecosystem. To be a part of this ecosystem, every service needs to do registration with the discovery server. We do have the services but we are still missing the most important component of our ecosystem, which is the *discovery server*.

Ways of providing service registry

There are different applications or frameworks designed, which can be used as a service registry. We will discuss a few of them in this chapter.

Zookeeper

The **Zookeeper** is written in Java to act as a centralized service to maintain the configuration information and naming, and it provides a distributed synchronization. Here, the service discovery is implemented by listing and then observing the namespace for the service. The clients on request receive all registered services. It also receives notifications when any service becomes unavailable or a new one gets registered. The clients also need to handle any load balancing or failover themselves. The **Zookeeper API** is a bit difficult to use properly and is specific to some languages. The **Curator Service Discovery Extension** might be helpful if we wish to use JVM-based language.

Etcd

Etcd is written in Go and is a highly-available key-value store for service discovery. It uses **Raft** and has an HTTP-based API. **Etcd** usually runs in the cluster. The clients use a *language-specific implementation*. The service registration relies on using a key and till the heartbeat is received from the service it ensures the key remains available. When a service *fails* and is not able to update the key, the **Etcd** will *expire* it. When a service is unavailable, the clients need to handle the connection failure and then try for another instance of the service. The *service discovery* does listings of the keys under a directory and then waits for the changes on the directory.

Consul

The **Consul** can be used as a centralized registry that enables *discovering*, *tracking*, and *monitoring* services. The Consul exposes the API for the clients to use for querying and discovering the service. It ensures all *inter-service communication* is authenticated, authorized as well as encrypted.

The discovery server

The **Spring Cloud Netflix** project provides Netflix OSS integrations typically for Spring Boot applications which we will be using. It supports auto configuration and binding to the Spring environment as well. One can use a couple of annotations to quickly enable and configure the commonly used service discovery in the application. Sometimes, we use the **Eureka server** or just **Eureka** for the discovery server.

Approaching location transparency using the Eureka discovery server

Let us create our discovery server (*Figure 6.7*). It is again a microservice that has the only responsibility to deal with services for the registration and then discovery:

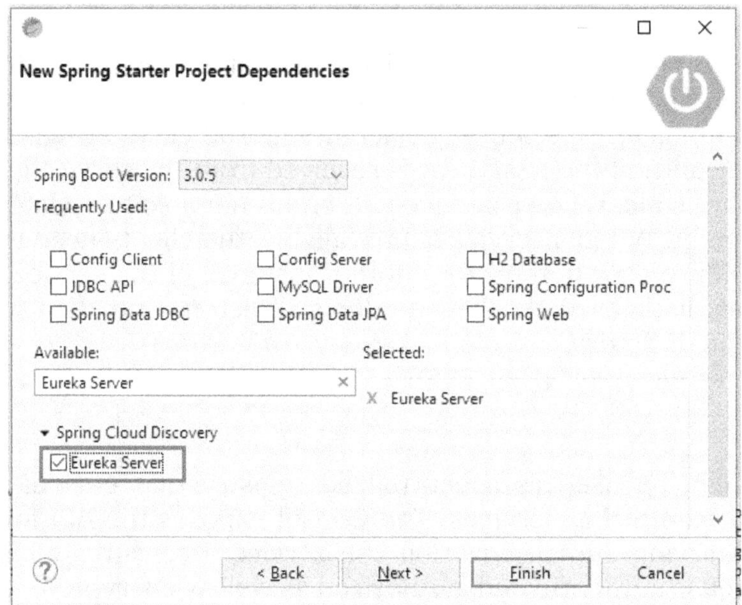

Figure 6.7: *Configuring Eureka server*

Figure 6.7 shows how to include a single dependency in the *Eureka-Server* in the application. By *default*, it is just a service. We will now convert it to a server by using **`@EnableEurekaServer`** annotation. The annotation enables auto configuration of bootstrapping, dashboard, and peer nodes related to the Eureka server. The following configuration shows the properties for the standalone Eureka server to configure:

```
spring.application.name=netflix-eureka-server
server.port=8761
eureka.client.registerWithEureka=false
eureka.client.fetchRegistry= false
```

Let us start the application. Once it is *up*, and *running* we will get a home page with a UI at **`http://localhost:8761`** which will have a table displaying all the registered services and other information as shown in *Figure* 6.8:

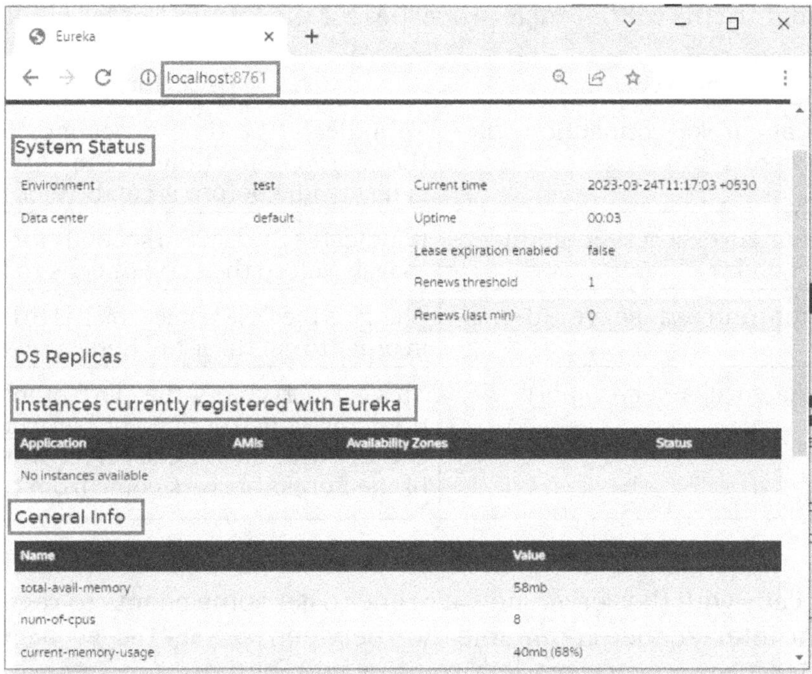

***Figure 6.8**: The Eureka dashboard*

The Eureka server does not have a backend store. The service instances in the registry have to keep on sending the heartbeats to the Eureka server, so that the server will keep them registered. Instead of going to the registry every time for requesting a service, the clients can have an in-*memory cache* of Eureka registrations. By default, every Eureka server is also a client to Eureka and it requires a service URL to locate a peer. The service still runs even if we do not provide it, but then we will get lots of logs about not getting registered with the peer. So, to run it in *standalone mode*, we have specified **eureka.client.registerWithEureka=false** in the configuration.

Apart from this, there are some other properties of the Eureka server, which can be configured.

The following are the *configurable properties* for the Eureka Server configuration:

Property	Description
Eureka.client.eureka-connection-idle-timeout-seconds	To indicate the time in seconds for which the HTTP connections to the Eureka server can stay idle before it can be closed.
Eureka.client.eureka-server-connect-timeout-seconds	It indicates the time in seconds for how long to wait before the server needs to timeout.
Eureka.client.eureka-server-d-n-s-name	This gets the DNS name which is to be queried in order to get the list of Eureka servers.
Eureka.client.eureka-server-port	This property gets the port number to be used for constructing the service URL to contact with the Eureka server when the list of the Eureka servers come from the DNS.

Table 6.1: *Eureka Sever configuration properties*

As we are ready with the server, now it's time to get some clients to register with. We want the inter-service communication between **`DoctorFind_By_DoctorId`** and **`Hospital_FindDoctors`** services, let's register both of these services with Eureka. The **`spring-cloud-starter-netflix-eureka-client`** dependency enables to Eureka client module. Let us add it in both of these services. Now, we need to register both these services as a client of Eureka by adding **`@EnableDiscoveryClient.`**

Finally, configure the property **`eureka.client.serviceUrl.defaultZone`** as **`eureka.client.serviceUrl.defaultZone= http://localhost:8761/eureka/`** to communicate with Eureka Server.

Now start both the instances of **`DoctorFind_By_DoctorId`** and one instance of **`Hospital_FindDoctors`**. Make sure the Eureka server is already up and running before we start these *two* services. Once the instances are *up*, re-visit the Eureka UI:

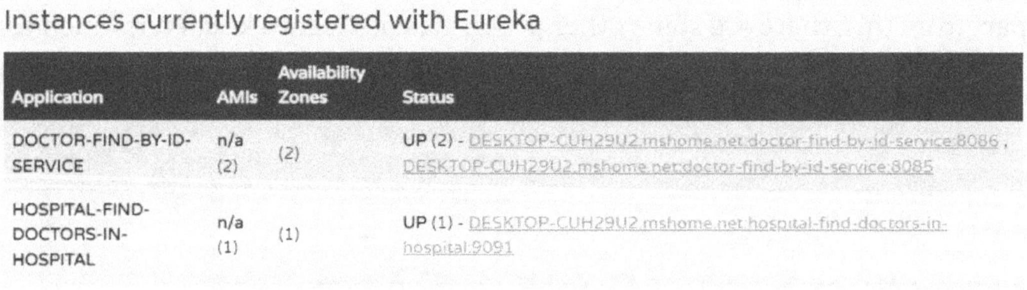

Instances currently registered with Eureka

Application	AMIs	Availability Zones	Status
DOCTOR-FIND-BY-ID-SERVICE	n/a (2)	(2)	UP (2) - DESKTOP-CUH29U2.mshome.net:doctor-find-by-id-service:8086 , DESKTOP-CUH29U2.mshome.net:doctor-find-by-id-service:8085
HOSPITAL-FIND-DOCTORS-IN-HOSPITAL	n/a (1)	(1)	UP (1) - DESKTOP-CUH29U2.mshome.net:hospital-find-doctors-in-hospital:9091

Figure 6.9: *Eureka server with service registration list*

Figure 6.9 shows very clearly that *two* instances of **`DoctorFind_By_DoctorId`** and one instance of **`Hospital_FindDoctors`** is registered in the server along with the associated URIs.

Revisiting RestTemplate as load balanced client

As now we have a service discovery ecosystem set, shall we try the endpoint once again for which we got the exception earlier?

GET http://localhost:9091/hospitals-balanced/12345

Params Authorization Headers (9) Body Pre-request Script Tests Settings

Body Cookies Headers (5) Test Results

Pretty Raw Preview Visualize JSON


```
{
    "hospitalRegistrationId": 12345,
    "hospitalName": "Not to Worry Hospital",
    "address": "Banglore,Karnataka",
    "doctors": [
        {
            "doctorId": 1,
            "doctorName": "ABC",
            "specialization": "Medicine"
        },
        {
            "doctorId": 2,
            "doctorName": "Doctor1",
            "specialization": "Medicine"
        },
        {
            "doctorId": 101,
            "doctorName": "Dr. Gajendra",
            "specialization": "Orthopedic"
        }
    ]
}
```


Figure 6.10*: Testing load balancer*

Hit the same endpoint one more time. Now, visit both the consoles of **`DoctorFind_By_DoctorId`** instances and observe the log of **`Hibernate`** query. You will observe that you are getting the queries on both consoles which show we are utilizing both instances at the same time. *Isn't it cool?* You can try a few more times to observe the instances responding to the requests.

Voila! We successfully communicated between services without the location in the URI. *You must be thrilled to see this!*

We have achieved horizontal scaling. But why are we getting the logs on both consoles? How does load balancing take place? Let us consider the following code:

```
restTemplate.getForEntity("http://doctor-find-by-id-service/doctors/
{doctorId}", Doctor.class, doctor_ids.get(i));
```

Here, the **RestTemplate** is load balanced enabled, as have used the **@LoadBalancer** annotation. The load balanced enabled **RestTemplate** will parse the URL. The name of the service in our case **doctor-find-by-id-service** is used to query the load balancer to find an instance of a service. The load balancer which is aware of being a client of Eureka will communicate with the Eureka server and try to find the instances associated with that service. From all the available instances the load balancer will apply the rule to choose one instance. This chosen instance's location now will be provided to the **RestTemplate**. The **RestTemplate** uses it and the inter-service communication will take place. By default, the load balancer uses a *round-robin rule* to choose the instances and that's why we got the queries alternatively getting displayed on the consoles.

Figure 6.11 shows how load-balanced enabled **RestTemplate** template that communicates to the **DoctorFind_By_DoctorId** service:

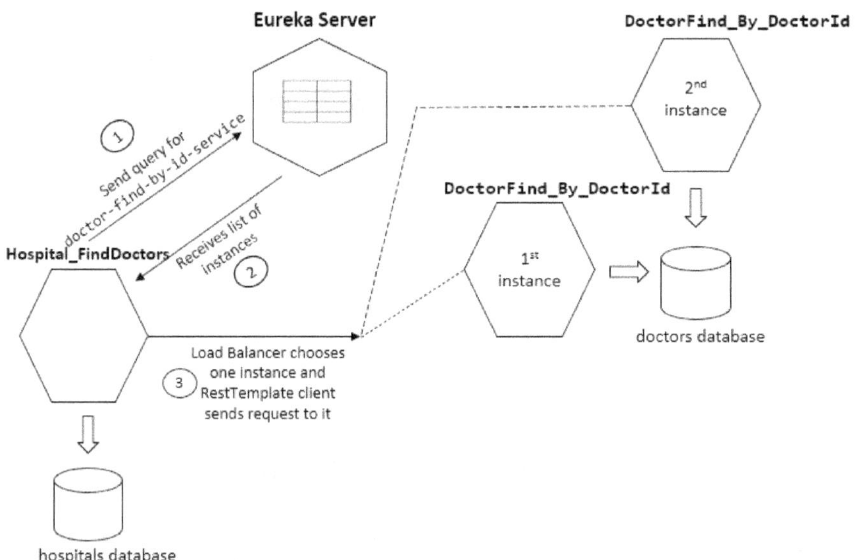

Figure 6.11: *Rest Template as load balanced client*

Feign client as load-balanced client

In *Chapter* 5, *Liaison Among Services*, under the *Shifting from RestTemplate to Feign client* section, we already have discussed inter-service communication using Feign client. Let us comment the URL from our code as shown in the following code which allows it to choose location transparency:

```
@FeignClient(name="doctor-find-by-id-service")//,url ="http://localhost:8085" )
public interface Hospital_Doctor_Feign {
      @GetMapping("/doctors/{doctorId}")
      ResponseEntity<Doctor> searchDoctorById(@PathVariable("doctorId")
                                              int doctorId);
}
```

Let us run the code and hit the **/hospitals-feign/{hospitalId}** endpoint to get the details of the *doctors* in the *hospital*. The response will be similar to *Figure* 6.10. It means we have Feign client communicating to the provider service without knowing where the service is.

Now, we know the Eureka server returns the list of instances based upon the name of application. It means it is exposing the endpoints. Let's discuss the endpoints exposed by Eureka.

REST endpoints exposed by Eureka

We can use the REST APIs exposed by Eureka to observe the contents of the registry. We can find all the instances of service by hitting the **http://<eureka_service>:8761/eureka/apps** endpoint. The **http://<eureka_service>:8761/eureka/apps/<APP_Name>** will provide information individual service specified by **APP_Name** as shown in *Figure* 6.12:

Figure 6.12: *Eureka registry for specific service*

Similarly, there are other REST endpoints to perform operations on Eureka. *Table* 6.2 lists all such endpoints:

Endpoint	Usage
`/eureka/v2/apps/appID with POST`	Registration of a new application instance.
`/eureka/v2/apps/appID/instanceID with DELETE`	De-registering an application instance.
`/eureka/v2/apps/appID/instanceID with PUT`	Sending application instance heartbeat.
`/eureka/v2/apps with GET`	Querying to fetch all instances.
`/eureka/v2/apps/appID with GET`	Querying for all instances with appID.
`/eureka/v2/apps/appID/instanceID with GET`	Querying for a specific appID or instanceID.
`/eureka/v2/apps/appID/instanceID/metadata?key=value with PUT`	Updating the metadata.
`/eureka/v2/vips/vipAddress with GET`	Querying for all instances of a particular VIP address.

Table 6.2: *REST API for querying Eureka server*

Till now, we have completed the first *two* stages which take place in the discovery ecosystem:

- **Service registration**: Every client of the discovery server gets registered with it at the time of startup.
- **Discovering discovery**: The client of discovery server can look up for other services by using the name of service to collect the associated information.

The remaining *two* are:

- Developing highly available Eureka and
- Health check-ups

Let us cover them one by one.

Developing highly available Eureka

Now the question is, if Eureka is also a service, there are chances of its failure. And when it fails everything in the application *fails*. The Eureka can be made highly available and resilient to failures by running its multiple instances and then registering them with each other. We can make Eureka aware of the peers. It is the default behavior which we changed in *standalone mode* by setting the properties:

```
eureka.client.registerWithEureka=false
eureka.client.fetchRegistry= false
```

The property **`eureka.client.serviceUrl.defaultZone`** allows Eureka to get registered with other instances of Eureka to form a kind of cluster:

```
spring.profiles= peer1
eureka.instance.hostname =name of host
eureka.client.serviceUrl.defaultZone= https://address of 2nd Peer/
                                      eureka/
spring.profiles= peer2
eureka.instance.hostname= name of host
eureka.client.serviceUrl.defaultZone= https://address of 1st Peer/
                                      eureka/
```

The preceding configuration shows a sample that has *two* peer configurations.

Health checkups

The Eureka server uses the *client's heartbeat* to determine the status of the client. Once the client is registered successfully, the Eureka server always announces the application with status as up. One can alter this behavior by enabling Eureka health checks. After enabling the health checks, the latest status of an application can be propagated to Eureka. This helps applications decide whether to send the traffic to the application or not. The application does not send traffic to applications that show a status other than up. One can set the following property which will enable the health checks for the client:

```
eureka.client.healthcheck.enabled= true
```

We can also customize the health checks for more control by implementing **`com.netflix.appinfo.HealthCheckHandler`** as per our scenarios.

Altering the load balancer algorithm

The **`RestTemplate`** as well as the Feign client both are using *Round Robin* as the default algorithm. *Shall we try changing the default algorithm*? Let us write a code to choose the same instance which served us earlier.

Before altering the algorithm, clear the console once and try hitting the endpoint a couple of times. You will observe the two **DoctorFind_By_DoctorId** instances are chosen alternatively one after the other. Now, instead of using *Round Robin*, the following code is writing the logic to use the same instance:

```
public class CustomLoadBalancerConfiguration {
  @Bean
  public ServiceInstanceListSupplier
    sameClientServiceInstanceListSupplier(ConfigurableApplicationContext
                                          context) {
      return ServiceInstanceListSupplier.builder().
      withBlockingDiscoveryClient().withSameInstancePreference().
      build(context);
  }
}
```

Finally, we need to register the load balancer in the configuration as:

```
@LoadBalancerClient(name = "doctor-find-by-id-service",
                    configuration=CustomLoadBalancerConfiguration.class,
                    value ="doctor-find-by-id-service")
```

The name attribute of **@LoadBalancerClient** annotation specifies for which service this load balancer is provided. The **configuration** attribute takes the class which provides the algorithm to choose the instance of the service.

Let us run the **Hospital_FindDoctors** service once again and hit the **/hospitals/{hospitaId}** endpoint. This time the query log will be displayed on the same instance, even if we hit the endpoint multiple times. Here, we set up the **LoadBalancer**, which prefers the instance that has been previously selected if that instance is available.

Load balancing based on zone

The **eureka.instance.metadata-map.zone** property can be configured for the **DiscoveryClient** specific zone configuration. This allows the clients to filter the available instances based on the zones. The filter **ZonePreferenceServiceInstanceListSupplier** retrieved instances and returns the instances within the same zone. When the zone doesn't contain instances within the same zone, then the filter returns all the retrieved instances. The following is the sample code for configuring *zone-based selection*:

```
@Bean
public ServiceInstanceListSupplier zoneBasedInstanceListSupplier(
            ConfigurableApplicationContext context) {
        return ServiceInstanceListSupplier.builder()
                    .withDiscoveryClient()
                    .withZonePreference()
                    .withCaching()
                    .build(context);
}
```

Weighted load balancing

To enable weighted load-balancing, we provide the **WeightedServiceInstanceListSupplier**.

The **WeightFunction** is used to calculate the weight of each instance. By default, the *weight* is parsed from the *metadata map* where the *key* is **weight**. When the *weight* is not supplied in the metadata *map*, the *weight* of that instance will be equal to **1**. Either we can set the property **spring.cloud.loadbalancer.configurations** can be configured for the *weight* or we can provide our *bean* as shown by the following code:

```
@Bean
public ServiceInstanceListSupplier weightedServiceInstanceListSupplier(
                            ConfigurableApplicationContext context) {
        return ServiceInstanceListSupplier.builder()
                    .withDiscoveryClient()
                    .withWeighted()
                    .withCaching()
                    .build(context);
}
```

The random weight can be configured by supplying the function as:

```
withWeighted(instance -> ThreadLocalRandom.current().nextInt(10, 20))
```

Health check-based load balancing

The **HealthCheckServiceInstanceListSupplier** enables a scheduled health check for the **LoadBalancer**. This verifies that the instances provided by a delegate **ServiceInstanceListSupplier**, are still alive and then returns the healthy instances only. In case , there are no *healthy* instances, then it returns all the instances that are retrieved. The **HealthCheckServiceInstanceListSupplier** uses properties prefixed with **spring.cloud.loadbalancer.health-check**. We can set the **initialDelay** and interval for the scheduler which is used by **HealthCheckServiceInstanceListSupplier** to check the instance **health**. The path for the health check URL can be set by configuring **spring.cloud.loadbalancer.health-check.path.default** property.

Observe the code as follows:

```
@Bean
public ServiceInstanceListSupplier healthCheckedInstanceListSupplier(
            ConfigurableApplicationContext context) {
        return ServiceInstanceListSupplier.builder()
                    .withDiscoveryClient()
                    .withHealthChecks()
                    .build(context);
}
```

This sample code shows the way that how health-checked instances will be returned. Using the health check-up is helpful, when one uses the **SimpleDiscoveryClient**. When the clients are backed by an actual service registry, then it is not necessary. It already has the list of healthy instances by querying the **ServiceDiscovery**. The recommendation is to use this when we have a minimal *number of instances per service* so that retrying calls on a failing instance can be avoided.

Request-based sticky session load balancing

Request-based Sticky Session prefers the instance with the provided **instanceId** in a request cookie. This is possible when the request is passed to the **LoadBalancer** through either **ClientRequestContext** or **ServerHttpRequestContext**. It is useful to have the selected service instance which is to be updated before sending the request forward. To enable this, we need to set the value for the property **spring.cloud.loadbalancer.sticky-session.add-service-instance-cookie** to **true**. The **sc-lb-instance-id** is used as the default name of the *cookie*. The property **spring.cloud.loadbalancer.instance-id-cookie-name** enables modification of the default name.

The following sample code shows how to choose an instance depending on the request-based sticky session:

```
@Bean
public ServiceInstanceListSupplier
stickySessionServiceInstanceListSupplier(
            ConfigurableApplicationContext context) {
        return ServiceInstanceListSupplier.builder()
                    .withDiscoveryClient()
                    .withRequestBasedStickySession()
                    .build(context);
}
```

Conclusion

In this chapter, we talk about load balancer and the discovery server in parallel. Discussing these two topics independently is possible. But at one point they will cross with each other. However, considering the real-time scenario they are tightly coupled. In this chapter, we discussed scaling to improve the performance by horizontal and vertical scaling. We in microservice architecture very often used **RestTemplate** and Feign client for interservice communication. By default, we use the location-specific URLs to communicate with another microservice. However, to enhance the performance, when we choose to adopt horizontal scaling the internal load balancer helps them to choose the instance to communicate and allows us to upscale or downscale the instance without worrying about the location where these instances to launch. Though by default, the *round robin rule* is applied by choosing the instance by the load balancer, we also discussed how to override the default mechanism by supplying **ServiceInstanceListSupplier**. We discussed the ways to configure the choice of instance based on *sticky session, health of instance, weighted instance*, and same instance preference.

Load balancer alone is not able to find all the available instances for any service and this is where the discovery server plays an important role. The discovery server performs four major tasks of registering the service instances at startup, allowing clients to look up for other service instances, being highly available by registering one eureka instance with another, and finally performing health check-ups. Every service which we write will launch a minimum *two* instances to be highly available. That proves both the load balancer and discovery server are two major concepts in the microservice architecture which enables us to develop highly available services along with maintaining the service performance.

In the next chapter, we will go one step ahead by adding a gateway API service which will act as a *single-entry point* for all other services. This service enables performing *centralized logging*, *security*, *transaction management*, and *exception handling* as a central point to avoid repetition in each and every individual service. As the service is a *single entry point*, it can also perform request routing to hide the services by getting exposed to the world.

Chapter 7
Gateway API Services

It was a typical day in one of the giant IT companies in Bangalore. The organization was developing a project for a *food delivery company* using the architecture of microservices. One team had completed the development of the logical parts of the microservices. The business logic was *ready*. One team was parallelly working on the UI part and it was also almost ready. The team was ecstatic to be able to finish tasks within the designated timeframe. Coincidentally, the presentation was diarized on the same evening. It was going swimmingly until the client tested the UI of the application on mobile devices. *Albeit* the application was the same, to everyone's *horror*, it was not the same product visually as it was on the system browser. The client as well as the product owner seemed worried. The client was expecting the team, to modify the UI of the application in such a way that it would be compatible with mobile devices as well. The stakeholders asked anxiously, *Can the team do that? Yes, we can. It should not be a problem*, we said confidently, unbeknownst to the fact that no *developer* on our team was completely sure about how we could fix this problem efficiently.

In the brainstorming session, the next morning, the team had very little idea about how to work with this new requirement from the client. It just seemed too complex of a task for us. Eventually, *Tejaswini, Team Lead* broke the underlying tension in the room, in an attempt to get the ball rolling again, *Instead of focusing on the end result, let's just look for the next step. Ultimately, you will miss every target that you do not attempt to hit. So, what do we do from here, to get closer to our ultimate goal? For now, let's just, lay out the requirements before us, single them out, and complete them one by one. First and foremost, the application's compatibility with mobile devices must be considered. Though the responses are received from the microservices, it contains a significant amount of data. The mobile version does not support it and that's mainly because it doesn't want or expect this elaborated data. It needs the data in a concise format. Secondly, this application needs the best network. Today's mobile networks are just not fast enough. In today's world, LAN still has the upper hand. Due to the slow network of mobile devices, latency is experienced. Does that mean the entire microservice needs to be rewritten? And this is just the tip of the iceberg. Let us say hypothetically, that we can fix this requirement. But technology is ever expanding. Hence there is always a scope for new devices or systems emerging in the market. What happens then? Will we need to revisit this when we need to provide support to the newer technology as well?*

Our team struggled to design an application that could support the frontends for different types of devices. There was another team that faced some other issues. This team followed **Domain Driven Design** (**DDD**) and wrote a minimum of *fifteen* services. They had deployed those services and now few of them had to undergo major changes. They didn't want to stop the usage of older APIs until the testing of the new ones was complete. The team had CI/CD pipeline in place and they now wanted to adopt a *blue-green deployment strategy*. However, once they decided to choose *blue-green deployment*, inter-service communication faced major issues. They constantly had to keep on toggling between the older and the newer versions of services.

The team had one more concern. They already had a logging mechanism in services. However, for better monitoring, they wanted to change their log messages to include a different format. They now had to go for individual service and change the logging. In the unfortunate event, that they missed even a single one, it would cause major issues in monitoring and they'd also need to go for redeployment. This will ultimately impact the clients. This is where the API *Gateway* service comes in handy. It can be used when the *developers* need a central place; a place where services like *routing*, API *exposure according to devices*, and *cross-cutting* concern implementations can be controlled. Instead of laboriously dealing with all these services ourselves, we can leverage the use of API gateway service.

Structure

In this chapter, we will be exploring the API gateway with the help of the following points:

- Exploring API server
- Setting up gateway API for request filtering

- Deep dive into the routing
- Point by point GatewayFilter factories
- Introducing Global filters

Exploring API server

The **API Gateway** is one of the components of the API management system. It is an API management tool that sits between a client application and the backend microservices. The API Gateway may act as a *reverse proxy* as well. It is equipped for intercepting all *incoming requests*, *processing* or *filtering* them, and then *routing* them through the API management system to the appropriate backend microservice. Once the response is received from the microservices, then finally it generates and returns the appropriate result.

The **Spring Cloud Gateway** project provides the API Gateway which is built on top of the *Spring* 6, *Spring Boot* 3, and the *Project Reactor*. The Spring Cloud Gateway equipped the developers with a simple but effective way of routing to APIs. It also supports *cross-cutting concerns* such as *security*, *logging*, and *monitoring*.

Need of API Gateway

Each kind of application is developed around providing a solution for a problem statement. The solution to the problem statement is the core focus of application development. However, along with providing the solution the application also needs to perform certain supportive implementations. This may include handling *data consistency by transaction management*, *writing the logs for monitoring the application*, *handling the exceptions*, and so on. These are not a part of any particular class, *layer*, or *microservices*. They span across classes, layers, or even microservices. These concerns are called **cross-cutting** concerns.

Following are a couple of cross-cuttings handled by API gateway:

Security

A *gateway* is our first line of defense against potential security threats. It can provide basic security functionalities such as *validation*, *encryption*, *decryption*, *antivirus scanning*, *token translation*, and so on. And the best part is we need to configure API gateway in only one place and apply it to all services.

Logging

An API Gateway can perform logging and keeps centralized detailed audit logs. These logs can further be used for *analyzing*, *debugging*, and *reporting purposes*.

Rate limiting

Sometimes the services are overused. We can provide policies against resource overuse in the API Gateway. This allows the services to be consumed at some specified rate.

Load balancing

The performance and availability of applications can be improved by adding more service instances. The API gateway can efficiently handle the requests by balancing the load between instances of a service.

API gateway implements *two* different approaches to cater to the preceding needs:

- Request routing from a single point of entry and
- Backends for front ends.

Request routing from a single point of entry

Gateway API is useful to protect the microservices by hiding the API endpoints. The client will communicate to the API gateway will then route the incoming request to a specific microservice depending upon some logic:

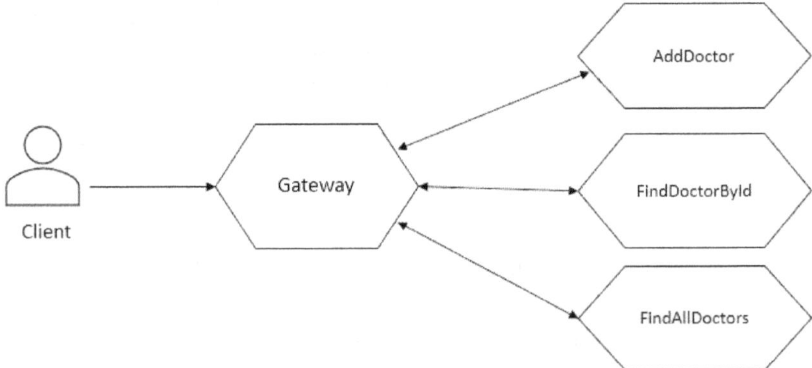

Figure 7.1: *Gateway routing pattern*

The client is least bothered about any internal changes to the service, as he is talking to API gateway. The client only needs to know about the API gateway as it's their single point of contact. It enables fast accommodation of any changes in the business by adding more microservices to the ecosystem. To go into detail about API Gateway, we need to know how the backends work for different frontends.

Backends for frontends

We may have different clients with different needs for the same services. The clients may need different communication protocols and different types of responses such as **GraphQL** or **REST API**. Our client may need different data, one may need concise data while the other is interested in elaborative data. One client may use a network that has different performance characteristics than the client which uses LAN.

For example, when we use a web application, it can make multiple requests to the backend services without hampering the user experience, however, when we use a mobile client, it makes few requests to the backend:

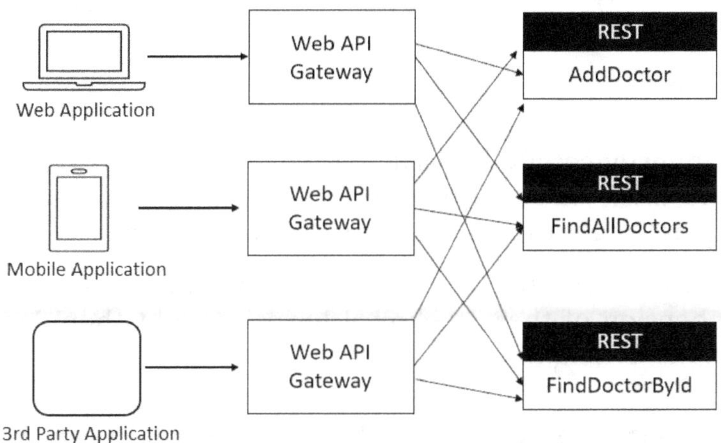

***Figure** 7.2: Backends for frontends*

We may have scenarios where we want to provide security by using different authentication mechanisms. Here, we need different API gateway services, each one of them having *authentication mechanisms* that are only used by a single client.

Now instead of communicating with the service directly, we will be communicating it via the API gateway service. The request is received by the API gateway first and then routed to the downstream service after matching the predicate by the filter. *What are routes, filters, and predicates*? These are very common terminologies that we will be using very frequently for discussing the gateway service. Let's get acquainted with these terminologies and how gateway works.

Route

The basic building block of the gateway is the **Route**. It represents the URL to which incoming requests will be forwarded. A *route* is defined by an *ID*, a *destination URI*, a *collection of predicates*, and a *collection of filters* either by the Java code or in the configuration. A route is matched against an aggregate **Predicate**.

Predicate

The Predicate is a Java 8 function **Predicate** that has the input type as a **ServerWebExchange**. The **ServerWebExchange** is a contract for an HTTP *request-response interaction*. This provides access to the HTTP request and response. It also exposes *server-side processing* for the properties and features such as request attributes. The Predicate allows matching anything from the *HTTP request*, such as *request parameters*, *query*, or *headers* by applying a condition. Once the predicate is matched, the incoming request is forwarded to a particular route URL.

Filter

The filter is an instance of GatewayFilter which is constructed with a specific factory. In the filter, one can modify requests and responses either before sending a request or after receiving the response from the downstream.

Would it be worth attempting to create a roadmap for our services to enhance their comprehension of these technical terms? Alright then! Let us start the journey by implementing the concept of routing first.

Setting up gateway API for request routing

The **Spring Cloud Gateway** can be included in the project by adding **spring-cloud-starter-gateway** as a dependency in the application. Sometimes, we may have a scenario where we have the dependency but we don't want to enable it for our application. In such case, you can set the property **spring.cloud.gateway.enabled** as **false**.

Let us develop our API gateway application. You can name the application, **API_Gateway_service** and add **spring-cloud-starter-gateway** and **eureka-client** as dependencies.

The properties of this service, such as the *port number*, *service name*, and *Eureka client registration*, must be configured as shown as follows:

```
spring:
  application:
    name: api-gateway-service
server:
  port: 9097
eureka:
  client:
    serviceUrl:
      defaultZone : http://localhost:8761/eureka/
```

Do not forget to add **@EnableDiscoveryClient** annotation. By doing so, we can ensure that the application functions as a client of the Eureka server. We already have services related to *doctors* and *hospitals* performing various tasks. Here we need to re-consider the services, **DoctorFind_By_DoctorId** and **Hospital_FindDoctors** that are intercommunicating with each other. Previously, the clients were accessing the service endpoints directly. We will now introduce a gateway that will handle requests to the actual service endpoints for either **DoctorFind_By_DoctorId** or **Hospital_FindDoctors**.

The gateway service uses the *Gateway Handler* to resolve the route configurations by using **RouteLocator**. Let's configure the RouteLocator bean in the **API_Gateway_service** which will match the path **/hospitals** and when it matches the request will be routed to **http://localhost:9091/hospitals** as shown by the following code:

```
@Configuration
public class GatewayRouting {
@Bean
public RouteLocator configureRoute(RouteLocatorBuilder builder) {
     return builder.routes()
        .route("hospital_route", r>r.path("/hospitals/**")
        .uri("http://localhost:9091/hospitals"))
        .build();
     }
}
```

Make sure you have the Eureka server *up* and *running* before you start **DoctorFind_By_DoctorId, Hospital_FindDoctors**, and **API_Gateway_service** services. It's time to check that we are able to get the response via gateway by hitting the endpoint **http://localhost:9097/hospitals/{ hospitalId}** as shown in the following figure:

GET http://localhost:9097/hospitals/12345

Params Authorization Headers (7) Body Pre-request Script

Body Cookies Headers (3) Test Results

Pretty Raw Preview Visualize JSON

```
{
    "hospitalRegistrationId": 12345,
    "hospitalName": "Not to Worry Hospital",
    "address": "Banglore,Karnataka",
    "doctors": [
        {
            "doctorId": 1,
            "doctorName": "ABC",
            "specialization": "Medicine"
        },
        {
            "doctorId": 2,
            "doctorName": "Doctor1",
            "specialization": "Medicine"
        },
        {
            "doctorId": 101,
            "doctorName": "Dr. Gajendra",
            "specialization": "Orthopedic"
        }
    ]
}
```

***Figure* 7.3**: *Using gateway services*

Here, we are not hitting **http://localhost:9091/hospitals/{hospitalId}**. But, we are hitting it via gateway which is running on **9097** which is routing us to the *downstream service*:

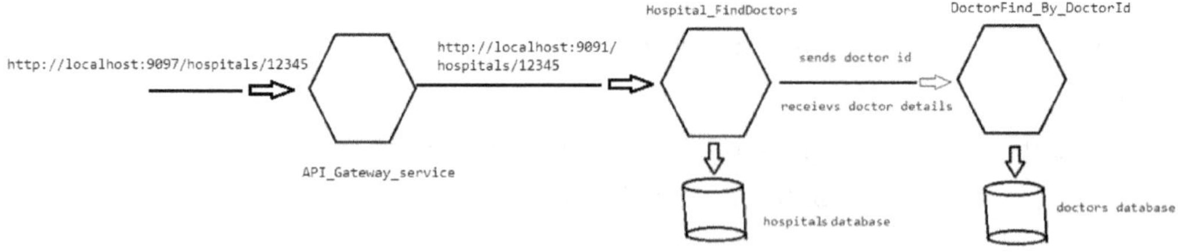

***Figure* 7.4**: *Routing using API Gateway service*

The API Gateway is positioned between the *services* and the *client*, as depicted in *Figure* 7.4. Once a request arrives, the gateway will handle it, and then utilize the **Predicate** to filter and direct the requests to their appropriate destinations.

Let's try to access, **http://localhost:9097/doctors/1**. Do not worry if you receive 404 *error* as there is no route configured by you. Let us add a route for, **/doctors**. Now, we need to keep in mind that **DoctorFind_By_DoctorId** has multiple instances running. So, the static URL will not work as it worked for **the Hospital_FindDoctors** service. To address this, we must request the load balancer by adding **lb://name_of_the_service** rather than the URL as shown here:

```
route("doctor_route",r->r.path("/doctors/**")
      .uri("lb://doctor-find-by-id-service/doctors"))
```

This dynamic routing allows the API server to route to one of the available instances though the service is running in multiple instances. A **RouteLocator** can have multiple routes specified. So, let's add it to our earlier code as:

```
@Bean
public RouteLocator configureRoute(RouteLocatorBuilder builder) {
       return builder.routes()
      .route("hospital_route",r->r.path("/hospitals/**")
      .uri("http://localhost:9091/hospitals"))
             .route("doctor_route", r->r.path("/doctors/**")
      .uri("lb://doctor-find-by-id-service/doctors"))
             .build();
}
```

Let's restart the **API_Gateway_service** and access the **http://localhost:9097/doctors/1** endpoint. We will get the response as expected.

You may want to use a configuration file rather than *Bean configuration* for routing. To achieve this, you can update the **application.yml** as:

```
spring:
  application:
    name: api-gateway-service
  cloud:
    gateway:
      routes:
      - id: hospital_route
        uri: http://localhost:9091/hospitals
```

```
        predicates:
        - Path=/hospitals/**
      - id: doctor_route
        uri: lb://doctor-find-by-id-service/doctors
        predicates:
        - Path=/doctors/**
```

Next, we must comment on the **Bean** configuration within the **GatewayRouting**. This is where we have consolidated all of our microservices under the API Gateway.

Note

Either use @Bean-based configuration or property-based configuration. Also, before trying the new routing configuration, make sure the comment is the existing one. This will help you to understand the routing in a better way. Once you get confident about applying the filters, feel free to add multiple filters together.

Deep dive into the routing

Spring Cloud Gateway employs the **Spring WebFlux** handler mapping to compare routes, which encompasses a range of pre-existing route predicate factories.

These predicates match the different attributes of the incoming HTTP request. The beauty is one can combine multiple route predicate factories using logical *and* statements:

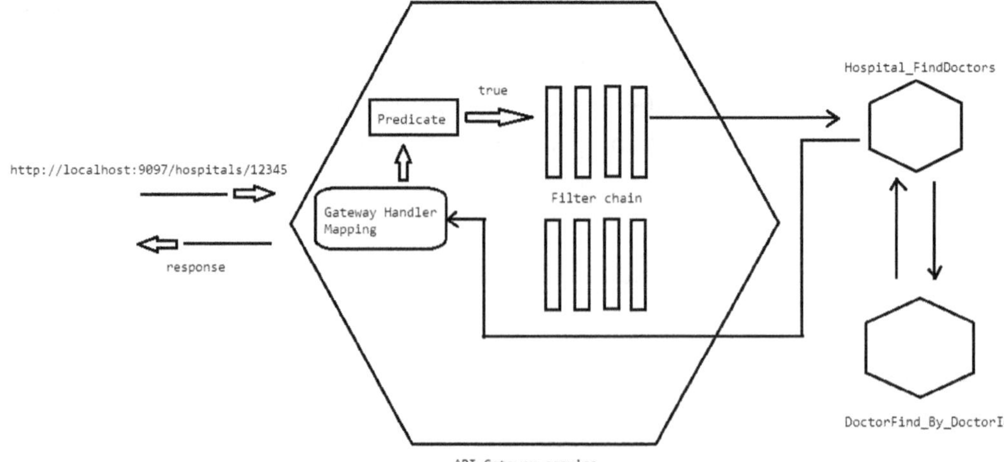

***Figure 7.5**: Integrating the Predicate*

When the client requests Spring Cloud Gateway, the first component in the act is **Gateway Handler Mapping**. It determines whether the incoming request matches a route. If it *matches*, then it is directed to the **Gateway Web Handler**. The *handler* propagates the request through a chain of filters. This chain is specific to the request and the handler decides which all filters will be applied. Filters can either be executed before sending the request to the downstream microservice or applied after obtaining the response from the downstream microservice. Depending upon whether the filters applied before or after they are categorized as pre-filters or post-filters. One can decide whether to execute only pre-filter, only post-filter, or even both. Once all the pre-filters are executed then the proxy request is made to the service and a response is produced. This response now may again pass through the post-filter chain. Ultimately, the final response is sent to the client.

Our basic demonstration provided us with insights into how request routing occurs. It is just one of the ways. However, we have different routing predicate factories such as **After**, **Before**, **Header**, and so on.

Let us cover some of the very commonly used predicates one by one.

The After Route Predicate Factory

The **After** route predicate factory utilizes a datetime parameter to match requests that occur following the specified datetime. Following is the sample configuration specified under the routes for the **After** predicate to route request after the specified date and time:

```
- id: after_route
  uri: lb://doctor-find-by-id-service/doctors
    predicates:
      - After=2023-04-02T20:16:10.420+05:30[Asia/Kolkata]
```

Please manage the *data* and *time* as per your time zone. Here, any request made before the time 2023-04-02T20:16:10.420+05:30 will produce 404 *as a response* as shown by the following figure:

Figure 7.6: *Responses received for un-matched After route predicate*

And after the specified time we will get the following response:

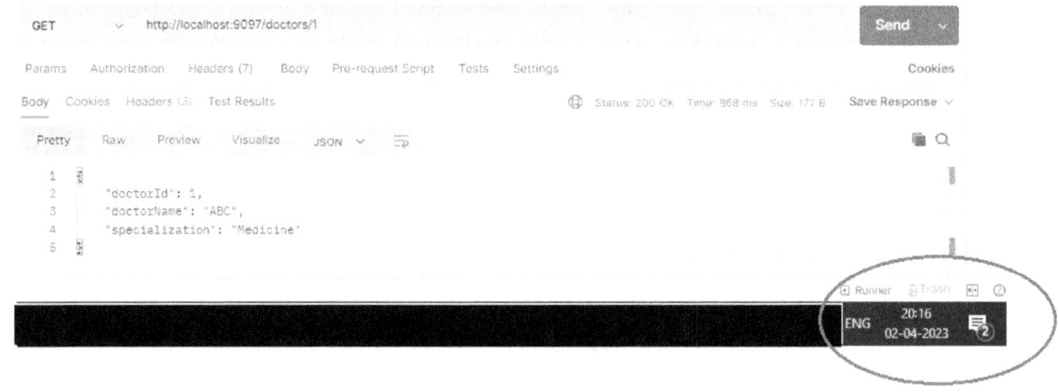

Figure 7.7: *Working of After route predicate factory*

The Before Route Predicate Factory

Similar to the **After** route predicate, we can configure the **Before** route predicate factory which also takes a datetime as a parameter specified in **ZonedDateTime**. All the requests will be routed before the specified **datetime**. The following is the configuration for the **Before** route predicate:

```
- id: before_route
  uri: lb://doctor-find-by-id-service/doctors
  predicates:
  - Before=2023-04-02T20:16:10.420+05:30[Asia/Kolkata]
```

Please adjust the date and time as per your respective zone. Any request made before the specified time will be routed and all others will produce 404 *as a response.*

The Between Route Predicate Factory

As the name suggests, the **Between** route predicate factory matches requests that occur between *two* dates. It takes **datetime1** and **datetime2** as *two* parameters specified in **ZonedDateTime** to match the condition. It is essential to ensure that the **datetime2** parameter must be specified as occurring after **datetime1**. The following predicate configuration can be added to route the request between the *1st of April* and the *30th of April 2023*:

```
predicates:
-Between=2023-04-02T20:16:10.420+05:30[Asia/Kolkata],
         2023-04-30T20:16:10.420+05:30[Asia/Kolkata]
```

The Cookie Route Predicate Factory

The **Cookie** route predicate factory matches cookies that have the given name with the values by the regular expression. It takes *two* parameters: a **name** and a **regexp**. The following example configures a cookie route predicate factory:

```
- id: cookie_route
  uri: lb://doctor-find-by-id-service/doctors
  predicates:
  - Cookie=book_name, Micro*
```

The preceding is a shortcut configuration. We also have the option to write the same configuration in the fully expanded format as follows:

```
- id: cookie_route
  uri: lb://doctor-find-by-id-service/doctors
  predicates:
  - name : Cookie
    args:
      name: book_name
      regexp: Micro*
```

The Header Route Predicate Factory

The **Header** route predicate factory matches headers that have the given name with the values by the regular expression. It takes *two* parameters namely a **header** and a **regexp**. The following example configures a header route predicate factory:

```
- id: header_route
  uri: lb://doctor-find-by-id-service/doctors
  predicates:
  - Header=book_name, Micro*
```

The Host Route Predicate Factory

The **Host** route predicate matches the host header to the pattern. It takes one parameter which is a list of the host name patterns. This pattern is an *Ant style pattern* having period (.) as the separator. It also supports the URI template variables. The following example demonstrates how to configure a host route predicate factory:

```
- id: host_route
  uri: lb://doctor-find-by-id-service/doctors
  predicates:
  - Host=**.abc.org,**.xyz.org
```

The Method Route Predicate Factory

The **Method** route predicate factory accepts the method as the parameter which is the name of one or more HTTP methods. The following example shows the configuration of the method route predicate factory which matches when the requested method was **PUT**, **POST** or **DELETE**:

```
- id: host_route
  uri: lb://doctor-find-by-id-service/doctors
  predicates:
  - Method=PUT,POST,DELETE
```

The Query Route Predicate Factory

The **Query** route predicate factory matches the request having a certain parameter. It takes *two* parameters namely a **param** and a **regexp**. The **regex** param is optional which takes Java regular expression. The following example shows how to configure the **Query** route predicate factory to route the request, if it contains a **book_name** as a **query** parameter:

```
- id: query_route
  uri: lb://doctor-find-by-id-service/doctors
  predicates:
  - Query=book_name
```

Sometimes along with the parameter name, we may be interested in matching the values with some regular expressions then we can also configure the **Query** with **regex**. The subsequent configuration corresponds to the query parameter **book_name** and matches the regular expression **Micro***:

```
- Query=book_name, Micro*
```

The RemoteAddr Route Predicate Factory

The **Remote** route predicate factory takes a list of sources having minimum size equal to one. The source is a **Classless Inter Domain Routing** (**CIDR**) notation of IP addresses. The following configuration configures a **RemoteAddr** route predicate when the request matches an address such as **192.168.1.10**:

```
- id: query_route
  uri: lb://doctor-find-by-id-service/doctors
  predicates:
  - RemoteAddr=192.168.1.1/24
```

The Weight Route Predicate Factory

The **Weight** route predicate factory takes *two* parameters **group** and **weight**. The weights are calculated per group. The following configuration configures a predicate that route a request traffic 70% *to* X and 30% *times to* Y:

```
- id: weight_route_high
  uri: X
  predicates:
  - Weight=group_high, 70
 - id: weight_route_low
   uri: Y
   predicates:
   - Weight=group_low, 30
```

The X-Forwarded Remote Addr Route Predicate Factory

The **Remote Route** predicate factory takes a list of sources having a minimum size equal to *one*. The source is a CIDR notation of IP addresses. This route predicate filters the requests based on the header **X-Forwarded-For** from the incoming request. It can be used with reverse proxies such as load balancers or web application firewalls where it allows the request when the request comes from a trusted list of IP addresses which can be used by the reverse proxies. The following configuration constructs a predicate for **X-Forwarded Remote Addr** route:

```
- id: xforwarded_remoteaddr_route
  uri: lb://doctor-find-by-id-service/doctors
  predicates:
  - XForwardedRemoteAddr=192.168.1.1/24
```

Thus, these are various approaches to constructing predicates that dictate the routing to specific downstream URIs. Implementing an API Gateway accomplishes two objectives:

- First, it places the services behind the gateway and directs them to their designated destinations, and
- Second, it alters the request before it arrives downstream.

Occasionally, there may be a need to modify the response obtained from the downstream service before its transmission to the client through the API Gateway. In such circumstances, we may wish to perform pre- or post-processing on the request based on the situation at hand. Let us proceed to examine the different approaches for achieving this.

Point by point GatewayFilter factories

The route filters allow the developers to modify the incoming HTTP request as well as the outgoing HTTP response as per the scenarios. The route filters are always scoped to a particular route.

The Spring Cloud Gateway includes a wide range of built-in **GatewayFilter** factories which are discussed as follows:

AddRequestHeader GatewayFilter Factory

The **AddRequestHeader** GatewayFilter factory takes a name and value parameter which adds a request header to the downstream request's headers for all matching requests. The following code describes how to use the **AddRequestHeader** GatewayFilter to add a header in case of a request match:

```
@Bean
public RouteLocator configureRoute(RouteLocatorBuilder builder) {
       return builder.routes()
            .route("doctor", r->r.path("/doctors/**")
            .filters(f -> f.addRequestHeader("sort", "Medicine"))
            .uri("lb://doctor-find-by-id-service")) //dynamic routing
            .build();
}
```

Regrettably, the endpoint which we already have in the **DoctorFind_By_DoctorId** service cannot utilize the header added by the gateway service. Therefore, let us proceed with updating the handler method for the endpoint. In the following code, an optional argument will be added to support all the code which we have written till now:

```
@GetMapping("/doctors/{doctorId}")
ResponseEntity<Doctor> findDoctorById(@PathVariable int doctorId,
  @RequestHeader(name = "sort",defaultValue = "all") String sort) {
  System.out.println(sort);
      Optional<Doctor> optional = repo.findById(doctorId);
        if (optional.isPresent()) {
            Doctor doctor = optional.get();
            if (sort.equals("all") ||
            doctor.getSpecialization().equals(sort))
                        return new
                          ResponseEntity<Doctor>(doctor,HttpStatus.OK);
            }
            return new ResponseEntity<Doctor>(HttpStatus.NO_CONTENT);
      }
}
```

The method will receive the header from the request which is added by the gateway API service and subsequently it returns only the *doctor* who is specialized in the relevant field. By the Gateway API service, we only are requesting a *doctor* who is specialized in *Medicine*. If the header is missing, the response will return to any *doctor* as shown in *Figure 7.8*:

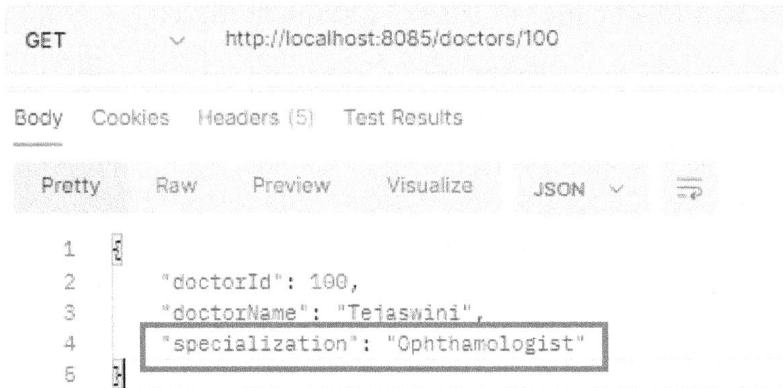

***Figure 7.8**: Response received if header is not set for AddRequestHeader GatewayFilter Factory*

On the other hand, if header is added, only the specialized *doctor* is returned as a *response*, demonstrated in *Figure 7.9*:

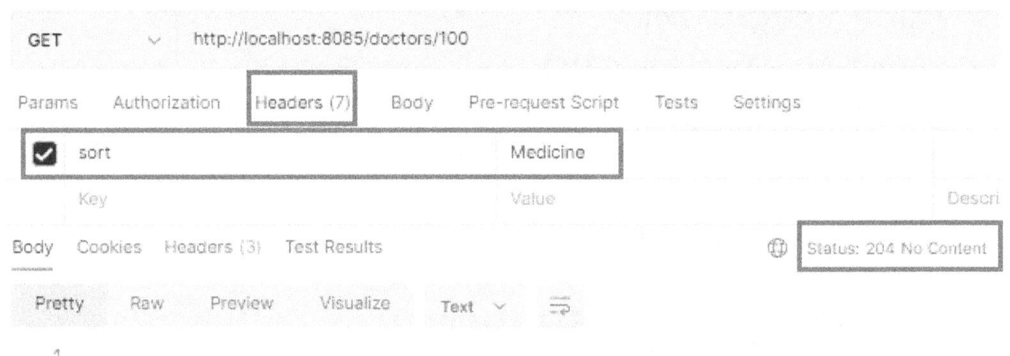

***Figure 7.9**: Response received for AddHeaderRequest GatewayFilter Factory*

Try to access the endpoint **http://localhost:9097/doctors/100,** via API Gateway service, you should receive a similar output as depicted in the preceding figure. This implies that routing is successful and additionally, the header also has been added. *Would this functionally work in the same manner when we attempt inter-service communication?*

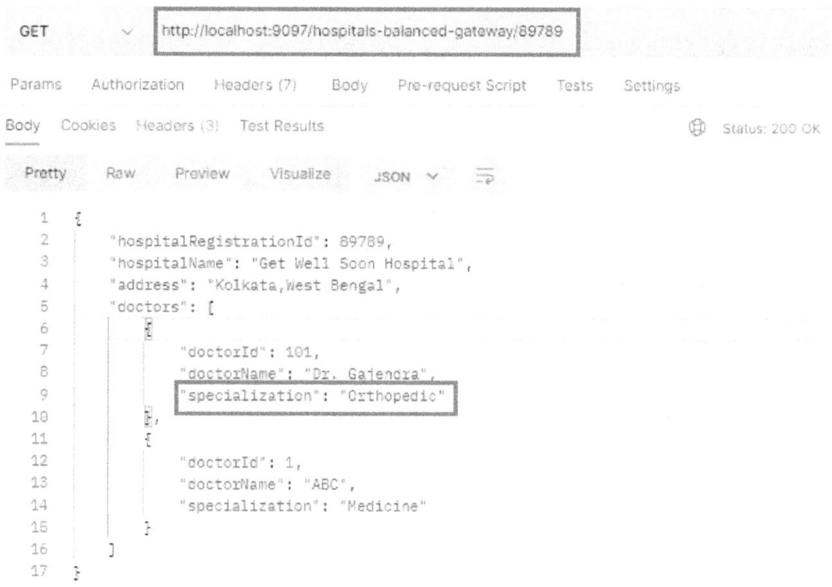

GET http://localhost:9097/hospitals-balanced-gateway/89789

Params Authorization Headers (7) Body Pre-request Script Tests Settings

Body Cookies Headers (3) Test Results Status: 200 OK

Pretty Raw Preview Visualize JSON


```
{
    "hospitalRegistrationId": 89789,
    "hospitalName": "Get Well Soon Hospital",
    "address": "Kolkata,West Bengal",
    "doctors": [
        {
            "doctorId": 101,
            "doctorName": "Dr. Gajendra",
            "specialization": "Orthopedic"
        },
        {
            "doctorId": 1,
            "doctorName": "ABC",
            "specialization": "Medicine"
        }
    ]
}
```


***Figure 7.10**: AddRequestHeader GatewayFilter Factory with inter-service communication*

No, it is *not*. We received a response of the *doctor* with a *specialization* in *Orthopedics* as well. This indicates that the headers added by the API Gateway are not getting forwarded. *Why the header will be forwarded?* The *Hospital* service is not forwarding the request to the *Doctor* service, instead, it is initiating a new call:

```
ResponseEntity<Doctor> entity =
  RestTemplate.getForEntity("http://doctor-find-by-id-service/doctors/
{doctorId}",
  Doctor.class, doctor_ids.get(i));
```

Furthermore, if you carefully observe the request initiated by the *Hospital* service is being sent directly to the *Doctor's* service and not via gateway API. *Is it a good or bad practice*? We cannot comment on whether it is *good* or *bad* as it depends on the scenario in our hands. Sometimes there is no necessity for routing via API Gateway service and also there is no need for modification of request. Therefore, it is acceptable to directly access the downstream service. On the other hand, when we wish to perform certain *transactions*, *logging*, or tracing through API Gateway as a central point, downstream service is nontrackable.

To achieve this, we need to modify the requesting code in **Hospital_FindDoctors** code as:

```
ResponseEntity<Doctor> entity =
  restTemplate.getForEntity("http://api-gateway-service/doctors/
{doctorId}",
  Doctor.class, doctor_ids.get(i));
```

After re-executing the **Hospital_FindDoctors** service and accessing the endpoint void API Gateway service, the output shown in the in *Figure* 7.11, clearly shows that the API service filters the requests to *hospital* service as well as *doctor* service and retrieves only the *doctors* who specialize in *Medicine*:

***Figure* 7.11**: *Request forwarding in inter-service communication for AddRequestHeader GatewayFilter Factory*

If we prefer not to use *annotation-based configuration*, we can opt for *configuration-based route* to modify the request and response in the configuration file as well. We will be able to achieve that as shown in the following configuration:

```
- id: doctor_route
  uri: lb://doctor-find-by-id-service/doctors
  predicates:
  - Path=/doctors/**
  filters:
  - AddRequestHeader= sort,Medicine
```

The **AddRequestHeader** also allows us to read the URI variable and to use it as a value of the header rather than setting up some static value as we did in the earlier example. To do so, we need to use the configuration as:

```
 - id: doctor_route
   uri: lb://doctor-find-by-id-service/doctors
   predicates:
- Path=/doctors-sort/{value}
  filters:
  - AddRequestHeader= sort,{value}
```

AddRequestHeadersIfNotPresent GatewayFilter Factory

This factory takes a collection of *name* and *value* pairs which are separated by a *colon*. And for all the matching requests this pair will be added to the downstream request's headers. This is very much similar to **AddRequestHeader** factory. However, unlike **AddRequestHeader**, it will not just add the *header*. It will first check the presence of the *header* in the request and if the header is *not* already there, then it will be *added*. If it is *present*, then the original value present in the *client request* is sent downstream.

If the *header* is *absent*, the following configuration will incorporate it:

```
- id: doctor_route_add_header_if_not_present
uri: lb://doctor-find-by-id-service/doctors
predicates:
- Path=/doctors/**
filters:
- AddRequestHeadersIfNotPresent= sort:Medicine
```

To verify this, we will append a header labeled **sort** with the value as **Orthepedic**, in the request. That will produce the response as shown in *Figure 7.12*:

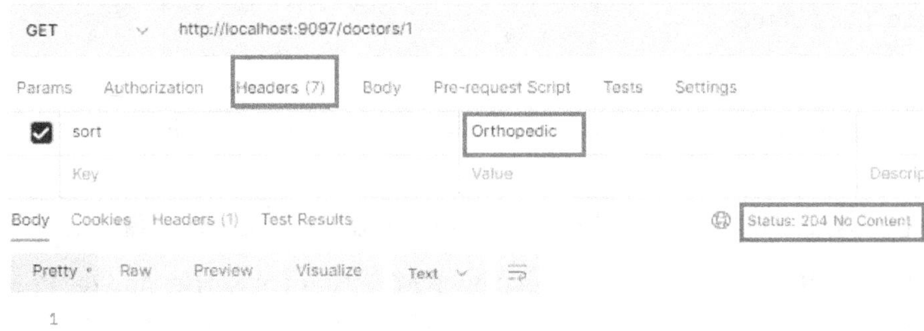

Figure 7.12: *Working of AddRequestHeaderIfNotPresent GatewayFilter Factory*

Subsequently, if we remove the header, the request header will be appended by the **Medicine** value. Much like how we can utilize the URI variable in place of a fixed value with **AddRequestHeader**, the same approach can be applied here.

AddRequestParameter GatewayFilter Factory

The **AddRequestParameter** GatewayFilter factory takes the *parameter name*, along with its *value*. The following configuration depicts a **request** query for the parameter to the downstream for all the matching requests:

```
- id: doctor_route_add_request_parameter
  uri: lb://doctor-find-by-id-service/doctors
  predicates:
- Path=/doctors/**
  filters:
- AddRequestParameter= value, Microservices
```

The **AddRequestParameter** is well aware of the URI variables that can be utilized to match the path or the host. At runtime, the URI variables within the path can be used as a value that gets expanded.

As anticipated, we require URI with a request parameter, so let's include an additional endpoint. In practice, we know about *incoming request parameters*, *path variables*, or *request body*, however, here we are adding the endpoint in the **DoctorFind_By_DoctorID** service for the sake of support as:

```
@GetMapping("/doctors-values/{doctorId}")
ResponseEntity<Doctor>findDoctorById(@PathVariable int doctorId,
            @RequestParam String value,
            @RequestHeader(name = "sort",defaultValue = "all") String
sort) {
  //logic goes here
}
```

Based on the scenario, we can use the value argument in the logic.

AddResponseHeader GatewayFilter Factory

Similar to **AddRequestParameter** GatewayFilter factory, the `AddResResponse Header` GatewayFilter factory takes the parameter name along with its value. The following configuration appends a response header **header_value** to the response for all the matching requests before the response is sent to the client.

This is the *post-processing* of the request, as it modifies the response received from downstream:

```
- id: doctor_route_add_response_header
  uri: lb://doctor-find-by-id-service/doctors
  predicates:
- Path=/doctors/{doctorId}
  filters:
- AddResponseHeader= header_value
```

Upon executing the request on the API service, the following response will be received:

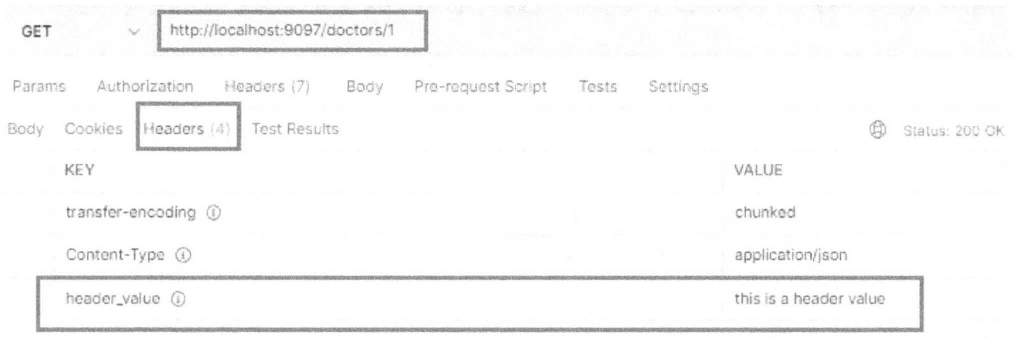

Figure 7.13: *Implementing AddResponseHeader GatewayFilter factory*

The preceding output displays that post-processing of the request occurred for the matched to add a header **header-value** to the response. In this case, we have appended a *static* value. However, as the factory is aware of URI variables utilized for matching a *path* or *host*, they can be employed within the value and are expanded dynamically at *runtime.*

DedupeResponseHeader GatewayFilter factory

The **DedupeResponseHeader** GatewayFilter factory eliminates the duplicate values from the headers. It removes the duplicate values from the headers when the gateway CORS logic as well as the downstream logic adds them. When both the gateway CORS and the downstream logic add headers, this factory removes the duplicate values from the added headers.

This factory takes name and strategy as parameters. The strategy is an *optional* strategy parameter. The name parameter can contain the list of header names that are space-separated. The accepted values for the strategy are **RETAIN_FIRST**, **RETAIN_LAST**, and **RETAIN_UNIQUE**. The **RETAIN_FIRST** is the default strategy. The following configuration shows how to remove the duplicate values of **Access-Control-Allow-Credentials** and **Access-Control-Allow-Origin** from the **response** headers:

```
-id: dedupe_response_header_route
 uri: http://doctors
filters:
-DedupeResponseHeader=
         Access-Control-Allow-Credentials Access-Control-Allow-Origin
```

LocalResponseCache GatewayFilter Factory

The **LocalResponseCache GatewayFilter** factory filter configures the local response cache as per the route, it is available only when we enable **spring.cloud.gateway.filter.local-response-cache.enabled** property. This feature also enables a local response cache according to configuration. It accepts *two* parameters:

- The first parameter overrides the time to expire a cache entry, which is expressed in **s**, **m**, and **h**, that is, in *seconds*, *minutes*, and *hours*, respectively.
- The second parameter sets the maximum size of the cache to evict entries for this route. This is expressed in **KB**, **MB**, or **GB**.

The rules that are followed by this filter which allows caching the response body and filter are as follows:

- This can cache bodyless GET requests only.
- It caches the response only for status codes **HTTP 200**, **HTTP 206**, or **HTTP 301**.
- If the **Cache-Control** header is present, then response data is not cached.
- If a new request is made with **no-cache** value in the **Cache-Control** header and the response is already cached then the bodyless response is returned with **304** as the status code.

We need to add **spring-boot-starter-cache** and **spring-boot-starter-cache** as dependencies in the **API_Gateway_service** application.

You must add the following configuration:

```
- id: doctor_local_response_cache
  uri: lb://doctor-find-by-id-service/doctors
```

```
  predicates:
  - Path=/doctors/**
    filters:
- LocalResponseCache=30m,500MB
```

We can now proceed with postman and send the request to **http://localhost:9097/doctors/1**. We will receive the response, as predicted. Here, the request made a round trip to the data from the downstream service. It increases the protocol's handshake latency, and time to get meaningful responses and the client may face the high latency of requests. We can avoid this by caching the endpoint's responses in API Gateway. By doing this, we can reduce the number of calls made to the endpoint which ultimately helps us to improve the latency of requests. Access the same URI couple of times and then observe the console of **DoctorFind_By_DoctorId**. Note that, despite making multiple requests to Gateway API service, there had been no hit on the service. But, *are we receiving the response? Yes*, we are getting the cached response but not by hitting the actual downstream endpoint.

MapRequestHeader GatewayFilter Factory

The **MapRequestHeader** GatewayFilter factory takes *two* parameters, namely **fromHeader** and **toHeader** parameter. From the incoming request the value of **fromHeader** is extracted and then a new header **toHeader** is created having the value of the **fromHeader**. In case the input header is not present, then the filter has *no* impact. Sometimes, the newly named header might already be available, in such cases, its value will be modified with the new values. The following code adds a route **doctor_map_request_header** which will take **spec** as an input header and then its value will be mapped to the header **sort** which will be added to the downstream. The following code illustrates how to achieve this:

```
@Bean
public RouteLocator configureRoute(RouteLocatorBuilder builder) {
  return builder.routes()
            .route("hospital",
                        r->r.path("/hospitals/**")
            .uri("http://localhost:9091/hospitals")) //static routing
            .route("doctor_map_request_header -", r->r.path("/
                                                      doctors/**")
            .filters(f -> f.mapRequestHeader("spec", "sort"))
            .uri("lb://doctor-find-by-id-service"))
            .build();
```

```
}
```

Now, you can execute the application in postman and access the URL **http://localhost:9097/doctors/1** along with **spec** as *header* and **Ortho** as its *value*. In this case, we will get 204 *as a response* because we do not have *doctor* with *doctorId* as **1**, and *Ortho* as **specialization** as shown in *Figure 7.14*:

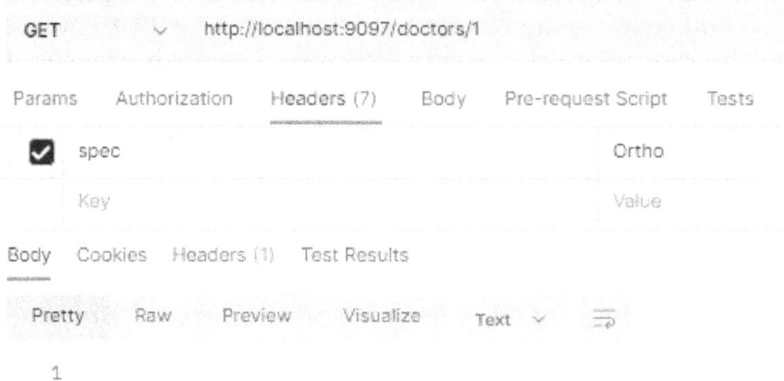

***Figure 7.14**: MapRequestHeader GatewayFilter factory with input header without matching record*

If the input header is not present, then the filter has no impact as shown in *Figure 7.15*:

***Figure 7.15**: MapRequestHeader GatewayFilter factory without input header*

And, when we add a header **spec** having value as **Medicine**, we will receive the response as shown in *Figure 7.16*. This is because the *doctor* with **doctorId 1**, has

Medicine as the **specialization**:

Figure 7.16: *MapRequestHeader GatewayFilter factory with input header matching record*

ModifyRequestBody GatewayFilter Factory

The **ModifyRequestBody GatewayFilter** factory modifies the request body before the Gateway API service forwards it downstream. We can configure it only by using the Java DSL as shown in the following code:

```
@Bean
public RouteLocator configureRoute(RouteLocatorBuilder builder) {
       return builder.routes()
       .route("doctor_modify_request_body -",
                  r->r.path("/doctors/**")
       .filters(f -> f.modifyRequestBody(Doctor.class, Doctor.class,
                  (exchange, s) -> Mono.just(new Doctor(s.getDoctorId(),
            s.getDoctorName().toUpperCase(),s.getSpecialization()))))
      .uri("http://localhost:8081"))
      .build();
}
```

The preceding code changes the name of the *doctor* to uppercase before sending the request to the **DoctorAddService**. Here, the request body will be changed so we are using the **DoctorAddService** to route the request. It is important to ensure that the service is registered to the Eureka server and it is running at **http://localhost:8081**. We will now add the POST request in the postman to receive the **doctorName** in *uppercase* as a part of the response as shown in *Figure 7.17*:

***Figure 7.17**: Implementing ModifyRequestBody GatewayFilter factory*

ModifyResponsetBody GatewayFilter Factory

Sometimes rather than modifying the request before sending it to downstream (which is referred as **request pre-processing**), we may need to use post-processing before sending the response to the client. The **ModifyResponsetBody** GatewayFilter factory allows us to modify the response body before it is sent back to the client. Instead of using **modifyRequestBody()** which we used earlier, we need to use the **modifyResponseBody()** method.

PrefixPath GatewayFilter Factory

The **PrefixPath** GatewayFilter factory prefixes **somevalue** to the path for all the matching requests. It takes `prefix` as a parameter. The following configuration adds a **PrefixPath** to all matching requests:

```
- id: prefix_path_route
  uri: http://localhost:8085/doctors
  filters:
  - PrefixPath=/my_prefix
```

PreserveHostHeader GatewayFilter Factory

The purpose of the **PreserveHostHeader** GatewayFilter factory filter is to enable the routing filter to make a decision about which host header to send with the request. It achieves this by setting a **request** attribute that can be used by the routing filter. This decision is based on whether the original host header or the host header determined by the HTTP client should be sent. This factory does not take any parameters. The following configuration configures **PreserveHostHeader** GatewayFilter:

```
- id: preserve_host_route
  uri: https://localhost:8085/doctors
  filters:
  - PreserveHostHeader
```

RedirectTo GatewayFilter Factory

The **RedirectTo** GatewayFilter factory is used to redirect to a new location. It takes *two* parameters namely, **status** and **url**. The **status** parameter is of a 300 *series* which is designed to redirect HTTP code. The **url** parameter takes the value of a valid URL. This is the value of the **Location Header**. When we want to use relative redirects, we should use **uri** with **no://op** as the **uri** in the **route** definition.

To perform redirect operation, the following configuration sends a status **301** with **http://localhost:8081** as the location header:

```
- id: prefixpath_route
  uri: https://localhost:8085
  filters:
  - RedirectTo=301, http://localhost:8081
```

RemoveRequestHeader GatewayFilter Factory

The **RemoveRequestHeader** GatewayFilter factory removes the specified header from the request. It takes a name as the parameter that will be removed from the request. By default, we don't have **sort** as the header in the request, so here we need to first add it, and then we will perform the remove operation.

The following configuration removes the header named **sort**:

```
- id: remove_request_header_route
  uri: lb://doctor-find-by-id-service/doctors
  predicates:
  - Path=/doctors/**
  filters:
  - AddRequestHeadersIfNotPresent= sort:Medicine
  - RemoveRequestHeader=sort
```

To test the functionality of API Gateway service, you can execute the service by sending a request to **http://localhost:9097/doctors/100**.

The following output shows the request header which was added by the configuration is removed by the **RemoveRequestHeader** filter and we received the response as the *doctor* with **Ophthalmologist** as the *specialization* which has the **doctorId** as **100**:

***Figure 7.18**: Implementing RemoveRequestHeader GatewayFilter factory*

RemoveJsonAttributeResponseBody GatewayFilter factory

The **RemoveJsonAttributesResponseBody** GatewayFilter factory provides a convenient method to apply a transformation to JSON body content by deleting attributes from it. It takes a collection of attribute names for searching an *optional* last parameter from the list which can be a *Boolean* suggesting the removal of the attributes just at *root* level which is the default value as *false* or recursively *true*.

RemoveRequestParameter GatewayFilter Factory

The **RemoveRequestParameter** GatewayFilter factory removes the specified parameter from the **request**. It takes **name** as the parameter to be removed. The following configuration shows how to *remove request parameter value* before sending it the downstream:

```
- id: remove_request_parameter_route
  uri: lb://doctor-find-by-id-service/doctors-values
  predicates:
  - Path=/doctors-values/**
  filters:
  - RemoveRequestParameter=value
```

Let us execute the API service again, and test it in the postman by requesting, **http://localhost:9097/doctors-values/1?value=100**. We will receive **400** *as response* as shown in *Figure* 7.19:

GET http://localhost:9097/doctors-values/1?value=100

Params Authorization Headers (7) Body Pre-request Script Tests Settings

Body Cookies Headers (3) Test Results Status: 400 Bad Request

Pretty Raw Preview Visualize JSON

```
{
    "timestamp": "2023-04-11T11:03:06.826+00:00",
    "status": 400,
    "error": "Bad Request",
    "path": "/doctors-values/1"
}
```

***Figure* 7.19**: *Implementing RemoveRequestParameter GatewayFilter factory*

If you visit **DoctorFind_By_DoctorId** console, you will observe the missing parameter as:

```
Resolved [org.springframework.web.bind.
MissingServletRequestParameterException: Required request parameter
'value' for method parameter type String is not present]
```

This console log gives clear evidence that the request parameter has been removed.

RewritePath GatewayFilter Factory

In some cases, for security reasons, it may be necessary to obscure the actual URL that is being accessed. So, when the client accesses a specific URL, it should be redirected to a different URL instead. The **RewritePath** GatewayFilter factory facilitates us to rewrite such a path. It takes an *actual path* and the *replacement path* as a parameter in the format of *regex* expression. This enables a flexible way to rewrite the request path.

The following code rewrites the path **/mydoctors** to **/doctors/{segment}** and **/myhospitals** to **/hospitals/{segment}** before making the request to downstream request:

```
@Bean
public RouteLocator configureRoute(RouteLocatorBuilder builder) {
  return builder.routes()
        .route("doctorById",r -> r.path("/mydoctors/**")
        .filters(rw -> rw.rewritePath("/mydoctors/(?&lt;segment&gt;/?.*)",
                                      "/doctors/$\\{segment}"))
        .uri("lb://doctor-find-by-id-service"))
        .route("hospitalById", r -> r.path("/myhospitals/**")
        .filters(rw -> rw.rewritePath("/myhospitals/(?&lt;segment&gt;/?.*)",
                                    "/hospitals/$\\{segment}"))
        .uri("http://localhost:9091"))
        .build();
}
```

Let's re-run the API service and access any of endpoint for which the **RewritePath** GatewayFilter is applied as shown in *Figure* 7.20:

Figure 7.20: *Implementing RewritePath GatewayFilter factory*

It is evident from the output that, we accessed the endpoint **/mydoctors** which had rewritten to **/doctors** endpoint, before getting forwarded the downstream without client being aware of actual URL.

We can achieve the same effect by configuring the **application.yml** file as follows:

```
- id: rewritepath_route
  uri: lb://doctor-find-by-id-service
  predicates:
  - Path=/mydoctors/**
  filters:
  - RewritePath=/mydoctors/?(?&lt;segment&gt;.*), /doctors/$\{segment}
```

Introducing global filters

The **global filters** are the special filters as they are applied to all the routes depending upon some conditions. The **GlobalFilter** interface has the same signature as that of the GatewayFilter. Once the gateway handler determines that the request matches a route, then the framework passes that request through a chain of filters. Few of these filters execute the logic before the request is propagated to the downstream service and others may be applied after the response is received from the service. This behavior is generally dependent on the conditions that have been configured for the route which are applied before or after the request has been processed. This is referred to as **pre-processing** and **post-processing** of the request.

Let us write our custom global filter **MyLoggingFilter.java** to add logging to perform pre-processing of the request. This class should implement the **GlobalFilter** interface and override the **filter()** method. Before writing the code, you should pay close attention to the **filter()** method:

```
public Mono<Void> filter(ServerWebExchange exchange, GatewayFilterChain
chain) {
  //pre processing logic
  return chain.filter(exchange);
  //post processing logic
}
```

Any operation that we perform through the code before invoking **chain.filter()** method is considered as *pre-processing of the request*. In this process, we can execute different tasks like *modifying the request body*, *adding some headers downstream*, and so on. Also, after receiving the response from the downstream, we can *add the headers*, *modify the response body*, and so on, before sending it to the client. This logic will be written after the invocation of **filter()** method. To perform the pre-processing of the incoming request, we can customize the behavior of the **filter()** method by overriding it. We will read the value of **spec** header from the request and then send this value in another header called sort to the downstream:

```
@Component
public class MyLoggingFilter implements GlobalFilter {
  final Logger logger = LoggerFactory.getLogger(MyLoggingFilter.class);
  @Override
  public Mono<Void> filter(ServerWebExchange exchange, GatewayFilterChain
                 chain) {
      logger.info("Global Pre Filter executed");
      ServerHttpRequest request = exchange.getRequest();
      logger.info("path: " + request.getPath());
      logger.info("address: " + request.getRemoteAddress());
      logger.info("method: " + request.getMethodValue());
      logger.info("URI: " + request.getURI());
      logger.info("Headers: " + request.getHeaders());
      ServerHttpRequest newRequest = exchange.getRequest().mutate()
            .headers(httpHeaders -> httpHeaders.add("sort",
                  request.getHeaders().get("spec").get(0))).build();
      return chain.filter(exchange);
  }
}
```

It is important to remember to annotate the class with **@Component** annotation to register it as a bean in the container. You can also register it by adding the method returning **GlobalFilter** annotated by **@Bean** annotation to register the custom filter as shown in the following code:

```
@Bean
public GlobalFilter requestFilter(){
  return new MyLoggingFilter();
}
```

Make sure to add the method in the class which acts as a configuration class or we can also add it in the main class. But, do not add **@Component** annotation as well as **@Bean** both otherwise we will be registering two separate beans performing the same task.

We are done with pre-processing filters, now we need to add the routes. We can do it in **.java** file as well as in the **.yml** configuration. We already have a route for `doctor` and `hospital` in the **application.yml** `file`. You need to just uncomment it.

The following configuration is just for your reference in case you don't have it yet:

```
spring:
  application:
    name: api-gateway-service
  cloud:
    gateway:
      routes:
      - id: hospital_route
        uri: http://localhost:9091/hospitals
        predicates:
        - Path=/hospitals/**
      - id: doctor_route
        uri: lb://doctor-find-by-id-service/doctors
        predicates:
      - Path=/doctors/**
```

Let us execute the API service and access the **/doctors** endpoint along with the header **spec**, with the value as **Ortho** as shown in the following figure:

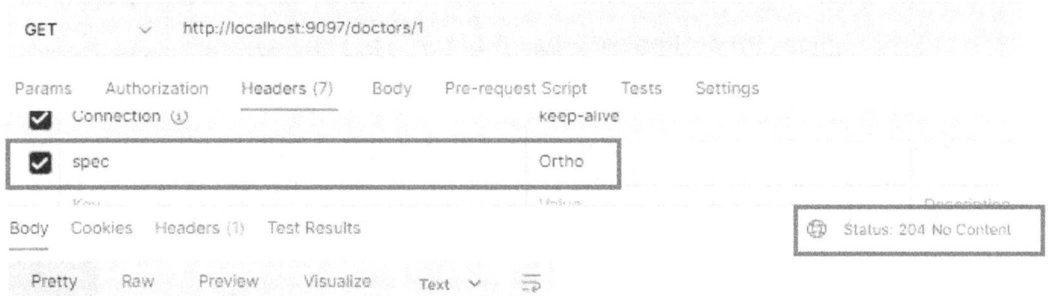

***Figure 7.21**: Implementing pre-processing of GlobalFilter for non-matching records*

The figure shows output which displays status code **204** because the *doctor* with **doctorId** 1, is having the specialization as **Medicine** but we sent the **spec** value as **Ortho** which got propagated downstream by our code.

The following console logs are displaying all the information about the request which is available in the API service. Make sure that you observe the value for **spec** header:

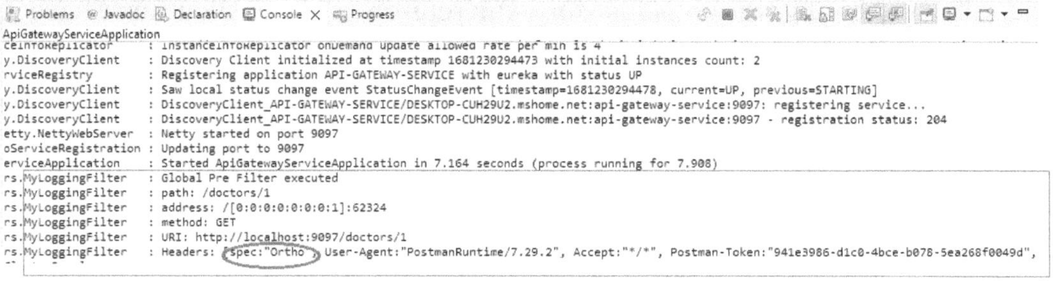

```
Problems  Javadoc  Declaration  Console X  Progress
ApiGatewayServiceApplication
ceInfoReplicator        : InstanceInfoReplicator onDemand update allowed rate per min is 4
y.DiscoveryClient       : Discovery Client initialized at timestamp 1681230294473 with initial instances count: 2
rviceRegistry           : Registering application API-GATEWAY-SERVICE with eureka with status UP
y.DiscoveryClient       : Saw local status change event StatusChangeEvent [timestamp=1681230294478, current=UP, previous=STARTING]
y.DiscoveryClient       : DiscoveryClient_API-GATEWAY-SERVICE/DESKTOP-CUH29U2.mshome.net:api-gateway-service:9097: registering service...
y.DiscoveryClient       : DiscoveryClient_API-GATEWAY-SERVICE/DESKTOP-CUH29U2.mshome.net:api-gateway-service:9097 - registration status: 204
etty.NettyWebServer     : Netty started on port 9097
oServiceRegistration    : Updating port to 9097
erviceApplication       : Started ApiGatewayServiceApplication in 7.164 seconds (process running for 7.908)
rs.MyLoggingFilter      : Global Pre Filter executed
rs.MyLoggingFilter      : path: /doctors/1
rs.MyLoggingFilter      : address: /[0:0:0:0:0:0:0:1]:62324
rs.MyLoggingFilter      : method: GET
rs.MyLoggingFilter      : URI: http://localhost:9097/doctors/1
rs.MyLoggingFilter      : Headers: [spec:"Ortho", User-Agent:"PostmanRuntime/7.29.2", Accept:"*/*", Postman-Token:"941e3986-d1c0-4bce-b078-5ea268f0049d",
```

Figure 7.22: *Console of API service for non-matching records*

Let us now try for post-processing. We will try to add *post-header* in the response as shown in the following code:

```
@Override
public Mono<Void> filter(ServerWebExchange exchange, GatewayFilterChain
chain) {
  return chain.filter(exchange)
.then(Mono.fromRunnable(() -> {
             ServerHttpResponse httpResponse= exchange.getResponse();
            HttpHeaders headers= httpResponse.getHeaders();
            headers.add("post_header", "this header is added by post
                                                              filter");
            logger.info("Post Global Filter");}));
}
```

We have commented on the earlier **filter()** method which is utilized for pre-processing and added a new **filter()** method. If you want, feel free to change the **filter()** method. Let us execute the service and access the URL as shown in *Figure 7.23*:

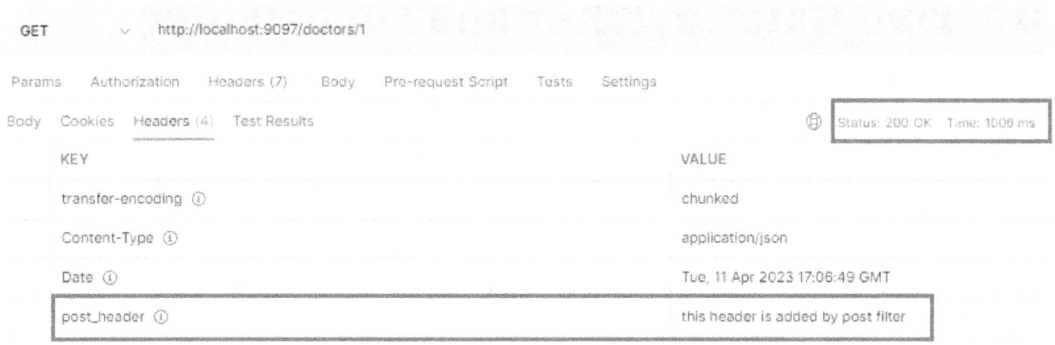

Figure 7.23: *Post-Processing in Global filters*

The preceding response clearly shows that we not only received the response but along with it, we have received modified response headers as well.

Finally, let us add both codes together to facilitate pre-processing as well as post-processing as shown in the following:

```
@Override
public Mono<Void> filter(ServerWebExchange exchange, GatewayFilterChain
                                                              chain)
  {
  logger.info("Global Pre Filter executed");
  ServerHttpRequest request = exchange.getRequest();
  logger.info("path: " + request.getPath());
  return chain.filter(exchange).then(Mono.fromRunnable(() -> {
       ServerHttpResponse httpResponse = exchange.getResponse();
       HttpHeaders headers = httpResponse.getHeaders();
       headers.add("post_header", "this header is added by post filter");
       logger.info("Post Global Filter");}));
}
```

On execution of the complete code, we will receive logs for both the pre-filters as well as post-filters on the console. You can try this using Postman.

We have *two* ways for filtering the request one is **GatewayFilter** factories and **GlobalFilter**. *Can we apply both?* And if *we apply both in which order they will be applied?*

Ordering GatewayFilter and GlobalFilter

When any incoming request matches a route, then the filtering web handler adds all instances of the **GlobalFilter** and all route-specific instances of the **GatewayFilter** to the chain. This chain is recognized as the filter chain. Now, **org.springframework.core.Ordered** interface will sort this combined filter chain. To order the filters we need to implement the **getOrder()** method. Any filter with the highest precedence will be the first in the *pre* phase. In the *post* phase, the filter chain is executed in reverse order. So, the first filter will be the last filter in the *post* phase.

The following code shows the modified **MyLoggingFilter.java,** which is used for ordering the filter:

```
@Component
public class MyLoggingFilter implements GlobalFilter, Ordered {
  @Override
  public Mono<Void> filter(ServerWebExchange exchange, GatewayFilterChain
                    chain) {
   //pre and post processing logic goes here
  }
  @Override
  public int getOrder() {
   // TODO Auto-generated method stub
   return -1;
  }
}
```

This filter being the lowest in the number will be executed first in the pre-phase and last in the post-phase.

We already have used the **ReactiveLoadBalancerClientFilter** right from the very beginning. However, being a *global filter*, earlier we had parked it. Now, is a *good* time to delve into it and discuss it thoroughly.

The ReactiveLoadBalancerClientFilter

The **ReactiveLoadBalancerClientFilter** looks into the exchange attribute named **ServerWebExchangeUtils.GATEWAY_REQUEST_URL_ATTR** to get the value of the URI. In case the URL has a lb scheme such **lb://doctor-find-by-id-service**, then it uses the **ReactorLoadBalancer** provided by Spring Cloud to resolve the name of service **doctor-find-by-id-service** to an actual host and port. Then it replaces the URI in the same attribute. Now, the unmodified original URL is appended to the list in the **ServerWebExchangeUtils.GATEWAY_ORIGINAL_REQUEST_URL_ATTR** attribute. The filter also observes in the **ServerWebExchangeUtils.GATEWAY_SCHEME_PREFIX_ATTR** attribute to find whether it also has **lb**. If it has, then the same rules are applied.

We have already used the following configuration number of times earlier:

```
- id: doctor_route
  uri: lb://doctor-find-by-id-service/doctors
  predicates:
  - Path=/doctors/**
```

If an instance of the service is not found by the **ReactorLoadBalancer**, it returns the status code **503**. If we want to change the status code to return **404**, we can configure the property **spring.cloud.gateway.loadbalancer.use404**, to **true**.

Conclusion

In this chapter, we discussed the role of API Gateway in microservice architecture. We explored different approaches used by API Gateway. **Request routing** is one of the important features of Gateway API. We discussed different ways to implement routing in this chapter. During this discussion, we talked about different predicate factories that are used by the Gateway API. Spring microservices can also pre-process or post-process the requests by using different GatewayFilters. We discussed different types point-by-point GatewayFilter factories. At the end of the chapter, we talked about Global filters which can be applied to all the routes based on some pre-defined conditions.

In the next chapter, we will discuss how to monitor the application using **Actuator**, **Logging**, and request tracing using **Zipkin**.

CHAPTER 8
Observability

Our team had completed the *development* phase and we are fortunate that the services are also deployed within the container successfully. *What a big relief, isn't it?* There's a great sense of satisfaction when you develop the application that is being used by many users and it runs without any issues. The DevOps team is in place and monitoring the instances of service. Till now everything was going well and so we all are relaxed. But as this is a *production* environment unexpected events may occur at any moment. And there was no exception in our case as well. Suddenly, the team noticed that the instances of **DoctorFind_By_DoctorId** service are getting unhealthy. The DevOps team retrieved the logs and tried to identify the reasons. But to their surprise, before the situation gets worse the instances of the service became healthy. Everything started working again flawlessly. The DevOps team was relieved and got engaged in some other tasks.

But then, on the following morning, the same incident was reported. The DevOps team was again clueless. Regretfully, on that day the team was unlucky and the instances didn't come back to the normal working state. The team panicked. The services need to return to a ready state before it's too late. The meeting invitation was sent on an urgent basis. The developers and DevOps team in the meeting room were trying to identify the root cause of this incident and why it was occurring repeatedly. *Why this is happening* was the only question in everybody's mind. The monitored logs were shared with the developers so that they reach the root cause. But that did not help as the microservices were combined with the containerized deployment which resulted in highly dynamic systems having various moving parts across multiple layers. After relentless efforts, they managed to figure out the bottleneck of inter-service communication when the requests were queued up it was creating the issue. But that is just speculation. They increased the CPU memory and services were back to work. Most of the team members continued their routine work, but few stayed back and brainstormed. They were eager to know the answer to the most important question, WHY?

The WHY, they were referring to was not the cause of the incident. They were already aware of the cause and anticipating to face such a situation. Moreover, they were expecting the monitoring system to identify the actual time and cause of that incident, but it was not functioning properly.

Manish from developer teams mentioned, "*we have the systems which emit enormous amounts of highly dimensional telemetry data. The data is generated from hardware, operating system, and Docker all the way to the application. Additionally, there are business performance metrics to consider as well. We currently are not getting help from the commonly used monitoring stack which we used earlier in monolithic applications.*"

Abhay, who was a colleague of Manish seemed to lose his patience, "Yes, *that's true, Manish. But why are you reiterating this, we all know this now. The used system is no longer sufficient to cover their backs. Why is that? And what we are going to do? What is the right approach to monitoring?*"

Manish exclaimed, "Well, *I am clueless too. We have too many things to work with. We have data and metrics from various systems. We have application-related data and metrics such as request rate and duration, which is one set of data. We also have infrastructure metrics available from the host CPU like available and utilized memory. Additionally, we have the container runtime metrics about the number of running pods, their memory, the node resource utilization, and so on. We have everything in our logs, but it's not helping us. It means we have to undergo significant transformation to overcome the challenges in the traditional approach towards monitoring. But the question is, HOW?*"

Mandar was listening to the conversation from the beginning and was anticipating this question. He stepped in, "*now we as a team have to meet these challenges and need to adopt the modern monitoring systems which will gear up with new capabilities and be flexible for querying and achieve high cardinality. It will efficiently automate metric scraping. And finally, it will enable scalability to handle large volumes of metrics scraping in the clustered scalable solution. We can't just rely on logs and log-based monitoring systems for such a complex environment. We need to first focus on how developers will collect and expose the data as well as metrics with minimum effort which will be effective to handle such situations. And then, once the data is available the DevOps team will monitor it easily and that to within the UI as it will be self-explanatory. I understand that physical monitoring is not possible every time. So, we are looking for a solution that will have some notification channel-based solution. A tool or set of tools which is easy to set, monitor, customize and use."*

Structure

In this chapter, we are focusing on microservice-based development so we will focus on the role of the developers to collect and expose the metrics to the monitoring tools with the help of the following points:

- Application monitoring
- Digging into Actuator
- Deep dive into observability
- Loggers
- Metrics
- Exploring distributed tracing
- A brief introduction to Micrometer
- Zipkin: The big picture

However, the picture is incomplete without knowing how our data is being used. Don't worry we will discuss how the exposed information is utilized by monitoring tools with their quick introduction. Let's get started then with what exactly is **monitoring** and its importance.

Application monitoring

By monitoring the application, we can identify *performance-related issues*, as well as other critical problems like *memory overload* and *excessive requests*, in their early stages, before they reach a critical point for the application. We need to resolve them in the early stage before they impact negatively the application and ultimately on businesses. We will be able to find the answers to some of the WH *questions* like *What, When, Where, and Why* something happened. While tracking performance is crucial, it's equally important to pinpoint when and where abnormalities occurred during the request process, and even more importantly, to determine why they happened. And that's why we developers consider reporting as the key aspect in monitoring any application for *performance*, *health*, and *request-response delivery*. Any monitoring system usually targets the *transaction time*, *system response*, *system response time*, *transaction volume*, and *rate error*.

Consider the scenario of attending a musical concert. *Have you ever noticed the extensive security measures at the entrance*? The reason behind this is to maintain safety and regulate the crowd, preventing any potential chaos. In a way, it is monitoring the event.

Importance of application monitoring

Nowadays, application monitoring has become an integral part of the day-to-day life in production environment-related operations. *Are you questioning the rationale behind this*? Don't forget that, if your application takes too long to respond, your customers may become *dissatisfied* and *frustrated*, potentially seeking out alternative options. Naturally, we want to avoid such a situation. We want our applications to respond to each request as quickly as possible and with accuracy. It's impossible to predict when demand will surge, and it's uncertain whether our application and environment have the necessary provisions to handle such a high demand. What we can help for sure is monitor the application 24/7. Monitoring the application facilitates the following advantages:

Alerts

There are millions of reasons why our application can become *unhealthy*. The application may face major outages, partial outages, or sometimes intermittent performance problems as well. Monitoring the application provides insights into the *server performance*, CPU *usage*, and *network traffic volume*. It also provides the application responses to requests to gauge the potential problems related to the performance. One can identify issues such as slow response times and errors very well before they make a major impact on the end-user experience. It helps us to understand the downtime before it occurs and we can take the majors to prevent the outages.

Pinpoints bottlenecks

Our application is complex with various independent modules working together. Observing them separately may be easy. However, if we combine all the modules, it becomes huge and complex. We can now combine the code level tracing, metrics exposed by the application, tracking exceptions, and understanding the error and event logs to monitor the applications as a complete picture. Once the information is exposed by the application, the DevOps teams can identify the bottlenecks causing the issues and can decide which issues are critical and need immediate resolution.

Improves stability

We are building enterprise microservice-based applications in a distributed environment. **Application monitoring** helps us to understand the application reaction when requests are made. It gives us insights into the applications in terms of performance when the load on a particular service increases.

Spring Boot provides several additional features which help to monitor and manage the application in production. We can choose to manage and monitor the application either by using `HTTP` **endpoints** or **JMX**. The module **spring-boot-actuator** provided by Spring Boot adds production-ready features to the application.

Digging into Actuator

Actuator provides us with the endpoints which allow us to monitor the application as well as interact with it. Spring Boot has a built-in set of endpoints and in addition to those, we also can incorporate our endpoints. The built-in endpoints are auto-configured but only when they are available. An endpoint is considered as available, only when it is both exposed as well as enabled. These endpoints are exposed over **HTTP** or **JMX**. However, we can't use them directly. We need to enable the endpoints to make them remotely accessible; otherwise, many of them are by default disabled. Most of the applications choose to expose the endpoints over **HTTP**. The **URL** to expose the endpoints is formed by adding **/actuator** as the prefix, followed by the **ID** of that endpoint. For example, one can find information about the application using the info endpoint, which is mapped to the URL as **/actuator/info**.

One can enable the feature just by adding **`spring-boot-starter-actuator`** dependency in the **classpath**. Let us add this dependency in our **`DoctorFind_By_DoctorId`** application and execute it. Ensure that the Eureka server is already in the *running* state, otherwise, you will get exceptions. Once the application is *up* and *running*, let us explore the endpoints provided by an actuator in our application by accessing **/actuator** as shown in *Figure 8.1*:

Figure 8.1: *Actuator end-points*

As we can observe, currently only the **health** endpoint is exposed which provides the health-related information as shown in *Figure 8.2*:

Figure 8.2: *Health status of the application*

The response received from the endpoint indicates that our application is *up* and *running* smoothly.

In the beginning, we mentioned that Spring Boot Actuator exposes several endpoints. However, when we accessed the **/actuator** endpoint, we noticed that only one or two endpoints were available. This raises the question of the whereabouts of the remaining endpoints and whether they are accessible. Your observation is *commendable*. Do you recall our earlier statement, *we can consider an endpoint is available only when it is both exposed and enabled*. By-default, only the **/health** endpoint is enabled and exposed over HTTP. Let us expose all the available endpoints by adding the following configuration in the **application.yml** file:

```
management:
  endpoints:
    web:
      exposure:
        include: "*"
```

On restarting the application, we will get access to additional actuator endpoints, precisely a total of 16 *endpoints* will be exposed by the actuator. *How are we so sure of the number of endpoints*? To ascertain this, let us visit the **`DoctorFind_By_DoctorId`** application console and observe the following piece of the log:

```
main] o.h.e.t.j.p.i.JtaPlatformInitiator       : HHH000490: Using JtaPlatform implementation: [org.hibernate.engine.tra
main] j.LocalContainerEntityManagerFactoryBean : Initialized JPA EntityManagerFactory for persistence unit 'default'
main] JpaBaseConfiguration$JpaWebConfiguration : spring.jpa.open-in-view is enabled by default. Therefore, database que
main] DiscoveryClientOptionalArgsConfiguration : Eureka HTTP Client uses RestTemplate.
main] iguration$LoadBalancerCaffeineWarnLogger : Spring Cloud LoadBalancer is currently working with the default cache.
main] o.s.b.a.e.web.EndpointLinksResolver      : Exposing 16 endpoint(s) beneath base path '/actuator'
main] o.s.c.n.eureka.InstanceInfoFactory       : Setting initial instance status as: STARTING
main] com.netflix.discovery.DiscoveryClient    : Initializing Eureka in region us-east-1
main] c.n.d.s.r.aws.ConfigClusterResolver      : Resolving eureka endpoints via configuration
```

Figure 8.3: *DoctorFind_By_DoctorId console*

The following table provides a list of the generalized endpoints which are available from the application when we add actuator dependency:

Endpoint ID	Description
`Auditevents`	It exposes the information related to the audit events for the application. However, it needs an **`AuditEventRepository`** bean.
`Beans`	It provides a complete list of all beans which are available in our application.
`Caches`	It exposes all available caches in the application.

Endpoint ID	Description
`Conditions`	It displays all the conditions that were evaluated on auto configuration and custom configuration classes along with the reasons why they did match or did not match.
`Configprops`	It displays a list of all properties exposed by the **`@ConfigurationProperties`** annotation.
`Env`	It shows all the properties available in the **`Configurable Environment`**.
`Flyway`	It displays any **`Flyway`** database migrations which have been applied. It needs a **`Flyway`** bean available in the application.
`Health`	It displays health information of an application.
`Httpexchanges`	It displays by default last **`100`** HTTP *request-response exchange* information. However, it requires an **`HttpExchangeRepository`** bean available in the application.
`Info`	It provides arbitrary information about an application.
	It displays the Spring Integration graph. We need to add a dependency of **`spring-integration-core`** in the application.
`Loggers`	It displays as well as modifies the configuration available for the loggers in the application.
`Liquibase`	It shows migrations that have been applied for any **`Liquibase`** database. We need to ensure that **`Liquibase`** beans are available in the application.
`Metrics`	This displays metrics related information of application.
`Mappings`	It displays a list of all available paths exposed by the **`@RequestMapping`** annotation.
`Startup`	It displays the startup steps data which is collected by the **`ApplicationStartup`**. To enable this information, we need to configure a **`BufferingApplicationStartup`** in the **`SpringApplication`**.
`Threaddump`	It performs a thread dump.

Table 8.1: *List of actuator end points*

Along with the preceding generalized endpoints, following additional endpoints are available when we have a web application:

ID	Description
`Hapdump`	This returns a heap dump file. If we are using a **HotSpot JVM**, an **HPROF-format** file is returned, and when we use **OpenJ9 JVM**, a **PHD-format** file is returned.
`Logfile`	It returns the contents of the log file. One need to be careful about setting the **`logging.file.name`** or the **`logging.file.path`** properties. It also supports the HTTP range header to retrieve part content of the log file.
`Prometheus`	It exposes the metrics in a format that a Prometheus server can scrape. We need to add **`micrometer-registry-prometheus`** in the classpath.

***Table 8.2**: Actuator end-points for web application*

Till now, we have exposed all the available endpoints. But *what if, we want to enable a few and disable the rest? Is it possible to accomplish that? Indeed*, we can. We can provide the list of endpoints instead of setting include to an asterisk which will enable only the configured endpoints.

Let's try it by updating the configuration in application.yml file as:

```
include: beans, mappings, env
```

This way we are exposing only **beans**, **mappings**, and **env** endpoints for our application. All the rest endpoints are *disabled*. Change the configuration and restart the application. Once it is up, try accessing **/actuator/beans**, **/ actuator/mapping**, or **/actuator/env**. You will observe that you are getting related information.

However, when we try for **/actuator/health**, we will receive the response as **404** status code, as this endpoint is not exposed. *Figure* 8.4 depicts the same:

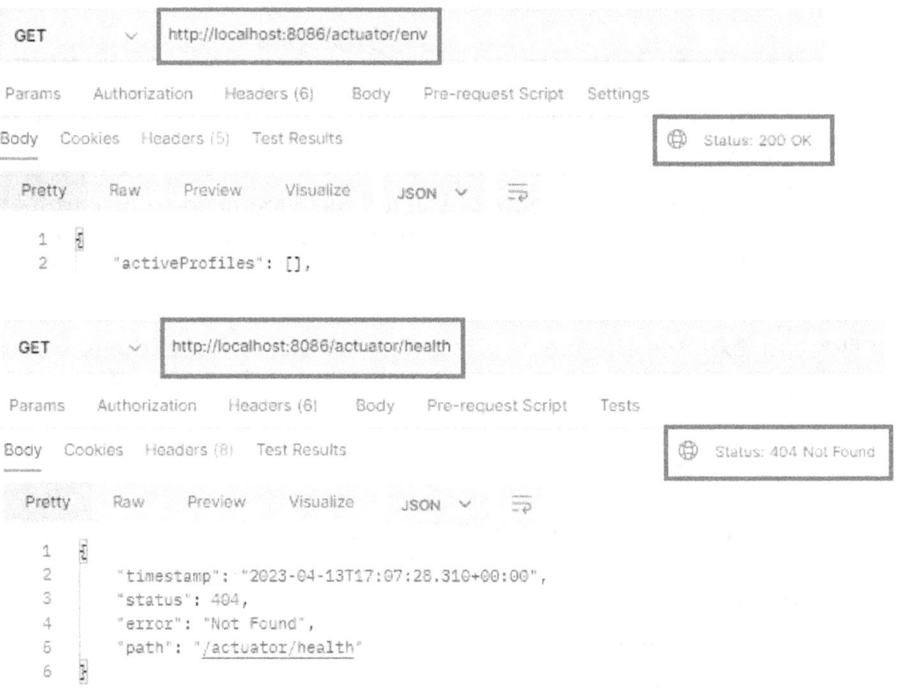

***Figure 8.4**: Accessing the enable and disabled endpoints of actuator*

We can exclude them, in the same manner that we included them.

Try the following configuration which will exclude **bean**, **env**, and **mappings** from exposing:

```
management:
endpoints:
    web:
      exposure:
        include: "*"
        exclude: beans,mappings,env
```

We can also expose the information over JMX by configuring the **jmx** instead of **web** in the preceding configuration. Now, we are aware of how to expose the endpoints. *Can we enable or disable the endpoints?*

We can also *enable* or *disable* the individual endpoints also by following the configuration:

```
management:
 endpoint:
    beans:
      enabled: true
```

This configuration will enable **/actuator/beans** only.

Remember when we want to change the technologies over which we intend to expose the endpoint, we need to use the **include** and **exclude** properties. Here we are exposing the actuator endpoints at the same port as that of the application. However, we can expose the application and the actuator on *two* different endpoints. And in this way, we are separating the application endpoints from the monitoring endpoints.

To accomplish this, we need to set management port as:

```
management:
  server:
     port: 8080
```

Till now we used the endpoints which were predefined. But what if we need to expose some custom information? Is it possible to customize the information that needs to be exposed? Yes, obviously! We can do this in two ways:

- The first is to customize the predefined endpoints to expose different sets of data and
- The second is to write a new endpoint.

Let us give a try to customize the information.

Customizing predefined endpoint

Before we start customizing, let us get the default response of **/actuator/health**. As predicted, we received the status: **UP** in the JSON format. Let us customize the response to get more information. The simplest thing we can do is to configure the property management:

```
endpoint:
    health:
      show-details : never or when-authorized or always
```

This property can be configured for one of the following *three* values:

- **never**: This is the *default* value, used when we do not wish to display any details.

- **when-authorized**: Used when we wish to display the details, only if the user is *authorized*. The *authorized* roles can be configured by using the property **management.endpoint.health.roles**.
- **always**: Used when we wish to display the details to all *users*.

Let us set the value to **always** and re-execute the service. The Postman will display more elaborate response including **db**, **discoveryComposite**, **diskSpace**, **ping**, **readinessState**, and **refreshScope** as shown in *Figure* 8.5:

***Figure* 8.5**: *Exploring more information about health endpoint*

If we want the response without details from the preceding response, we need to configure show-components as:

```
management:
  endpoint:
    health:
      show-components : never or when-authorized or always
```

When we want more controlled output, we can even customize the response by adding a **CustomHealthIndicator**, as shown in the following code:

```
@Component
public class CustomHealthIndicator implements HealthIndicator {
      private static final String URL = "http://localhost";
      @Override
      public Health health() {
            try (Socket socket = new Socket(new java.net.URL(URL).
                                                  getHost(), 8761)) {

            } catch (Exception e) {
                  System.out.println("Failed to connect to: " + URL);
                  return Health.down().withDetail("Eureka connection
                                                         is down",
                                              e.getMessage()).build();
            }
            return Health.up().build();
      }
}
```

As you might have noticed, we are trying to access the Eureka endpoint and depending on that we are deciding whether to set the status as **UP** or **DOWN**. Re-execute the service. For the time being stop the Eureka service. So that, we will be able to observe the prominent response as shown in *Figure 8.6*:

***Figure 8.6**: Customized health indicator*

In the same way, we also can have the **DataSource** health indicator which will display the *health* of both standard data sources and routing data source beans. If you prefer not to include routing data sources and **db** in the indicator's output, set the following in the configuration:

```
management:
  health:
    db:
     enable : false
     ignore-routing-data-sources : true
```

In this section, we discussed how to customize the predefined endpoint. Now, let us add our endpoint.

Adding custom endpoint

This endpoint will expose the operating system-related information. Let us add a POJO class **SystemInfo**, to expose the desired information. Here, we are exposing OS *name*, *version*, and *architecture* shown in the following code:

```
@Component
public class SystemInfo {
  private Map<String, String> systemDetails;
  public SystemInfo() {
       systemDetails =new LinkedHashMap<>();
              // Operating system name
              String osName = System.getProperty("os.name");
              // Operating system version
              String osVersion = System.getProperty("os.version");
              // Operating system architecture
              String osArchitecture = System.getProperty("os.arch");
              systemDetails.put("os.name", osName);
              systemDetails.put("os.version", osVersion);
              systemDetails.put("os.arch", osArchitecture);
}
       @JsonAnyGetter
       public Map<String, String> getsystemDetails() {
              return this.systemDetails;
       }
```

```
        public void setSystemDetails(Map<String, String> systemDetails) {
                this.systemDetails = systemDetails;
        }
}
```

Here we have used the **@JsonAnyGetter** annotation, which allows us to use map fields as standard properties flexibly.

Now, let us add a class **MyCustomEndpoint** annotated by **@Endpoint** annotation having a method **system()** annotated by **@ReadOperation** as shown in the following code:

```
@Component
@Endpoint(id = "system-endpoint")
public class MyCustomEndpoint {
  @Autowired
  SystemInfo;
  @ReadOperation
  public SystemInfo system() {
             return systemInfo;
  }
}
```

When we have added a bean with the **@Endpoint** annotation, then any methods annotated with **@ReadOperation**, **@WriteOperation**, or **@DeleteOperation** will be automatically exposed over JMX. If we have a web application the endpoints are exposed over HTTP as well.

Let us execute the service and check the **/actuator** for our custom endpoint:

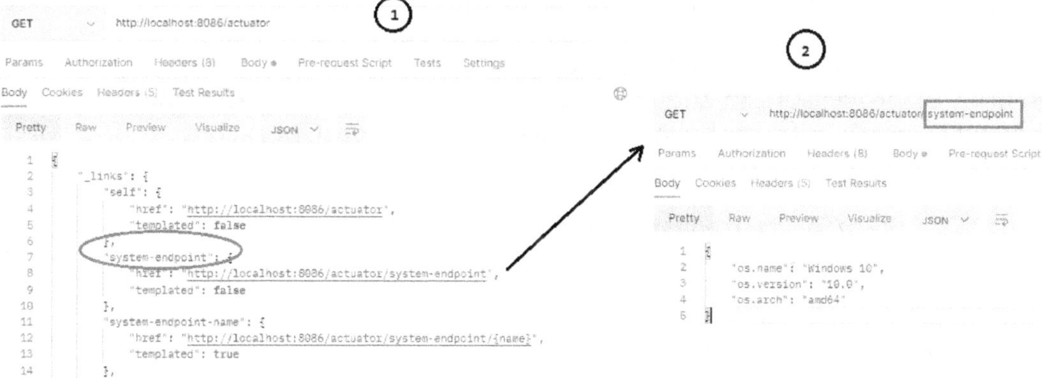

Figure 8.7: *Creating custom endpoint*

As shown in *Figure* 8.6, our endpoint is added as a name **system-endpoint** as provided by the **@Endpoint** annotation. And when we use the custom endpoint system related information is exposed as shown by second image, as **@ReadOperation** adds an endpoint to expose entire information. We can also expose *on-demand information* by annotating the method argument by **@Selector** annotation. The client can request the information using the pathvariable. Let us add the following code in the **MyCustomEndpoint** class to expose on-demand information:

```
@ReadOperation
public String readSystemInfoByName(@Selector String name) {
  String info = systemInfo.getsystemDetails().get(name);
  return info;
}
```

Re-execute the service and access **/actuator**, which generates the following response with endpoint having a name as **system-endpoint-name**. When we access the endpoint having name equal to **os.name** or **os.version** or **os.arch**, we will get relevant information as shown in the following figure:

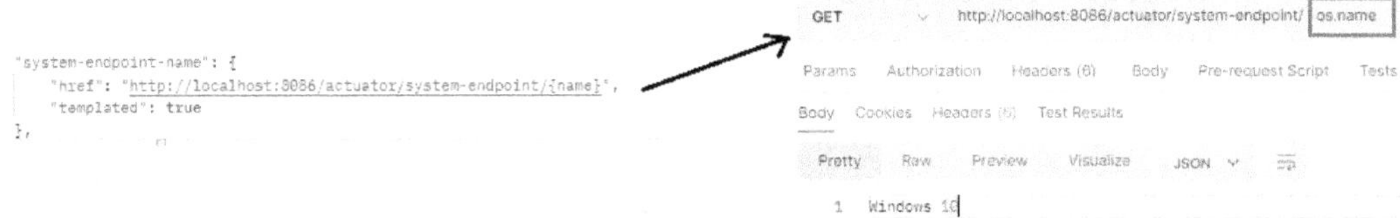

***Figure* 8.8**: *Customized endpoint with path variable*

If we enter a value in the URL that does not exist in the specified location, a status code **404** will be returned.

Now, let us add an endpoint to *update* or *delete* the information. We will add the number of processors in the system information using **@WriteOperation** and then will remove it from the system info using **@DeleteOperation**:

```
@WriteOperation
public SystemInfo updateSystemInfo_statusOK(String name) {
  // perform write operation
  System.out.println(name);
  if (name.equals("processors")) {
      System.out.println("adding extra info");
      Map<String, String> details = systemInfo.getsystemDetails();
```

```
        details.put(name, Runtime.getRuntime().availableProcessors() +
                                                                   "");
        systemInfo.setSystemDetails(details);
    }
    return systemInfo;
}
@DeleteOperation
public void modifySystemInfo_queryParam(String name) {
    // delete operation
    systemInfo.getsystemDetails().remove(name);
}
```

After updating the code, re-execute the application. Launch Postman and visit @ **WriteOperation** which is exposed at **HTTP POST** method as shown in *Figure* 8.9:

Figure 8.9: *Testing @WriteOperation*

As you can notice, the output now includes the processor as an added key in the map. You can also access HTTP GET on **http://localhost:8086/actuator/system-endpoint** which is used to retrieve the processor-related information added in the response.

Let us attempt to access **@DeleteOperation** as depicted in *Figure* 8.10:

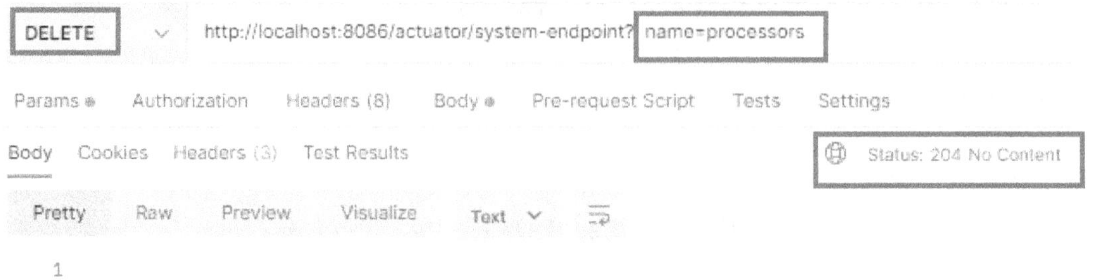

***Figure* 8.10**: *Testing @DeleteOperation*

Observe the way we are sending the name in the **query** parameter rather than sending it as a **path** variable. If we want to send it as a **path** variable, we need to add **@Selector** to the method argument. Strangely, the status code in the preceding figure is **204**. *Does that mean we did not find the matching content to delete*? That is not the case actually. Try accessing **/actuator/system-endpoint**. As shown in *Figure* 8.11, we will not receive any processor-related information:

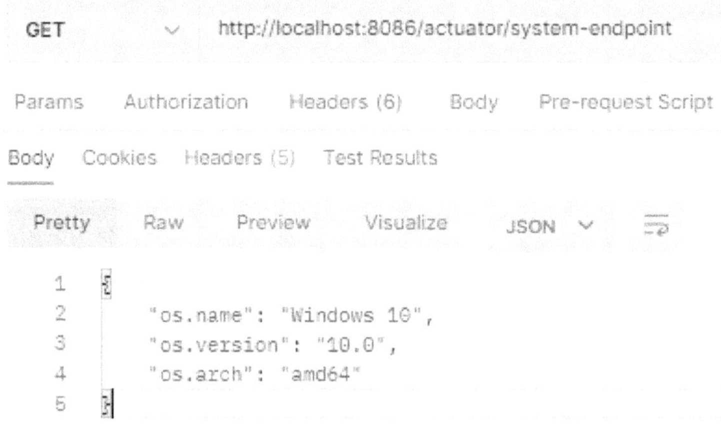

***Figure* 8.11**: *Testing system-endpoint after @WriteOperation and @DeleteOperation*

This is because we have removed that by using **@DeleteOperation**. *Are you still wondering about* **204**, *which was received as the status code*? When we perform **@WriteOperation** or **@DeleteOperation** in a method and the method returns a value, we get the response status as **200 (OK)**. However, when the method has a return type as *void*, indicating that it does not return any value, the response status will be **204 (No Content)**. Before moving further, we need to discuss the actuator in terms of API Gateway.

The Gateway API exposes **/gateway** as an actuator endpoint, which allows us to monitor and interact with an API Gateway application. We can remotely access the endpoints that have over **HTTP** or **JMX**, if they are enabled in the application properties. We can enable it in the configuration as:

```
management:
  endpoint:
     gateway:
         enabled: true
```

As discussed earlier, along with it we are also configuring the management port by adding **management.server.port=8080**. It is not necessary though. We already discussed this but didn't try it earlier. Maybe this is the right time to explore it. So, let us observe what we have on **/actuator** endpoint as shown in *Figure 8.12*:

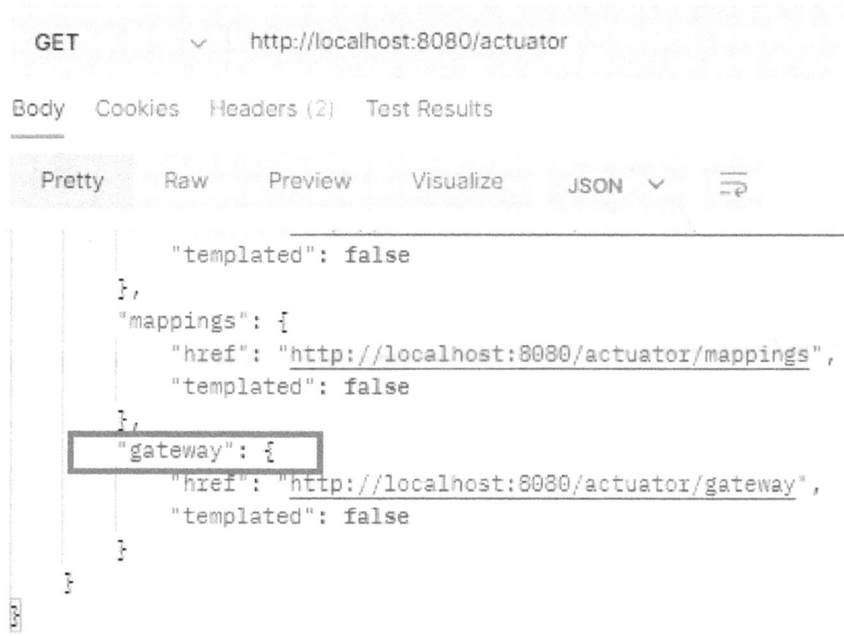

Figure 8.12: *Enabling gateway endpoint*

If you have noticed, we were not having the information about the gateway earlier. But now we have it because we have enabled it. This endpoint allows us to find route-related information at **/actuator/gateway/routes** as shown in *Figure 8.13*:

GET http://localhost:8080/actuator/gateway/routes

Params Authorization Headers (8) Body ● Pre-request Script Tests Settings

Body Cookies Headers (2) Test Results

Pretty Raw Preview Visualize JSON

```
[
    {
        "predicate": "Paths: [/hospitals/**], match trailing slash: true",
        "route_id": "hospital_route",
        "filters": [],
        "uri": "http://localhost:9091/hospitals",
        "order": 0
    },
    {
        "predicate": "Paths: [/doctors/**], match trailing slash: true",
        "route_id": "doctor_route",
        "filters": [],
        "uri": "lb://doctor-find-by-id-service/doctors",
        "order": 0
    },
```

Figure 8.13: *Display route information*

You can also use the global filters which are available at **/actuator/gateway/globalfilters** as shown in *Figure 8.14*:

Figure 8.14: *Retrieving the global filters in the actuator*

You can observe that, the response received also includes our custom filter along with the order which is assigned to it. In the same way, we also have the following endpoint for specific information:

- **http://localhost:8080/actuator/gateway/routefilters provides information about all the route filters.**
- **http://localhost:8080/actuator/gateway/refresh with POST is used to clear the routes cache.**
- **http://localhost:8080/actuator/gateway/actuator/gateway/routes/hospital_route to get information using route ID where hospital_route is the route ID.**
- **http://localhost:8080/actuator/gateway/actuator/gateway/routes/first_route to find information about the first route.**

We can also create a route at runtime using POST request to **`/gateway/routes/{id_for_route_to_create}`**. Here, we are creating and endpoint having **`my_hospital_route`** as route ID:

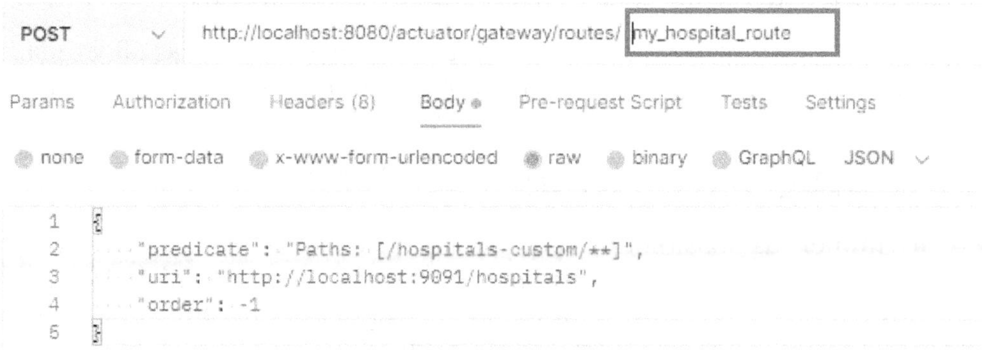

POST http://localhost:8080/actuator/gateway/routes/my_hospital_route

Params Authorization Headers (8) Body Pre-request Script Tests Settings

none form-data x-www-form-urlencoded raw binary GraphQL JSON

```
{
    "predicate": "Paths: [/hospitals-custom/**]",
    "uri": "http://localhost:9091/hospitals",
    "order": -1
}
```

***Figure 8.15**: Dynamic route creation for actuator*

We can confirm the addition of route at **/actuator/gateway/routes**.

As we can create a route, we can also remove it by sending the *Delete* request as **`/gateway/routes/{id_to_route_to_delete}`**.

By configuring the actuator, our endpoints are making the application-related information available. But, *should the DevOps persons keep on accessing the actuator endpoints every now and then?* It's so complicated. Don't there, *isn't any built-in UI for easy monitoring*? Unfortunately, we don't have a built-in UI. But we can set up the system to achieve that:

***Figure 8.16**: Communication with Prometheus and Grafana*

As shown in *Figure* 8.16, we have actuator-enabled services. The metrics exposed by the actuator will be scraped by **Prometheus**. Prometheus doesn't have a beautified UI and one needs to know Prometheus query language to get application-related information. We further can set up **Grafana** to make it easy to monitor the application.

Note

Prometheus: Prometheus is a time series database that can collect metrics. You can download it from **https://prometheus.io/download/**.

Grafana: Grafana provides dashboards for displaying the metrics collected from Grafana. You can download it from **https://grafana.com/grafana/download**.

Deep dive into observability

There are numerous possibilities to explore in terms of actuators. Here, we have tried to give you the best insight into how to enable, and customize the actuator to share the information over endpoints. Moving ahead we aim to monitor the internal state of our service from the external environment. We can do this by adding **logging**, **metrics**, and **traces** in our application.

Loggers

The Spring Boot Actuator enables us to configure and view the log levels of the application at runtime. We can either view the entire list or an individual configuration of the logger. **Logging** framework assigns the logging level to each logger. If needed we can also explicitly configure the logging level as well by choosing different levels like **TRACE**, **DEBUG**, **INFO**, **WARN**, **ERROR**, **FATAL**, **OFF**, and so on. Assigning a logging level to null implies that no explicit configuration has been established for the logger. We can retrieve the information about all loggers by accessing **/actuator/loggers** endpoint as shown in *Figure* 8.17:

GET http://localhost:8086/actuator/loggers

Params Authorization Headers (8) Body Pre-request Script

Body Cookies Headers (5) Test Results

Pretty Raw Preview Visualize JSON

```
{
    "levels": [
        "OFF",
        "ERROR",
        "WARN",
        "INFO",
        "DEBUG",
        "TRACE"
    ],
    "loggers": {
        "ROOT": {
            "configuredLevel": "INFO",
            "effectiveLevel": "INFO"
        },
        "SQL dialect": {
            "effectiveLevel": "INFO"
        },
        "_org": {
            "effectiveLevel": "INFO"
        },
```

Figure 8.17: *Retrieving loggers from the actuator*

Along with it, we can also access the endpoint with the name of the logger in the path to retrieve information about a specific logger. The following output shows information about the SQL dialect logger:

Figure 8.18: *Retrieving specific logger from actuator*

We obtained this information from the configuration file as well. But, *can we accomplish this in a different manner*? Indeed, *we can*. We can change the logging level at runtime. Yes, during runtime. Now the **effectiveLevel** is **INFO** and there is no any configuration for **configuredLevel**. *Shall we attempt to set the* ***configuredLevel*** *to* **DEBUG**? Let us do it as demonstrated in *Figure* 8.19:

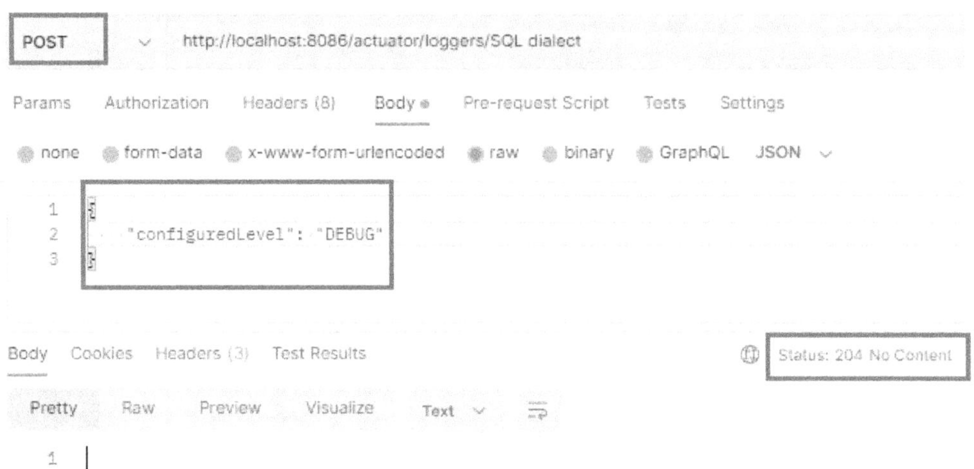

Figure 8.19: *Setting up the configuredlevel*

This seems familiar! But, *where did we post the information to the endpoint*? If you recall, while creating a custom actuator endpoint we discuss **@WriteOperation**. The implementation is precisely the same. Therefore, we won't be discussing it again. If you wish to refresh your memory on this concept, please refer to our earlier section, *Adding Custom Endpoint*.

You can verify, if the level has been added or not, by accessing the **/actuator/loggers/SQL** dialect endpoint. You will obtain the same response as shown in *Figure* 8.20:

Figure 8.20: *Adding levels to the logger*

Occasionally, we wish to reset the logging level. If you do so, the default value for the logger will be utilized. To reset any specific level, we just need to pass a value as null for the **configuredLevel** as shown in the following figure:

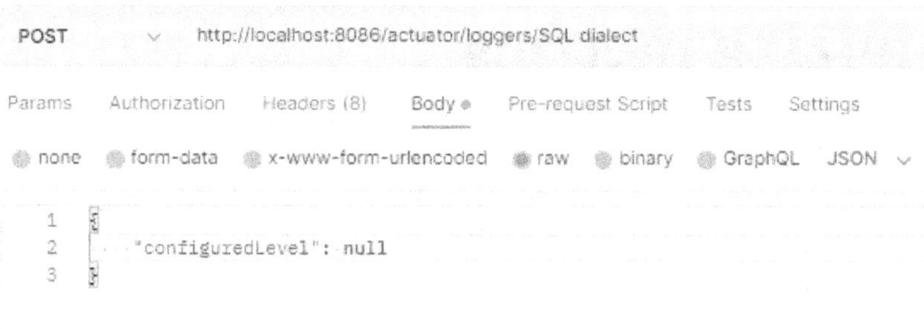

***Figure 8.21**: Resetting the level*

In our case as there is no default value set up, the **configurationLevel** will be removed.

Metrics

Metrics is one of the ways to explore how the application is performing. The application performance can be evaluated on various parameters such as **JVM**, **System**, **Application startups**, **loggers**, **Spring MVC**, **HTTP client**, **Jersey server**, **Tomcat**, **DataSource**, and so on. This metrics information is exposed at **/actuator/metrics** endpoint. Using this endpoint, we can retrieve metrics related to **JVM**, **System**, **Application Startup**, **Logger**, **TaskExecution and scheduling**, **Spring MVC**, **Spring webflux**, **HTTP Client**, **Tomcat**, **Cache**, **DataSource**, **Hibernate**, **Spring Data Repository**, **RabbitMQ**, **MongoDB**, **Redis**. All these are supported metrics. However, we can also register custom metrics.

We have different use cases, which demand distinct types of metrics. However, we can categorize metrics provided by Micrometer into *three* main types:

- **Counter**: It is used to measure the number of events. The counter has the value in increasing order and it never decreases. It is useful to find the total number of *orders processed*, *tasks completed*, or *requests processed.*
- **Gauge**: It allows us to measure resource usage, capacity, and so on. The gauge values can *rise* and *fall* which have some fixed upper bounds. It is useful to find the size of a collection, the number of threads that are in the running state, the number of messages that are in a queue, and memory usage, and so on.

- `Timer`: The time is used to measure short-duration events along with their frequency. We can find the time taken by a method to execute, the request duration, and so on.

Customizing metrics

To gather the information about controller method's execution time and the frequency of the client requests, let us annotate the method by **@Times** annotation. Here, we are updating the **FindDoctorByIdController**'s handler method. We can follow the same thing for all other methods as well. The updated handler method is as follows:

```
@Times(value = "execution.time", description = "Time taken to return
                                                              Doctor")
@GetMapping("/doctors/{doctorId}")
ResponseEntity<Doctor> findDoctorById(@PathVariable int doctorId,
                                           @RequestHeader(name = "sort",
                                        defaultValue = "all") String sort) {
}
```

Here, the **@Times** annotation exposes the information on the **execution.time** as **tag**. Let's re-execute the service and visit Postman to obtain the **execution.time** metrics as follows:

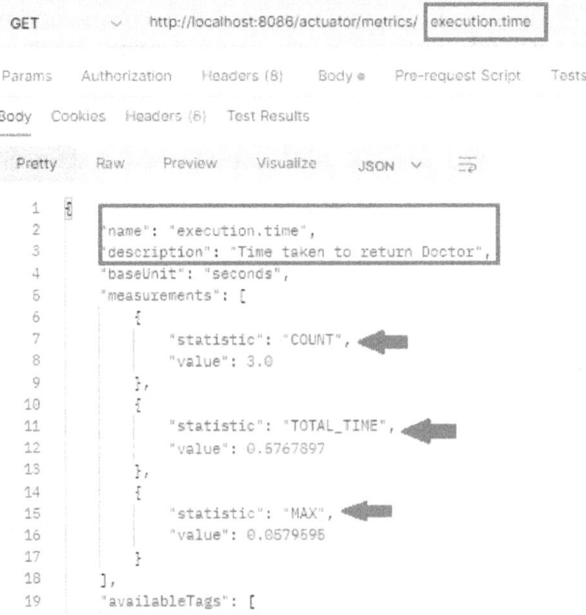

Figure 8.22: *Retrieving execution.time through Postman*

Now, the final one in the list is tracing.

Exploring distributed tracing

Request tracing is a technique to explore sub-requests that occur across multiple services when a single service endpoint is requested. We already have discussed *inter-service communication* which can make multiple requests to the underlying service to collect some data. As we know, a microservices architecture is a distributed application where a service often needs to integrate with other services, databases, as well as third-party dependencies. In a microservices architecture, we have multiple inter-communicating services. So, tracing *end-to-end requests* is necessary to identify the bottleneck in request processing and obtain accurate performance metrics.

Importance of distributed tracing

As the use of microservices architecture has increased in recent days, the demand for distributed tracing has increased. Starting from the frontend engineers, backend engineers along with site reliability engineer's use distributed tracing for observing the services.

The following are the benefits that make distributed tracing most important:

- **Insite of inter-service relationship**: In a microservices architecture, we develop services that follow SRP and the services communicate with each other to perform certain tasks. **Distributed tracing** can help the developers to get insight into the relationships between services along with the causes and effects of their performance degradation. Let us say, we have an inter-service communication for adding a new record in the database. If these services are under request tracing, then we can view a span generated by a database call, which reveals that there is latency in the upstream service when we are attempting to add a new record.
- **Understanding the bottlenecks**: Distributed tracing also provides the time elapsed to complete the execution of a certain task. The tracing helps the developers to identify backend bottlenecks, as well the reasons which are affecting the user experience.
- **Improved developer productivity**: In microservice architectures, specialized teams may design independent microservice. In other words, these teams claim ownership of their services. Simultaneously, the other might have developed another microservice which utilizes inter-service communication to produce a full-fledged response to a client request. If everything goes well everyone is happy. However, when something doesn't work as predicted, it is complex to identify the reason

as we are working in a distributed environment. In addition, the services involved are not owned by your team. Here, distributed tracing helps the developers to identify the exact location of the error and which team is responsible to fix it.

- **Mean time to resolution**: Distributed tracing helps us to map an entire flow of a request which also goes across network boundaries or it has a security context. When we come across any complex issue, we debug the application to identify the reason. The data retrieved from tracing helps us to debug complex issues. This is quicker, as it pinpoints the source of the issue and then identifies which trace logs on which we should focus. This certainly reduces the **Mean Time to Resolution** (**MTTR**) to our issue.

- **Microservice tracing**: Till now, we have developed various microservices related to *doctor* and *hospital* operations. We have also used the Eureka service, Gateway API service. This completes our ecosystem. Some requests were served well, while some were not. Sometimes we received the responses and sometimes the requests failed to receive the response. One way to tackle this scenario is to implement **exception handling**. However, as discussed earlier after knowing the cause of failure, if we wish to debug it in MTTR, we need to set up a tracking system for our microservices. Let us accomplish it without wasting time. We first need to decide about which traces we want to *log*, to identify the dependencies to include in our application. Spring Boot supports the auto-configuration for **OpenTelemetry** with **Zipkin** or **Wavefront** and **OpenZipkin Brave** with **Zipkin** or **Wavefront** as tracers.

When we aim to implement tracing for any application, we have to add **spring-boot-starter-actuator** as a common dependency. Then, to collect the data and report the trace we need to choose either **Zipkin** or **Wavefront** as distributed tracing systems. We also need to choose the metrics collector either as **Micrometer** or **Opentelemetry**. Depending upon our selection, we have the following choices to add dependencies:

- For OpenTelemetry with Zipkin:

  ```
  io.micrometer:micrometer-tracing-bridge-otel
  io.opentelemetry:opentelemetry-exporter-zipkin
  ```

- For OpenTelemetry with Wavefront:

  ```
  io.micrometer:micrometer-tracing-bridge-otel
  io.micrometer:micrometer-tracing-reporter-wavefront
  ```

- For OpenZipkin Brave with Zipkin:

  `io.micrometer:micrometer-tracing-bridge-brave`

  `io.zipkin.reporter2:zipkin-reporter-brave`

- OpenZipkin Brave With Wavefront:

  `io.micrometer:micrometer-tracing-bridge-brave`

  `io.micrometer:micrometer-tracing-reporter-wavefront`

Remember:

- Metrics data will denote the observed *throughput of every service*, *overall average latency*, *maximum latencies*, and other distribution statistics in a period.
- The *distributed tracing system* will inform us of the time in milliseconds the particular service took to process the given request.

Note

Change in version: Spring Cloud Sleuth will not work with Spring Boot 3.x onwards. We were using Sleuth with Spring Boot 2.x. However, here we will be using Micrometer instead of Sleuth.

Micrometer in brief

The **Micrometer** is a metrics instrumentation library for JVM-based applications. The **Micrometer Tracing** provides data for the most popular libraries which can be used to trace the request and enables us to instrument our application code. It is designed in such a way that it adds very little or no overhead to our tracing collection activity. The Micrometer Tracing contains a core module with an instrumentation SPI. The Micrometer adds a rich set of meter primitives to the counters and gauges which was available from *Spring Boot 1.X*. Now, we have a single Micrometer Timer which is capable of producing time series related to *throughput, total time, maximum latency of recent samples, percentile histograms*, and so on. It supports **Netflix Atlas**, **CloudWatch**, **Datadog**, **Ganglia**, **Graphite**, **InfluxDB**, **JMX**, **New Relic**, **Prometheus**, **SignalFx**, **StatsD**, and **Wavefront** as monitoring systems. The Micrometer Tracing borrows **Dapper's** terminology.

Let us discuss a few of the terminologies:

- **Span**: Span is the basic unit of work. The **Span** has the data such as *descriptions*, *timestamped events*, and *key-value* annotations provided by the *tags* and the *ID*. The **Spans** can be *started* and *stopped*. They can keep track of timing information. When we create a span, we must stop it at some point in the future when a unit of work is done. The **SpanId** may or may not be the same as the **traceId**.

- **Trace**: The Trace is a set of spans forming a tree-like structure. The trace has **traceId** which is the overall 64 or 128-bit ID of the trace. Every span in a trace shares this ID.
- **Parent ID**: The parent ID is an *optional* ID, which will only be present on the child spans. When we have the span without a parent id it is considered the root of the trace.
- **Annotation** or **Event**: **Annotations** and **Events** are used to record the existence of an event that happened in time.
- **Tracer**: A **Tracer** is a library, which handles the lifecycle of a span. The tracer can *create*, *start*, *stop*, and *report* spans to an external system using the reporters.

Now we know the basics of tracing, the library which provides the instrumentation and the distributed system to trace our service request. Let us explore Zipkin in detail:

Big picture with Zipkin

We have many services running. So, it is time to trace the requests. We may have the dependencies either at the time of application creation or if we need to add them later. None of our services has them yet. Let us add the configuration as shown in the following code which will add the dependencies in the **classpath** in addition to the actuator:

```
<dependency>
       <groupId>io.micrometer</groupId>
       <artifactId>micrometer-tracing-bridge-brave</artifactId>
</dependency>
<dependency>
       <groupId>io.zipkin.reporter2</groupId>
       <artifactId>zipkin-reporter-brave</artifactId>
</dependency>
```

Now, let us explore the implementation of tracing. There are various scenarios where we can implement the tracing. To begin with we will explore the implementation of simple tracing. Let us concentrate on the **DoctorFind_By_DoctorId** service. We have already added `actuator`, **micrometer-tracing-bridge-brave** and **zipkin-reporter-brave** as dependencies. If you want to go with a different collector or bridge, you are free to add the respective dependencies. Also, make sure to enable the actuator endpoints as discussed earlier.

If we are targeting to trace the request on Zipkin, we must ensure that a Zipkin server *up* and *running*. You can visit **https://zipkin.io/pages/quickstart** and choose how you want to launch the Zipkin server. If you have Docker, you can use the command as,

`docker run -p 9411:9411 openzipkin/zipkin:latest` to launch the Zipkin.

Once the Zipkin server is *up* and *running*, visit **http://localhost:9411** to launch the Zipkin `UI`. We are all set. Let us also launch `Eureka` Server, if it is *not up* and *running*. Then start the **DoctorFind_By_DoctorId** service.

Now, visit the Zipkin UI and click on the **Service Name** drop-down. We do not have any services listed there as shown in *Figure* 8.23:

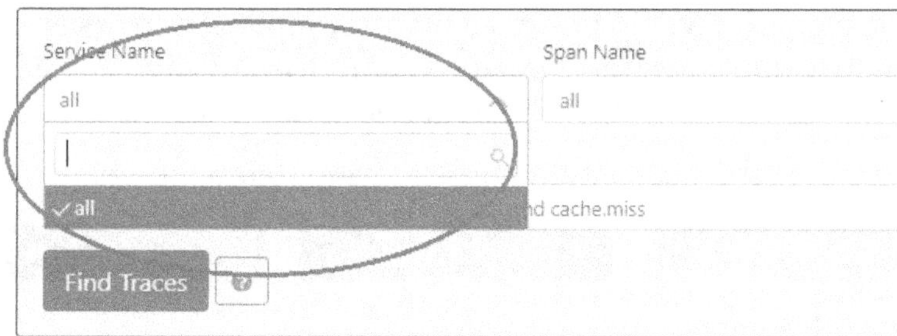

***Figure* 8.23**: *Zipkin UI*

Now you can launch Postman and make a request to *`doctor`* service as **http://localhost:8085/doctors/`1`.** As predicted, we received the response. But our focus is to trace the request. Re-visit the Zipkin UI and refresh the browser.

If you click the **Service Name** again, you will notice that the service names which are requested are listed as shown in *Figure* 8.24:

Select the **Service Name**, for which you want to accomplish the request tracing and click on **Find Traces**:

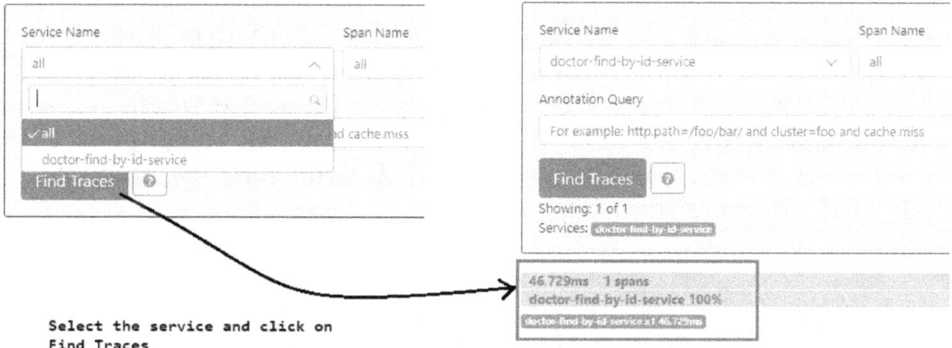

***Figure* 8.24**: *Finding the trace of service*

On clicking any entry, you can explore the detailed information about it. By default, Spring Boot does the sampling of only 10% *of requests* which prevents overwhelming the trace backend. However, we are starving to get all our requests traced.

The following configuration enables 100% *sampling* and every request is delivered to the trace backend:

```
management:
  tracing:
      sampling:
      probability: 1.0
```

In the current scenario, we do not have many complications, as it is a *standalone service*. Let us also add the configurations for **Actuator**, **Zipkin**, and **Micrometer** in **Hospital_Find_Doctors** and **API_Gateway_service**.

We are trying to set the ecosystem shown in the following image:

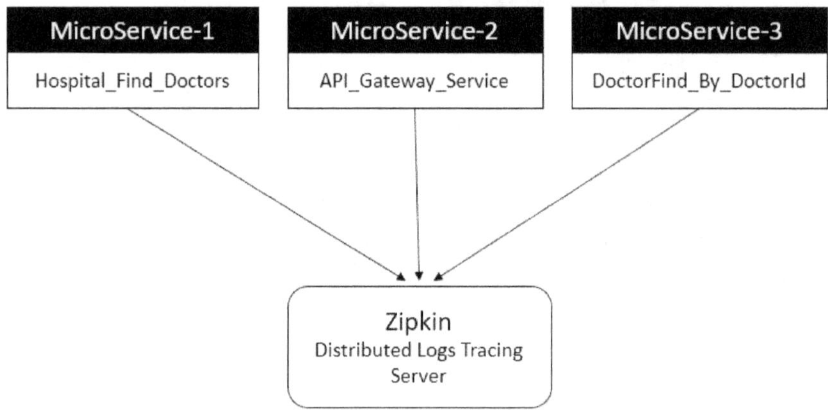

***Figure* 8.25**: *Zipkin ecosystem*

Make sure that you enable the actuator in every service that you intend to trace. Also, configure the sampling probability property and cross-check does the gateway service has the correct configuration of the route which we want to test. For the time being, you can disable the custom **MyLoggingFilter**. Once everything is set, launch Eureka, gateway API, **DoctorFind_by_DoctorId,** and **Hospital_Find_Doctors** services.

Note

We do not want to get confused with the cumulative Zipkin server output and want to observe the Zipkin console on every change. For this reason, on every change we will restart it. In practice, this is not recommended.

Now, access the hospitals endpoint via Gateway API service as **http://localhost:9097/hospitals/12345**.

Now, visit the `Zipkin UI` and refresh it. Notice that, instead of only one service, we are now getting all services in the dropdown. Select **api-gateway-service** and click on the **Find Traces**. Now click on the entry mentioned as follows to obtain the description as depicted in *Figure 8.26*:

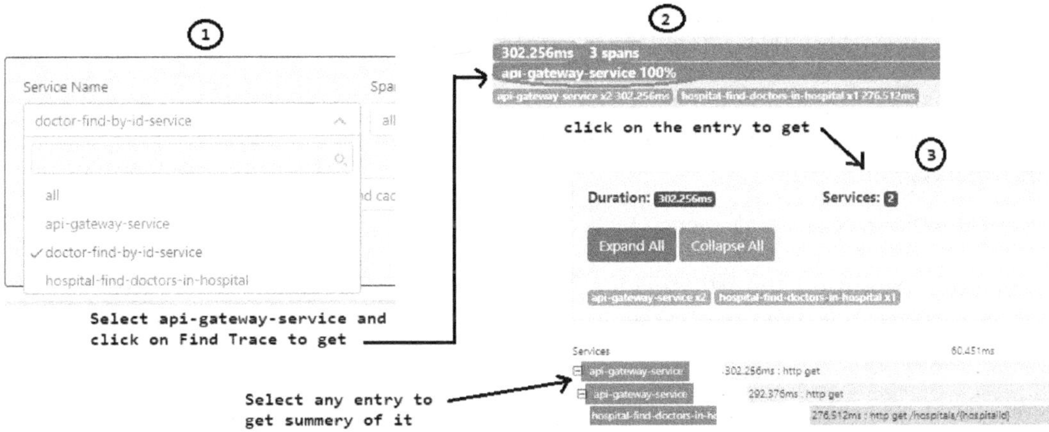

***Figure 8.26**: Obtaining the summary of services*

Hey, you can notice that the API service invokes the *hospital* and it invokes the *doctors*. We received the response, but *why the* ***doctor-find-by-id-service*** is *not available in the trace*? Indeed, *great observation!*

The request we made to the API service was then routed to the hospital service and then the *doctor's* service was requested using **RestTemplate**. Regretfully, it is not possible to trace the request made by the instance of a **RestTemplate**. If we intend to trace the request made by the **RestTemplate**, then instead of just creating the instance of the **RestTemplate** we need to build the instance using **RestTemplateBuilder**. It is a *helper* class which provides convenient methods for building and configuring and instances of the **RestTemplate**. Let us change our code in **Hospital_Find_Doctors** service to retrieve the instance of **RestTemplate** in the **MyConfiguration** class as:

```
@LoadBalanced
@Bean
public RestTemplate getRestTemplate(RestTemplateBuilder builder) {
      return builder.build();
}
```

Once, we modify the code let us restart the service. We haven't touched the controller code and there is no need to do so as well. We already have **hospital-balanced** endpoint mapped for the **findAllDoctorsInHospitals_loadBalanced()** method which uses the preceding configured instance. Let us now focus on API service. *Does our service have a route configured for `hospitals-balanced` endpoint?* No, we do not have it. Ideally, if you already have the configuration for a **hospital-balanced** endpoint, there is no need to modify anything in the code. However, as we do not have such a configuration, we need to add the following configuration under the gateway routes section:

```
- id: hospitals_balanced-route
  uri: http://localhost:9091/hospitals-balanced
  predicates:
  - Path=/hospitals-balanced/**
```

As we have modified the API service, we obviously need to restart it. Before you test endpoints ensure that all three services, Eureka server and Zipkin server are *up* and *running*.

Now, access **http://localhost:9097/hospitals-balanced/12345** URL from Postman. Once you receive a response, visit Zipkin UI. Notice that, now the *doctor*'s service is also listed as request tracing. You will receive the detailed tracing of any entry if you click it as shown in *Figure 8.27*:

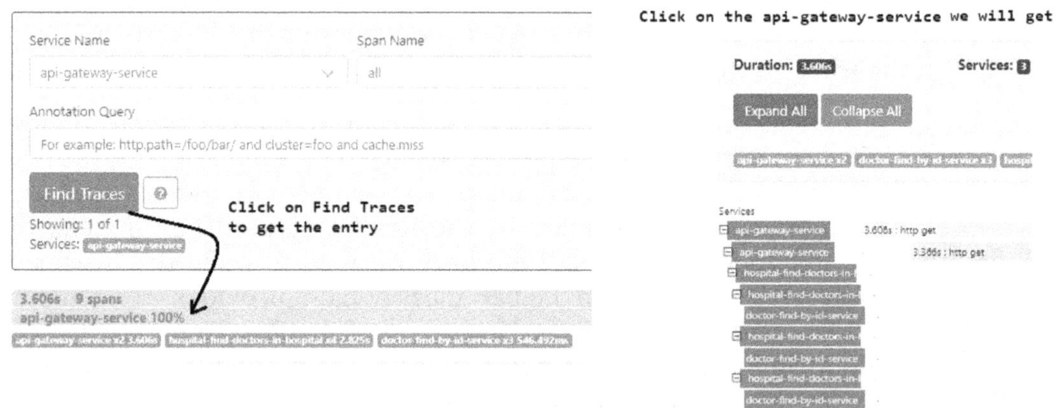

***Figure 8.27**: Registering the services in Zipkin*

Now, let us stop the *doctor's* service. And try accessing the same endpoint. Do not worry if you receive the response as **500** status code. Visit the Zipkin UI and search for the recent entry for **api-gateway-service**. You will notice that it is displayed in red color as shown in *Figure 8.28*:

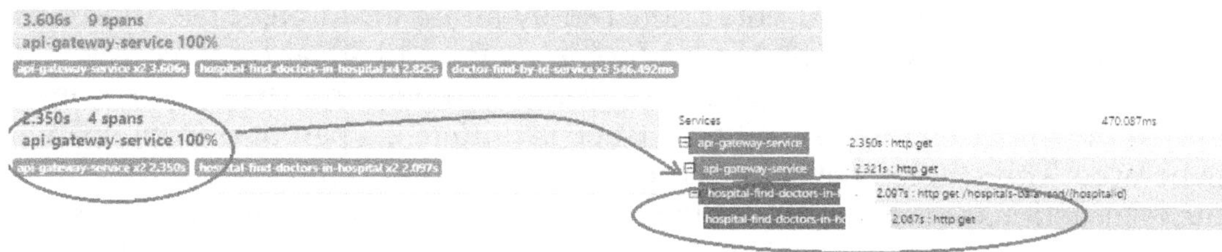

***Figure 8.28**: Status of the failed services*

Let's go one step ahead and click on **hospital-find-doctors-in-hospital** to get the following output:

hospital-find-doctors-in-hospital.http get: 2.067s

Services: hospital-find-doctors-in-hospital

Date Time	Relative Time	Annotation	Address
4/15/2023, 10:14:15 PM	48.437ms	Client Start	172.31.208.1 (hospital-find-doctors-in-hospital)
4/15/2023, 10:14:17 PM	2.115s	Client Finish	172.31.208.1 (hospital-find-doctors-in-hospital)

Key	Value
client.name	doctor-find-by-id-service
error	I/O error on GET request for "http://doctor-find-by-id-service/doctors/1": Connect to http://172.31.208.1:8085 [/172.31.208.1] failed: Connection refused: no further information
exception	ResourceAccessException
http.uri	http://doctor-find-by-id-service/doctors/1
method	GET
outcome	UNKNOWN
status	CLIENT_ERROR
uri	/doctors/{doctorId}

Show IDs

traceId	643ad45fc845f9125d5d90abe9e7dd59
spanId	4d510e7751b40019
parentId	444128ab9c3160ec

***Figure 8.29**: Tracing the details of failed service*

It justifies clearly *why we received the status code 500 as a response*. Additionally, we also received the information that the service is down for some reason. Notice the IDs in the preceding figure. *How do they get associated, what is the process, and what is the working of distributed tracing*? Let us explore that.

Internal working of tracing

A **trace** is a set of related events triggered by an input. In our case, the trace is generated when we access the endpoint. Every individual trace consists of multiple spans. Each of the spans represents an operation that is performed due to the initiating request. When a trace is *initiated*, a parent or root span is generated. This trace encapsulates the entire end-to-end transactions. If any of the transactions comprises multiple inter-service communication, a child span is created for each of the services. When this operation is broken down further, then each descendant is considered as a *grandchild span*. As discussed in the terminology, the **span** is a hierarchical tree structure that starts from the *root span*, with descendants for each dependent inter-service communication. At the time of root span generation, it is assigned a *context* or *identifier*, which is then propagated to each child span. Along with the identifier each span also records the *start* and *end* time of the operation. It may also contain *optional* additional attributes, such as the service instance identifier. This allows us to identify *every request*, the *request call*, and a particular transaction in which they occurred followed by the time taken at each stage.

Note

To add `spanId` and `traceId` to the log, we can add the property `logging.pattern.level = %5p[${spring.application.name:},%X{traceId:-},%X{spanId:-}]` in the configuration

Conclusion

In this chapter, we discussed different approaches to monitoring the microservice-based application. We learned how to utilize the services of actuator to check the status of our application. While discussing this, we studied different endpoints provided by Actuator which provide details about the **audit events**, **beans**, **conditions**, **configprops**, and so on. We also studied that we can even customize the behavior of pre-existing endpoints of the actuator. Additionally, we explored the different ways to implement observability such as **Loggers**, **Metrics**, and so on. At the end, we delved into the concept of distributed tracing. While we did not discuss the Micrometer in great detail, we discussed thoroughly how to work with Zipkin for distributed tracing.

In the next chapter, we will explore how to ensure that the microservices are reliable. We will learn how to ensure that our services are not failing.

Chapter 9
Reliability

"*Tejaswini*, I don't think it's going to work", *Manish* approached me furiously. He was *angry*, *frustrated*, and more than that he was disappointed. I asked him, "*What happened?* You were so elated yesterday, when we had the conversion. *What happened suddenly?*" He sat in front of me and said, "*We transformed our application from monolithic to microservices. Correct?*" I replied, "Yes, *that's true*". He asked, "*Why?*" I was in a dilemma. I wasn't sure about the sudden change in this demeanor. I was completely clueless. Why is he raising this question now? I replied, "Of course, it is easy to develop, and reuse. You can modify it whenever required. Additionally, we can leverage the feature of high availability of microservices as well." He jumped in his chair, "*Exactly! They should be available all the time and provide the service for which they are designed. But in reality, we can't predict real-world issues. We rigorously performed testing. But ultimately, we are human beings. We can't anticipate every situation, under which our service may fail to perform the services. Tejaswini, we were under the impression that we tested against everything, against every odd. Still, sometimes we are facing occasional issues and observing that some instances are unavailable. On one hand, we are happy that the unavailable instances are being restored to the 'live state', but on the other hand, the requests that are received by those unavailable instances are failing. And that's quite a number. We simply can't afford it. My team and I were thinking that if we have multiple instances of the services which follow SRP, it should be reliable. But our assumption was incorrect. What should we do now?*"

"*Manish*, we can only expect that all services will be *up* and in the *running* state all the time. But you said it *right*, that real-world scenarios could be very *unpredictable*. It is almost impossible to comprehend every cause of the failure. When they failed, we can handle them by *exception handling*, or *ensure to log* that as well. But, instead of raising the exception and then asking the client to deal with it, *wouldn't it be good to just hold the request for some more time till the result is prepared? Or instead of dealing with exceptions, can we try to send the request more than once?*", I responded to Manish.

With a cheerful note, Manish exclaimed, "Yes! That will alleviate most of our concerns."

To achieve this, we need services to be equipped with reliability. This can be accomplished by implementing **circuit breakers** in the services.

Structure

In this chapter, we are going to study the following topics:

- Understanding microservice reliability and its importance
- Reasons for service failure
- Approaches to handle failure
- Circuit Breaker Design Pattern
- Resilience4J as a savior

We started this journey by discussing monolithic applications. We can't stop considering this architecture whenever we discuss microservices. We were having some hiccups and we decided to move on with a new partner. The most important among many reasons was we were willing to have our services up all the time. Earlier it was a myth, but now it's possible. I guess before discussing how to make it let's start with the meaning of reliability in microservices and its importance.

Understanding microservice reliability and its importance

We had an application. Instead of discussing the complexities that occur during development, let us take into consideration the post-deployment disasters. I said disasters not because I don't want to criticize them. It's because when something goes *wrong debugging*, *identifying*, *correcting*, and then *pushing* it into the production environment takes a long time with enormous complexity.

Though for years we were using it, suddenly we started feeling the size of monoliths causing issues. I will consider when we want to hit down a mammoth and we don't have a canon/mortar. Instead of hitting and getting him down in one shot, we will start hitting it part by part. And the same thing we are dealing with in microservices. As the piece of application is *independent* and the memory requirement will be *less* and the task it is going to deal with will be *limited.* This means the service is going to handle very less requests as compared to the monolith. And that makes the service less loaded, *less work equally proportional to fewer chances of being overwhelmed to serve more requests.*

But sometimes the situation gets beyond our control and service starts feeling unhealthy. We all know and understand it's not just about the service; the service might be used by many other services and when one does not feel well many others do the same. It's not about why; it's all about the reason for which we are choosing microservices architecture. Now, the question is *why is it so important to be reliable?*

As already discussed, a couple of times, we develop microservices that follow SRP, we don't want to invest the time again and again to develop the same kind of solution. So, we as developers choose the available services which will be able to provide us with the solution. The whole ecosystem is based upon collaboration. If I am not wrong, most of the time to fulfill the request the services collaborate with *one-to-many downstream* services to produce the final response. Now, if collaboration is the backbone, I don't have to tell you what will happen if it breaks. You all can predict that for yourself. We expect services to be up 100% *times*. However, we can just anticipate it, in reality, the behavior of the service is unpredictable. The services that are available 100% *times* is a myth. They might be either busy serving other requests, talking to the database, or, even talking to other resources, and it just continues. We want our services to have the ability to stand robust against all the odds and then bounce back from the issue. We expect our services to be resilient.

Reasons for service failures

We expect our services to be available all time in order to label them as reliable. Before discussing the failures, we need to understand what do we understand by failure. *What does it mean by service failure? When are we going to say the service failed to serve?* The service is said to be in the phase of failure when it is not able to perform the promised task. After failing, the service starts recovering. It tries to get back on track to serve but still, it doesn't start serving the request in normal ways. We can implement most of the measures to handle the situation to ensure that service will not fail. But, even after all our attempts to make it reliable, the service might *fail.* In such cases, we can provide helping hands by deploying additional service instances. Of course, there are other ways to deal with *failures*, which we will discuss in due course of time. For now, let us focus on the reasons for the service failures one by one.

Overloaded traffic

The major reason for service failure is the **request overload**. We can identify the usual traffic which any service handles. During *production*, the memory will be allocated to the service which is used to handle the load. However, occasionally the service receives more requests than expected. Such requests will be queued and handled sequentially. The situation persists till the threshold where the requests exceed the response and the load becomes overwhelming. This causes service to respond slowly and ultimately that may *fail*.

Unavailability of resources

The service usually communicates with the *database* or LDAP *servers* or **Kafka** or **RabbitMQ** or a combination of them. These *third-party services* are located on a separate dedicated server. Occasionally, these services are busy serving others or they may take more time to respond. In the worst situation, these services are unavailable and our service can't reach them. As our services are tightly coupled with them, the unavailability of these services impact on normal working of our services and they may *fail* to serve.

Deployment strategies

The best and ideal situation is to deploy a service per host or an instance per host with sufficient memory. But, it's too ideal and in practice, we usually adopt the strategy of utilizing a single host which hosts multiple service instances. When we have one service that takes more time, sometimes it starts utilizing more resources than normal, and because of this other services will thrive for the required resources. In case, the service keeps the *resources allocated*, other services may require *more memory to execute* and the *memory is unavailable* then that will cause issues.

Unavailability of services

Third-party resource failure is one of the causes of failure. At the same time, as we follow SRP each service has its dedicated responsibility. Many times, the service requires help from *one or more services* to serve the request. On normal days, we might be fortunate to be served quickly by all the services. But, sometimes one of the downstream services is busy serving another request. This causes queuing up of our service and our service may face failure. Additionally, if there are more than one downstream microservices to invoke sequentially, there is a possibility that one or more services take more time due to logical execution or resource communication. This can ultimately cause the failure of our service.

The availability of *third parties*, *resource allocation*, or *memory requirement* can be managed separately and the developer doesn't have a big role to play in it. But that's not true in the case of unavailable downstream services. As we know pretty well, services communicate with each other very often either with the help of **RestTemplate** or the Feign client. If the communication is smooth, it will impact the response. And this is a major cause of service failure which is a direct impact of unavailability of the services. A developer can play a major role to handle the situation.

It is curious to know, who in development desires their code to fail. Indeed, No *one! Why would someone desire their efforts to be wasted?* A developer always wishes to develop a long surviving code. The same is *true* for our microservices as well. We must develop it in such a way that it will stand by its commitment of always being available! But in reality, it may *fail* and we may require to *modify* the code if the failure is because of the code. We might need to check the configuration if the failure is due to the environment. In the chatper 8: Observabillity, we have already taken the measures to elucidate the failures along with their causes and pinpoint the location of the same. Once we have the knowledge about it, we need to focus on how to recover from this failure. Let me clarify a crucial point before we proceed with the discussion. There is no inherently right or wrong approach. It may work for us in a given scenario and we may adopt it. But be careful about the long runs. Don't get settled with short-term solutions, think about the future and take action. Here are some common approaches which we can adapt to handle the failures.

Approaches to handle failures

There are different approaches that we can adopt to handle the failure are discussed in the upcoming subsections.

Handling third-party services

Our services heavily rely on the *persisted data*, *messaging servers*, file *handling servers*, and so on. We need to ensure these services must be UP and running all the time. Whenever possible try to set up the cluster, to avoid *failures*. The cluster enables the high availability of these *third-party services*. Even if one of the nodes fails, it gets replaced by the sub-ordinate node. In terms of the persistence layer, setting up a cluster is one approach. Additionally, we need to be careful about the data it stores. It is a very important asset and must be preserved properly. Usually, data backup strategies save us from data loss.

Hardware

Our microservices will be deployed somewhere; may it be a server maintained by us or some cloud provider. Ultimately, it is a system that runs on top of the hardware. It is a mechanical part that may get *non-functional* at any moment due to *electricity fluctuations*, *natural calamities*, *overheating*, *improper handling*, and many more. We must try to avoid all such scenarios by setting up our systems in a controlled environment. We can also install the instances of our services in different locations which are physically separated from each other, to ensure that all the systems will not face the same issue for hardware failure.

Setting up instances

High availability is the commitment to service and we must stand by it. Failures are *unavoidable* and also *unpredictable*. One instance may get overburdened by multiple requests. The load will be *distributed*, if we have more than one instance of the same service also, the performance will be enhanced. We need to ensure that such instances are launched in separate regions, to avoid failures due to environmental reasons. We will discuss the deployment strategies in detail in our upcoming chapters. However, we need to also consider that we are not talking about *one* or *two* services, we are talking about a bunch of services. Each one of them has minimum of *two* instances. Additionally, we also have a **discovery server**, **Config client server**, and **API service**, the list is *countless*. It is unrealistic for any human to handle all this alone. Even if we have a team of technocrats, it is still pretty complex and difficult. So, we have to consider the tools to automate all this. We will be discussing it as well, but the point here is we need a *plan* and *system* in place.

Exceptions and their handling

Microservices normally *fail* due to hardware and we already discussed how to deal with it. Apart from this, microservices are also dependent on the input they receive from client requests. A *service* may expect a typical data type, or may have conversion in place for certain scenarios. Additionally, it may also have the validation applied to the data. If any of the component of this is not in place, it will cause an exception. Also, if the *third-party services* are not available and the response from these services is not timely it leads to exceptions. Sometimes, in the worst scenarios, these services are unavailable and we may end up with more and more *exceptions*.

The best way to deal with it is to implement an *exception handling mechanism*. This will lead the client in the proper direction along with the reason why he is not getting the expected response. We already have discussed exception handling in *Chapter 2, Decipher the Unintelligible*, under the section, *Exception Handling in the* REST.

Our services normally follow SRP. Along with this we also design the services in such a way that they will be *re-usable*. We already discussed the concept of inter-service communication earlier. We were in learning mode and discussed the ideal situations where the downstream services are available. At that time, we did not consider the possibility of the service with whom we are communicating is being unavailable. But if our service response is dependent on the response from *downstream service*, we will be in a *mess*. Our intention is not to just inform the client of the status code or the exception that had occurred and ask them to re-send a request after some time. What is expected is, we handle that using *exception handling*. But the approach of exception handling is different; it is not identical to traditional exception handling. This is accomplished by circuit breakers, which we are going to discuss in detail in our next section.

Circuit breaker design pattern

Our services being SRP collaborate with other services while handling the requests. As we know, service communication can be **synchronous** or **asynchronous**. When our service synchronously communicates with other service the failure chances are high as the other service might be unavailable or take unexpectedly more time to respond. Such situation is tough to handle. The service which received the request is waiting for another service to respond and before the earlier service is served another request starts bombarding. It might lead to *resource exhaustion*. And we might end up with failure. Our service has no issue. However, due to the cascading to other non-responding services we are facing the failure.

We will take *two* services here into consideration. The *first service* acts as a client which raises the request and the *other* is a service that receives the *raised requests* and *serves the response*. A service acting as the client should invoke the downstream service via a proxy which will work similarly to an electrical circuit breaker. When we switch on the circuit the electricity flows and when the switch is off it stops. In our services, as well when the number of *back-to-back failures* crosses a threshold then the circuit breaker trips. Then, for the duration of the *timeout period*, all the consecutive attempts to invoke the downstream service will fail immediately. Once the timeout expires, then the circuit breaker allows a limited number of requests to pass through, which we call **test requests**. If the *test requests succeed*, then the circuit breaker resumes the normal operation. If not, then the timeout period is initiated again. The pattern provides the solution to prevent *network* or *service* failure, which occurs due to cascading calls to other services. It makes the services resilient against failures. Accept that, services will *fail*. But the resilience feature will make them *bounce* back. *Figure* 9.1 displays different states of circuit breaker as **Closed**, **Open**, and **Half Open**:

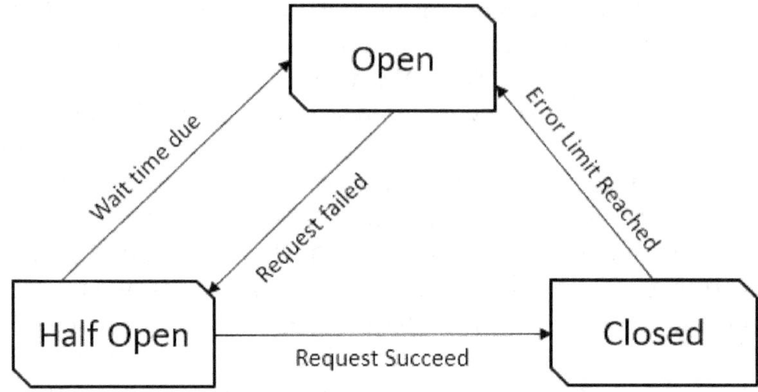

***Figure* 9.1**: *States in circuit breaker*

- **Closed**: When the service requests another service which is *up* and it receives an appropriate *response* then the circuit breaker remains in the *Closed* state and all the calls to that microservice will go normally. When the calls *fail back-to-back* and exceed a *threshold* that is set by us, then the circuit breaker goes into the next state, the *Open* state.
- **Open**: When the circuit breaker returns an *error* for calls without successfully executing the call it is called an *Open* state.
- **Half-Open**: Once the configured timeout period is over the circuit breaker switches to a state known as *Half-Open* state. It checks whether the problem with the client service still exists. Here, even if a single call fails in the *Half-Open* state, then the breaker will trip once again to an *Open* state. And in case, the call succeeds then the circuit breaker will be reset back to the *normal* state, that is, the *Closed* state.

Types of circuit breaker

Circuit breakers are classified as **time based circuit breaker** and **count based circuit breaker**. Let us discuss both one by one:

- **Time based**: The *time-based circuit breaker* switches from a *Closed* state to an *Open* state when it tries to communicate to another service and it fails for the *last* N *time unit* or it *fails* because of *timeout*.
- **Count based**: The *count-based circuit breaker* switches from the *Closed* state to an *Open* state when the service keeps on requesting N *times*, however, the requests have *failed* or *timeout*.

I believe you have very well understood the issue in interservice communication and how to handle it with the circuit breaker design pattern. It is the time to implement it. But before starting with implementation, we need to discuss the Spring Boot support for the circuit breaker.

The project **Spring Cloud Circuit Breaker** comprises the implementations for **Resilience4J**, **Spring Retry**, and **Sentinel**. All the APIs implemented from the Spring Cloud Circuit Breaker are *live* in the Spring Cloud Commons. Based on the type of application and the implementation we need to include the starters.

We will be using *Resilience4J-based* implementation. You need to include one of the following starters for application:

- If the application is *non-reactive* **include org.springframework.cloud:spring-cloud-starter-circuitbreaker-resilience4j** as the starter.
- If the application is *reactive* include **org.springframework.cloud:spring-cloud-starter-circuitbreaker-reactor-resilience4j** as the starter.

Once we include any one of these starters it enables the Resilience4j. In case we intend to *disable* the auto-configuration, we need to set the property **spring.cloud.circuitbreaker.resilience4j.enabled** to, **false**.

Note

The `Spring Cloud Hystrix` project is now deprecated and new applications will not be able to use it. We have Resilience4j as a new option for implementing the circuit breaker.

Resilience4J as a savior

We have **Resilience4J** as a new option for implementing the circuit breaker. It is a *lightweight library* to enable *fault tolerance*. It is designed based on **Java 8** and hence supports functional programming. It provides higher-order decorators to enhance any functional interface, Lambda expression, or method reference using **Circuit Breaker**, **Rate Limiter**, **Retry**, or **Bulkhead** implementations. It is possible to use more than one decorator on any functional interface, Lambda expression, or method reference. The beauty is we need to just select decorators and everything else is provided to us.

The Resilience4j provides **TimeLimiter**, **Bulkhead**, **Retry**, **RateLimiter**, and **Circuit Breakers** as decorators. So, let us discuss them one by one:

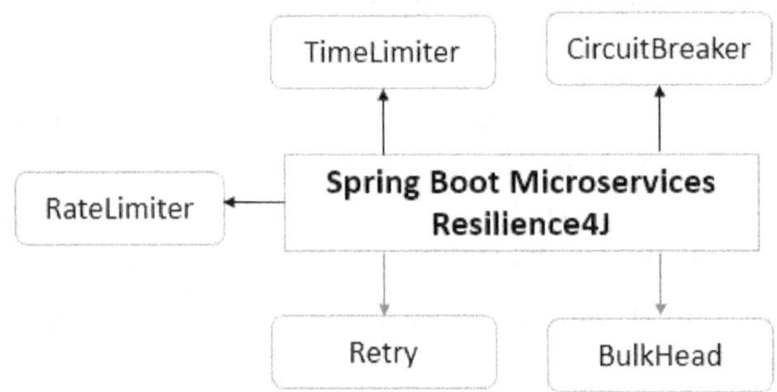

Figure 9.2: *Decorators of Resilience4J*

Circuit breaker

This is the same which we already discussed in the circuit breaker design pattern with three states viz: *Closed*, *Half-Open*, and *Open*. The circuit breaker uses a sliding window which stores and then aggregates the outcome of the calls. We can choose between a *count based* and a *time-based sliding* window. The outcome of the *last* N *calls* gets aggregated in the *count-based sliding window* and the outcome of the calls of the last N *seconds* will be aggregated in the *time-based sliding window*.

- **The count-based sliding window**: The **count-based sliding window** is implemented using a circular array with N *measurements*. When the count window size is 5, then the circular array always has 5 *measurements*. Incrementally, the sliding window updates a *total aggregation*. This total aggregation is updated when a new call outcome gets recorded. Now on the basis of subtract on *Evict principle*, when the oldest measurement is evicted, it is subtracted from the *total aggregation* and then the bucket is *reset*.

- **The time-based sliding window**: The **time-based sliding window** is implemented with a circular array having N *partial aggregations* or *buckets*. When the time window size is 10 *seconds*, then the circular array always has 10 *partial aggregations*. Every bucket aggregates the outcome of all calls that take place in a certain period of seconds. And the head bucket of the circular array stores the call outcomes from the current *epoch* second. We also have the other partial aggregations which store the outcome from the call in the previous seconds. The sliding window does not store call outcomes individually. However, it incrementally updates the *partial aggregations* and the *total aggregation*. The total aggregation gets updated incrementally when a new call outcome is recorded. The bucket is *reset* by subtracting the partial total aggregation of that bucket from the total aggregation and the bucket is reset. This takes place when the oldest bucket is *evicted*.

Failure rate and low call rate thresholds

As discussed already, the state of the circuit breaker changes from *Closed* to *Open* state when the request failure rate is either *equal* to or *greater* than the value of the threshold which we have configured. We also need to know that, by default whenever any exception occurs, it is counted as a *failure*. So, in case we don't wish to consider some kind of exceptions as failures then we can define a list of exceptions that should count as a failure. Once we configure the list then all other exceptions will be treated as a *success*. The exceptions can also be ignored so that such exceptions will neither be counted as a *failure* nor as a *success*. When the percentage of slow calls is equal to or greater than a configurable threshold then also the circuit breaker changes its state from *Closed* to *Open*. This enables the load reduction on an external system when it is just facing more request load and still is *responsive*.

One can calculate the *failure rate* and *slow call rate* when a minimum number of calls were recorded. For example, if the minimum number of required calls is 10, then at least 10 *calls* must be recorded, before which the failure rate can be calculated. If only 9 *calls* have been evaluated the circuit breaker will not trip to *Open*, even if all 9 *calls* have failed.

Circuit breaker with RestTemplate

Let us attempt to use circuit breaker in our code. Before we start ensure that you have included the actuator dependency and **spring-cloud-starter-circuitbreaker-resilience4j** in the **pom.xml** file.

We have the following scenario:

```
Hopital_FindDoctors service-----> DoctorFind_By_DoctorId service
```

Under ideal scenarios, the call from **Hospital_FindDoctors** would be able to make a successful call to the **DoctorFind_By_DoctorId** service and the response received will be sent to the client. But, *what if the* ***DoctorFind_by_DoctorId*** *is not responsive*? Obviously, the exception will be generated. To verify the *real-*

time scenario, we can simply stop the **DoctorFind_By_DoctorId** service and make the call to it:

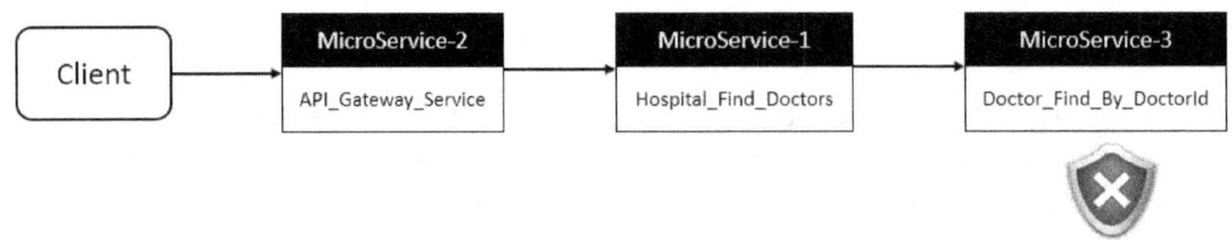

***Figure* 9.3**: *Flow of inter-communicating microservices*

When **DoctorFind_By_DoctorId** service is unavailable and it fails to *respond.* This failure gets propagated and the entire application *goes down.* We are using microservices which are *fine-grained* services having their responsibility. This means even if we have a partial failure or fault or exception in one or more of these inter communicating services that should not bring down the entire application.

Let's update the system to make it *fault tolerant.*

To begin with, we must add **resilience4j** dependency in the application. In our case, we are adding this dependency to the **Hospital_Find_Doctors** service. Ensure to add the same in every service where we intend to facilitate fault tolerance.

Here we are duplicating an existing endpoint **/hospitals-balanced**. There is no need to modify the business logic. But to track all the code conceptually we are going to add a new endpoint **/hospitals-circuit-breaker** with **@CircuitBreaker** annotation as shown in the following code:

```
@CircuitBreaker(name = "circuit-breaker-for-doctor")
@GetMapping("/hospitals-circuit-breaker/{hospitalId}")
ResponseEntity<Hospital> findAllDoctorsInHospitals_cricuitBreaker
                        (@PathVariable int hospitalId) {
  List<Doctor> doctors = new ArrayList<>();
  Hospital hospital = repo.findHospitalById(hospitalId);
  if (hospital != null) {
        List<Integer> doctor_ids = repo.findDoctorIds(hospitalId);
        for (int i = 0; i < doctor_ids.size(); i++) {
             ResponseEntity<Doctor> entity = restTemplate.getForEntity(
               "http://doctor-find-by-id-service/doctors/{doctorId}",
               Doctor.class, doctor_ids.get(i));
```

```
            if (entity.getStatusCode().equals(HttpStatus.OK)) {
                                doctors.add(entity.getBody());
            }
        }
        hospital.setDoctors(doctors);
        return new ResponseEntity<Hospital>(hospital, HttpStatus.OK);
  }
  return new ResponseEntity<Hospital>(HttpStatus.NO_CONTENT);
}
```

You don't have to create a new endpoint. Just update the earlier method **findAllDoctorsInHospitals()** mapped for **@GetMapping("/hospitals/{hospitalId}")** endpoint by applying the **@CircuitBreaker** annotation. We already had set up the *fault tolerance* mechanism by these steps. Our circuit breaker is all set. But now to switch between the *states* we need to set some properties. Let us add the following properties to start with:

```
resilience4j.circuitbreaker.instances.circuit-breaker-for-doctor.
                                                   failure-rate-threshold=50
resilience4j.circuitbreaker.instances.circuit-breaker-for-doctor.
                                                   minimum-number-of-calls=5
```

The property **failure-rate-threshold=80**, indicates that, if 50% *of requests* made by the client are getting *failed* then open the circuit which will make the circuit b reaker state to change from *Closed* to *Open*. In the configuration, we used **circuit-breaker-for-doctor** which is the **name** attribute of the **@CircuitBreaker** annotation.

We can also set the property **minimum-number-of-calls=5,** which indicates that to calculate the *failure rate threshold*, we need at least 5 *calls*.

Let's try this first. We need to make the requests to hospital service by accessing **/hospitals-circuit-breaker/{hospitalId}** endpoint. But here the request making is a bit different, as we aim to observe the change in the circuit breaker's state. As per the configuration, the state will change from *Closed* to *Open*, if 50% *of the requests* made by us are failed. Also, to calculate the threshold, the system has to get a *minimum of* 5 *concurrent calls*. So, execute the **Hospitial_FindDoctors** service and access the enabled endpoint with the circuit breaker for *minimum of* 7-8 *times*. While making the calls observe approximate the response time. You will observe the *first* 5 *requests* take significant time to respond but then onwards we are receiving a comparatively quick response. The *first* 5 *requests* were made to **/hospitals-circuit-breaker/{hospitalId}**. You tried to call the downstream **DoctorFind_By_DoctorId** service. In terms of circuit breaker, this is a *Closed* state and that's why calls have been made. After that our condition of threshold calculation is made, the threshold is calculated which obviously is 100% *way* more than the configured value. It means now the circuit breaker state will be changed from *Closed* to *Open*. We can certainly prove this change in the state. Let us open the console for **HospitalFind_Doctors** service and observe the description of the most recent exception as shown in *Figure* 9.4:

```
io.github.resilience4j.circuitbreaker.CallNotPermittedException: CircuitBreaker 'circuit-breaker-for-doctor' is OPEN and does not permit further calls
	at io.github.resilience4j.circuitbreaker.CallNotPermittedException.createCallNotPermittedException(CallNotPermittedException.java:48) ~[resilien
```

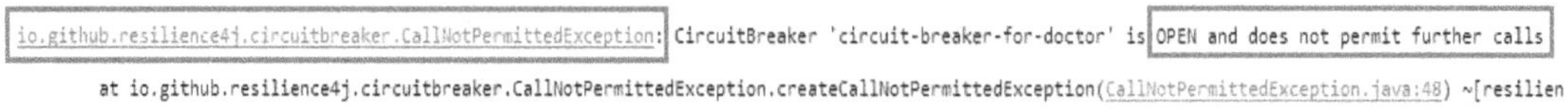

Figure 9.4: *Exception for Open State*

The state is *Open* and no more calls to the downstream will be made. The circuit breaker rejects all further calls made with a **CallNotPermittedException** as shown in *Figure* 9.4 when it is in *Open* state. That's the reason all the subsequent calls made by us from the *6th request* onwards received a *quick* response.

Once the wait time duration is over the circuit breaker state will change from *Open* to *Half Open* and permits the further call. You can just wait for 30 *sec* before making the request to verify the exception **org.apache.hc.client5.http. HttpHostConnectException** which says the call to downstream had been made.

We can also configure how many calls we need to make to observe if the backend is still unavailable or has become available again. After that further calls will be rejected with a **CallNotPermittedException** until all permitted calls have been completed.

You can again give a try to requests consecutively 7-8 *times* to the **/hospitals-circuit-breaker/{hospitalId}** endpoint. Notice the console stacktrace to ensure that we received *Open state*. Return and make a request to the same endpoint. Yes, we need to wait more, access the console and observe the stacktrace. You will notice the exception **org.apache.hc.client5.http.HttpHostConnectException**. And *why is it trying to connect downstream*? As the wait period is over, it can verify if the service is available.

We are repeating the process again and again because that is the only way we can explore *threshold*, *minimum calls* or *permitted-number-of-calls-in-half-open-state*.

Right now, we have not set up any more properties. So, let us set the *permitted-number-of-calls* and other properties as follows:

```
resilience4j.circuitbreaker.instances.circuit-breaker-for-doctor.wait-
            duration-in-open-state=10s
resilience4j.circuitbreaker.instances.circuit-breaker-for-doctor.
            permitted-number-of-calls-in-half-open-state=3
resilience4j.circuitbreaker.instances.circuit-breaker-for-doctor.
            sliding-window-size=10
resilience4j.circuitbreaker.instances.circuit-breaker-for-doctor.
            sliding-window-type=COUNT_BASED
resilience4j.circuitbreaker.instances.circuit-breaker-for-doctor.
            automatic-transition-from-open-to-half-open-enabled=true
```

Here we have set up **sliding-window-type=COUNT_BASED** to indicate that we are using a **COUNT_BASED** sliding window. We can also use **TIME_BASED** sliding window. **The automatic-transition-from-open-to-half-open-enabled=true** is used to ensure the states will switch to *Half-Open* rather than directly shifting from the *Open* state to the *Closed* state. The property **permitted-number-of-calls-in-half-open-state=1**, indicates that when the circuit breaker is in *Half-Open* state, consider *sending 3 requests* to downstream. If 50% *of them* are failing, then switch back to *Open* state. Finally, we have **wait-duration-in-open-state=1s** property which indicates the *waiting time interval* to switch between the *Open* state and the *Closed* state is **1sec**.

We can now restart the service and try executing the requests. It will mostly work on the same pattern as we discussed earlier but with a major change. This time once the state is shifted to *Open*, then 3 *requests* will be sent to downstream to identify whether the downstream service is available on the server or *not*.

The shift in between the states can also be observed using the actuator. That's why we have included the actuator dependency in the service. Before observing, please ensure that you have enabled the endpoints as:

```
management.endpoints.web.exposure.include=*
```

Additionally, we can manage the *health-related information* of circuit breakers using the following property:

```
management.health.circuitbreakers.enabled=true
```

Now, restart the application and access the **/actuator** endpoint to obtain the information as:

```
"circuitbreakers-name": {
    "href": "http://localhost:9091/actuator/circuitbreakers/{name}",
    "templated": true
},
"circuitbreakers": {
    "href": "http://localhost:9091/actuator/circuitbreakers",
    "templated": false
},
"circuitbreakerevents-name-eventType": {
    "href": "http://localhost:9091/actuator/circuitbreakerevents/{name}/{eventType}",
    "templated": true
},
"circuitbreakerevents-name": {
    "href": "http://localhost:9091/actuator/circuitbreakerevents/{name}",
    "templated": true
},
"circuitbreakerevents": {
    "href": "http://localhost:9091/actuator/circuitbreakerevents",
    "templated": false
},
```

Figure 9.5: *endpoints /actuator*

Let us explore the state in the very beginning before we start requesting the endpoint as shown in *Figure* 9.6:

Figure 9.6: *Actuator endpoints for circuitbreakers*

Now access **http://localhost:9091/hospitals-circuit-breaker/12345** endpoint for 6 *to* 7 *times* consecutively, and revisit **actuator/circuitbreakers**, and observe the change in the state as shown in *Figure* 9.7:

Figure 9.7: *Failed endpoint and its circuitbreaker state*

The first part of the image shows the transition from *Open* state to *Half-Open* state after **10sec**. When we make a couple of calls, the second part of the image shows the *failed* calls.

In this way, we can manage the circuit breaker. But what if instead of returning the exception we intend to return some values after switching to Open state? We can also achieve that.

So, the task is, we wish to return some logical value when the downstream is down. This will be enabled by the attribute **fallbackMethod** of the **@CircuitBreaker** annotation. This attribute accepts the *name of the method* which will be invoked and execute some logic to generate the response for the client request.

Let us update our earlier annotation as:

```
@CircuitBreaker(name = "circuit-breaker-for-doctor",
   fallbackMethod = "getDoctorFallback")
```

Now, we must declare this method. The method signature must be as that of the method which we have annotated by the **@CircuitBreaker**. And make sure to have the trailing argument of type **Exception** as shown in the following code:

```
public ResponseEntity<Hospital> getDoctorFallback(int hospitalId,
                                                   Exception e) {
  Hospital hospital = repo.findHospitalById(hospitalId);
  if (hospital != null) {
      return new ResponseEntity<Hospital>(hospital, HttpStatus.OK);
  }
  return new ResponseEntity<Hospital>(HttpStatus.NO_CONTENT);
}
```

The logic totally depends on the scenario which a developer is handling.

Let us try it. Please make sure you have the Eureka server, **Hospital_FindDoctors** and **Zipkin** server are *up* and *running*. Once you have this setup, initiate the request. In Postman, let us initiate the request and observe the response as shown in *Figure* 9.8:

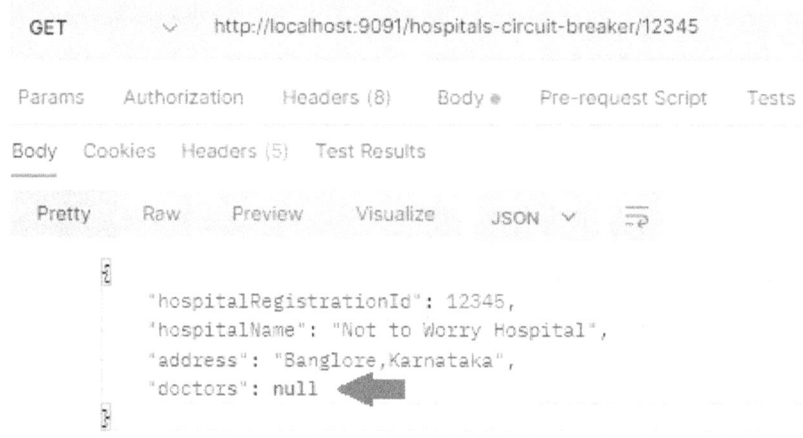

***Figure* 9.8**: *Working of fallback method*

Notice that, there is no more 500 *Internal server* error received as a response is generated from the exception handler. We obtained the response from the fallback method. When the client requests **/hospitals-circuit-breaker/{hospitalId}** endpoint, it tries to connect to the downstream **DoctorFind_By_DoctorId** instance to obtain doctor details. As the downstream is unavailable, an exception will be generated. But as we have specified **fallbackAttribute** in the @ **CircuitBreaker** annotation, it will call the method associated with that and the response will be generated from it.

We have just used **@CircuitBreaker** annotation, which facilitates us to change the state of the circuit depending on the availability of the downstream services.

If the downstream services are *down*, instead of throwing exceptions it uses an exception handling mechanism to generate custom response for the client.

This is so good. Isn't it? But, if you have noticed, we have used a circuit breaker as a fault tolerant mechanism with **RestTemplate**. Does it mean we can't use it with the Feign Client? Or do we need to take a different approach to implement it?

Circuit breaker with FeignClient

Feign Client supports *fault tolerance*. In order to enable the fault tolerance, we need to add **Spring Cloud Circuit Breaker** dependency in the class path. Additionally, we need to also set the property **spring.cloud.openfeign.circuitbreaker.enabled** to **true**. Once we set this, Feign will equip all the methods with a circuit breaker. In case we want to enable the Spring Cloud Circuit Breaker group, we need to set the **spring.cloud.openfeign.circuitbreaker.group.enabled** property to **true**, as the default value of this property is **false**.

So, let us use it for our Feign Client. Here, we will be using fault tolerance with a **fallback** method for the Feign Client. The very first thing you need to ensure that circuit breaker dependency is available on the *class path*, and we already have that. Now, we need to add the support of circuit breaker to the Feign Client by adding the configuration. Additionally, we also will be adding a **fallback** method.

Let's first add the **fallback** method as:

```
@FeignClient(name="doctor-find-by-id-service",
        fallback = FeignClient_FallBack.class)
```

The **fallback** method which will be invoked after the *failure*, is provided by the **FeignClient_FallBack** class. So let us add it. The class simply implements the Feign Client interface and overrides the methods from it as shown in the following code:

```
@Component
public class FeignClient_FallBack implements Hospital_Doctor_Feign{
@Override
public ResponseEntity<Doctor> searchDoctorById(int doctorId) {
  return new ResponseEntity<Doctor>(
      new Doctor(1, "ABCD", "No spec"),HttpStatus.OK);
  }
}
```

Note

If you are confused with the declaration of Hospital_Doctor_Fein, please revisit section: Shifting from RestTemplate to Feign Client from *Chapter* 5, *"Liaison Among Services"*.

In our *control code*, we have written a test against the status code **OK** and that's the reason I have written **HttpStatus.OK** in the preceding code. So, the logic of what to return and how to return is decided depending on the scenario.

Now, it's time to add the configuration. The only property which is different than that of **RestTemplate** with fault tolerance is enabling circuit breaker for **OpenFeign**.

The complete configurations are described as follows:

```
spring.cloud.openfeign.circuitbreaker.enabled= true
resilience4j.circuitbreaker.instances.
  HospitalDoctorFeignsearchDoctorByIdint.minimum-number-of-calls=5
resilience4j.circuitbreaker.instances.
  HospitalDoctorFeignsearchDoctorByIdint.failure-rate-threshold=50
resilience4j.circuitbreaker.instances.
  HospitalDoctorFeignsearchDoctorByIdint.wait-duration-in-open-state=10s
resilience4j.circuitbreaker.instances.
  HospitalDoctorFeignsearchDoctorByIdint.permitted-number-of-calls-in-
  half-open-state=3
resilience4j.circuitbreaker.instances.
  HospitalDoctorFeignsearchDoctorByIdint.sliding-window-size=10
resilience4j.circuitbreaker.instances.
  HospitalDoctorFeignsearchDoctorByIdint.sliding-window-type=COUNT_BASED
resilience4j.circuitbreaker.instances.
  HospitalDoctorFeignsearchDoctorByIdint.automatic-transition-from-open-
  to-half-open-enabled=true
```

Observe the name of the instance. It follows the pattern as:

`name_of_interface+name_of_Method+the_type_of_argument_the_method_accepts`, that is, **`HospitalDoctorFeignsearchDoctorByIdint`**.

Note

Here, we used the style adopted from 2020.0.2 as `<feignClientName>_<calledMethod>`. If you want to switch back to the circuit breaker names used prior to Spring Cloud 2022.0.0 you can set `spring.cloud.openfeign.circuitbreaker.alphanumeric-ids.enabled` to, `false`.

Let us execute the service and access the endpoint more than 5 *times*. You should send consecutive 6 *to* 7 *requests* to the **http://localhost:9091/hospitals-feign/12345**. We very well aware of how we are getting the response. It is time to focus on the actuator. Let us access the **/circuitbreakerevents** as shown in *Figure 9.9*:

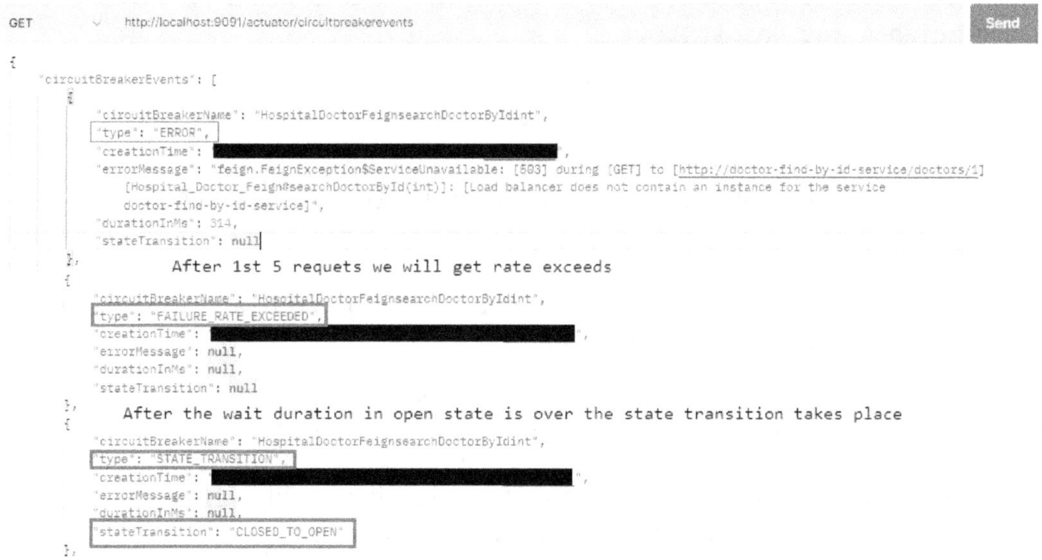

```
GET    http://localhost:9091/actuator/circuitbreakerevents    Send
{
    "circuitBreakerEvents": [
        {
            "circuitBreakerName": "HospitalDoctorFeignsearchDoctorByIdint",
            "type": "ERROR",
            "creationTime": "",
            "errorMessage": "feign.FeignException$ServiceUnavailable: [503] during [GET] to [http://doctor-find-by-id-service/doctors/1]
                [Hospital_Doctor_Feign#searchDoctorById(int)]: [Load balancer does not contain an instance for the service
                doctor-find-by-id-service]",
            "durationInMs": 314,
            "stateTransition": null
        },        After 1st 5 requets we will get rate exceeds
        {
            "circuitBreakerName": "HospitalDoctorFeignsearchDoctorByIdint",
            "type": "FAILURE_RATE_EXCEEDED",
            "creationTime": "",
            "errorMessage": null,
            "durationInMs": null,
            "stateTransition": null
        },     After the wait duration in open state is over the state transition takes place
        {
            "circuitBreakerName": "HospitalDoctorFeignsearchDoctorByIdint",
            "type": "STATE_TRANSITION",
            "creationTime": "",
            "errorMessage": null,
            "durationInMs": null,
            "stateTransition": "CLOSED_TO_OPEN"
        },
```

Figure 9.9: *circuitbreakerevents for Fein Client*

As you can observe in this figure, we have the transition in the states as per the configuration, the rate exceeded *error* and so many other things. And after the 6th *request* onwards you will also observe the type as **NOT_PERMITTED**.

Retry

Though **@CircuitBreaker** annotation equipped us to handle the unavailability of the downstream service and *what if instead of exception we want to retry calling the services*? The **@CircuitBreaker** changes the states from *Closed* to *Half-Open* and from *Half-Open* to *Open*. We can also configure a condition of attempt the availability of the downstream instances depending upon the configuration of **permitted-number-of-calls-in-half-open-state** property. The **@Retry** annotation will retry sending the request 2 *to* 3 *times* specified by the **max-attempts** property to increase the chances of getting response from the downstream.

We can update the earlier endpoint by applying **@Retry** in place of @ **CircuitBreaker**. As we already specified, we are adding a new endpoint for a new configuration. This will ensure that every configuration will be available as a ready reference. You can just update the earlier endpoint. But in this demonstration, we are adding a new endpoint as shown in the following code:

```
@Retry(name = "retry-for-doctor")
@GetMapping("/hospitals-retry/{hospitalId}")
ResponseEntity<Hospital> findAllDoctorsInHospitals_retry(
@PathVariable int hospitalId) {
  System.out.println("Method called");
  List<Doctor> doctors = new ArrayList<>();
  //the same code as we have written already.
  return new ResponseEntity<Hospital>(HttpStatus.NO_CONTENT);
}
```

The only purpose of the output statement in the method is to allow us to observe, if the **Retry** works and how it happens.

After updating the *Hospital* service, please rerun it and access **http://localhost:9091/hospitals-retry/12345** endpoint. Observe 500 *Internal Server Error* as a response, *which is very similar to what we receive when* we apply **`@CircuitBreaker`** annotation. So, what is the difference here? Let us observe the console of **`Hospital_Find_Doctors`** service which is displayed here:

```
<terminated> HospitalFindDoctorsApplication [Java Application]
2023-04-22T11:17:19.314+05:30  INFO[hospital-find-doctors-in-hospital,
2023-04-22T11:17:19.315+05:30  INFO[hospital-find-doctors-in-hospital,
2023-04-22T11:17:19.321+05:30  INFO[hospital-find-doctors-in-hospital,
Method called
2023-04-22T11:17:19.468+05:30  INFO[hospital-find-doctors-in-hospital,
2023-04-22T11:17:20.036+05:30  INFO[hospital-find-doctors-in-hospital,
2023-04-22T11:17:20.042+05:30  INFO[hospital-find-doctors-in-hospital,
2023-04-22T11:17:20.379+05:30  WARN[hospital-find-doctors-in-hospital,
Method called
2023-04-22T11:17:20.939+05:30  WARN[hospital-find-doctors-in-hospital,
Method called
2023-04-22T11:17:21.471+05:30  WARN[hospital-find-doctors-in-hospital,
```

***Figure 9.10**: Working with Retry*

Though the client makes a single request the handler method is invoked *thrice* as a default behavior retrying to access the downstream service consecutively. Sometimes depending upon the availability, the downstream service may take more time. So, the requests need to wait for some time before giving the next call.

Observe the following configuration setting:

```
resilience4j.retry.instances.retry-for-doctor.max-attempts=5
resilience4j.retry.instances.retry-for-doctor.wait-duration=15s
```

The **max-attempts** property enables us to override the default behavior of retrying only *three times*. Here we have specified to retry it 5 *times* and then the waiting period between the two calls is specified as 15 *sec* by configuring the **wait-duration** property as shown by the preceding configuration.

So, we keep on trying sometimes. But still, if the downstream service is unavailable and we do not wish to receive any exception, *how do we achieve that*? In such a case, you can configure a **fallback** method. This will ensure that even after retrying if the service is unavailable the fallback method will be invoked and response will be generated. For this we need to update the code as:

```
@Retry(name = "retry-for-doctor", fallbackMethod = "getDoctorFallback")
```

We are using the same **fallbackMethod**. If you intend to write another **fallback** method you are *free* to do so. Once the updates are done, rerun the service, and access **http://localhost:9091/hospitals-retry/12345** endpoint again. The console will prove the retrial and the Postman response will show the Hospital details provided by the **fallback** method.

Here the retrying is taking place in all the scenarios of exceptions. *Can we achieve retry on a specific exception? Indeed*, your observation is accurate and to accomplish it we have a property **retry-exceptions**. We need to configure this property when we intend Resilience4j to retry only when some typical type of exception occurs.

Observe the following configuration:

```
resilience4j.retry.instances.retry-for-doctor.retry-exceptions
  =org.springframework.web.client.RestClientResponseException
```

This configuration ensures that the retrial is performed only when the **`org.springframework.web.client.ResourceAccessException`** occurs.

Let's focus on actuator endpoints. You will get all retry-related endpoints under **/actuator**.

If we access **/actuator/retryevents** before we access **/hospitals-retry/{hostpitalId},** you can notice that there is no any retry event associated as shown in the following figure:

Figure 9.11: *Actuator without Retry*

Now try requesting **/hospitals-retry/{hospitalId}**. Please wait patiently to get the *response*. Now again hit the **/actuator/retryevents** to observe **numbreofAttempts** as shown in the following figure:

Figure 9.12: *Actuator with Retry*

Observe the 5th try for the type. It's an error as shown in *Figure* 9.13:

```
{
    "retryName": "retry-for-doctor",
    "type": "ERROR",
    "creationTime": "                                    ",
    "errorMessage": "org.springframework.web.client.ResourceAccessException: I/O error on GET reque
        doctor-find-by-id-service/doctors/1\": Connect to http://172.31.208.1:8086 [/172.31.208.1]
        refused: no further information",
    "numberOfAttempts": 5
}
```

Figure 9.13: *Error for Retry*

And after this, the **fallback** method is invoked to generate the response. Along with this, we also have other endpoints that provide us more information as shown in *Figure* 9.14:

```
"retries": {
    "href": "http://localhost:9091/actuator/retries",
    "templated": false
},
"retryevents": {
    "href": "http://localhost:9091/actuator/retryevents",
    "templated": false
},
"retryevents-name": {
    "href": "http://localhost:9091/actuator/retryevents/{name}",
    "templated": true
},
"retryevents-name-eventType": {
    "href": "http://localhost:9091/actuator/retryevents/{name}/{eventType}",
    "templated": true
},
```

Figure 9.14: *Fallback for handling error in Retry*

You can further delve deeper into this for additional information. Let us move on exploring the rate limiting.

> **Note**
>
> When we are using retry with a Feign Client then we need to add the same properties and instead of using the instance name from the @Retry annotation, we need to add the Feign Client `interface_name+name_of_the_method+the_argument_type` in the configuration.

Rate limiting

The **Rate Limiting** is an imperative technique that is used to prepare the API for scaling and establishing high availability and reliability of our microservice.

This technique comes with a whole bunch of different options for handling a detected limit surplus or type of requests we intend to limit. We can simply decline this *over-the-limit request* or *build a queue* to execute them later or even can combine both of these approaches in some way.

The **Rate Limiter** limits the *number of requests for a given period*. Sometimes, we wish to protect the resources from *spammers*, or *minimize the overhead*, or *meet* a *service level agreement*. In such case, we may choose to limit the requests to that endpoint for a particular time duration. Undoubtedly, we can achieve this functionality with the help of annotation **@RateLimiter** provided by `Resilience4j` without writing the explicit code.

Let's add the **@RateLimiter** annotation instead of **@Retry** as shown here. As stated earlier, you can just update the earlier endpoint. One thing which we will be changing here is the **fallback** method. Again, it is not necessary. We are adding a new method to demonstrate **TOO_MANY_REQUESTS**, as the status code.

Both methods are as follows:

```
@RateLimiter(name = "rate-limiter-for-doctor",
                    fallbackMethod = "getDoctorFallback_rateLimiter")
@GetMapping("/hospitals-rate-limiter/{hospitalId}")
ResponseEntity<Hospital> findAllDoctorsInHospitals_rate_limiter
                         (@PathVariable int hospitalId)
{
       System.out.println("Method called");
       //same implementation as past
       return new ResponseEntity<Hospital>(HttpStatus.NO_CONTENT);
}
public ResponseEntity<Hospital> getDoctorFallback_rateLimiter(
                                int hospitalId, Exception e)
{
       System.out.println(e.getMessage());
       return new ResponseEntity<Hospital>(HttpStatus.TOO_MANY_REQUESTS);
}
```

It is totally based on the scenario to choose the implementation. Now, it's time to set the *configuration* of for *how many requests* are in a period of a specific time as shown by the following configuration:

```
resilience4j.ratelimiter.instances.rate-limiter-for-doctor.limit-for-
period=2
resilience4j.ratelimiter.instances.rate-limiter-for-doctor.limit-
refresh-period=5s
resilience4j.ratelimiter.instances.rate-limiter-for-doctor.timeout-
duration=0
```

To test the working of **`@RateLimiter`** we first need to start the **`DoctorFind_By_DoctorId`**, the **`HospitalFind_Doctors`**, Eureka services, and Zipkin server. Once you ensure this, access the endpoint more than 2-3 *times* within **5 sec** as we set it as, **limit-refresh-period**. We will receive the status code **429**, which is for **`TOO_MANY_REQUESTS`**. You can also visit the console of the **`HospitalFind_Doctors`** service to observe the exception.

In terms of the actuator, we will receive the following end points:

```
/actuator/ratelimiters,
http://localhost:9091/actuator/ratelimiterevents/{name}, /actuator/
metrics/resilience4j.ratelimiter.available.permissions and
/actuator/metrics/resilience4j.ratelimiter.waiting_threads
```

This is very much similar to the earlier discussion we had. We need to enable the **metrics** and **health** information as:

```
resilience4j.ratelimiter.metrics.enabled=true
management.health.ratelimiters.enabled=true
```

Figure 9.15: *Actuator for Rate Limiter*

We can also enable health-related information as:

```
resilience4j.ratelimiter.instances.rate-limiter-for-doctor.register-health-indicator=true
```

***Figure 9.16**: Health information of actuator*

Note

When we are using Rate Limiter with a feign client then we need to add the same properties and instead of using the instance name from the @RateLimiter annotation, we need to add the `feign_client_interface_name+name_of_the_method+the_argument_type`, in the configuration.

Bulkhead

When we have microservices, one microservice utilizes another service and it can then further utilize another service. Occasionally, two different microservice may communicate with the same downstream service concurrently. These concurrent requests may put an extra burden on the service. When we intend to limit the number of concurrent requests, **Bulkhead** is the choice. The *Bulkhead* enables us to limit the number of concurrent requests within a specific period. The *question* is then, *how is this different from Rate Limiting*? The answer is it was also limiting the requests. *Why do we have two different decorators to accomplish the same task*? Indeed, they are not identical. When we discussed **Rate Limiter**, we didn't mention concurrent requests. However, when we discuss Bulkhead, we always focus on concurrent requests. We limit the number of concurrent requests. **@Bulkhead** annotation enables it without writing customized code. We need to include the **`resilience4j-bulkhead`** dependency in the class path to enable the support for the bulkhead. Once we include the **`resilience4j-bulkhead`** dependency on the class path, the Spring Cloud Circuit Breaker will wrap the methods with the support of Bulkhead. As it is by default *enabled*, we can choose to disable it by setting the property **`spring.cloud.circuitbreaker.bulkhead.resilience4j.enabled=false`**.

A **`SemaphoreBulkhead`** and **`FixedThreadPoolBulkhead`** are the *two* implementations provided by the Spring Cloud Circuit Breaker Resilience4j for the bulkhead pattern.

SemaphoreBulkhead

The **java.util.concurrent.Semaphore** is used internally by **`SemaphoreBulkhead`** to control the number of concurrent calls along with executing code on the currently executing thread. The **`maxConcurrentCalls`**, **`maxWaitDuration`**, **`writableStackTraceEnabled`**, and **`fairCallHandlingEnabled`** configurations are encapsulated in Bulkhead configuration.

The **maxConcurrentCalls** determine the number of maximum concurrent calls allowed to the downstream service. The value of **`maxConcurrentCalls`** specifies the number of permits which is used to initialize the Semaphore. The default value for the same is **25**. When this limit is over and a thread makes an attempt to invoke the downstream service either a **`BulkheadFullException`** is raised *immediately* or the thread *waits for some time*. This ensures that the other thread completes the invocation and the service requests will be back in limit. Now, this waiting duration of the thread is decided by the value of **`maxWaitDuration`**. The default setting of **`maxWaitDuration is 0 (zero)`** second. Many times, multiple threads might be waiting for permits. The value for **`fairCallHandlingEnabled`** in the configuration decides whether the waiting threads acquire the permits in a *First-in-First-out* order or not, the default value of which is set as **true**. When the **BulkheadFullException** exception occurs our console or log may get flooded by the stack trace. The **`writableStackTraceEnabled`** configuration allows us to reduce the amount of information in the stack trace. It is also set by default to **true**.

It is time for the code. Let us add an endpoint. (You can also modify the **@RateLimiter** annotation to **@Bulkhead** keeping the rest code as it is.).

The sample code is as follows:

```
@Bulkhead(name = "bulkhead-for-doctor",
         fallbackMethod = "getDoctorFallback_rateLimiter")
@GetMapping("/hospitals-bulkhead/{hospitalId}")
ResponseEntity<Hospital> findAllDoctorsInHospitals_bulkhead (
                        @PathVariable int hospitalId) {
  System.out.println("Method called");
  List<Doctor> doctors = new ArrayList<>();
  return new ResponseEntity<Hospital>(hospital, HttpStatus.OK);
  //the implementation is same
  return new ResponseEntity<Hospital>(HttpStatus.NO_CONTENT);
}
```

Now it's time to configure the properties for **SemaphoreBulkHead** as shown here:

```
resilience4j.bulkhead.instances.bulkhead-for-doctor.max-concurrent-
                                                            calls=5
resilience4j.bulkhead.instances.bulkhead-for-doctor.max-wait-duration=1
```

Now, start the **DoctorFind_By_DoctorId**, **HospitalFind_Doctors**, Eureka services, and Zipkin server and then access the endpoint more than 2-3 *times* from Postman or from multiple browser tabs. As we have set the **max-concurrent-call** to **5**, the method called will be displayed on the console 5 *times*, and for the 6th *concurrent request* we will receive **Bulkhead full** exception as highlighted in the following figure.

```
HospitalFindDoctorsApplication [Java Application]
2023-04-22T18:12:12.512+05:30  INFO[hospital-find-doctors-in-hospital,,] 27436 -
2023-04-22T18:12:29.682+05:30  INFO[hospital-find-doctors-in-hospital,,] 27436 -
2023-04-22T18:12:29.683+05:30  INFO[hospital-find-doctors-in-hospital,,] 27436 -
2023-04-22T18:12:29.688+05:30  INFO[hospital-find-doctors-in-hospital,,] 27436 -
Method called
Method called
Method called
Method called
Method called
Bulkhead 'bulkhead-for-doctor' is full and does not permit further calls
2023-04-22T18:12:29.867+05:30  INFO[hospital-find-doctors-in-hospital,6443d6357a
```

Figure 9.17: *Bulkhead setup*

Once you have gathered information about **Semaphore**, let us now concentrate on **ThreadPoolBulkhead**.

ThreadPoolBulkhead

A **thread** from a **ThreadPool** is used to execute our code in the **ThreadPool Bulkhead**. The execution of the number of concurrent calls will be internally controlled by **java.util.concurrent.ArrayBlockingQueue** and a **java.util.concurrent.ThreadPoolExecutor**. The properties **coreThreadPoolSize, maxThreadPoolSize, keepAliveDuration**,and **queueCapacity** are the configurations associated with the **ThreadPoolBulkhead**. As we know it internally uses these configurations to construct a **ThreadPoolExecutor**. The internal **ThreadPoolExecutor** executes incoming requests on one of the available threads from the pool. When all threads are *busy* and no thread is *free* to execute the request, then the task is *enqueued*. This enqueued task will be executed once a thread becomes available. In case, the **queueCapacity** is reached then the remote call is *rejected* and a **BulkheadFullException** is raised. We also can configure the **writableStackTraceEnabled** to limit the information in the stack trace of a **BulkheadFullException**.

We will not change anything in the code. However, the configuration needs to be updated, to move from **Semaphore** to **ThreadPool** by configuring the following properties:

```
resilience4j.thread-pool-bulkhead.instances.bulkhead-for-doctor.
                                              maxThreadPoolSize= 3

resilience4j.thread-pool-bulkhead.instances.bulkhead-for-doctor.
                                              coreThreadPoolSize= 1
```

Similar to **semaphoreBulkHead**, after starting all the required services, execute 6-7 *requests* consecutively. After the 5th concurrent request, we will receive the **Bulkhead full** exception as highlighted in the following figure:

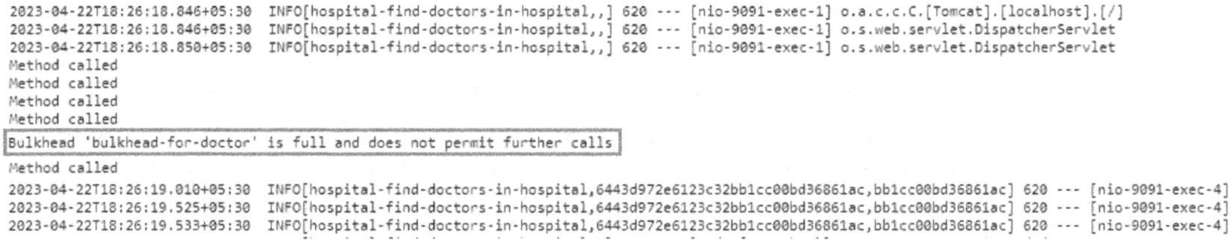

```
2023-04-22T18:26:18.846+05:30  INFO[hospital-find-doctors-in-hospital,,] 620 --- [nio-9091-exec-1] o.a.c.c.C.[Tomcat].[localhost].[/]
2023-04-22T18:26:18.846+05:30  INFO[hospital-find-doctors-in-hospital,,] 620 --- [nio-9091-exec-1] o.s.web.servlet.DispatcherServlet
2023-04-22T18:26:18.850+05:30  INFO[hospital-find-doctors-in-hospital,,] 620 --- [nio-9091-exec-1] o.s.web.servlet.DispatcherServlet
Method called
Method called
Method called
Method called
Bulkhead 'bulkhead-for-doctor' is full and does not permit further calls
Method called
2023-04-22T18:26:19.010+05:30  INFO[hospital-find-doctors-in-hospital,6443d972e6123c32bb1cc00bd36861ac,bb1cc00bd36861ac] 620 --- [nio-9091-exec-4]
2023-04-22T18:26:19.525+05:30  INFO[hospital-find-doctors-in-hospital,6443d972e6123c32bb1cc00bd36861ac,bb1cc00bd36861ac] 620 --- [nio-9091-exec-4]
2023-04-22T18:26:19.533+05:30  INFO[hospital-find-doctors-in-hospital,6443d972e6123c32bb1cc00bd36861ac,bb1cc00bd36861ac] 620 --- [nio-9091-exec-4]
```

***Figure 9.18**: Working with Threadpool*

Now it's time to visit the actuator. We will get all the endpoints such as **/bulkheads, /bulkheadevents, /bulkheadevents/{/bulkheadname},** and so on. Let's execute the **/actuator/bulkheadevents** to find what all events taking place:

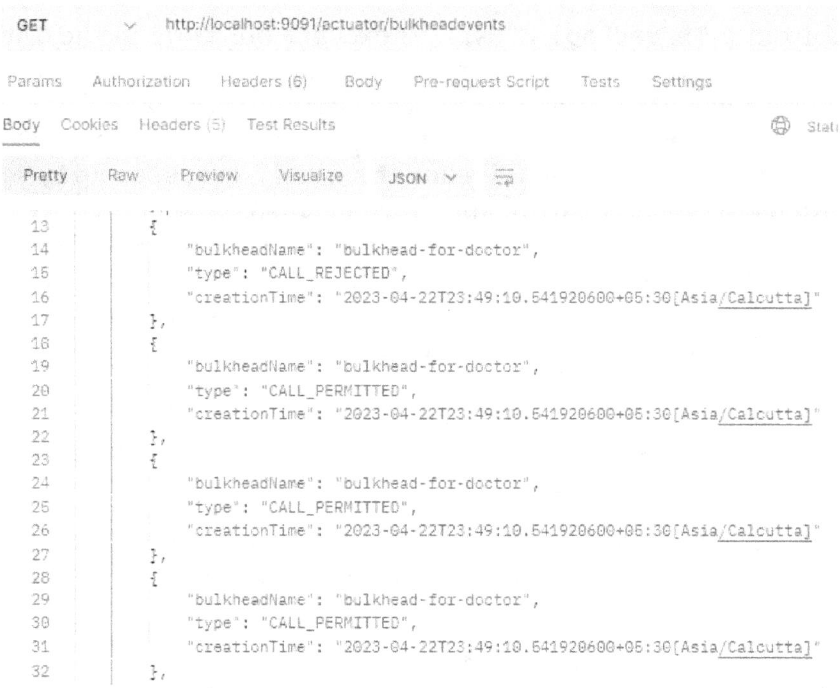

GET http://localhost:9091/actuator/bulkheadevents

Params Authorization Headers (6) Body Pre-request Script Tests Settings

Body Cookies Headers (5) Test Results

Pretty Raw Preview Visualize JSON


```
    {
        "bulkheadName": "bulkhead-for-doctor",
        "type": "CALL_REJECTED",
        "creationTime": "2023-04-22T23:49:10.541920600+05:30[Asia/Calcutta]"
    },
    {
        "bulkheadName": "bulkhead-for-doctor",
        "type": "CALL_PERMITTED",
        "creationTime": "2023-04-22T23:49:10.541920600+05:30[Asia/Calcutta]"
    },
    {
        "bulkheadName": "bulkhead-for-doctor",
        "type": "CALL_PERMITTED",
        "creationTime": "2023-04-22T23:49:10.541920600+05:30[Asia/Calcutta]"
    },
    {
        "bulkheadName": "bulkhead-for-doctor",
        "type": "CALL_PERMITTED",
        "creationTime": "2023-04-22T23:49:10.541920600+05:30[Asia/Calcutta]"
    },
```


***Figure 9.19**: Actuator for bulkheadevents*

As you can observe from the output, *first 5 calls* are permitted, and once we reach the limit, that is, on the execution of 6th or 7th request consecutively we will receive the **Bulkhead full** exception and the events will show **CALL_REJECTED** in the type.

Note

When we are using Bulkhead with a Feign Client, we need to add the same properties and instead of using the instance name from the `@Bulkhead` annotation we need to add the `feign_client_interface_name+name_of_the_method+the_argument_type`, in the configuration.

TimeLimiter

Many times we experience that, the applications are responding late for no apparent reason. In *microservice architecture*, when services communicate with each other it is very obvious to experience *latency*. This may be due to network issues or service code itself taking more time in execution or the service is again dependent on another service and that is slow. It is a very common issue and needs serious consideration.

A *limit* on the amount of time which we anticipate to wait for a function to complete the task is known as **Time Limiting**. When the operation does not get completed within the specified time, we intend to get a notification about it with a *timeout error*. Usually, the **Resilience4J's TimeLimiter** can be used to set timeouts on the asynchronous operations which have been implemented using **CompletableFuture**. The **TimeLimiter** allows us to limit the duration of receiving the response of a request.

Now as just discussed the method must be asynchronous to use **@TimeLimiter**. However, we do not have such an endpoint or method. So, let us add an endpoint that handles the asynchronous request. The logic is the same as earlier. We just have updated the return type and refactored the code a bit as shown in the following code:

```
@TimeLimiter(name = "timelimiter-for-doctor", fallbackMethod =
                                            "getDoctorFallback_timeLimiter")
@GetMapping("/hospitals-timelimiter/{hospitalId}")
CompletableFuture< ResponseEntity<Hospital>>
findAllDoctorsInHospitals_timelimiter(@PathVariable int hospitalId) {
  return CompletableFuture.supplyAsync(() -> {
      return this.getDetails(hospitalId);
  });
}

public ResponseEntity <Hospital> getDetails(int hospitalId) {
  System.out.println("Method called ");
  List<Doctor> doctors = new ArrayList<>();
  Hospital hospital = repo.findHospitalById(hospitalId);
  if (hospital != null) {
      List<Integer> doctor_ids = repo.findDoctorIds(hospitalId);
      for (int i = 0; i < doctor_ids.size(); i++) {
        ResponseEntity<Doctor> entity = restTemplate.getForEntity(
            "http://doctor-find-by-id-service/doctors/{doctorId}",
                         Doctor.class, doctor_ids.get(i));
        if (entity.getStatusCode().equals(HttpStatus.OK)) {
            doctors.add(entity.getBody());
        }
```

```
        }
        hospital.setDoctors(doctors);
        new ResponseEntity <Hospital>(hospital, HttpStatus.OK);
    }
    return new ResponseEntity<Hospital>(HttpStatus.NO_CONTENT);
}
```

Now as we change the endpoint, we also need to update the **fallback** method as well to match the signature of the methods. Following is the updated code which will return **408** status code:

```
public CompletableFuture<ResponseEntity<Hospital>> getDoctorFallback_
timeLimiter(int hospitalId, Exception e) {
    System.out.println(e.getMessage());
    return CompletableFuture.supplyAsync(() ->
           new ResponseEntity<Hospital>(HttpStatus.REQUEST_TIMEOUT));
}
```

Let us update the configuration to set the timeout duration to **1 ms** as follows. This specifies the maximum amount of time a request can take to respond:

```
resilience4j.timelimiter.instances.timelimiter-for-doctor.timeout-
  duration=1ms
resilience4j.timelimiter.instances.timelimiter-for-doctor.cancel-
  running-future=false
```

The **`cancel-running-future=false`**, specifies not to cancel the running CompletableFuture even after the timeout. Now, raise the request to hit the endpoint **http://localhost:9091/hospitals-timelimiter/12345.** Just after the 1ms you should receive the exception as highlighted by the following console:

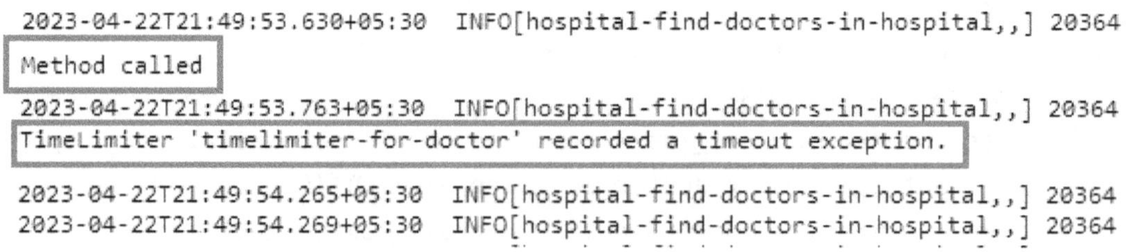

```
2023-04-22T21:49:53.630+05:30  INFO[hospital-find-doctors-in-hospital,,] 20364
Method called
2023-04-22T21:49:53.763+05:30  INFO[hospital-find-doctors-in-hospital,,] 20364
TimeLimiter 'timelimiter-for-doctor' recorded a timeout exception.
2023-04-22T21:49:54.265+05:30  INFO[hospital-find-doctors-in-hospital,,] 20364
2023-04-22T21:49:54.269+05:30  INFO[hospital-find-doctors-in-hospital,,] 20364
```

***Figure 9.20**: Timeout exception*

The Postman also will show the **408** as status code for request timeout as shown in *Figure 9.21*:

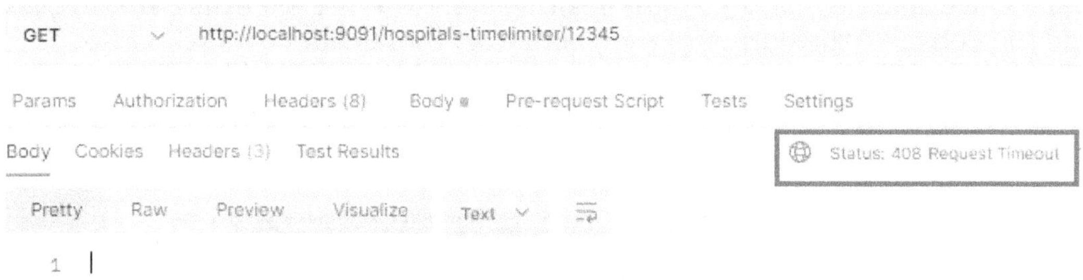

```
GET        http://localhost:9091/hospitals-timelimiter/12345

Params   Authorization   Headers (8)   Body   Pre-request Script   Tests   Settings

Body   Cookies   Headers (3)   Test Results                 Status: 408 Request Timeout

Pretty   Raw   Preview   Visualize   Text

1 |
```

***Figure 9.21**: Implementing TimeLimitter*

If we observe the actuator, we will have the following endpoints that also show the details of the bulkhead as follows:

```
"bulkheads": {
    "href": "http://localhost:9091/actuator/bulkheads",
    "templated": false
},
"bulkheadevents": {
    "href": "http://localhost:9091/actuator/bulkheadevents",
    "templated": false
},
"bulkheadevents-bulkheadName": {
    "href": "http://localhost:9091/actuator/bulkheadevents/{bulkheadName}",
    "templated": true
},
"bulkheadevents-bulkheadName-eventType": {
    "href": "http://localhost:9091/actuator/bulkheadevents/{bulkheadName}/{eventType}",
    "templated": true
},
```

***Figure 9.22**: Actuator for bulkhead*

And the metrics will provide the information about *number of threads*, *available thread count*, *pool size*, and so on as shown in the following figure:

```
"resilience4j.bulkhead.active.thread.count",
"resilience4j.bulkhead.available.concurrent.calls",
"resilience4j.bulkhead.available.thread.count",
"resilience4j.bulkhead.core.thread.pool.size",
"resilience4j.bulkhead.max.allowed.concurrent.calls",
"resilience4j.bulkhead.max.thread.pool.size",
"resilience4j.bulkhead.queue.capacity",
"resilience4j.bulkhead.queue.depth",
"resilience4j.bulkhead.thread.pool.size",
```

***Figure 9.23**: Bulkhead metrics*

We will focus on the **bulkheadEvents**. The process is very much similar. After executing the service observe the output for the **/actuator/bulkheadevents**. We will receive an empty array of **bulkheadEvents**. Now, fire 6-7 *concurrent request* and then observe the output of the **/actuator/bulkheadevents** response:

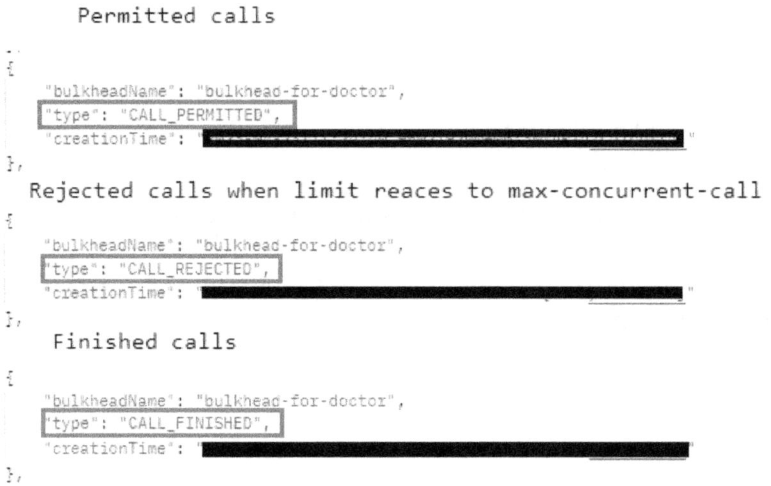

```
Permitted calls
{
    "bulkheadName": "bulkhead-for-doctor",
    "type": "CALL_PERMITTED",
    "creationTime": "                    "
},
Rejected calls when limit reaces to max-concurrent-call
{
    "bulkheadName": "bulkhead-for-doctor",
    "type": "CALL_REJECTED",
    "creationTime": "                    "
},
Finished calls
{
    "bulkheadName": "bulkhead-for-doctor",
    "type": "CALL_FINISHED",
    "creationTime": "                    "
},
```

***Figure 9.24**: Bulkhead for concurrent requests*

We made *six concurrent requests*. For all *six requests*, we received **`CALL_PERMITTED`** as type, then 1 *call* got rejected with type as **`CALL_REJECTED`** as only 5 *concurrent* calls are allowed. Finally, 5 *calls* will get the type **`CALL_FINISHED`** as shown in *Figure* 9.24. The figure shows only the type of calls as the response is lengthier.

Note

If we are using the Time Limiter with a Feign Client then we need to add the same properties. Additionally, instead of using the instance name from the `@TimeLimiter` annotation we need to add the `Feign_Client_interface_name+name_of_the_method+the_argument_type` in the configuration.

Applying multiple decorators for a single method

We learned in detail to implement the fault tolerance in microservices using **Resilience4j** with the help of various decorators such as **`Bulkhead`**, **`Time Limiter`**, **`Retry`**, and so on. But we applied them individually. Now, the question is *can we apply multiple decorators for a single service*? Indeed, we can. We can apply multiple decorators for a single method. Now, the more significant point is the order in which they execute. *Will it be the order in which they are applied?* The answer is very straightforward. The order is decided by the configuration. Generally, we follow the default order specified by **`Resilience4J`** as **`Bulkhead`**,

`Time Limiter`, **`Rate Limiter`**, **`Circuit Breaker`**, and finally **Retry**.

This can also be configured as shown by the following configuration:

```
resilience4j.bulkhead.bulkheadAspectOrder=1
resilience4j.timelimiter.timeLimiterAspectOrder=2
resilience4j.ratelimiter.rateLimiterAspectOrder=3
resilience4j.circuitbreaker.circuitBreakerAspectOrder=4
resilience4j.retry.retryAspectOrder=5
```

Conclusion

In this chapter, we discussed the factors making a service unhealthy and the approaches to handling the failure. Developing highly available services is the promise made by microservice architecture. A service may *fail* and we can't avoid it from happening, so there are always chances of failure. The failure doesn't mean that the service is unavailable or down but it failed to respond to the request to certain factors. These factors may be related to the code, service being busy, or responding late along with some scenarios that make services unhealthy and it cannot serve. We also explored the Circuit Breaker design pattern and different states of it.

Fault tolerance is one of the important mechanisms that we must apply to Spring Boot application. In this chapter, we discussed the **Resilience4J-based** fault tolerance mechanism which provides **Circuit Breaker**, **Retry**, **Rate Limiter**, **BulkHead**, and **Time Limiter** as decorators. We discussed the configuration of these decorators, and different annotations which help to wire them to a specific method. We also implemented a **fallback** method to provide an alternative response to the client request when the request fails to obtain the actual response from the downstream service. We also utilized the fault tolerance approach for **RestTemplate** and Feign Client for inter-service communication. Earlier in case of service failure, we provided alternate responses to the client by using the **fallback** method or a status code. But, *how could we neglect the service maintenance in the production environment*? When a service fails the fault tolerance is triggered but we need to ensure that it is registered and monitored. We utilized the services of actuator intermittently to monitor the application by enabling the *health* and metrics associated with each decorator.

Our all endpoints are freely available to access and it is not a good practice at all. It makes the endpoints vulnerable. We need to protect not all but at least some endpoints. In the next chapter, we will introduce the mechanism to secure our endpoints. We will also explore the differences between securing *microservice* and *monolith*.

CHAPTER 10
Keep it Safe

It was *Thursday* at 4.00*pm*; *Mandar* was enjoying a *latte coffee* with *Manish*. Simultaneously, they were discussing the recent microservices project they were working on. While they were deep in their conversation, their colleague *Abhay* joined them to share an important update about the project. "*Mandar, we have done significant progress in the project. Recently, we have added an* API *Gateway to facilitate a single-entry point for all our backend microservices. Now, none of our endpoints are exposed directly, they are all exposed via* API *Gateway. Additionally, we have implemented the rewrite path, because of which some of the actual endpoints are completely hidden from the clients*". Intrigued, Mandar asked, "*Abhay, as per my understanding, we already have the logic in place so that the endpoints can be accessed by the clients who provide the correct credentials. So, what's the purpose of implementing the rewrite path?*"

Abhay explained, "*The rewrite path allows us to obscure the true endpoint from clients. It adds an extra layer of security and improves the overall architecture. However, there are a few endpoints that we don't want to expose to the public. We've implemented authentication and authorization mechanisms to secure such endpoints. It works well for independent services where clients provide the necessary credentials. However, the challenge arises when we have multiple services, each with different security requirements*".

Manish was nodding his head in complete disagreement, "*I still don't understand your point, Abhay*". Abhay continued expressing his views with more excitement now, "*The concept of authentication and authorization works well with independent services since the client provides the credentials. But we have numerous services, each requiring different paths to secure and the need for different roles to access them. We are using different databases in different subdomains. We are duplicating similar logic for various paths and roles each time. This is not a maintainable solution at all. Somehow, we need to streamline this*".

Mandar seemed surprised by this view. Deeply concerned, he raised a question, "*Manish, are we using basic authentication for microservices? And why in microservices we are rewriting the logic of securing endpoints again and again?*" Manish was prompt in replying this, "Not *at all, Mandar. We have written the security service and bundled the same in a jar. The same jar is reused in every service. But Abhay had his own perspective. He continued, We have a large, complex code. Each service is independent and it may or may not need securing the endpoints. We can't manage the state of the service. This statelessness is increasing the complexity. In our previous monolithic application, we had an in-memory context, such as* `ThreadLocal`*, which is used to pass the information or typically user identities. Our services don't share a memory which makes it difficult to use an in-memory security context for identities. We need a different mechanism so that identities are from one microservice to another microservice. In monolith, we also may use centralized sessions and then by accessing a database, this session can be preserved. However, for us, we use a database per domain and all services might not be using the same database which means in our microservices architecture, we require a different session mechanism. We may independently be able to secure the services, but the same technique might not work for interservice communication*".

Realizing the complexities of the situation, Mandar nodded and replied, "*We have the API Gateway as an entry point. All requests to all downstream services are passed via the API Gateway. We have already used it for logging, pre-processing, and post-processing of requests. Why don't we leverage its services to implement security as well? But the point of concern is how we notify the services that the request is authenticated. And what about interservice communication requests? Where are we going to add the credentials?*"

"*Mandar, do you remember that we generated a token and then forwarded it within the request to secure the service?*" Manish asked. Mandar was impressed, "*Oh, yes. We generated a token and then used it for authentication. Also, once the token expires, the user can ask for a new token with refresh_token as well. We can implement the same here. Though the services are isolated and the requests are filtered from the API Gateway, we can add the refresh_token in each request and then only the API Gateway will be responsible for securing the endpoints. This will also solve the issue of adding the security logic in individual services.*"

Abhay was overjoyed when he heard about tokens and jumped in the chair, saying, "*This means we don't have to include the logic every time. The token will be passed on securely within the body or header. And if I am correct, we can even use the* IAM *tool to ensure that only authorized clients have access to resources*".

Excited by the possibilities, the trio decided to further explore the idea of a centralized security service. As the team delved into the project, they realized that this central security service would not only address their immediate concerns but also pave the way for future *scalability* and *extensibility*. It would enable them to seamlessly add new services, adapt to evolving security requirements, and simplify the *development*, and *maintenance* of their microservices architecture.

Structure

In this chapter, we are going to discuss the following topics:

- Exposing resources
- Revealing secret
- Revisiting microservice architecture
- Exploring ways of securing microservices
- Understanding token-based security and their available options
- Digging into OAuth 2 token

Exposing resources

We have already discussed microservice architecture in detail. The main objective of any service is to expose the data. This data may be in the form of **text**, **String**, **Object**, **JSON**, **XML**, **HTML**, or **PDF**. Any data that a service exposes is considered a resource. We have designed various endpoints till now which were utilized to expose resources.

Consider *doctor-related services*. They are exposing the *doctor* as a resource and the best part is that these are *independent services* which can be requested by any client. We also have *hospital-related services* exposing and handling *hospitals* as a *resource*. However, a *hospital* cannot be considered a completely *independent* service since some of the *hospital-related services* communicate with downstream *doctor-related services* to perform some operations. We have already discussed different scenarios, such as *establishing communication downstream*, *managing the failure of downstream services*, *handling the load*, and most importantly, *ensuring location transparency for our services.*

One of the major concerns regarding all these endpoints is **security**. Our resources are exposed publicly. The resources consist of data, which is the most important thing, which should be handled carefully. Unfortunately, till now, we have been ignorant about it. We haven't paid any attention to who is accessing the *resource* and the manner in which it is being accessed. We have only been focusing on exposing the resources. The resources which do not cause any issue can be exposed publicly to everyone. However, the endpoints that expose vulnerable resources must be handled with utmost care. We need to validate the client requesting the resource before sending it.

Revealing secret

Security! When we hear this word, *what comes to mind*? For me it's the lock of my phone, the credentials of my bank account or email address, the list is unending. Normally, we carry our own mobiles and laptops with us. If we are aware of our credentials, then *why do we need to protect them*?

Let's imagine a scenario: you are working at your desk and inadvertently leave your device behind as you depart from your workstation. In such cases, someone may steal your device and gain access to your personal information. *What if, on social media, we don't want any anonymous person to read our posts or see our photos or videos because they are highly personal? How would you achieve that?*

The same is true about the applications. In any application, the data is of utmost importance and we intend to handle it with utmost care. Our resources are exposed over the network and it is very important to protect them against *malfunctions*, *phishing*, *cybercrimes*, or any other kind of *cyberattacks* to avoid *data loss*. Nowadays, due to smart attackers and advanced attacking tools, we need to ensure that we scan our endpoints for vulnerabilities. This makes security testing crucial to defend them against attacks. We definitely need to expose the resource to the client, but sometimes it's very important to keep the resource safe. These resources should be available only to the authenticated client and not to everyone. We will reveal the resource to only those clients who prove their identity.

In *monolithic applications*, most of the time, the frontend is also part of the application. The requests and responses are part of one transaction, so just by managing the sessions on login to the application and ending it on logout. In the case of microservices, things are very different. *Firstly*, we don't have a front end. *Secondly*, in services, communication is between applications rather than between humans and services. So, in such a case, *who is going to log in and how?* This is just the tip of the iceberg much more to reveal yet.

Revisiting microservice architecture

We need to write the logic for *authentication* and *authorization* in all microservices whose endpoints need to be protected. This means that part of the logic needs to be implemented repeatedly. We can bundle the code and create a JAR out of it, which facilitates the code reusability. Though we are not repeating the code, these microservices will have a dependency on that code base, taking out the flexibility of our microservice.

As we all are aware, *HTTP is a stateless protocol*. This means that each request made by HTTP is an *independent* request, and the server will not keep track of any request and will not be able to make the connection between *two* consecutive requests from the same client. Consider a scenario where the user is browsing the *webpages* of a news portal. In such scenario, user will make a new request every time and no details need to be shared between *two* requests. However, sometimes some details from the first request might need to be transferred to another. Typically, when the user experience needs to be enhanced, the *authentication information* and other data needs to be passed on, the *stateless requests* cause issues.

Now consider an *online shopping application*. When a user adds some item to a *cart* in one request, that information must be available in the next requests to keep track of the same cart. But by default, it's *not* possible due to the *stateless HTTP protocol*. We need to arrange something due to which some piece of information will transfer from one request to another and the client doesn't need to enter it again and again. Now on top of statelessness, our microservices are distributed over the network, which will add complexity:

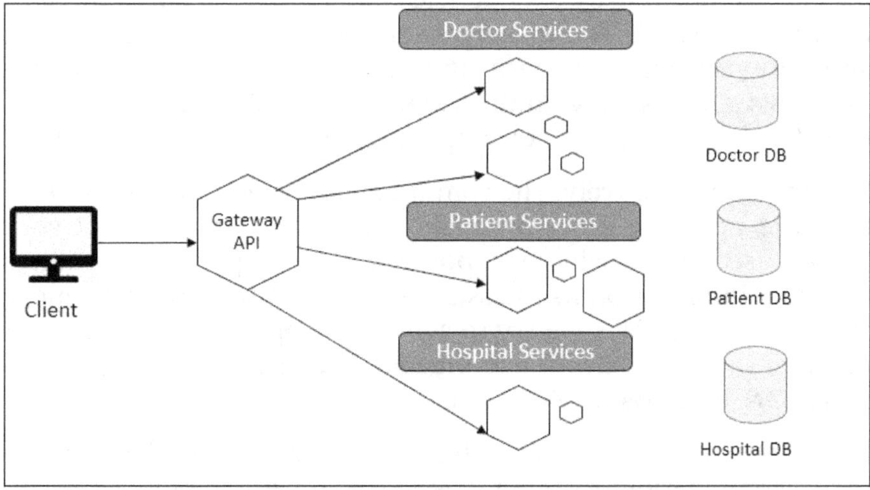

Figure 10.1: *Microservice architecture*

As shown in *Figure* 10.1, we have microservices under the **Doctor** subdomain, **Hospital** subdomain, and **Patient** subdomain. Many of the endpoints of hospital-related services are *public*, but we want the *doctor* and *patient-related* endpoints to be available for users only. We don't want them to be accessed by anonymous clients. So, when we say *doctor* services to be protected, we need a protection logic. The same is true about *patients*. We don't want to add another layer. All calls are routed via API Gateway. *Oh, yes! How could I forget Eureka and Cloud config servers?* We need all of them to be under protection.

But, *how*? The very easy thing we can do is to ask the user to enter credentials in the same exact way when someone tries to check their emails or tried to visit the bank account. This is a straightforward example of login base security. *Can we use the login in our services?* In a way YES, we can. But *when we say we will ask the client to prove who he is, where and how he is going to enter the credentials?* We don't have a front end, so *how are we going to ask to enter the credentials?* For us, its inter-services communication and using credentials is quite difficult and we can't do this for our microservices. Our services are not consumed by human beings, so *who will enter the credentials?*

Exploring ways of securing microservices

There are different ways to secure the microservices. Let us explore them:

- **Track the dependencies**: It is very common to use external dependencies in our services. These dependencies can make up for more than 70% *of our code* in production. If you have observed keenly, many of these dependencies have their own dependencies and they may have their own and so on. These dependencies may contain security vulnerabilities. It's very crucial for us to keep them *up-to-date* in order to make our application secure, as these updates often fix security vulnerabilities. The tools such as **NPM Audit**, **GitHub Dependabot**, or **Synk** allow us to keep track of and update outdated dependencies automatically.

- **Communicate securely**: The communication with microservices happens over the network. But we usually use HTTP which is *not* secure. We should use HTTPS wherever possible in our application while sending sensitive information like *passwords*, *keys*, or *secrets*. Also, encrypt it as soon as possible. We will try to avoid sending this kind of information in plain text. Instead, try to use **Mutual Transport Layer Security** (**mTLS**) and **JSON Web Token** (**JWT**) while communicating.

- **Limit the traffic**: Many times the attacker tries to send multiple requests with a combination of credentials to gain access to our secure resources. When we use limiting traffic, we are trying to limit the number of requests hitting the endpoint. We can prevent certain endpoints from using most of the application bandwidth. We can monitor requests per IP or time and then take action accordingly.

- **Secure the containers:** Most of the microservices are usually deployed inside containers. We must ensure the security of the containers. Here are some good practices which we can follow:
  - Try to avoid using the **sudo** command while running the application:
  - Provide only the required and minimum permissions.
  - Try not to store secrets inside containers.
  - Try to ensure that our container images are downloaded from secure sources only.
  - Try to keep our container image up-to-date.
  - Always limit access to available resources.
  - Scanning regularly for security and vulnerability.
  - Scan the Dockerfile, using the Docker scan.
- **Be careful about secrets:** We should keep our secrets such as *login credentials*, *passwords*, and API in a secure place. We can store them in an external store such as **AWS Secretes Manager**, **AWS KMS**, **Vault**, or **AWS Parameter Store**, and so on. Avoid committing them with your code.
- **Add a security layer**: We wish to control access to a couple of our resources so that only a group of intended users can access them. For such settings, we need to implement security. Security implementation can be done in various ways. In general, we have basic authentication, **form-based authentication**, **digest authentication**, and **Token-based authentication**. As we cannot stop any developer from using any of them in a code, all of them are applicable. However, it is easy to use *Token-based security* in distributed environments such as microservice and we will be implementing the same. But you might be having the question everywhere we usually provide the authentications by entering the credentials, so *what's wrong with it? Why are we taking the same approach*? This is a *legitimate question* for sure. But we should not forget about the fact that we are developing services for other applications. *The services are rarely consumed by human beings from browsers*! So exactly *what's different*? Let's dig it.

In the *traditional monolith, client server-based applications* were also comprised of restricted resources. Whenever such restricted resources were requested by the client, the request must include client credentials. These *credentials* are then used by the server against the resource owner's credentials to validate the client. In this model to provide third-party applications access to restricted resources, the resource owner shares its credentials with the client and then the client will use it. *Isn't it harmful*? Yes, *it is*! That's not all, there are other dots to connect as well.

Issues while using passwords to grant access

The *third-party application* has to store the resource owner's credentials so that they can be used in the future. The issue is the *password* is in clear text and can be available for use. These passwords will then be sent to the servers and the servers are required to support *password authentication* even though it has the security weaknesses inherent in passwords. Once the client applications gain access to the restricted resource, the resource owner doesn't have the ability to restrict the duration for which the access is allowed. Unfortunately, once the access is granted, the resource owners cannot revoke the access to an individual third party. It can be done only by changing their password and by revoking access to all third parties. It means we can use it, but *we should not!*

In a microservices architecture, we have centralized and decentralized access control as *two* different approaches to managing user access. Obviously, each has its own advantages as well as disadvantages. *Which one of them to select* is totally dependent on the requirements of the microservices implementation.

Understanding token-based security and their available options

The *centralized access controls* all the decisions regarding which resource to be accessed by whom are stored at a centralized location. It makes things simpler to manage to add security policies while we use it in smaller applications. However, when the same is considered in large-scale implementations, it may become a bottleneck, causing issues in scalability. And *how could we forget a potential single point of failure in the system when the centralized system fails*? Using *centralized access control* may be difficult when we consider high-level coordination for inter-microservice communications and the access control service.

The *second* approach is to use *decentralized access control*. It allows for more scalable access control as compared to a centralized approach. The decisions on access control are made at the service level. The access control decisions can be made by multiple services in the event of a failure, which directly reduces the risk of a single point of failure. But we can't overlook the fact that each microservice must implement its own access control logic.

The selection between *centralized* and *decentralized* access management is totally dependent on the requirements of the *microservices implementation*. The size makes it complicated, as security is required at every level, along with the need for resilience.

The *tokens* enable *decoupled authentication* as the *authentication* and *authorization* details are stored in a separate service and then can be easily shared between other microservices. These tokens are *stateless* as they do not store any data on the client as well as the server, which reduces the risk of security incidents.

We are using tokens so frequently. Aren't you keen to know exactly *what is a token*? Let us explore it. A **token** is a piece of data which is meaningless and useless on its own. However, when it is combined with the correct tokenization system, it enables the most important factor for an application, **SECURITY**. The *token-based authentication* works by ensuring each request to a server must be accompanied by a signed token. The server receives the token and verifies its authenticity, if and only if the token is valid response is sent.

Types of tokens

You may have heard about **access tokens** or **bearer tokens**. We have different types of tokens to use in various environments, access tokens and bearer tokens are a few of them. *Which one will we be using*? Let us look into types before we decide which one to use:

- **Access tokens**: Access tokens are opaque tokens which are conforming to the **OAuth2.0 framework**. Usually, an access token contains authorization information without identity information. We use these tokens to authenticate and provide authorization information to the APIs. The good part is we don't need to manage these access tokens. The libraries automatically retrieve the credential and exchange it for an access token. If needed, the refresh of the access tokens can also be issued.
- **ID tokens**: ID tokens are JSON web tokens which conform to **the OpenID Connect** specifications. Usually, an ID token is composed of a set of *keys* and their associated *value pairs* which are also called a **claim**. The ID tokens are meant for *application-level* use. These tokens will be inspected and used by the applications. The token contains the information about who signed the token, and the identity for whom the ID token has been issued which can be used by the application. **Self-Signed JSON web tokens (JWTs)**: Self-signed JWTs are required for authenticating the APIs which are deployed with API Gateway. Some Google APIs without having to get an access token from the authorization server allow us to use self-signed JWTs for authentication.

- **Refresh tokens**: We as a client will be having an access token or ID token to access the resource. Providing a token with unlimited validity is a security threat. Fortunately, both these tokens come with some validity, which is by default an hour. Here comes our savior refresh token which will be used to obtain additional tokens. So, *are we going to request the refresh token after our token expires?* No, when our application is authenticated for the very first time, it will receive a token as well as a refresh token. Now, whenever our issued token expires, the application will use the refresh token to request a new token. Remember one thing: the *refresh tokens can expire.*
- **Federated tokens**: Federated tokens are used as an intermediate step by the **Workload Identity Federation**. The special thing about them is they are issued the Security Token services and cannot be used directly and we need a service account for it.
- **Bearer tokens**: The access tokens, ID tokens or even JWT tokens are all bearer tokens which grant access to the applications which have possession of the token. When someone uses the bearer tokens for authentication, we are relying on the security provided by an encrypted protocol, such as **HTTPS**. Sometimes it won't provide the required level of security, then we must consider adding another layer of encryption. We can also use a mutual **Transport Layer Security** for limiting access to only authenticated users on a trusted device.

So, now we understand what tokens are and their types. The use of tokens is so common over the traditional methods as it has the following *benefits*:

- The tokens are *stateless*. As just discussed, each token is *self-contained*, having all the information it needs for authentication. As the token makes our server free from storing the session state, it enables more scalability.
- The tokens can be generated from anywhere and the best part is the token generation is decoupled from *token verification* which allows us to handle the signing process of the tokens on a separate server. One can even provide a different server for authentication.
- The token provides the most flexible and fine-grained control as we can add the payload specifying the user roles, the permissions, and which resources a specific user can access.
- Tokens act as a barrier to prevent attacks from hackers accessing user data and resources. When we use *password-based authentication* alone, it's very easy for hackers to intercept user accounts. However, when we use the tokens, the users can verify their identity via physical tokens. This adds an extra layer of security and prevents the hacker from accessing the account even somehow discovering the login credentials.

When we start thinking of using tokens and we know bearer tokens will help us in accessing the resources, we need to make a decision about which kind of token are we going to use and how the module will be implemented.

JWT token

Here, we will be using the **JSON Web Token** known as **JWT**. It's an open standard which defines a *compact* and *self-contained* method for transmitting the information encoded as a JSON object between the parties securely. It can be easily transmitted via query strings, header attributes as well as within the body of a POST request.

The JWT token consists of **Header**, **Payload**, and **Signature** as *three* distinct parts. The *header* and *payload* are first encoded to **Base64** and then concatenated by a *period*. Finally, the result is algorithmically signed to produce the final token in the form of **header.claims.signature**. The *header* consists of *metadata*, which includes the *type of token* and the hashing algorithm which is used to sign the token.

The tokens are not encrypted but are signed to protect against manipulation. It unfortunately can be easily decoded to reveal its contents. We will be generating such a token very soon to discuss this further.

Digging into OAuth2 token

To address the issues faced while using passwords to authenticate the clients OAuth has introduced an *authorization layer*. The authorization layer separates the role of the client from that of the owner of the resource, which we call as **resource owner**. In OAuth, the *client* requests access to the restricted resources which are controlled by the *resource owner* and hosted on the resource server using the *access token*. These tokens are issued to third-party clients by an *authorization server*. This access token has a string denoting a *specific scope*, *lifetime*, and other *access attributes*. The client after obtaining the access token uses it to access the protected resources hosted by the resource server.

The OAuth defines *four* major roles. It's important for every developer who intends to use OAuth to understand these roles. So, let us discuss them before proceeding:

- **Resource owner**: The *resource owner* is an entity which is capable of granting access to a protected resource. Usually, when we use the resource owner, we are considering a *person* typically an *end user*.
- **Resource server**: The *protected resource* is hosted on the server. The *host server* which is capable of accepting the request with a token and then responding accordingly is the resource server.

- **The client**: The *client* is any application which requests the protected resource on behalf of the resource owner along with authorization. Here, the *client* does not denote any particulars like whether the application is getting executed on the server, a desktop, or another device.
- **Authorization server**: We need the access token to be issued by an *entity*. The *server* issues the access tokens to the client after *successful authentication* of the *resource owner* and obtains the *authorization*.

Now we have an idea of the OAuth roles. Let's look at how these roles generally interact with each other with the help of *Figure 10.2*:

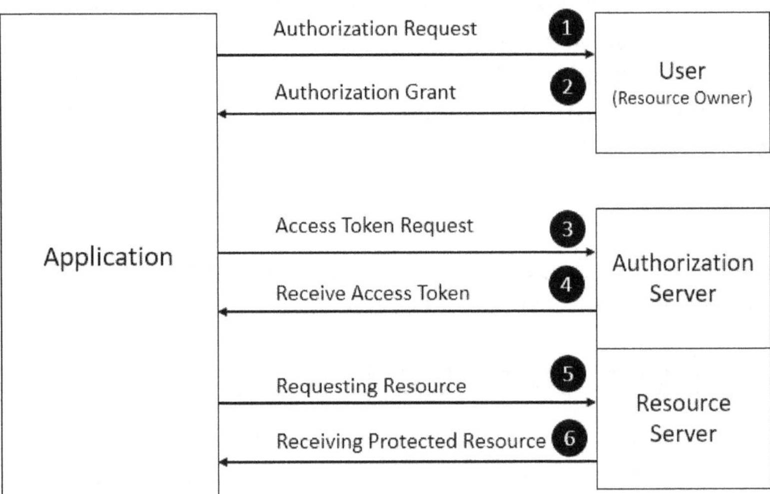

Figure 10.2: Abstract protocol flow

The entire process is illustrated by the following steps:

1. **Sending authorization request**: The client requests authorization to access protected resources from the *resource owner* or *user*.
2. **Receiving authorization grant**: If the resource owner authorized the request, then the client application will receive an authorization grant.
3. **Requesting for access token**: The client application now will send a request for an access token from the authorization server along with its own *identity* and the *authorization grant*.
4. **Receiving access token**: After successfully authenticating the application identity and validating the authorization grant, the *authorization server* issues an access token to the client application. Here, the process of authorization is complete.

5. **Requesting the resource with access token**: Once the client application has the access token it will make a request for the protected resource from the resource server along with the access token for authentication.
6. **Receiving the protected resource**: If the access token presented by the client application is *valid* the resource server sends the resource as a response.

Now, you might be wondering about the *grant types*, why the resource owner will issue it, what are the types, and so on. So, let's discuss the process in general.

The very first step is the **application registration**. We need to register our application with the service application or resource owner. Usually, this is done by filling up a registration form by the *developer* or in the UI. The form collects information such as the name of the application, the redirect URI, or the callback URL. These are the URLs where the service will redirect the user after authorizing our application.

Once our application is *registered*, the resource owner or the service will issue the credentials in the form of a *client identifier* and the *client secret*. The **Client ID** is a string which is used by the services to identify the application. It is used to build the authorization URLs which are presented to users. The *resource owner* will also send the grant. The authorization grant type depends on the method used by the application to request authorization.

The OAuth2 defines *three* primary grant types: **Authorization Code**, **Client Credentials**, and **Device Code**:

- **Authorization code**: This grant type is the most commonly used, as it is optimized for *server-side applications*. This is a *redirection-based flow* and the application must be capable of interacting with the user's web browser and then receiving the API authorization codes which are routed via the browser.
- **Client credentials**: The client credentials grant type provides an application with a way to access applications that have API access. One can use an application which wants to update the registered redirect URI, access the stored data, and so on.
- **Device code**: This grant type is used when devices lack browsers or have input limitations. It provides a means for such devices a way to obtain an access token and access details. It makes the process easier for the users to authorize the applications on such devices to access their accounts. It is usually used to sign into a video streaming application from a smart television or a video game console, which does not have a keyboard for input.

OAuth or JWT

Both **OAuth** and **JWT** have *pros* and *cons*. The **OAuth** is widely used and many *plug-and-play* OAuth solutions are available in the market. Most authentication services understand and use those. It has well-tested client libraries for almost every language along with the web framework. When we use OAuth, it allows us to *code isolation*. But it is complicated for beginners to understand the different OAuth flows. This makes it more difficult to decide which one to use. The OAuth can be a privacy concern for the end users, as the authentication server has knowledge of all the sites the end-user has logged into.

The JWTs can transfer the user details which eliminates the need to use *DB-based query* for authenticating every request and makes the process more efficient and quicker. The JWTs tokens are only stored on the *client side* and it's the responsibility of the client to send it with each request allowing us to save the database storage space. They are *digitally signed* and cannot be modified by clients or attackers, which guarantees strong security.

However, the JWTs can be revoked with significant additional engineering work only as there are *no* database calls when validating. When the signing key is compromised, the attacker can use it to construct a valid JWT and that is a concern.

So, *can we use them together*? Let us discuss the same. As we are very well aware the JWT and Oauth2 serve different purposes, we still can use them together. As the Oauth2 protocol does not specify a token format, it can be combined with JWT. The *access token* which is returned from the Oauth2 authorization server can carry JWT with additional information in the payload. This enables us to improve the performance by reducing the round trips which are required between the resource server and the authentication server. So, it's quite possible to use them together.

The **issuer-url** provided is used by the *Resource Server* allowing it to discover *public* keys of the authorization server and validate the token as well. This is similar to the URL present in the **iss** claim.

Note

The iss claim denotes the identity of the party that issued JWT. It comprises a simple string, which is decided by the issuer. Any consumer must always ensure that the iss claim matches the expected issuer.

```
Spring:
  security:
    oauth2:
```

```
resourceserver:
  Jwt:
   issuer-url: http://localhost:8080/auth/realms/{realm}
```

At startup, the Resource Server will automatically configure itself to validate JWT encoded as the **bearer token**. When we start the Resource Server, it queries the authorization server metadata endpoint for the **jwks_url** property. It provides access to the supported algorithm as well as its valid *public* keys. However, this setup has a drawback. In case the authorization server is *down* or *not already up*, then the Resource Server startup will also *fail*. Here **jwk-set-uri** property helps us. Once it is *set*, the Resource Server will not ping the authorization server at the startup. However, **issuer-uri** is configured for the validation of the JWT **iss** claim on the incoming access token. Once we configure this, the Resource Server will not ping the authorization server at startup. The **issuer-uri** is used to validate the JWT **iss** claim on the incoming token. Spring Security provides extension points to customize the default behavior of the implementation.

Figure 10.3 shows the flow of client registration, client login, and the process of authorizing the client before sending the response:

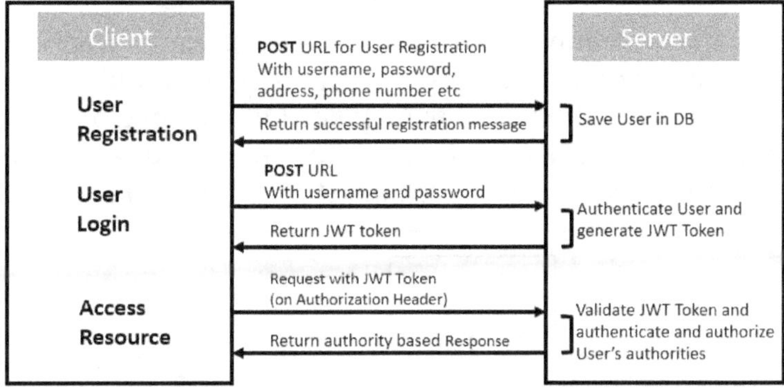

***Figure 10.3**: Process flow for using JWT Token*

In our service, we skipped *Step* 1 of registering the client and added the users directly in **Keycloak**. But in practice, we can write a separate microservice for registration.

OAuth2.0 protocol is based upon industry standards to perform authorization. It focuses on client developer simplicity along with providing the authorization flows for applications such as for *web*, *desktops*, *mobile phones* as well as the devices in our living rooms.

This authorization framework enables *third-party applications* to obtain access to the resources exposed by HTTP services. The *token* can be obtained either on behalf of a resource owner or by the application itself.

Keycloak

Keycloak is an open-source *Identity and* Access *Management tool*. It enables authenticating users rather than individual applications. It means now the application need not have to deal with the login forms, the logic for authenticating the users or storing credentials, etc. for the users.

Single-Sign-On, Identity Brokering and Social Login, User Federation, Client Adapters, Admin Console, Account Management Console, Multi-Factor authentication, and Social Login are some features provided by Keycloak.

The Keycloak can be integrated into the application and enables us to set up the policies for *authentication* and *authorization*, configuring the Keycloak server, and client. It also provides the Keycloak client libraries which can be used in the application to perform the Keycloak integration process. Keycloak offers a reliable and safe approach for managing user identities and access to the applications. It enables the developers to focus on the main concerns of the application without worrying about security issues. It provides a wide range of authentication protocols such as **OAuth2**, **SAML**, and **OpenID** Connect which makes it compatible to use a variety of applications.

When we create a new realm by *default*, it has no *password policies* associated with it. The users can choose to create a *short*, *long*, or *complex* password as per their choice. Although simple settings may suffice for development or learning purposes, when working with Keycloak, they are unsuitable for production environments where *robust security*, *scalability*, and *performance* are essential:

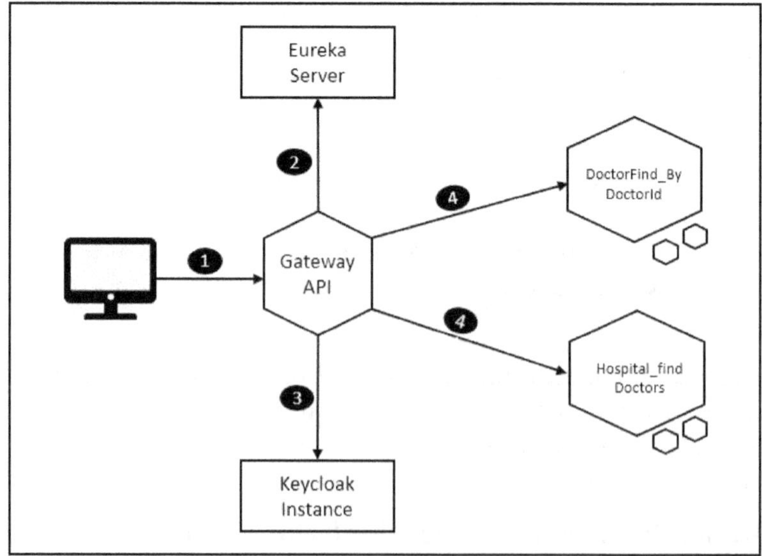

Figure 10.4: *Resource communication with Eureka and Keycloak*

Keycloak can be downloaded from **https://www.Keycloak.org/downloads**. If you have a Docker and you want to use Docker image, refer to the page **https://www.Keycloak.org/getting-started/getting-started-docker**.

Note

Our Keycloak is by default starting on `8080`, as we haven't customized the default port. So, please make sure before starting the Keycloak, port `8080` is available or make it available. You can opt to change the default port as well.

Once you have **Keycloak** *up* and *running*, the very first thing we need to do is to create **Realm**. Let's now explore how to use the **Keycloak**.

Setting up Keycloak

1. From the browser, open the URL **http://localhost:8080.** The dashboard is shown in *Figure* 10.5:

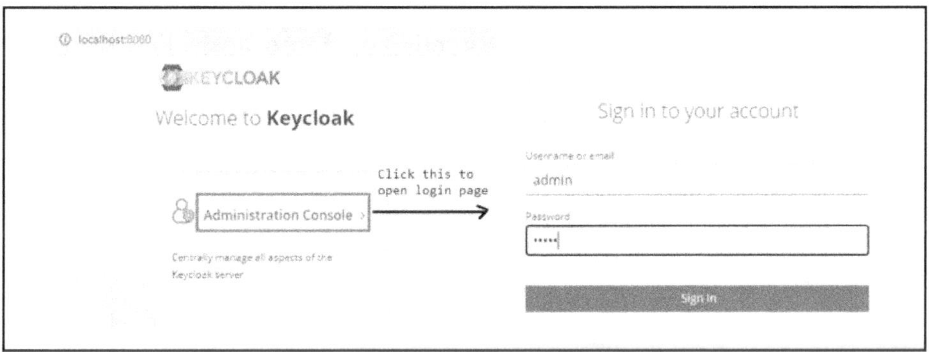

***Figure* 10.5**: *Keycloak dashboard*

2. Enter the *username* as **admin** and the *password* as `admin`.

   Once *successfully logged in*, we will be landing on the admin console page where the default realm **master** is displayed as shown in *Figure* 10.6:

***Figure* 10.6**: *Keycloak admin console*

3. The very first thing we will be doing is to *create a realm*. We will get **Create Realm** button by clicking the *drop-down arrow* next to the **master** realm as shown in *Figure 10.7*:

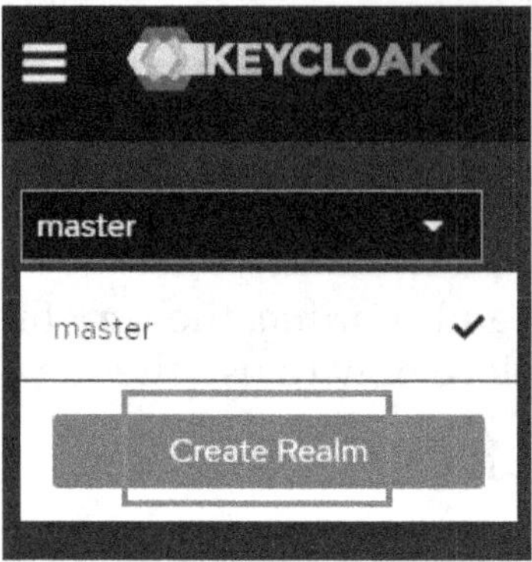

Figure 10.7: *Creating Realm - I*

4. Add the name of the realm as **security_demo** and click on the **Create** button, as shown in *Figure 10.8*:

Figure 10.8: *Creating Realm - II*

5. *Congratulations!* We have just created a Realm *successfully*. Now, we need to add *clients* and *register users* under the Realm.

Make sure you have selected the newly created Realm, and then click on **Clients** to add a *client*, and then click on **Create Client** button as shown in *Figure 10.9*:

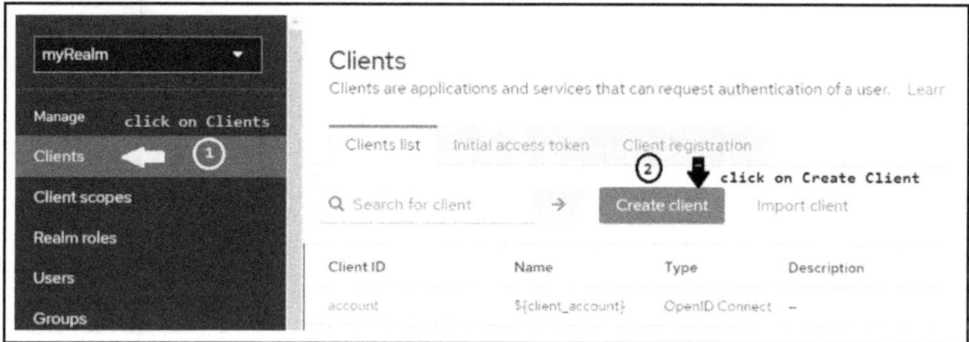

Figure 10.9: *Creating Client - I*

6. In a populated form, add the information as shown in *Figure 10.10*:

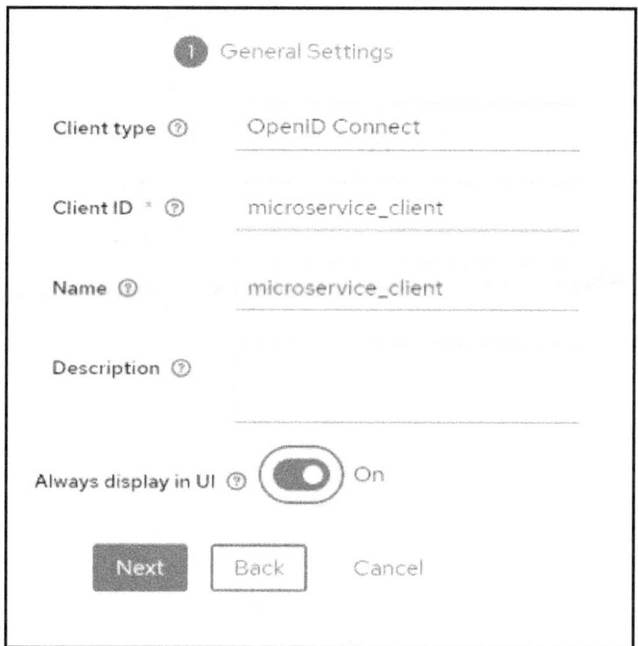

Figure 10.10: *Creating Client - II*

7. Select **Client type** as **OpenID**, **Client ID** as **microservice_client**, name as **microservice_client** as shown in the preceding figure, and then click on the **Next** button. You will observe the screen as shown in *Figure 10.11*:

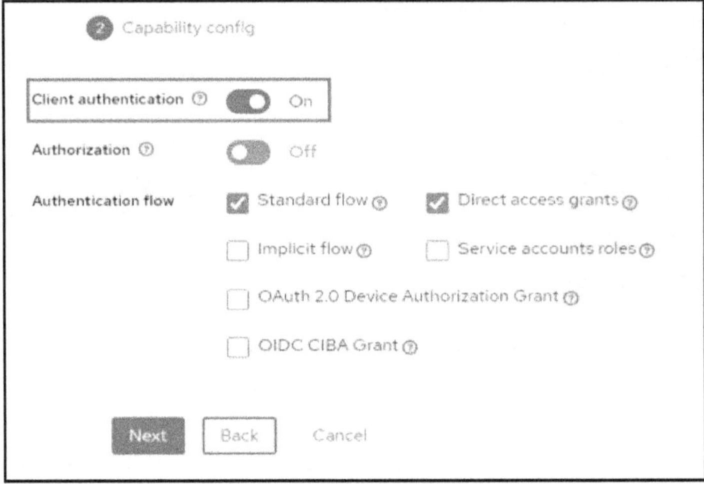

***Figure 10.11**: Capability configuration*

8. As shown, enable **Client authentication** and click on the **Next** button.
9. In the final stage, we will keep everything default and simply click on the **Save** button. We will get a message **Client added successfully**.
10. Click on **Credentials** and then click on **Copy to clipboard**. Paste it somewhere. We need it in further steps. The step is depicted in *Figure 10.12*:

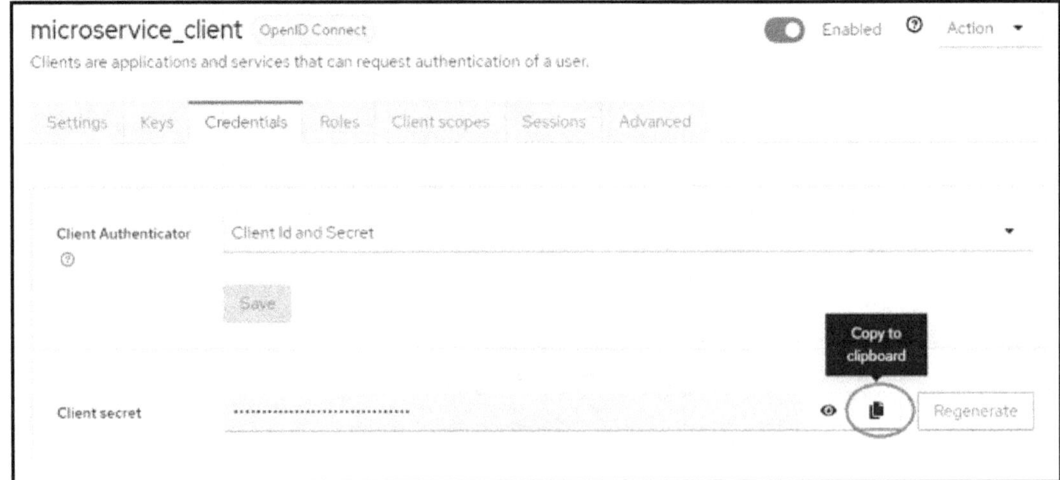

***Figure 10.12**: Generating credentials*

11. Now, we will add a few users, and to do so we need to click on **Users** and then **Add user** button as shown in *Figure 10.13*:

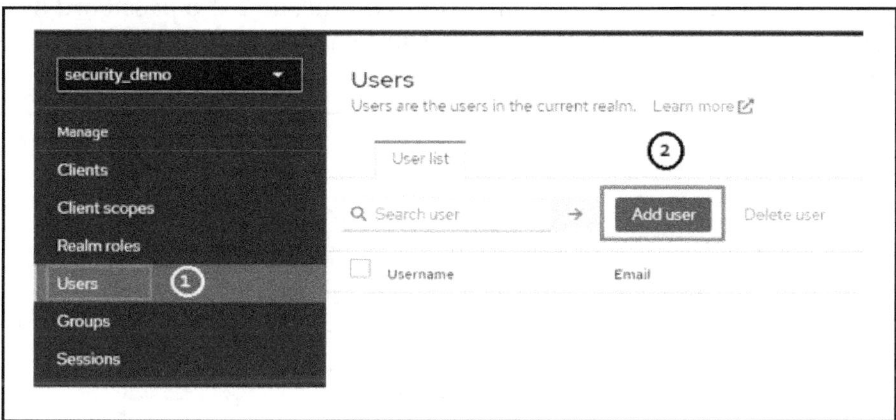

Figure 10.13: *Adding user – I*

12. Fill in the create user form with **client1** as username. And then click on the **Create** button:

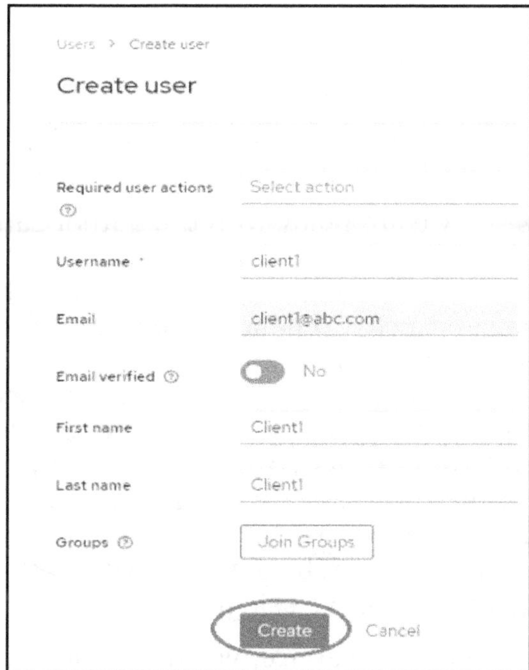

Figure 10.14: *Adding User – II*

13. We will get the message **User added successfully** and we will land on the **client1** home page. Click on the **Credential** tab as shown in the figure and click on **Set Password**. Once the popup opens, add the *password* as **client1** and ensure that you have disabled the **Temporary** as summarized in *Figure 10.15*:

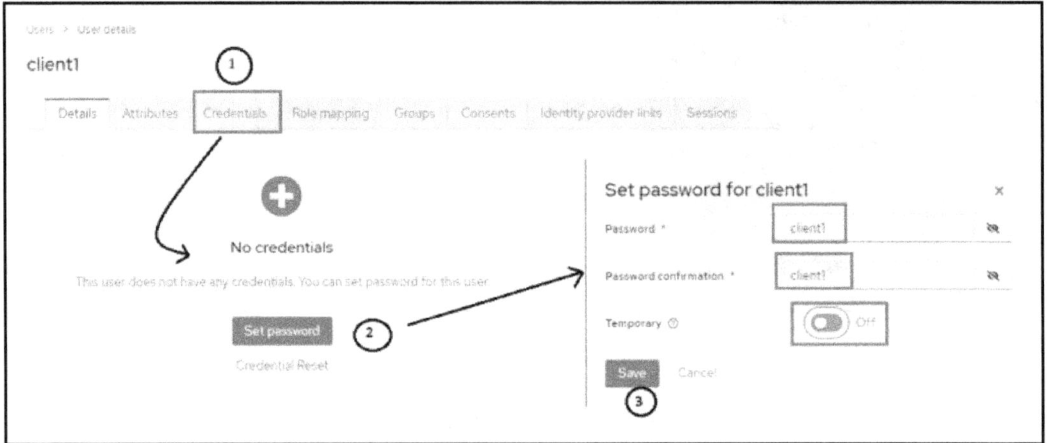

Figure 10.15: *Setting user password*

14. After clicking on **Save**, it will ask for a *set password*. Similarly, you can add a few more users. This is actually a registration process which happens on demand. However, we just did it for learning purposes. Note down your *client IDs* and *credentials*. We need them very soon.

Once the **Keycloak** is set, we are ready with the Authorization Server. Now it's time to focus on configuring the security for our endpoints. As already discussed, we intend our endpoints to be secure and we just want them to be accessed by the authenticated users such as **client1**. To enable the security, we need to configure information about which endpoints to *keep secure* and *who can access them*, and so on. This can be done in an individual microservice. However, if we do so, then the security will be a part of various services and we need to repeat the configuration. We have already written API Gateway and all our requests are filtered from the same point. So, if we write the security configuration on the API service, it will be applied to all the requests. The configuration will be loaded only once. So, there will not be any repetition and in case any changes are needed, we can do them easily at a single point.

Though we already have an API service, we are writing another service. This will make the responsibility of the services clearer. If you wish, you can update the configuration and add classes in the same API service. The newly created service **Security_Provider_Service** is having **spring-boot-starter-oauth2-**

resource-server as a new dependency on top of all which we already added for **`API_Gateway_service`.**

We will now enhance the security of our endpoints by implementing a configuration class that restricts *public* access to them. To add the configuration, we need a bean of the type **SecurityWebFilterChain** as shown in the code snippet:

```
@Bean
public SecurityWebFilterChain configureResourceServer(ServerHttpSecurity
      httpSecurity) throws Exception {
  return httpSecurity.authorizeExchange().pathMatchers(HttpMethod.GET,
                                                "/doctors/**")
                     .authenticated().and()
                     .oauth2ResourceServer().jwt()
                     .and().and().build();
}
```

Anyone who has access tokens will be able to get access to **/doctors/**** resources with OAuth2 Resource Server for JWT tokens.

Spring Boot does not deal with *plain text passwords*, it supports *multiple password encoding* implementations. Each of them has their own set of strong and weak points and we can easily choose any of them. Here we are including the **BCrypt algorithm** by adding the following bean:

```
@Bean
public PasswordEncoder passwordEncoder() {
      return new BCryptPasswordEncoder();
}
```

When a client makes a request with a *token*, we need to verify the token's validity by performing a *cross-check*. To determine the Authorization Server to use, we rely on the following configuration defined within the **spring** tag:

```
security:
  oauth2:
  resourceserver:
    jwt:
      issuer-uri: http://localhost:8080/realms/security_demo
```

If you have created a different Realm, you can fetch the issuer URI from the Keycloak admin console. Go to *Keycloak admin console–> Select your Realm–*

>*Realm Settings* menu. Under the **General** tab, you will notice the **Endpoints** tag. Click on **OpenID Endpoint Configuration**:

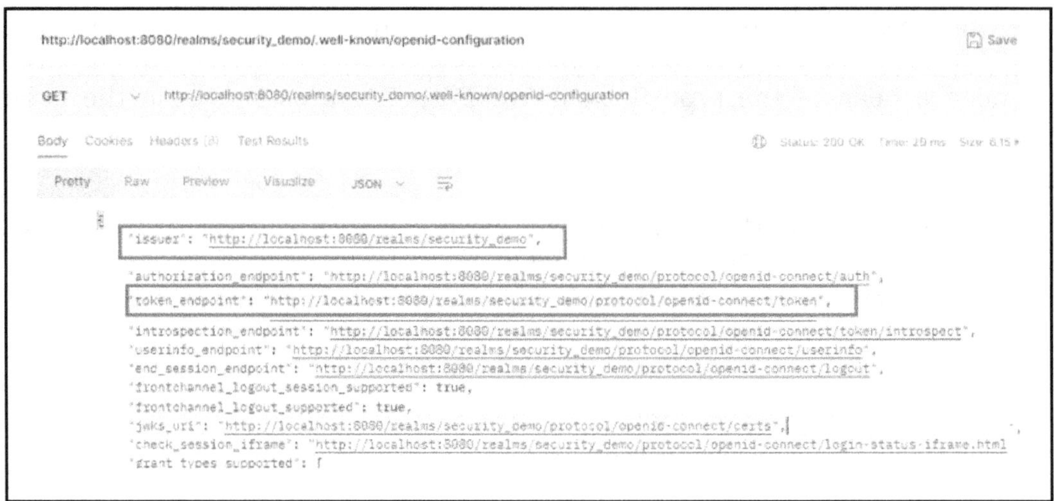

Figure 10.16: *OpenID endpoint configuration*

Figure 10.16 displays all the information you are searching for. As we are going via API Gateway, we need *routing*. So, before moving ahead, check the *route configuration*. Here, we are providing the final route configuration. For simplicity, you can just add for **/doctors/**** as well:

```
spring:
  application:
   name: api-gateway-service
  main:
     allow-bean-definition-overriding: true
cloud:
   gateway:
     routes:
     - id: hospital_route
       uri: http://localhost:9091/hospitals
       predicates:
       - Path=/hospitals/**
       filters:
      - id: doctor_route
        uri: lb://doctor-find-by-id-service/doctors
        predicates:
```

```
          - Path=/doctors/**
      - id: hospital_balanced_route
        uri: http://localhost:9091/hospitals-balanced
        predicates:
        - Path=/hospitals-balanced/**
      - id: hospital_balanced_gateway_route
        uri: http://localhost:9091/hospitals-balanced-gateway
        predicates:
        - Path=/hospitals-balanced-gateway/**
```

And the moment of truth. Let's execute the Eureka server, **DoctorFindByDoctorId**, **SecurityProvider** services, and Zipkin server as well. Once all services are *up* and *running*, fire the request for **http://localhost:9097/doctors/1** resource:

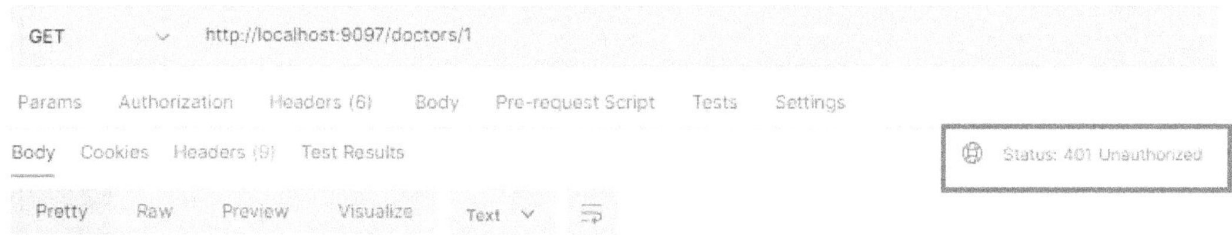

***Figure 10.17**: Accessing unauthorized resource*

We will get status code **401** as shown in *Figure* 10.17. The reason is very simple; we have added the endpoint under *security* and need a valid JWT token. It means first we need a token from the Keycloak:

To generate the token, follow these steps:

1. Select the **Authorization** tab from Postman.
2. Select **OAuth2.0**, as the **Authorization type**.
3. Under the **Configuration**, edit the values for the new token as:

```
Token Name: Token_gateway (Any valid token name can be added)
Grant Type: Password Credentials
Access Token URL:
http://localhost:8080/realms/security_demo/protocol/openid-
connect/token
Client ID: microservice_client (use the client ID created earlier
under
realm security_demo)
```

```
Client Secret: SECRET COPIED EARLIER (client secret copied on the
      clipboard)
Username: client1 (User created in Keycloak)
Password: client 1 (Password assigned to client1 user in
Keycloak)
Scope: openid
```

4. Select **Client Authentication** as **Send as Basic Auth header**.

   Figure 10.18, depicts the entire process of generating the token:

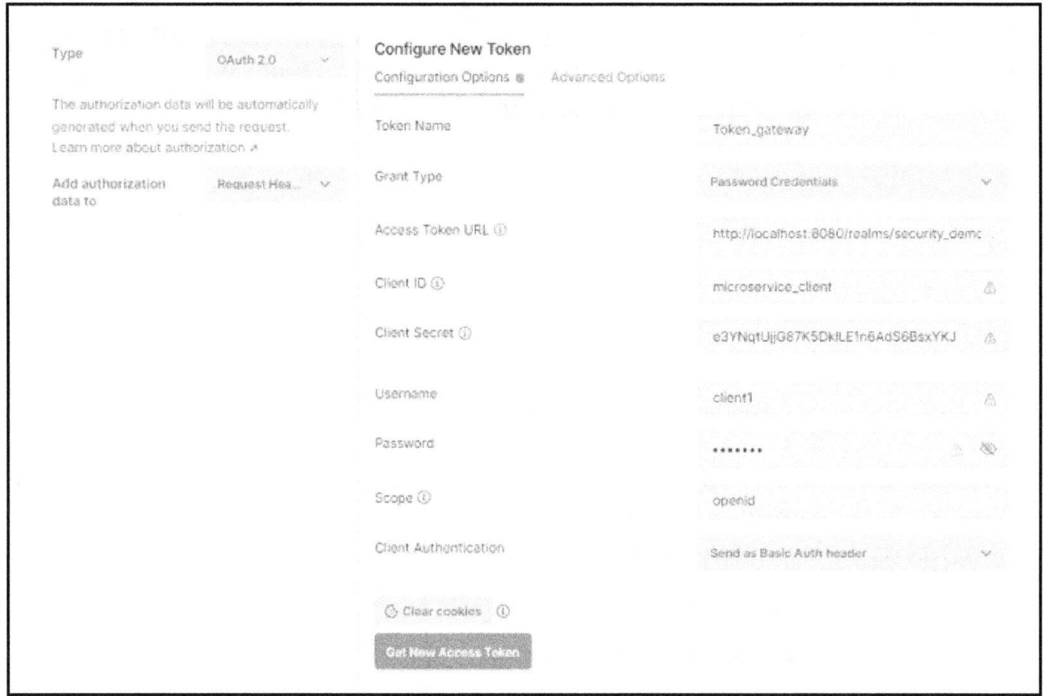

***Figure 10.18**: Token generation*

When the authentication is *successful* with Keycloak, the popup labelled **Get new access token** will appear, as shown in *Figure* 10.19:

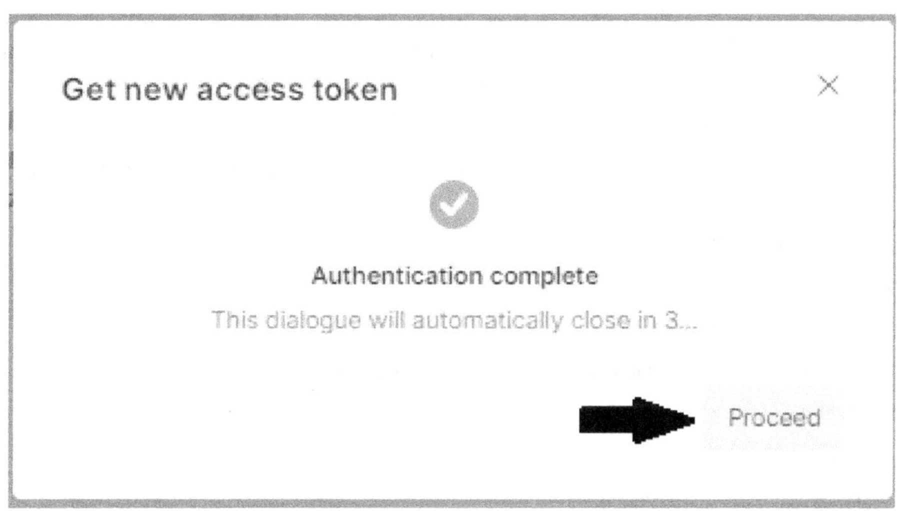

***Figure 10.19**: Getting a new access token*

Click on the **Proceed** button so that you can retrieve the access token from Keycloak as shown in *Figure 10.20*:

***Figure 10.20**: Retrieving access token*

We will be using it to request the resource by clicking on **Use Token**. Once clicked, it will be added to **Current Token** and when we request the resource, it will be added as a **Bearer token**. The final step is to request the **/doctors** resources once again, but this time we have added the token. You will notice that we received the *doctors* details, *which means our security works*!

Now, we have a secure endpoint. In the same way, we can configure the rest of the endpoints as well. But before that, we have to make sure that we intend only **/doctors/**** URL to be authenticated and others to be available freely. Try accessing the **/actuator** endpoint, we will receive **401 Unauthorized** as the *status code. What does that mean?* It means we need to update the configuration to specify which URLs to allow and which need authentication. Let's update the configuration for **/actuator** to allow without authentication by invoking the **permitAll()** method as shown by the following code:

```
return httpSecurity.authorizeExchange().pathMatchers(HttpMethod.GET,
  "/doctors/**")
  .authenticated()
  .and()
  .authorizeExchange()
  .pathMatchers(HttpMethod.GET, "/actuator/**")
  .permitAll()
  .and()
  .oauth2ResourceServer()
  .jwt()
  .and().and()
  .build();
```

Great! You will notice that the code is working well when we communicate with doctors services directly. But *what about inter-service communication?* In the **Find_Doctors_in_Hospital_Controller** we have **/hospitals/{hospitalId}**, **/ hospitals-balanced/{hospitalId}** endpoint which are directly communicating with the **/doctors** service. It's *not* a good idea as it makes the *doctor* service insecure and can be used by everyone. We also have the **/hospitals-balanced-gateway/{hospitalId}** endpoint which is communicating with the *doctor* service but is routed via API Gateway where we have configured security. If we try to access **http://localhost:9097/hospitals-balanced-gateway/{hospitalId}** we will get a **401** status code. This is because we are trying to access the **/doctors** endpoint without any token. Now, we first need to obtain the token and that token needs to be forwarded to the API Gateway. The process is very much the same as we did from POSTMAN. The only change is here we will be doing it programmatically. In order to achieve it, we need to update the controller code for the **Hospital_FindDoctors** microservice. You can either update the code or create a new application as we are doing here. We have created another microservice **Hospital_FindDoctors_FeignClient_Security** which is the same as **Hospital_FindDoctors**. All the security-related updates we will be adding to this service:

```
@GetMapping("/hospitals-balanced-gateway/{hospitalId}")
ResponseEntity<Hospital> findAllDoctorsInHospitals_loadBalanced_
gateway(@PathVariable int hospitalId, @RequestHeader(name = "sort",
defaultValue = "all") String sort) {
```

```
List<Doctor> doctors = new ArrayList<>();
    Hospital hospital = repo.findHospitalById(hospitalId);
    if (hospital != null) {
                //step 1: set the clientId, secrete, username,
                                                     password,
                          grant_type etc to obtain the token
            MultiValueMap<String, String> map =
                         new LinkedMultiValueMap<String, String>();
            map.add("username", "client1");
            map.add("password", "client1");
            map.add("grant_type", "client_credentials"); //
            map.add("client_secret",
                         "e3YNqtUjjG87K5DklLE1n6AdS6BsxYKJ");
            map.add("client_id", "microservice_client");
            map.add("scope", "openid");
            HttpHeaders headers = new HttpHeaders();
            headers.setContentType(MediaType.APPLICATION_FORM_
                         URLENCODED);
            HttpEntity<MultiValueMap<String, String>>
              requestBodyFormUrlEncoded
                 = new HttpEntity<>(map, headers);
            String access_token_url =
              "http://localhost:8080/realms/security_demo/protocol/
                 openid-connect/token";
//step 2:  Use RestTemplate to obtain the token from Keycloak
            RestTemplate restTemplate = new RestTemplate();
            ResponseEntity<MyToken> response_token = restTemplate.
               exchange(access_token_url, HttpMethod.POST,
                 requestBodyFormUrlEncoded, MyToken.class);
//set 3: Set the token as Bearer token to the header
            HttpHeaders headers_token = new HttpHeaders();
            headers_token.setBearerAuth(response_token.getBody().
                               getAccess_token());
            HttpEntity<MultiValueMap<String, String>> reqest_doctor_
              header_entity = new HttpEntity<>(headers_token);
            List<Integer> doctor_ids = repo.findDoctorIds(hospitalId);
            System.out.println(doctor_ids.size());
              for (int i = 0; i < doctor_ids.size(); i++) {
```

```
//step 4 : access the resource via Gateway API along with headers
           with Bearer token using exchange()
           ResponseEntity<Doctor> entity = restTemplate1.
            exchange("http://api-gateway-service/doctors/{doctorId}",
                   HttpMethod.GET, request_doctor_header_entity,
                   Doctor.class,doctor_ids.get(i) );
               if (entity.getStatusCode().equals(HttpStatus.OK)) {
                    doctors.add(entity.getBody());
               }
           }
      }
           hospital.setDoctors(doctors);
           return new ResponseEntity<Hospital>(hospital, HttpStatus.
                                                                 OK);
}
```

As you can observe in the preceding code, the code is implemented in *four* steps. In the *first* step, we have set up the **clientId**, **secrete**, **username**, **password**, **grant_type**, and so on to obtain the token. In the *second* step, we used **RestTemplate** to retrieve the token from Keycloak using the **exchange()** method. Here, we have obtained the **ResponseEntity** which is added to **Mytoken** type for simplicity. This token has **access_token, expires_in**, **refresh_expires_in, token_type**, **not_before_policy**, scope as its members. In the *third* step, we have set up this obtained token from *Step* 2 as a bearer token to the *header* and access the resource via Gateway API along with headers which contain the Bearer token using **exchange()**. The method **getForEntity()c**is unable to add new *headers*. So, instead of it we have used the **exchange()** method here.

Now we need to update the security configuration to specify whether to authenticate **/hospitals-balanced-gateway** endpoint. We are adding a few more endpoints which we will be using in upcoming demos. So that we don't have to update the service again and again:

```
return httpSecurity.authorizeExchange().pathMatchers(HttpMethod.GET,
"/doctors/**").authenticated().and().authorizeExchange()
  .pathMatchers(HttpMethod.GET, "/hospitals/**",
              "/hospitals-balanced/**",
              "/hospitals-balanced-gateway/**", /hospitals-feign/**",
              "/hospitals-feign-interceptor/**")
  .authenticated().and().authorizeExchange()
  .pathMatchers("/actuator/health/**")
```

```
.permitAll().anyExchange().authenticated()
.and().oauth2ResourceServer().jwt().and().and().build();
```

It's time to observe how it works. Before testing, make sure in the API Gateway you have added the route for **/hospitals-balanced-gateway** endpoint. Make sure the Eureka server, **DoctorFind_By_DoctorId**, **Hospital_Find_Doctors**, or **Hospital_FindDoctors_FeignClient_Security**, **API_Gateway_Service**, or **Security_Provider_Service**, **Zipkin**, **Keycloak** are *up* and *running.*

Before visiting the POSTMAN, we need to update the service accounts settings in Keycloak otherwise we will *not* get authenticated. To enable it, visit the *Keycloak Admin Console* and select the realm, in our case **security_demo**. Then go to **Clients → microservice_client → Settings→** Select the checkbox of **Service account roles** as shown in *Figure 10.21:*

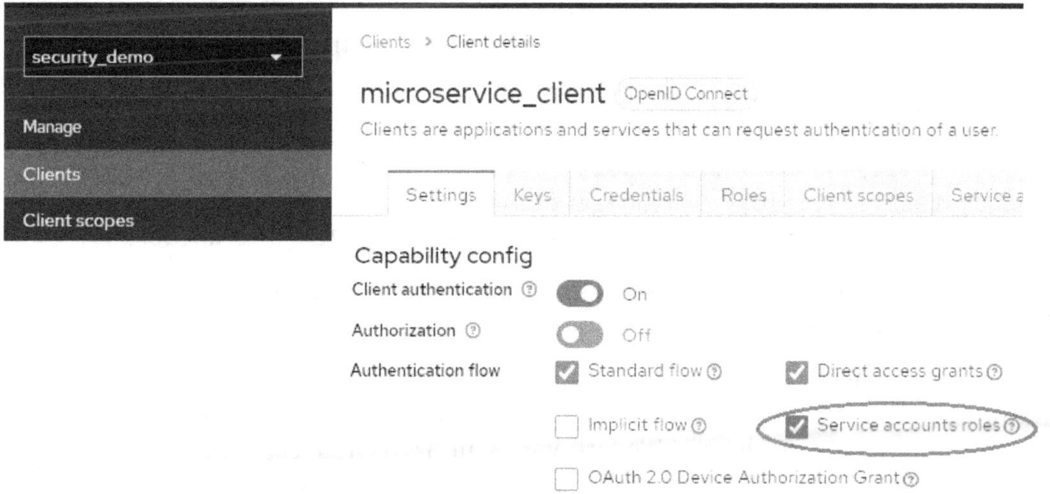

***Figure 10.21**: Service account settings*

Why do we need service accounts? The Service accounts are great for administrative tasks. When the tasks are executed on behalf of the service instead of being executed by an individual user, service accounts come as a savior. As we know OAuth2 provides an *Authorization code*, *Client credentials*, and *Resource owner password*, and *Implicit* four major kinds of grant types which can be used with Keycloak. In Keycloak, we can enable *Client Credential Grant Type* by selecting the checkbox for **Service Accounts Enabled**. *We are all set!*

Now in POSTMAN access the **http://localhost:9097/hospitals-balanced-gateway/12345** URL along with the Bearer token in the same way as we did in the earlier demo. We will receive our resources and status as success. You can also use the Feign Client to achieve this instead of **RestTemplate**.

Tokens and Feign Client

As already discussed, and demonstrated the Feign Client is a much easier way for inter-service communication. Earlier, when we used Feign Client, the provider service endpoint was publicly available, and we didn't have to do anything extra. However, now when *hospital* service communicates with the *doctor* service, they need secure communication. The process of communicating securely is very much the same as we did with **RestTemplate**. In terms of Feign Client, we can pass the token using the headers directly or we can write a **RequestInterceptor** which will pass on the headers.

Sending the authorization header within method arguments

When we decide to pass on the headers to Feign Client, we need to change the signature of the method to accept the **Authorization** header as shown by the following code:

```
ResponseEntity<Doctor> searchDoctorById(
 @RequestHeader(value = "Authorization", required = true)
 String authorizationHeader,@PathVariable("doctorId")int doctorId);
```

The method will make a request along with **AuthorizationHeader** having the access token obtained by the Keycloak. *Isn't it easy?*

Now to demonstrate this we will be modifying the **Hospital_Doctor_Feign** definition. Earlier code was communicating to the **/doctors/{doctorId}** directly, and the call was not going via API Gateway, which was *non-secure communication*. Now, we will update the definition to always go via API Gateway as:

```
@FeignClient(name="api-gateway-service",
             fallback = FeignClient_FallBack.class)
public interface Hospital_Doctor_Feign {
//Using Authorization header to pass on access token
  @GetMapping("/doctors/{doctorId}")
  ResponseEntity<Doctor> searchDoctorById(
    @RequestHeader(value = "Authorization", required = true)
    String authorizationHeader,@PathVariable("doctorId")int doctorId);
//Authorization Header will be added by the RequestInterceptor
  @GetMapping("/doctors/{doctorId}")
  ResponseEntity<Doctor> searchDoctorById(@PathVariable("doctorId")
                                         int doctorId);
}
```

We have declared another **searchDoctorById()** method so that we can pass on the access token within the header. As the Feign Client definition is changed, we need to change the **fallback** class as well and here is the updated definition. Unfortunately, to try sending the header, we all have to update it:

```
@Component
public class FeignClient_FallBack implements Hospital_Doctor_Feign{
@Override
public ResponseEntity<Doctor> searchDoctorById(String
                                          authorizationHeader,
int doctorId) {
          return new ResponseEntity<Doctor>(new Doctor(1, "ABCD",
                                          "No spec"),HttpStatus.OK);
    }
    @Override
    public ResponseEntity<Doctor> searchDoctorById(int doctorId) {
          return new ResponseEntity<Doctor>(new Doctor(1, "ABCD",
                                          "No spec"),HttpStatus.OK);
    }
}
```

We already have discussed **fallback** in detail so I am not discussing it here. In case you have any queries, you can refer to *Chapter 9, Reliability*.

Let's concentrate on the handler method now, which is shown in the following code snippet:

```
@GetMapping("/hospitals-feign/{hospitalId}")
ResponseEntity<Hospital> findAllDoctorsInHospitals_feign(@PathVariable
int hospitalId) {
//step 1: Get the Token
//Code to get the token using RestTemplate from Keycloak as we did
//earlier.
    List<Doctor> doctors = new ArrayList<>();
    Hospital hospital = repo.findHospitalById(hospitalId);
    if (hospital != null) {
    List<Integer> doctor_ids = repo.findDoctorIds(hospitalId);
    for (int I = 0; i < doctor_ids.size(); i++) {
//step 2: send the token as Authorization Header
    ResponseEntity<Doctor> entity = feign_client.
```

```
searchDoctorById(String.format""%s %""""Beare"", response_token.
getBody().getAccess_token()),doctor_ids.get(i));
    if (entity.getStatusCode().equals(HttpStatus.OK)) {
                doctors.add(entity.getBody());
          }
    }
    hospital.setDoctors(doctors);
    return new ResponseEntity<Hospital>(hospital, HttpStatus.OK);
    }
    return new ResponseEntity<Hospital>(HttpStatus.NO_CONTENT);
    }
```

As we did and discussed earlier, we will request the token from the *Authorization server* and then will send it as a *Bearer token* in the **Authorization** header and we achieve this using:

```
@RequestHeader(value =""Authorization"", required = true)
String authorizationHeader
```

as shown in the code.

Let's start the *hospital* service and use POSTMAN to check whether the request receives a *successful* response or not. *Bingo!* It's working when we pass an access token from a POSTMAN request, otherwise, we will receive **401** as a status code.

Things go smoothly until there is a scarcity of Feign Client requests. However, as the number of Feign Clients *increases* and secure communication becomes necessary, the code for generating tokens must be duplicated. It becomes necessary for a developer to explicitly invoke the token generation process and include it in the headers. Here, the **RequestInterceptor** facilitates us to make the process much smoother.

Sending the authorization header using RequestInterceptor

The Feign provides a **RequestInterceptor** interface, which we can use for *adding*, *removing*, or *mutating* a part of the request, so that we can update it implicitly. At a time, we can write more than one **RequestInterceptors**. This will ensure that all the requests will get updated. But it's not guaranteed in which order the interceptors will be applied. A **RequestInterceptor** can be added either as a

Bean in the configuration class or we can write it as an interface implementer class. Here we are adding it as a bean:

```
@Bean
public RequestInterceptor feinRequestInceptor() {
return new RequestInterceptor() {
   private static final String AUTHORIZATION_HEADER = "Authorization";
   private static final String BEARER_TOKEN_TYPE = "bearer";
   @Override
   public void apply(RequestTemplate template) {
   //step 1: Using RestTemplate Obtain the token
   //step 2: Send the token in the Header
   template.header(AUTHORIZATION_HEADER,
   String.format("%s %s", BEARER_TOKEN_TYPE,
   response_token.getBody().getAccess_token()));
  }
 };
}
```

Now, we don't need to send the token in the Feign Client method signature. So, let us add another endpoint to see how it all works together. If you wish, you can just update the existing method. Here we are adding **/hospitals-feign-interceptor** as a new handler in the **Find_Doctors_in_Hospital_Controller** controller as follows:

```
@GetMapping("/hospitals-feign-interceptor/{hospitalId}")
ResponseEntity<Hospital> findAllDoctorsInHospitals_feign_interceptor
   (@PathVariable int hospitalId) {
  List<Doctor> doctors = new ArrayList<>();
  Hospital hospital = repo.findHospitalById(hospitalId);
  if (hospital != null) {
    List<Integer> doctor_ids = repo.findDoctorIds(hospitalId);
    for (int i = 0; i < doctor_ids.size(); i++) {
      ResponseEntity<Doctor> entity=
        feign_client.searchDoctorById(doctor_ids.get(i));
      if (entity.getStatusCode().equals(HttpStatus.OK)) {
        doctors.add(entity.getBody());
      }
  }
  hospital.setDoctors(doctors);
```

```
    return new ResponseEntity<Hospital>(hospital, HttpStatus.OK);
  }
  return new ResponseEntity<Hospital>(HttpStatus.NO_CONTENT);
}
```

Indeed, it is identical to our older implementation that is because the **RequestInterceptor** works in the background to update the request and the Feign Client interface implementer needs no knowledge about it.

Note

We can request the Authorization server and subsequently add the token to the request header when a class implements security or has access to the security context. An alternative approach is to retrieve the token from the Authentication object. This can be achieved by using the `getTokenValue()` method of the `OAuth2AuthenticationDetails` class to extract the token.

In all the preceding cases, we obtained the token in POSTMAN as well as in the hospital service. If our client is authenticated once, then *why do we need to repeat the process of authentication? Can't we just use the same token in the downstream service again*? Indeed, we can do so.

Using TokenRelay

We wish to forward the available token to the downstream service. This is facilitated by **TokenRelayGatewayFilterFactory**. The **TokenRelay** is where the OAuth2 consumer acts as a *client* to forward the token received in the request to the outgoing requests to the downstream service. A Resource Server or any SSO application can act as a *client*. Our API Gateway acts as a client to forward the OAuth2 access tokens to the downstream services. We can apply it using the **TokenRelayGatewayFilterFactory** as follows:

```
@Autowired
private TokenRelayGatewayFilterFactory filterFactory;
@Bean
public RouteLocator routeLocator(RouteLocatorBuilder builder) {
    return builder.routes()
            .route("resource", r -> r.path("/doctors")
                    .filters(f -> f.filter(filterFactory.apply()))
                    .uri("http://localhost:9091"))
            .build();
}
Or we can use it in YAML configuration as:
```

```
- id: hospital_hospitals-feign_relay_route
  uri: http://localhost:9091/hospitals-feign-relay
  predicates:
  - Path=/hospitals-feign-relay/**
  filters:
  - TokenRelay=
```

Time to get into action! For this demonstration, we need to update the **API_Gateway_service** or **Security_Provider_service** depending on whether you are implementing the codes in the new API service or an older application. Make sure that you have included the s**pring-boot-starter-oauth2-client** as a dependency to use **TokenRelay** in Spring Cloud Gateway. In the YAML file add a route **hospital_hospitals-feign_relay_route** to add TokenRelay as a filter shown in the following configuration:

```
- id: hospital_hospitals-feign_relay_route
  uri: http://localhost:9091/hospitals-feign-relay
  predicates:
  - Path=/hospitals-feign-relay/**
 filters:
  - TokenRelay=
```

Now either you can add a new handler method or update the earlier one as per your choice in the **Hospital_FindDoctors_FeignClient_Security** or **Hospital_FindDoctors** depending on where you have added all earlier codes for security:

```
@GetMapping("/hospitals-feign-relay/{hospitalId}")
ResponseEntity<Hospital> findAllDoctorsInHospitals_feign_relay(
  @RequestHeader(value = "authorization", required = true)
  String authorizationHeader,@PathVariable int hospitalId) {
List<Doctor> doctors = new ArrayList<>();
Hospital hospital = repo.findHospitalById(hospitalId);
if (hospital != null) {
  List<Integer> doctor_ids = repo.findDoctorIds(hospitalId);
  for (int i = 0; i < doctor_ids.size(); i++) {
  ResponseEntity<Doctor> entity = feign_client
    .searchDoctorById(authorizationHeader,doctor_ids.get(i));
          if (entity.getStatusCode().equals(HttpStatus.OK)) {
                    doctors.add(entity.getBody());
            }
```

```
            }
            hospital.setDoctors(doctors);
          return new ResponseEntity<Hospital>(hospital, HttpStatus.OK);
      }
    return new ResponseEntity<Hospital>(HttpStatus.NO_CONTENT);
  }
```

As you can observe in the preceding code, the method **findAllDoctorsInHospitals_feign_relay()** has an argument **authorizationHeader** as a **RequestHeader** which will accept the incoming authorization header and then forward it to the downstream service as:

```
feign_client.searchDoctorById(authorizationHeader,doctor_ids.get(i));
```

Finally, it's time to use the endpoint **http://localhost:9097/hospitals-feign-relay/12345**. Don't forget to generate a new token before you hit the URL.

Conclusion

In this chapter, we discussed in detail the importance of security and how exposing all the resources will be a security threat. In a *monolithic application*, applying a security layer is much easier. However, in a distributed environment like microservices, it is complicated. During our discussion, we explored the concept of applying security to endpoints belonging to different services without the need for duplicating the security configuration. We also discussed why basic authentication is not useful in microservices and how token-based authentication helps us to overcome the limitations of basic authentication. Moving forward, we discussed in detail different tokens such as **JWT tokens**, and **OAuth2 tokens** and their uses. We added **SecurityWebFilterChain** bean with **BCryptPasswordEncoder** to enable OAUth2 token-based security for endpoints such as **/doctors**, **/hospitals**, **/hospitals-balanced**, and so on. We also learnt how to set up the Keycloak as an authorization server by adding new realms, clients, and users. Then we set up handler methods in the *Hospital* controller to generate a new token from Keycloak and then forward it to downstream service in the **RestTemplate** as well as Feign Client. After adding the security features, we used POSTMAN to generate the token and add it as a Bearer token to the request.

We have made significant progress by creating our services for various operations, configuring filters, implementing logging, ensuring high availability with Resilience, and achieving location transparency through the Eureka server. Now, the next step is to deploy these services. In the next chapter, we will discuss the *deployment*, *deployment design patterns*, *image creation and deploying instances* using the created image. I am excited to explore it, *aren't you*? See you all in the next chapter.

CHAPTER 11
Deployment

Abhay was a little panicked as he was about to attend the review meeting of the ongoing project. He called one of his colleagues *Vishwas* and asked, "*Vishwas, the team was expecting a new version of* Hospital_Update_Details *microservice in production. But just now they informed me we still have the older version in production. What happened?*" *Vishwas* was looking worried. He replied, "*Abhay, I and the team tried to deploy the new version. However, every time we were getting a 'version not supported' message. When we did the deployment of the first version everything went very smoothly. Even we deployed another service and it went very well.*" *Abhay* was surprised by this. This was not what was planned and predicted. He told *Vishwas* that he will look into the matter and get back to him in some time.

After a while, *Abhay* had a long discussion with *Manish*, who was equally surprised to know this. But then he recalled that the new version of Hospital_Update_Details microservice is built with *Spring Boot* 3.0.1 version and the other service is still using the 2.7.8 *version*. *Manish* reconfirmed it with the team. Unfortunately, the team didn't inform the DevOps team about the changes which caused this issue. *Abhay* mailed *Vishwas* and explained what happened and also sent the changes to the software version requirements. *Vishwas*'s team started working on the deployment with the changes but was a bit upset with the re-installation. This is the *third* time when they faced a similar hurdle. One of the team members was furious, "*Vishwas, why are we doing the installation of a new version of Java? It is the same project. So why are they changing the system requirements every time? This time they gave us a WAR file which we weren't able to deploy on the earlier Tomcat 8. We downloaded and installed a new Tomcat and then we set up all the configurations."* Another team member added, "Yes Vishwas, *why don't they stick to the same configuration?"* Anticipating the situation, Vishwas responded in a composed manner, "I *acknowledge that we are adhering to the same configuration, but it is essential for the project's needs, and we will provide our support to the team. I understand your concerns, and the excessive time wasted was due to system requirements. Our conventional approach, which worked well during monolith deployments, is proving insufficient in this case. I have been actively seeking a solution for some time and have had discussions with others. Fortunately, Mandar has proposed an excellent solution. Mandar, would you kindly explain it to us?"*

Mandar was ready with his view, "*Hello team. I am not surprised by what you are facing now. It is a very common issue, and it is going to increase as we go on developing more microservices. Sometimes we may need to upgrade some microservice to a newer version and sometimes because the upgraded services cause issues we may decide to use the older versions. It's a continuous process. Earlier in monolithic applications, once the version, platform and system configuration are decided, we hardly do any changes to it. And if the changes are required, those will be just once. The microservices are different applications and they do not necessarily have to follow the same version, platform or system requirements. Every time a new configuration and setting causes an issue. Who is responsible for this? It's not you, but all the developers are more responsible for letting you know the system requirements. We are now going to change this traditional approach. Rather than that, we will adopt container-based deployment using images*", "Images?" Everyone shouted in surprise. Mandar continued, "*Yes, images. Not ordinary images, but Docker images. These Docker images will take care of all the necessary platform or Java version-specific requirements along with the actual applications. The DevOps team will only use this image in a clustered environment and set up the required instances. No more system, platform, version-related issues*" Vishwas was overjoyed, "*Wow that's a really good, time-efficient and easy approach.*"

Many of you might have faced similar bottlenecks in your teams and expecting a better approach to deal with this. Some of you are very new to the deployment process itself and require an in-detail understanding. Some of you might have done deployment on servers but are not familiar with Docker. This chapter will provide you with the detailed *process of deployment*, *various ways*, and *approach right from bundling the application to exposing it from the cluster* with the help of the following points.

Structure

In this chapter, we will discuss the following concepts:

- Revisiting microservices architecture
- Deployment patterns
- Choice of deployment
- Using Kubernetes to deploy service

Revisiting microservices architecture

We already discussed on several occasions *why we moved from monolithic to microservice-based architecture*. We also know *what are the benefits due to which we are shifting*. We are also aware of the different components that we need to manage in the microservices architecture. I am quite sure now you can talk for hours on this topic. So, let us not repeat it. I will prefer to revisit it to understand what happens in the *production phase* when we intend our applications to go live in both of these architectures.

Let's start with a monolithic architecture. Observe *Figure 11.1*:

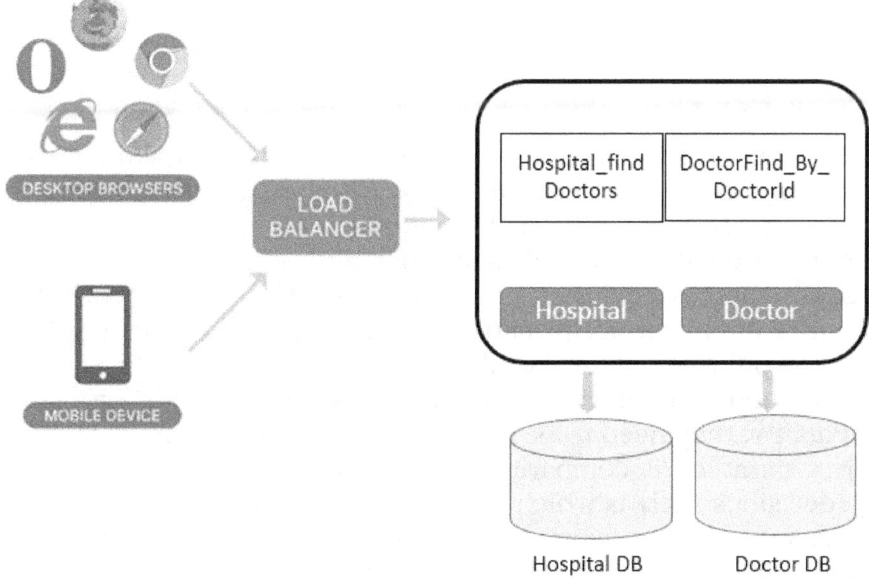

Figure 11.1: *Revisiting monolithic architecture*

In monolithic applications, we develop the application as *one single* unit having its *business logic*, *database*, and *utility layers*. The *application* communicates to one or more databases but needs to have a single configuration which is used by the DB layer. The application consists of various modules and needs a large code base for support. The size of the application creates challenges at the time of deployment. However, the system configuration will remain the same all the time, making it easy for the DevOps team.

Now let's consider microservices architecture:

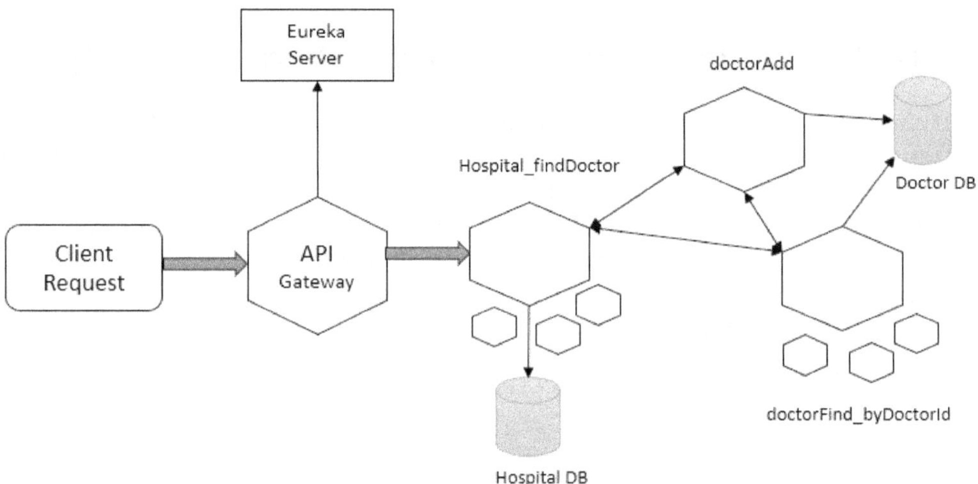

***Figure 11.2**: Microservice architecture*

As we can observe, we have *multiple small-size monolithic applications* communicating to the respective databases. Some may share databases, some may not. Some services choose to communicate with other services. The microservices are *independent* of each other, allowing developer independence. The isolation supports fault tolerance, additionally, the *scalability* of bottlenecked microservices improves performance and overall development will be much faster. But the point of concern would be, *what about their deployment?* We need to deploy numerous independent services. Also, to enhance *performance* and *high availability*, they need to be deployed in more than one location, which is physically separated. As compared to *monolithic deployment*, we need to take strategic decisions such as which component or service must be deployed first and expose it over the network. We need to also think about *how the databases will be deployed and when they should be backed up.*

Let's take an example of the Eureka Server. To maintain location transparency, we have the Eureka server, but it's again a service and we can't guarantee its availability. A single instance will not be sufficient in production; we need a Eureka cluster. In the same way, **Cloud config server** instances need to be deployed. These *two* services are needed and utilized by other microservices, so we need to start with them. And then one by one start deploying other microservices by updating the properties of the production environment.

We now are well aware of microservices deployment, and how is it different. Now, it's time to discuss different available deployment patterns.

Deployment patterns

The following patterns are available in the deployment process:

- **Single service per host**: We started with microservices so that we will be able to take advantage of faster development, easy deployment, and most important highly available services. When we install an instance per host, it faces less competition for the resources, and more memory to utilize. In case, the server hosting the instance *goes down*, only that instance will be unavailable, as it's isolated from one another. It won't affect the rest of the system. Being a single instance it's very much straightforward for monitoring, managing as well as redeploying the service instance. On top of all the advantages, *what about the resources we allocated*? You all will agree with me when we choose *one instance per host*, we are not utilizing the resources efficiently.
- **Multiple services per host**: As we just discussed, we are underutilizing the available resources when we just deploy *one service per host*. The best way to utilize the resources is to launch multiple services. While launching multiple instances, we need to be careful in choosing the services as we are interested in achieving high availability. We need to take care not to install multiple instances of the same service on the same host. In this way, we are separating the instances physically and reducing the chances of service getting completely down. Though we manage to utilize the resources, we can't overlook the fact of having the risk of conflicting resource requirements. Some service instances may race to use the resources, as it's very difficult to limit the resources consumed by each service instance. As multiple services are running on the same host, it is almost impossible when we intend to isolate them from each other. This makes their monitoring more difficult as an individual instance.
- **Service instance per container**: When we decide to use container-based deployment, we need to package our services as a container image and then deploy each service instance *as a container using the packaged image. Nowadays,* ***Docker*** *is a very* well-known packaging tool allowing

us to package the service as a Docker image and then use it to launch an instance within the Docker container. As we are working with the containers, scaling up and down a service by changing the number of container instances is easy. Each service instance is isolated and monitoring becomes easier. The containers are extremely fast to build and permit us to launch instances faster.

Using orchestrators

As we are dealing with a bunch of services and wish to launch them on a minimum of *two* separate instances, we need to take a strategic decision to easily manage the *updating*, *deploying*, and *versioning* process. The **Docker swarm** enables the clustering for easy management of different services and their individual instances in the containers. We also have the orchestrators which are specialized in distributing container workloads over a group of servers distributed over the network. **Kubernetes** and **Openshift** are well-known *container-managed tools*. The orchestrators provide *container management*, *routing*, *security*, *load balancing*, as well as centralized logs which is very much required in a microservice architecture.

Microservices as a serverless function

Microservices, as a *serverless* function, is very different from everything we have discussed so far. Till now we used *servers*, *containers*, and *orchestrations*, but now we will use the cloud to simply run code on demand. The cloud, such as AWS offers **AWS Lambda**, and *Google Cloud* offers **Google Cloud** functions to handle all the infrastructure details. It also enables scaling and high availability services so that the developers can focus on business logic development.

Now we intend to deploy the microservice, but *the question is how* we are going to bundle the application either for deployment or for distribution. Let us talk about the packaging services and their usage.

Packaging services

We are developing multiple *small*, *independent* microservices. We have successfully run the services in the local system. But we were working in the *development* phase and can access the code from the IDE. Now we have completed the *development* phase and are looking forward to production. Many of you earlier worked in **Servlets** and **JSPs**, **Struts**, **JSF**, or **Spring MVC-based applications**, created a WAR file and then deployed it on the server. *Are we going to do the same? How are we going to convert* JAR *to a* WAR? We can do so, but that's not the only option, actually, we are going to discuss various ways of bundling the microservices and then how to use the bundled packages to get an instance of them. So, *let us proceed!*

Packaging as JAR

We developed so many services along with some supportive services as well. The most important thing of all is to bundle microservices so that the distribution will be easy. As we are developing a web application which needs a server where the deployment happens. We packaged all the services which we developed in this book as a separate JAR file which has a self-contained Tomcat server. It means, as per the Tomcat server, we are deploying a single instance of the service. Let's consider a **DoctorFind_By_DoctorId**. When we run the service, our application is deployed on the internal Tomcat server. We didn't think of distributing the service earlier as we were in development. Now we are moving to *production* and must be aware of all possible options. We can package this service as a JAR and then use the JAR to launch an instance of the service. It can be considered a *service-per-host* pattern. Before we move on to the next step, let us achieve this first.

It's very easy to package the JAR as we are using **Maven** and already choose to bundle the service as JAR at the time of application creation. This is similar to what is shown in *Figure* 11.3:

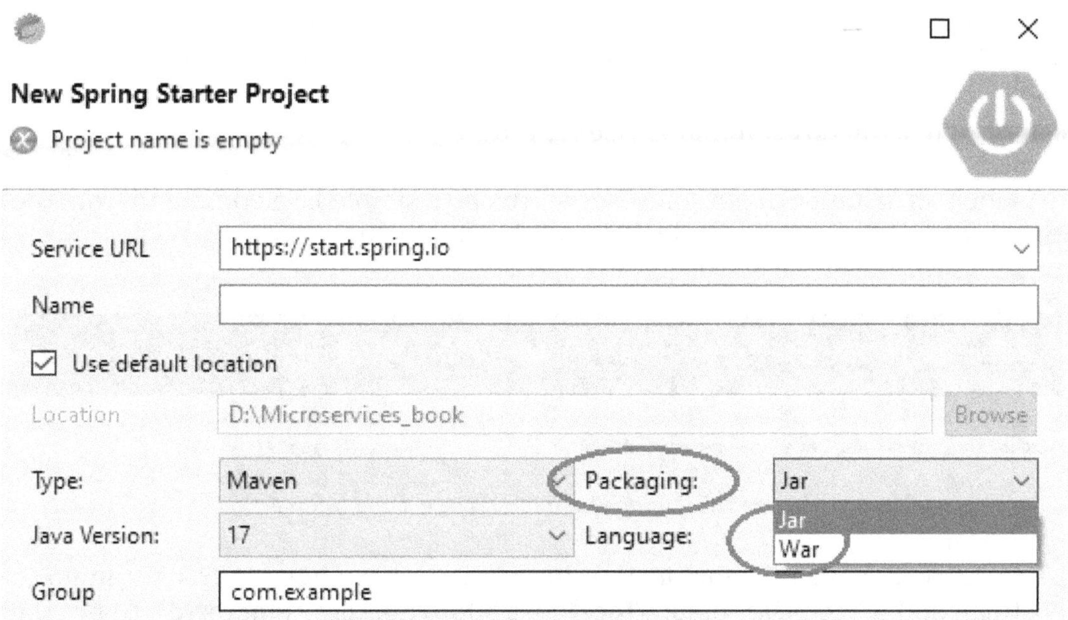

***Figure* 11.3:** *Setting up packaging*

We already have selected packaging our microservice as JAR and our service is a Maven project, so nothing to worry about it. Now, we just need to use the command **maven clean install** so that the application will be cleaned up and a new JAR will be generated under the *target* folder as shown in *Figure 11.4*:

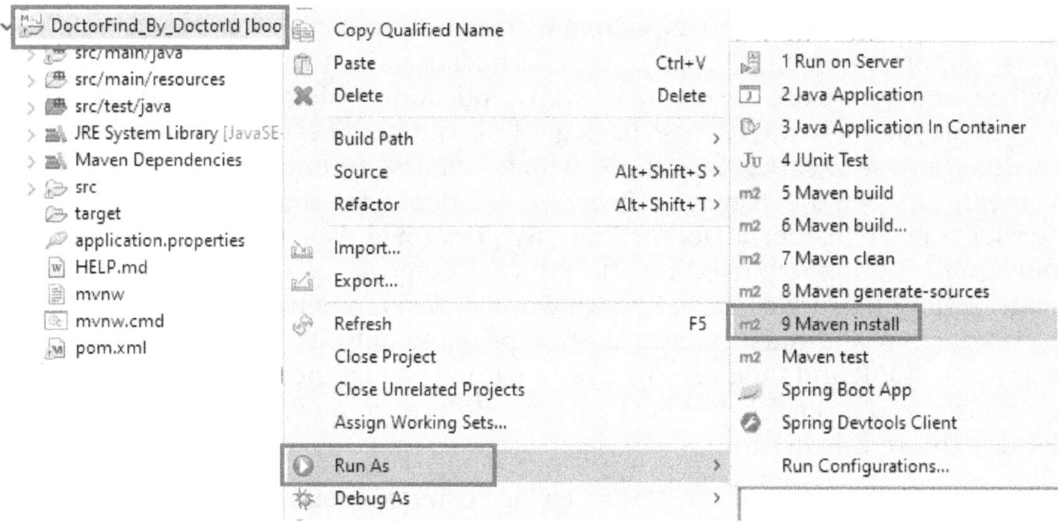

Figure 11.4: *Generating the JAR file*

The **Maven install** command will generate a JAR file under the *target* folder. Sometimes the *target* folder is not visible. In this case, simply *refresh* the application. To refresh the application, right click on the application and select **Refresh**. Once the *target* folder is visible, you can retrieve your JAR file. Before we move on, make sure the Eureka server is running. Let us use the generated JAR to launch an instance of our microservice using a simple Java command from the directory where we have the JAR file, as shown in *Figure 11.5*:

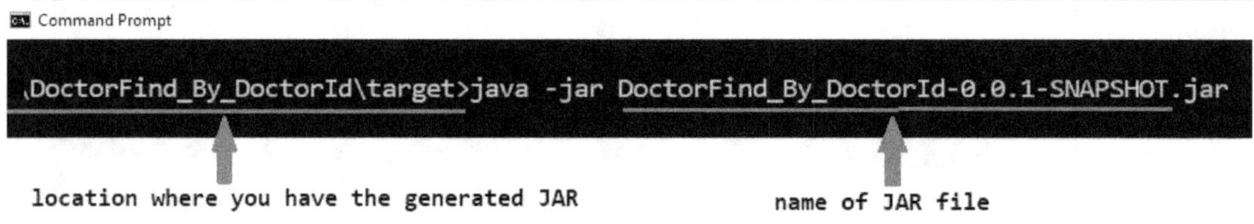

Figure 11.5: *Launching microservice using JAR file*

Isn't it easy to launch the application instance once you have JAR? We can go to Postman and hit the URL **http://localhost:8085/doctors/{doctorId}** to get the details of the *doctor*. The only problem in this way is per JAR we need to launch a new instance of Tomcat and it increases the memory requirement. Also, being a server, it can host more than one microservice.

Packaging as WAR

Here, we got different Tomcat servers which will eat up lots of memory of the host. We can create a separate WAR file for each of the microservice and then deploy all the WARs to the server. We can use the Tomcat server to host more than one service, which can be considered as *multiple services per host*. We need to do some changes while developing and then package them as WAR.

Let's do it then. It all starts when we create an application. We need to choose to package the application as WAR instead of JAR as shown in *Figure* 11.6:

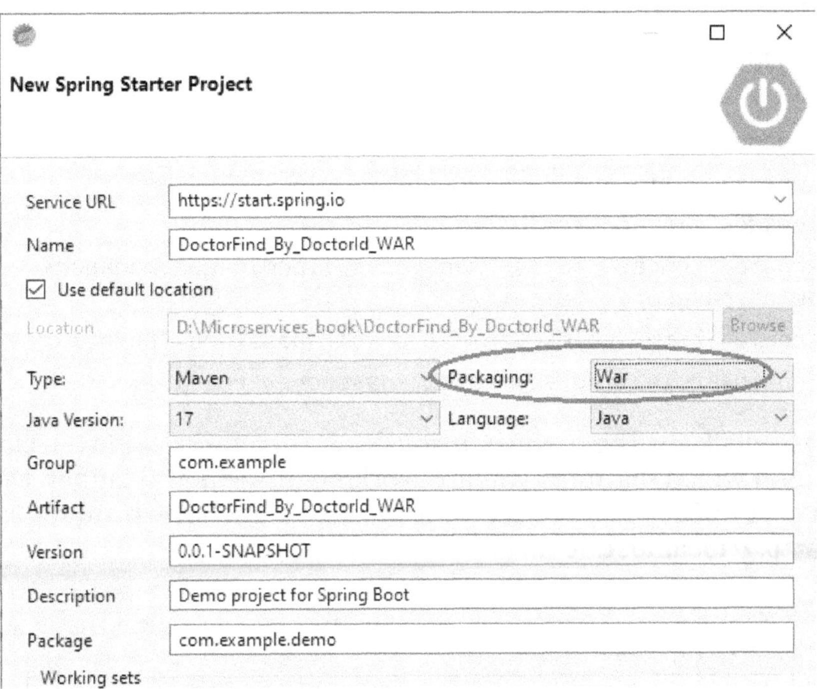

***Figure 11.6**: Generating WAR file*

We have already added the same dependencies as that of the **`DoctorFind_By_DoctorId`** application. We have simply copied all the files from the **`DoctorFind_By_DoctorId`** application. Additionally, you can simply add a controller with some handler methods. As we did at the time of JAR creation, here also we will select **Run As** → **Maven install**, to generate the WAR file.

The very first thing we need now is to have a server to deploy this WAR file. Currently, we are using **Tomcat 10**, but we can choose any server of our choice. Please make sure the selected version of the server support **jakarta.*** instead of **javaee.***. We have downloaded a **`.zip`** file of Tomcat from **https://tomcat.apache.org/download-10.cgi**.

Some of you might be already using the **8080** port, for some other purpose. In such case, we can update the Tomcat server port to a new port by modifying the **Connector port** property of **server.xml** as follows:

```
<Connector port="8083" redirectPort="8443" connectionTimeout="20000"
                                           protocol="HTTP/1.1"/>
```

By default, we don't have any registered users for Tomcat. So, we need an *admin* role and a *user* registered as an *admin* in Tomcat. To achieve this, we can edit **tomcat-users.xml** available at the Tomcat installation **directory/conf** to add roles and users as follows:

```
<role rolename="tomcat"/>
<role rolename="role1"/>
<role rolename="manager-gui"/>
<role rolename="admin-gui"/>
<role rolename="manager-script"/>
<user username="tomcat" roles="manager-gui,admin-gui,manager-
script,admin" password="tomcat"/>
<user username="both" roles="tomcat,role1" password="both"/>
<user username="role1" roles="role1" password="role1"/>
```

Now double-click on the *Tomcat installation directory* → *bin* → *startup* file, depending on which platform you are working on. This will launch the Tomcat server on port **8083**. Once the server is started, launch the browser and access the URL **http://localhost:8083**:

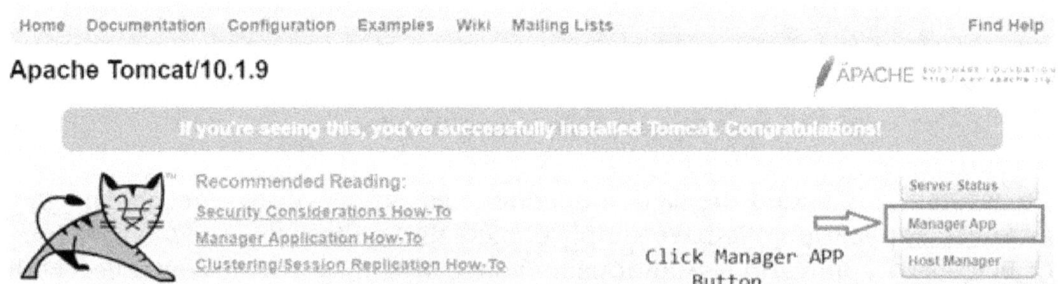

Figure 11.7: *Tomcat dashboard*

We will be on a page to upload the generated WAR file under the **Deploy** section as shown in *Figure 11.8*:

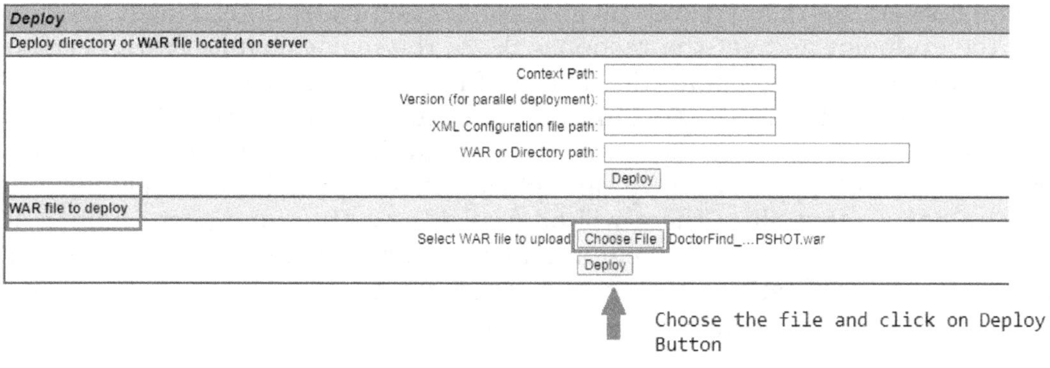

Choose the file and click on Deploy Button

Figure 11.8: *Deploying the WAR*

Notes

Sometimes the size of our WAR exceeds the default uploading limit set in Tomcat. We can change the size by changing the configuration in the `webapps/manager/web.xml` file as shown:

```
<multipart-config>
    <max-file-size>68662404</max-file-size>
  <max-request-size>68662404</max-request-size>
  <file-size-threshold>0</file-size-threshold>
</multipart-config>
```

Once the WAR is uploaded, we can start the application by clicking the **Start** button located in front of the application name as shown in *Figure 11.9*:

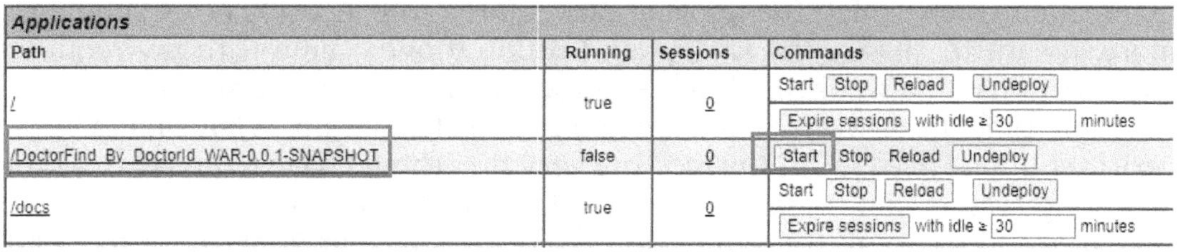

Figure 11.9: *Launching the app*

We need to do this process only once. Next time if the server is *restarted*, the application will be started automatically. You can visit the *Tomcat console* to confirm the launch of the application. One more very important thing, before you start the application, you must have the **Eureka** and **Zipkin** server already *running* otherwise the console will give connection exceptions. Finally, we can visit the endpoint and get the response. Here the major change is we need to append the name of the application in the URL as it now acts as the base path as: **http://localhost:8080/DoctorFind_By_DoctorId_WAR-0.0.1-SNAPSHOT/doctors/1**. You can choose the name of WAR and that becomes your base path. Similar to *doctor's* application we can upload other applications as well. But, we need to ensure that all of them will be available on the same port number of the server, which means now we don't need to choose a different port number for every new application. Keep one thing in mind, as all the applications are running on the same host, *once the host is down everything will be down!*

Packaging as Docker image

For years, we were deploying our enterprise applications on either a *direct* system or in the cloud on bare metal. One may directly execute the application on the operating system in the same way as we are launching it on our system. Sometimes instead of launching an instance on the system, one may choose to launch it on the virtual machine. In either of the situations, the environment which was available in the development must be replicated on the cloud system as well, otherwise the application will not work well in the production environment. We may also face issues while updating the instances to new versions and in case the instances are unhealthy, we have to interfere and launch another instance manually. All this makes it hard for the production environment to respond to ever-changing demands in business.

The containers work very similarly to VMs. However, the containers are more specific and handle the deployment in a granular way. The containers are *isolated* and may have a single application along with its dependencies, the external software which the application requires to execute. Let us simplify it more. I want to change my laptop, so I ordered one online with my required specifications. In a week, my brand-new laptop arrived. I was so happy, but at the same time, I was overwhelmed when I was setting it up. *What should be the very first thing I need to do? Correct*, the very first thing I have to do is install the operating system and then, according to that, all other software like *Java*, *IDE*, *database*, and so on. In the same way, when we want our application to install anywhere, we need to set up all the requirements of it. For example, if I want to launch Doctor's service, I need at least a *database* and *Java* 17 installed on the system, otherwise, the execution of our microservice is impossible. All these are requirements one must fulfil before performing the launching task and that is always dependent. Some applications may need **Java 8**, **Java 11**, or even **Java 17**. So, dependencies are important and Docker sorts them out as the Docker image contains all the basic software and then on top of it, the application will be launched. This removes the major constraints in production.

As described in Docker documentation, Docker is an open platform for developing, shipping, and executing applications. Docker allows us to separate the applications from our infrastructure and enables quicker software delivery. Managing the infrastructure is very much the same as managing our applications. The Docker methodologies allow us to ship, test, and deploy the applications with a significant reduction in time. Deploying microservices is best as it minimizes the delay in developing services and then running them in production. You might be wondering what a Docker image is!

Docker image

The application developed by the developer will be packaged for easy distribution. The Docker image is the starting point when we start using Docker. A **Docker image** is a file which is used to execute the application code in a Docker container. The Docker image is like a template which has a set of instructions to build a Docker container.

A **Dockerfile** is a very simple text file which contains all the commands to assemble the Docker image along with a packaged application and how to execute it to install it. The very first line in a **Dockerfile** is the base image on top of which we will install our application or its dependencies. We normally find this base image in the **Docker hub**. Now, we may want to use a specific directory where all our files will be kept. It can be done by using **WORKDIR**. It's *optional*. Now we want our **JAR** file to be made available in the container. The **COPY** command allows copying files from the base system to the Docker image. Finally, we wish to unpack the application and launch the instance. It is done by the **ENTRYPOINT** command. We can also use the **CMD** command to perform a set of commands once we execute the run command. *Shall we create our Docker image? What are we waiting for?* Let us do it. Take note that this chapter is not to master Docker or Kubernetes. We want to get an idea about what exactly happens in *deployment* and what is our role as a *developer*. Let's create a Docker image for the **DoctorFind_By_DoctorId** service. We need to start writing a **Dockerfile** as follows:

FROM openjdk:17-alpine

```
COPY DoctorFind_By_DoctorId-0.0.1-SNAPSHOT.jar DoctorFind_By_DoctorId.
jar
CMD ["java","-jar","DoctorFind_By_DoctorId.jar"]
```

Practically, we don't need any specific location to save the file. For simplicity, I am creating a folder **Deployement_Docker** and storing the file in it. The file doesn't have any extension, not even **.txt**.

You can use any editor to create the file and, once done, save the file as **Dockerfile**. We can use the older **JAR** file. However, there is a practical difficulty. Our service needs to communicate with the MySQL server, which is running outside of the Docker container. The network, by default, will not be able to communicate outside of the container. Let us change local host to **host.docker.internal:3306**. This is a recommended way using which we can connect to the special DNS named **host.docker.internal**. This resolves to the internal IP address used by the host on which our MySQL DB is running. Again, this is only for *development* purposes and we should not use it in a *production* environment. In *production*, we will have everything in the container, not in a hybrid. Once you make the changes in the **application.yml** file either to connect to MySQL, Eureka, and Zipkin, generate a new JAR file.

Now, copy the JAR file from **/target** folder in the same folder **Deployement_Docker**. It's not compulsory but in the Docker file, we did not specify where the **DoctorFind_By_DoctorId-0.0.1-SNAPSHOT.jar** is kept. This means it is available locally. Now, we need to generate a Docker image from the file. Let's execute the **build** command as shown in *Figure 11.9*:

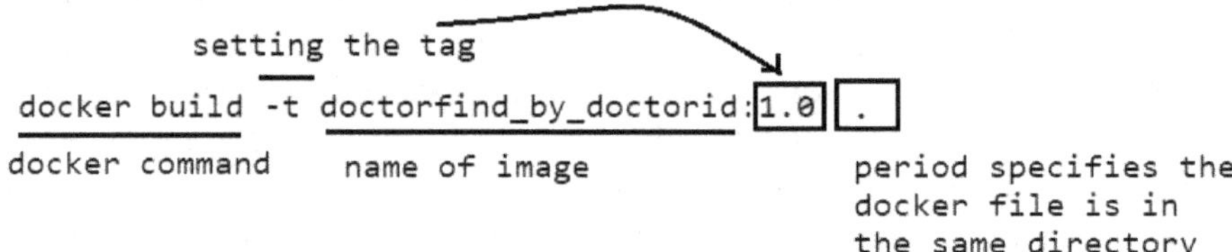

Figure 11.10: *Generating Docker image*

Hope now you got the point, *why we copied JAR and Dockerfile at the same location*? On the execution of the build command, step by step the image will be generated. All the intermediate layers generating this process can be observed in *Figure 11.11*:

Figure 11.11: *Exploring Docker build*

We can confirm the creation of the image using the Docker images command. The preceding figure confirms the creation of the **doctorfind_by_doctorid** image. We are just a step away from launching our application with the help of the **docker run** command. Before that, ensure that you have the Eureka server and Zipkin server *up* and *running*. Let us launch the **run** command. It will execute the CMD written in the Dockerfile. However, it's not exposed to the outside world and is available to use within the Docker container only. We will use **-p** to expose the internal port to the external world as:

```
docker run -p 8085:8085 doctorfind_by_doctorid:1.0
```

The command will launch the application and when we make the request from outside the container to the **8085** port, it will be forwarded to the service running in the Docker container on port **8085**:

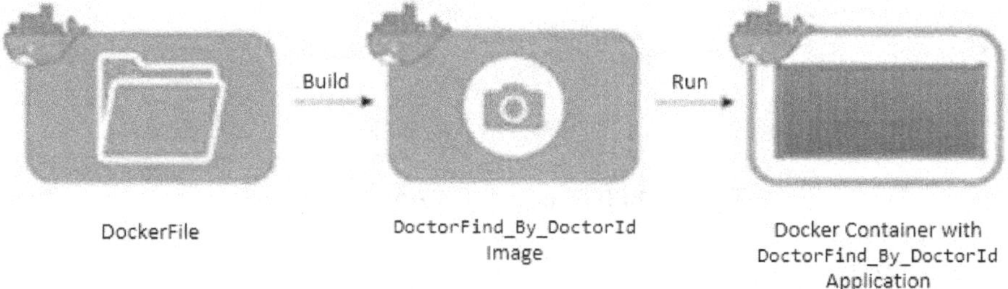

Figure 11.12: *Docker Image to container*

You can observe the **DoctorFind_By_DoctorId** application launching on the Command Prompt with a major difference. We are not running it on the host system; it is launched in the Docker container. Once the application is *up* and *running*, we can request POSTMAN by accessing **http://localhost:8085/doctors/{doctorId}** URL. Notice that we are receiving the response in the same old way.

You just observed that the Doctor service is *running* in the Docker container. *Can't we run* `Eureka` *as well in the container*? Yes, *why not*! We just need to repeat the same steps of generating the JAR and referring it from the Dockerfile as:

```
FROM openjdk:17-alpine
COPY Eureka-Server-0.0.1-SNAPSHOT.jar Eureka-Server.jar
CMD ["java","-jar","Eureka-Server.jar"]
```

Use the **`docker build -t eureka_server:1.0`** command to generate the Docker image. Before you launch the Eureka server using a **build,** please stop the running Eureka server on the host. The **build** command will be, **`docker run -p 8761:8761 eureka_server:1.0`**.

The entire infrastructure is depicted in *Figure* 11.13:

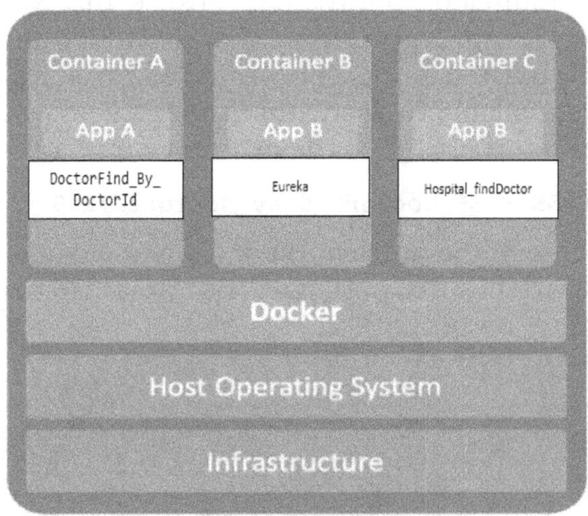

Figure 11.13: *Docker infrastructure*

You can use MySQL image also to launch MySQL in the Docker container as well. I am using the MySQL server running on the host system.

Docker registry

A developer develops an application and now to shift into the production phase, the application instance needs to be launched on different systems easily. To make this distribution easy a Docker image is created and added to the **Docker Registry** which is a system for *versioning*, *storing*, and *distributing* Docker images. **DockerHub** is a hosted registry which is used by default when we install the Docker engine. Along with DockerHub, the clouds such as **AWS** and **Google** have their own registries for public use. So, you can also create an account and push your image to the Docker repository for further distribution. In practice, we add all our images to the Docker Registry so that accessing from anywhere will be easy.

Being a developer, Dockerfile creation is our role as we know *what are the requirements, such as Java version, execution command, and so on*. And we just did it. *Now what?* You can just upload the images to DockerHub so that they can be accessed easily. But we just launched the instance on a single system. We know that, for *high availability*, we need a minimum of *two* instances. *Are we going to go to an individual system and repeat the same process which we did here?* No! If we want to launch the instance in a clustered environment, we can choose to go with **Docker Swarm**.

Docker Swarm

When developers work with limited services and their instances using Docker to launch individual applications might be feasible. However, it's actually a very complex and lengthy process. Docker provides a **Docker Swarm mode**. The *swarm mode* is a container orchestrator which we can use on any host having Docker Engine installed. We can create Docker Swarm and use it for replicating the containers across various systems. The *swarm* allows us to add multiple manager nodes to enhance performance and enable fault tolerance. Though the Docker Swarm is *lightweight*, it offers limited *customizations* and *extensions* and offers fewer functionalities along with fewer automation capabilities. Along with Docker Swarm, we can also use tools such as **Kubernetes** or **OpenShift** to manage clustered deployment. I am leaving Docker Swarm to you for self-exploration and moving on to Kubernetes.

Using Kubernetes to deploy services

Kubernetes is an *open-source, portable platform* which enables the management of containers, and their production workloads along with scalability. Kubernetes allows the DevOps team to *schedule*, *deploy*, and *manage* applications in highly available flexible clusters. The **worker nodes** in the cluster are managed by a Kubernetes master. The **master** controls and monitors all the resources in the cluster.

Kubernetes offers functionalities for *service discovery*, and routing using ingress as well as *load balancing*, *storage*, *scalability*, *automatic rollouts*, or *rollbacks* of the images. The best part is, it is available on the *public* cloud. It is available for on-premises use and many cloud providers such as **AWS**, **Azure**, **IBM Cloud**, and **Google Cloud Platform**, and so on provide their support to set and manage the Kubernetes cluster in the easiest way.

Let us have a look at standard Kubernetes cluster to manage instances of microservices as shown in *Figure* 11.14:

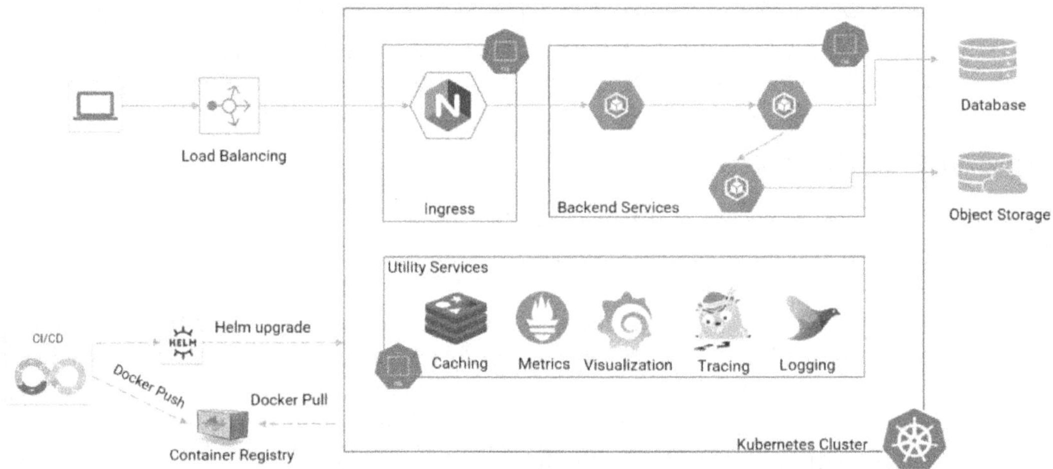

Figure 11.14: *Kubernetes Cluster*

We already have discussed **Docker**, **Docker image creation**, and **Docker Registry**. The following are a few more components from the cluster.

Ingress

The **Kubernetes Ingress**, is an API object which provides the routing rules to manage access to the services which are running in the Kubernetes cluster. The **Ingress** is ideal in a *production* environment. It uses HTTPS as well as HTTP protocols for enabling routing. Let us take an example. When the ingress rule path is **/doctors**, we can access it from the outside of the Kubernetes cluster using the **/doctors** API, as it is the responsibility of the Ingress controller to fulfil the ingress rules:

- **Load balancer**: The Load Balancer helps in managing the load on any particular instance. It routes the incoming requests to Ingress. The Load Balancer is always configured with *public* IP and it sits in front of the Ingress controller. We can also map the DNS to the public IP of the load balancer.

- **Observability**: Along with the backend services which are involved in the business logic we need various additional utility services such as *database*, *caching*, *ELK stack*, *Prometheus*, and *Grafana*. Either we need to set them up or we can choose a cloud-managed observability stack.

- **Container Registry**: We can set up the Container Registry enabling us to store *private* container images which can be deployed on the Kubernetes cluster. The best part is most of the cloud providers have their own Container Registry.

- **CI/CD pipeline**: The world is of automation. The job of a developer is to develop the business logic and then the rest is taken care of by the tools which will *build*, *test*, *package*, and *deploy* it. The CI/CD pipeline does the same for us without any interference. The tools such as Jenkins allow for to automate the builds and deployments

- **Helm**: Using Kubernetes, we manage the PODs one by one. It is complex and time-consuming when we intend to make some decision about rolling out, scaling up and down in some instances. The **Helm** is a package manager for Kubernetes allowing bundling of the Kubernetes objects into a single unit so that it can be *deployed*, *versioned*, or *updated*.

We can set up a Kubernetes cluster on the cloud, here we are setting it up locally. The major difference is we don't need to do the provision for a Load Balancer locally and then no need for DNS mapping. The rest of the steps remain the same when you set up on the cloud.

Here, we will set up the Eureka server and the **DoctorFind_By_DoctorId** service and then use POSTMAN to request the resource as shown in *Figure 11.15*:

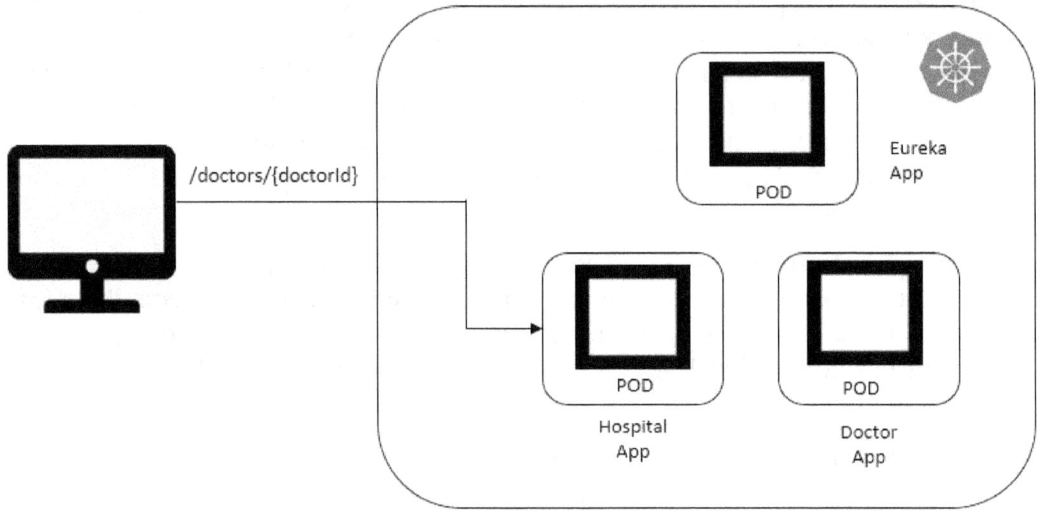

Figure 11.15: *Running applications in container*

As shown in *Figure 11.15*, we need the pods and then service to expose them to the world. But *hold on! What are these pods and services?* We haven't used it before. Let us know about these terms as well.

- **Pod**: The **Pods** are the smallest deployable units which we can create and manage in Kubernetes. A Pod may contain one or more containers with shared storage and network resources along with a specification of how to run these containers. The Pod can be considered as a host which will contain more than one application container which is relatively tightly coupled. A standard definition of Pod contains the *kind of Pod, the name of the Pod, a label associated with it, a container with a name, the name of the image* which is going to run with that container and a policy which decides how to fetch the image.
- **Service**: In Kubernetes, **pods** are ephemeral, which means they last for a very short time. The Pods are created and sometimes even destroyed to match the number of replicas defined in deployment. Every pod will get its own *IP address*, but unfortunately, it is *not permanent*.

This creates an issue for us. *When some pods need to communicate with other pods how are they going to keep track of the IP addresses?* Let's take an example. We have a Pod for the Eureka server and the Pod which hosts **DoctorFind_By_DoctorId** needs to communicate with Eureka for registration. *How is it going to keep track?* This is where **Kubernetes Service** plays an important role.

A **Kubernetes Service** defines a set of pods and the policy using which the pods can be accessed. Usually, a logical set of pods is determined by a selector. We have *four* different types of Kubernetes services:

- **ClusterIP**: The default service type is **ClusterIP** which exposes the service on the internal IP of the cluster. When the type of service is **ClusterIP**, it is only accessible within the cluster.
- **NodePort**: The **NodePort** exposes the service at each node's IP on a *static* port and enables the service accessible from outside the cluster using the **IP_of_node:NodePort**.
- **Load Balancer**: **Load Balancer** is the most commonly used type which creates an external Load Balancer in the cloud and assigns a *fixed external* IP to the service. When we want to access service directly from the *external cluster*, we use Load Balancer.
- **ExternalName**: The **ExternalName** type of the service maps the **Service** to the contents of the field as **externalName**. Usually, this type of service is used when we wish to access an external resource such as a database which is not part of our cluster.

Demonstrating pod and service

Before we start, make sure you have already built the image for the Eureka server and what is the name of the image along with its tag. You can easily find it out using the command, **docker images**. Now we are ready to write the definitions. Following is a sample definition of a Pod which will host a Eureka server and a service exposing the server to the *public*. We have written both definitions in the same file **eureka.yml** which is separated by three dashes (**---**). In this way, we can easily *manage* and *maintain* related configurations associated with the Eureka server. If you wish, you can create *two* separate files, but then you need to execute them separately:

```
apiVersion: v1
kind: Pod
metadata:
  name: eureka-server
  labels:
    app: eureka-server
    release: "0"
spec:
  containers:
```

```
  - name: eureka-server-container
    image:  eureka_server:1.0   # name of your eureka server image along
                                          with tag
    ports:
      - containerPort: 8761
    imagePullPolicy: Never     # we don't want to pull the image from
                                          docker hub
---
apiVersion: v1
kind: Service
metadata:
  name: eureka-server-service
  labels:
    app: eureka-server-service
spec:
  type : NodePort
  ports:
  - port: 8761
  selector:
    app: eureka-server
```

Before we execute the Kubernetes command, make sure you have started the Kubernetes cluster in Docker. Now, we will execute this file from the directory which has the **eureka.yml** file as:

`kubectl apply -f name-of-the-file`

Execution of our **eureka.yml** will create the *pod* and *services* as shown in *Figure* 11.16:

```
D:\Deployment_Demo>kubectl apply -f eureka.yml
pod/eureka-server created
service/eureka-server-service created
```

Figure 11.16: Executing eureka.yml

We can confirm the pod and service creation using the **kubectl get all** command, as shown in *Figure* 11.17:

```
D:\Deployment_Demo>kubectl get all
NAME                              READY   STATUS    RESTARTS        AGE
pod/eureka-server                 1/1     Running   0               14s

NAME                             TYPE       CLUSTER-IP      EXTERNAL-IP   PORT(S)          AGE
service/eureka-server-service    NodePort   10.106.230.13   <none>        8761:30429/TCP   14s
```

***Figure 11.17**: Displaying all the Pods and Services*

Now it's time to update the **DoctorFind_By_DoctorId** service. Find the port exposed by the **eureka-server-service** as shown by the preceding figure to update the **DoctorFind_By_DoctorId** service's properties to communicate with Eureka on the specific port number. In our case, it is **30429** as shown in *Figure* 11.16. Once the port number is modified in the **application.yml** file, create a new JAR of it, and then a new image. You can use a different name for the image, instead using the tag makes it easy to manage images of the same application. So, we have built an image using the tag 2.0 as shown by the following command:

```
docker build -t doctorfind_by_doctorid:2.0 .
```

Note

I have changed the same `application.yaml` file to communicate with Eureka in production. We already have discussed application profiling which enables us to maintain different configurations under different circumstances. So here we can create another configuration file. For example, `application-prod.yaml` and use it at the time of instance launching.

We will be using the image to create a pod and a service as shown by the following **doctorfind-doctorid.yml** file:

```
apiVersion: v1
kind: Pod
metadata:
  name: doctorfind-by-doctorid
  labels:
    app: doctorfind-by-doctorid
    release: "0"
spec:
  containers:
  - name: doctorfind-by-doctorid-container
    image:  doctorfind_by_doctorid:2.0
    ports:
      - containerPort: 8085
```

```
    imagePullPolicy: Never
---
apiVersion: v1
kind: Service
metadata:
  name: doctorfind-by-doctorid-service
  labels:
    app: doctorfind-by-doctorid-service
spec:
  type : NodePort
  ports:
  - port: 8085
  selector:
    app: doctorfind-by-doctorid
```

Time to apply the configuration to launch the Pod and Service. Here, is the output when we executed the **doctorfind-doctorid.yml** file:

```
D:\Deployment_Demo\kubernetes>kubectl apply -f doctorfindby-doctorid.yml
pod/doctorfind-by-doctorid created
service/doctorfind-by-doctorid-service created
```

***Figure 11.18**: Executing doctorfind-doctorid.yml*

And then find the port exposing the pod by the service as:

```
D:\Deployment_Demo\kubernetes>kubectl get all
NAME                          READY   STATUS    RESTARTS   AGE
pod/doctorfind-by-doctorid    1/1     Running   0          8s
pod/eureka-server             1/1     Running   0          24m

NAME                                    TYPE       CLUSTER-IP      EXTERNAL-IP   PORT(S)          AGE
service/doctorfind-by-doctorid-service  NodePort   10.99.144.54    <none>        8085:30536/TCP   8s
service/eureka-server-service           NodePort   10.106.230.13   <none>        8761:30429/TCP   24m
```

***Figure 11.19**: Displaying all the Pods and Services*

Let's visit the Eureka service as shown in *Figure* 11.20.

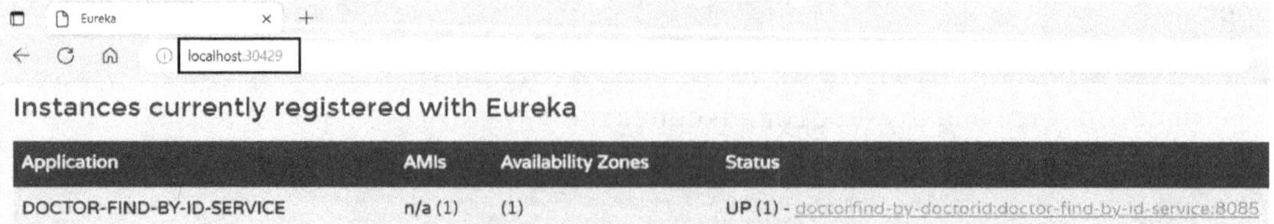

***Figure 11.20**: Eureka dashboard*

You will notice that our service got registered to Eureka. Now, we can request the *doctor* service running in the Kubernetes cluster from the POSTMAN as shown in *Figure 11.21*:

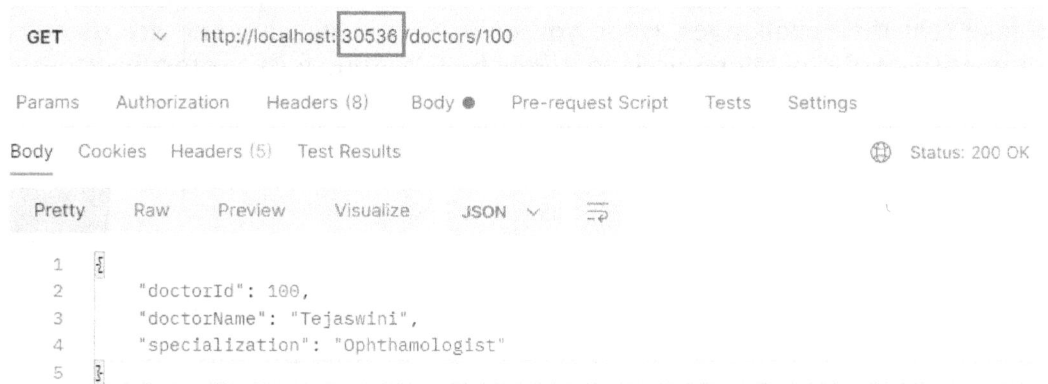

Figure 11.21: *Connecting to Kubernetes cluster from* POSTMAN

Observe the *port number*. This is the same port to which the application has deployed within Kubernetes and you can find it by using the **kubectl get all** command.

Conclusion

In this chapter, we discussed in detail the microservice architecture from a deployment perspective. We discussed service per host, multiple services in a host, and serverless and orchestration-based deployment. Whatever may be the deployment pattern we choose, we need the application packaged as a unit. This makes application sharing easy. We discussed how to package an application in a JAR or a WAR. We also learnt how to use it to launch the application either as a standalone application with an embedded server or multiple services in a single server by deploying a WAR. Though we were able to launch and consume our microservices in both ways, we observed that the process was a bit complicated and, on a large scale, very time-consuming. We move on to the modern way of packaging an application which helps developers to bundle applications with all its required platforms, frameworks on which the application is built and so on. **Docker** helps not only developers but the DevOps team as well to distribute and launch the application easily. However, in microservices, we need high availability which is possible by deploying multiple instances of a microservice in physically separated locations. **Docker Swarm**, **Kubernetes**, and **OpenShift** make this task easy. In this chapter, we demonstrated how to launch the application on the Kubernetes cluster and then expose it using a **Service**.

It's a deep ocean of deployment. Covering each point is really difficult and beyond the scope of this book. We tried touching the corners which will help you in understanding the end-to-end process from development to deployment. So, with the successful deployment of our services in the container, now it's time to take real-time challenges. Hope you enjoyed this learning and are ready to conquer the world of microservices. *All the best*! Waiting for your feedback. *Good Luck*!!

Appendix 1

Steps to create the spring boot project in VSCode:

1. Install the java extension pack

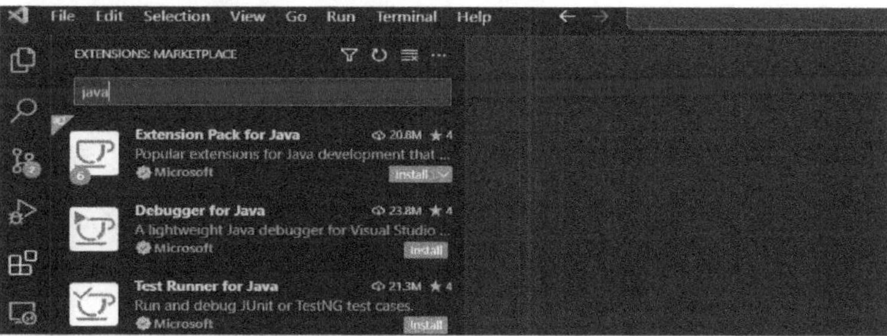

2. Install Spring boot Extension Pack

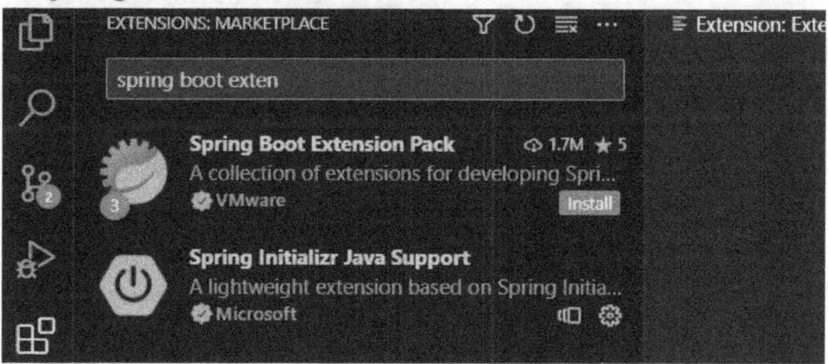

3. Select the Command Pallet from View menu
4. Select Spring Initializ: Create maven project option

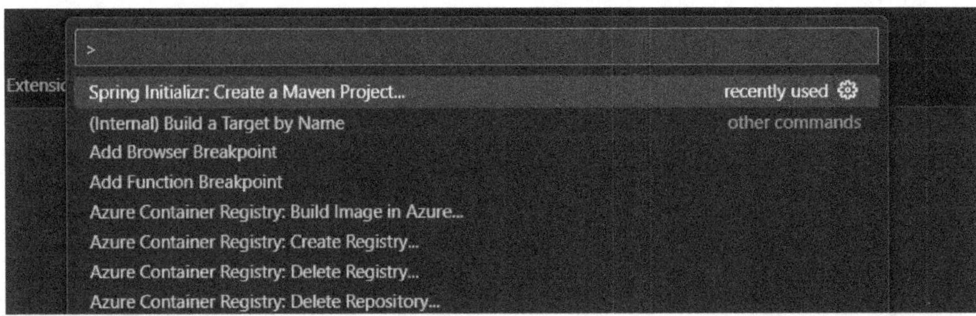

5. Select Spring Boot version

6. Select the project language as Java

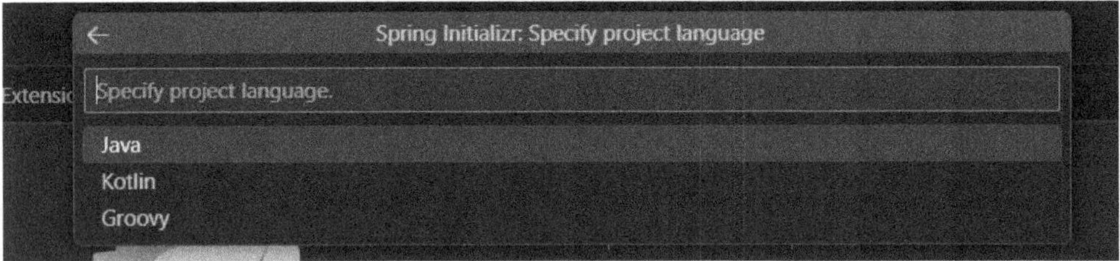

7. Input group Id

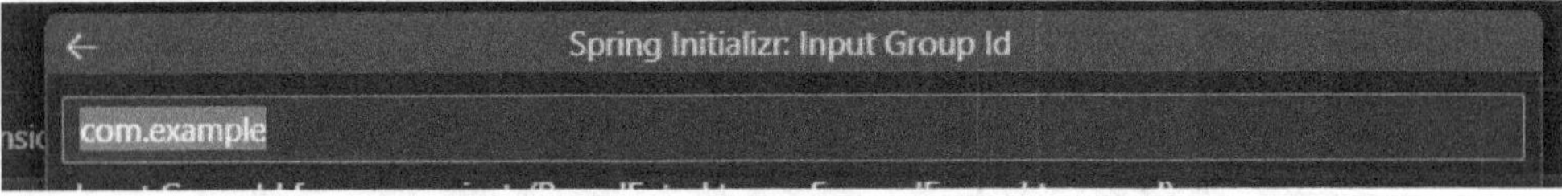

8. Input artifact Id

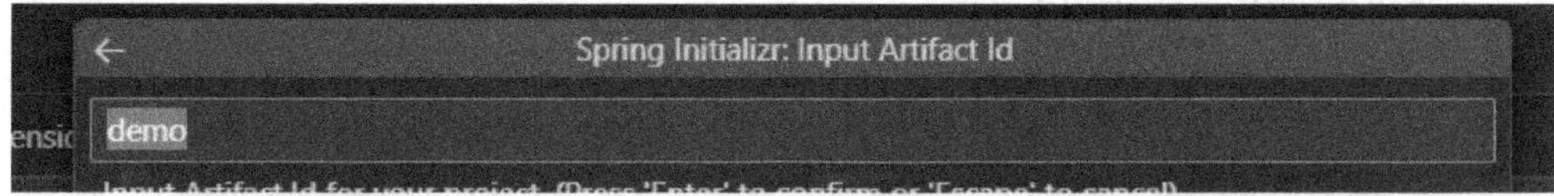

9. Specify packaging type

10. Specify Java Version

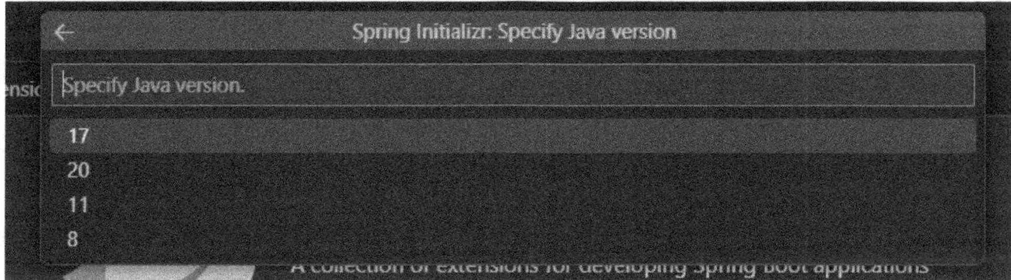

11. Choose Dependencies

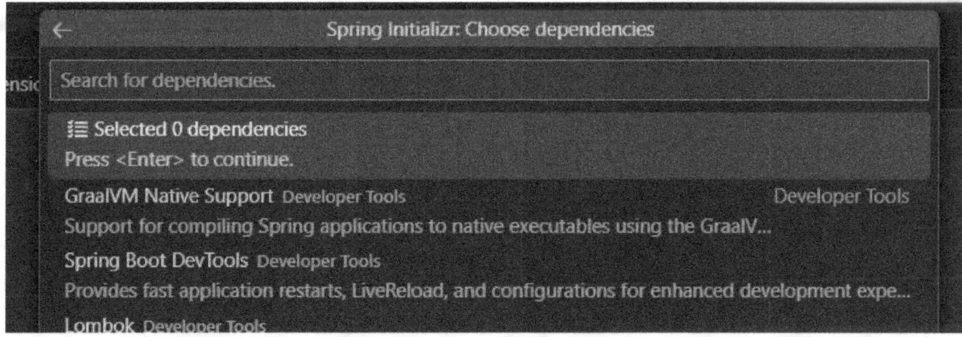

12. Select the desired location to create the project structure as shown in the following screenshot:

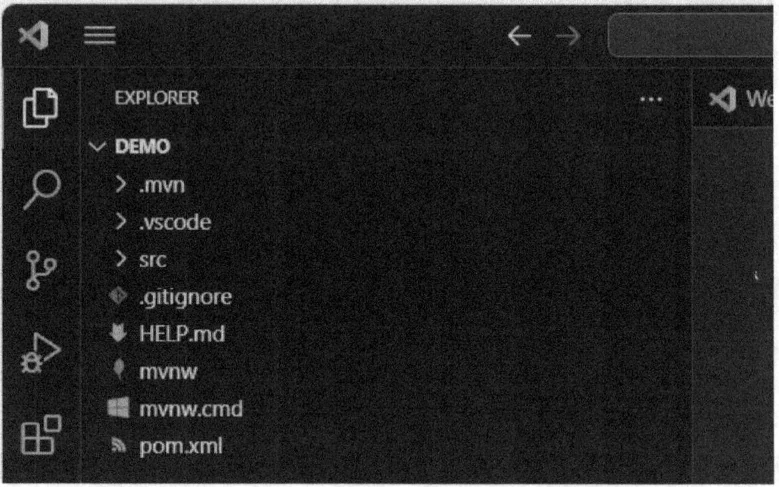

Appendix 2

Rest End Point Testing Tools:

1. Postman : **https://www.postman.com**
2. Soap UI : **https://www.soapui.org/**
3. Swagger : **https://swagger.io/**
4. Rapid API: **https://rapidapi.com**
5. Curlx: **https://www.curlx.dev**

Steps to download and install Postman as stand along application

1. Go to **https://www.postman.com/downloads/ and download the postman app**.
2. Install the setup file, which pops up the screen as shown:

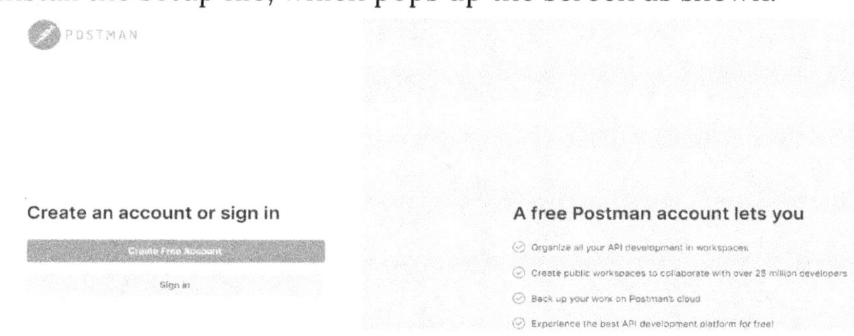

3. Select Create free account and register with your email
4. Alternatively, you can also sign up with your google account directly.
5. Once you login successfully, you will get the home screen as shown:

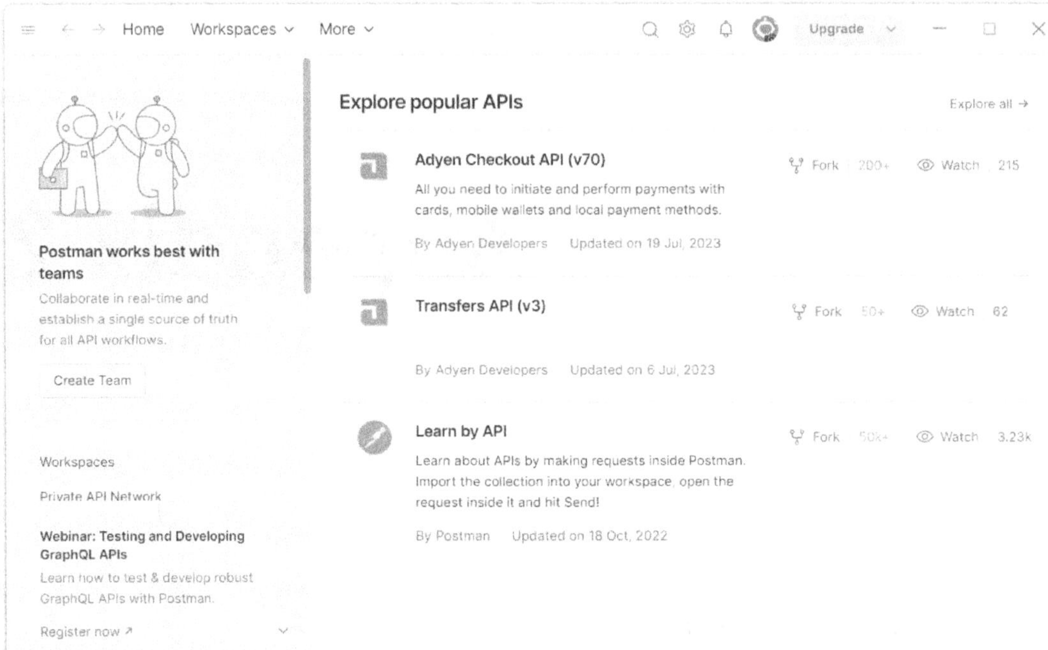

6. Select the option -> **`Workspaces`** from left panel
7. Select **`MyWorkspace`** as shown in the following figure:

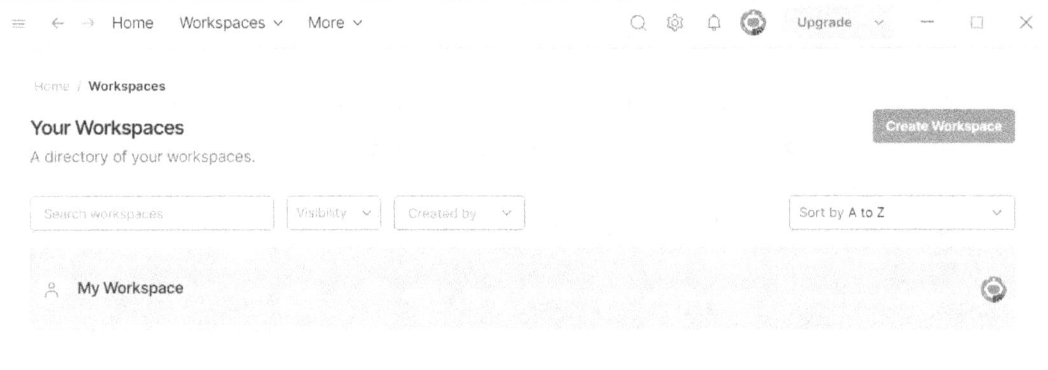

8. Select the + tab, adjacent to overview tab to test your API

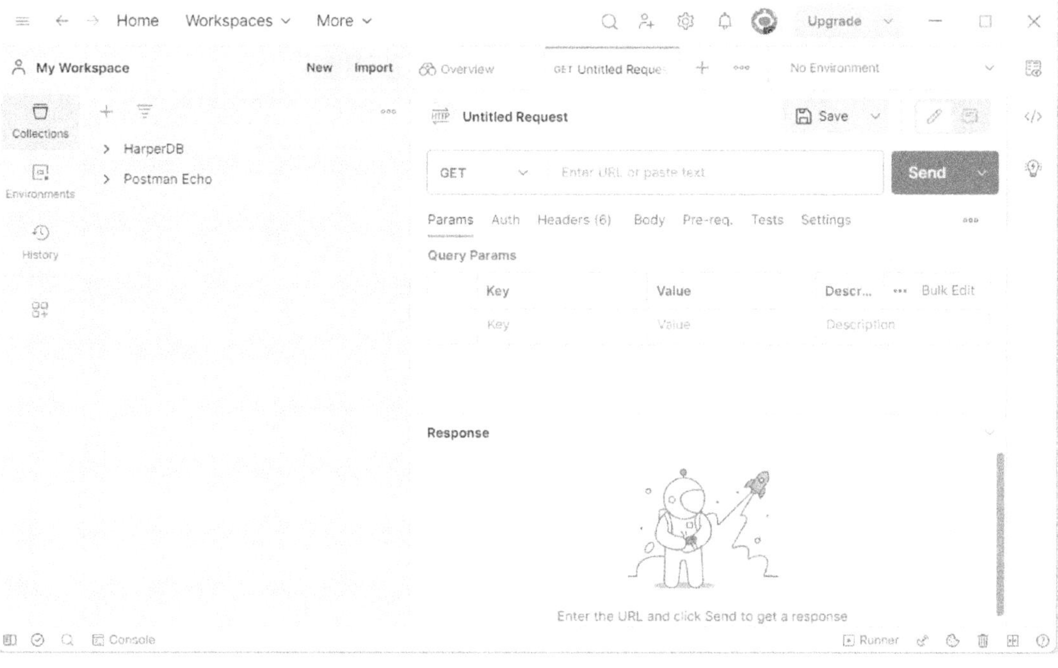

Index

Symbols

A

H

I

J

K

L

M

N

O

P

Q

R

www.ingramcontent.com/pod-product-compliance
Lightning Source LLC
LaVergne TN
LVHW061931220826
846092LV00004B/1004
* 9 7 8 9 3 8 8 5 9 0 9 1 4 *